Communicating Racism

Communicating Racism

ETHNIC PREJUDICE in THOUGHT and TALK

Teun A. van Dijk

49-714

SAGE PUBLICATIONS
The Publishers of Professional Social Science
Newbury Park   London   New Delhi

For information address:

SAGE Publications, Inc.
2111 West Hillcrest Drive
Newbury Park, California 91320

SAGE Publications Ltd.
28 Banner Street
London EC1Y 8QE
England

SAGE Publications India Pvt. Ltd.
M-32 Market
Greater Kailash I
New Delhi 110 048 India

Printed in the United States of America

Library of Congress Cataloging-in-Publication Data

Dijk, Teun A. van (Teun Adrianus), 1943-
    Communicating racism.

    Bibliography: p.
    Includes index.
    1. Racism.   2. Communication.   3. Prejudices.
4. Ethnic attitudes.   5. Race discrimination
I. Title.
HM291.D496   1986   305.8   86-15514
ISBN 0-8039-2674-X (CLOTH)
ISBN 0-8039-3627-3 (PAPER)

SECOND PRINTING, 1989
FIRST PRINTING, PAPER, 1989

Contents

Preface

Racism and ethnocentrism are major problems in our society, requiring permanent and persistent critical inquiry. This book reports on a study of a crucial, and hitherto neglected, dimension of these problems: How are ethnic prejudices expressed, communicated, and shared within the dominant, White in-group? The answer to such a question should tell us something about the everyday reproduction of racism in society. Whereas most other work on racism has a more abstract, macro-level nature and focuses on historical or socioeconomic aspects, this study examines some of the micro phenomena of racism or "ethnicism." And whereas earlier work on prejudice is often limited to individual social psychology, we extend its analysis to a more explicit study of social cognition and communication. We analyze how White people think and talk about ethnic minority groups, and how they persuasively communicate their ethnic attitudes to other members of their own group. Such an analysis requires a multidisciplinary framework. Therefore, I try to integrate and apply new theoretical developments from such disciplines as discourse analysis, cognitive and social psychology, microsociology, and communication.

The research reported here is part of an ongoing project being carried out at the University of Amsterdam about the expression of ethnic prejudice and racism in various types of discourse. This book focuses on everyday conversations and interpersonal communication. Interview data for this study were collected in Amsterdam, the Netherlands, and in San Diego, California. Whereas some of our earlier studies of these interviews focus on their discourse properties and on the cognitive structures and strategies of prejudice, this book integrates and further expands these results in a more social-psychological and communicative direction. Thus, we are specifically interested in the cognitive, discursive, and communicative strategies White people use during the positive self-presentation and negative "other-presentation" that characterize talk about "foreigners." Also, the sources, such as the media or personal contacts and experiences that people mention in their discursive reproduction of prejudiced beliefs are examined.

Although the interviews have been held mainly in the Netherlands, as well as in California, there is reason to assume that the results have a more general nature, and also hold for other countries in Northwestern Europe and Northern America where racial or ethnic minorities always have been or recently have become prominent. For Europe, the rise of racism in the last decade has been spectacular, and overtly racist parties are obtaining increasing support among a White population that feels both superior to, as well as culturally or economically "threatened" by, the new citizens. Yet, racism should not be identified only with such relatively small extremist groups. On the contrary, more widespread and subtle forms of prejudice, discrimination, and ethnicism occur among all groups and all institutions of our societies. The interviews that were conducted and analyzed bear witness to the content and forms of this more general and structural type of everyday racism and its reproduction in thought and talk.

The serious and widespread social problems of prejudice, discrimination, and racism, as well as the multidisciplinary approach of this study, should make this book relevant for students and scholars in most of the humanities and social sciences. To make it more accessible to all those interested, each theoretical analysis has been prefaced by a brief introduction for nonspecialists. At the same time, this study also provides many new theoretical and methodological proposals for the study of discourse, cognition, persuasion, and communication, aside from its results for the study of prejudice and racism in society. It may, therefore, be useful as an advanced text in upper-division and graduate courses in, for example, linguistics (discourse analysis), cognitive and social psychology, microsociology, anthropology, speech and communication, as well as in ethnic studies.

This research has been accomplished in collaboration with, and with the assistance of, many people of whom only a few can be mentioned here. First, I would like to thank my students, both at the University of Amsterdam and at the University of California, San Diego. They are the ones who helped me collect and transcribe more than 150 interviews during the past five years, and also contributed to the interviews' analysis. The names of these students are mentioned separately in a list of acknowledgments. Next, I am indebted to the earlier members of the Amsterdam project, funded by the Netherlands Organization of Pure Research (ZWO), on the expression of ethnic prejudice in conversation: Eva Abraham-van der Mark, Rob Rombouts, Martijn den Uyl, and Adri van der Wurff. As always, Piet de Geus, my assistant, has provided invaluable help with administrative and computer chores. To Mark Knapp, I am grateful for considering the manuscript for publication in his series on interpersonal communication, and for his magnanimous acceptance to have the book published by Sage outside of his series, so that the book could reach a wider public in other disciplines as well.

For extensive discussions on the nature of racism, on its theoretical analysis as well as on the sociopolitical fight against it, I am particularly indebted to Chris Mullard, one of the first and few Black professors appointed at the University of Amsterdam, and director of its new Center for Race and Ethnic Studies.

I am grateful for the help Luis Moll gave in stimulating students from his classes at UCSD to participate in this research. The Center for Human Information Processing at UCSD, its director, George Mandler, and especially its secretary, Arlene Jacobs, provided me with the necessary home-base and assistance for my research in San Diego, for which Aaron Cicourel also provided important help.

Finally, more than gratitude and indebtedness are due to Philomena Essed, my wife, whose pioneering work on everyday racism and the experiences of Black women, has been a stimulating, instructive, and revealing background to this study. Without her advice, her comments upon the first version of this book, our innumerable discussions about racism, and without her permanent support for my work, this book would undoubtedly have had less value, if it could have been written at all.

—Teun A. van Dijk
La Jolla, California

Acknowledgments

I am indebted to the following students who helped me collect, transcribe, and analyze the interviews on which this study is based:

Group I (Amsterdam):

Nico Hergaarden, Marianne Pruis, Jan Krol, Marion Oskamp, Henk Verhagen, Giovanni Massaro, Leny Schuitemaker.

Group II (Amsterdam):

Marion Algra, Wilmy Cleyne, Hans Deckers, Trudi Konst, Lyanne Lamar, Myra Kleindendorst, Arghje de Sitter, Evelien van der Wiel.

Group III (Amsterdam):

Cees Braas, Annette Berntsen, Gerrie Eickhof, Rob Hermes, Martin van Iersel, Robertine Luikinga, Ton Maas, Monica Robijns, Margriet Schut, Eva Stegemann, Evelien Tonkens, Saskia Ven, Bep van der Werf.

Group A (San Diego):

Laurie Ambler, Linda De Leon, John Gjerset, Larry Green, Chiaki Ishimura, Jennifer Keystone, Teenie Matlock, Molly Schwartz, Susan Wallace.

In general, interviews or interview fragments recorded and transcribed by these students are identified in this book by the group number (I, II, III, or A) followed by the initials of the student (except in Group II, where a combination of last name initial and street name initial was used), followed by the interview number of each student, followed by "a," "b," or "c," in case more people were interviewed, and (for group III) sometimes followed by an "x" when the "ethnic topic" was eXplicitly mentioned during presentation.

1

Introduction

1. Background and goals of this study

In this book, the way racism is reproduced through everyday talk is analyzed. Dominant group members regularly engage in conversations about ethnic minority groups in society, and thus express and persuasively communicate their attitudes to other in-group members. In this way, ethnic prejudices become shared and may form the cognitive basis of ethnic or racial discrimination in intergroup interaction.

Whereas racism is usually studied as a structural, macro-level phenomenon of society, we are interested in its micro-level, interpersonal enactment in everyday communicative situations. This does not mean that we conceive of prejudice and discrimination as individual properties of people. On the contrary, ethnic attitudes, their formulation in discourse, their persuasive diffusion, as well as their uses as the cognitive basis for action, are all essentially social. They characterize groups and intergroup relations and exhibit sociocultural, historical, political, and economic dependencies. They embody and signal dominance and power. It is the task of this study to show how these group-based properties of racism are cognitively represented in and reproduced among dominant group members. An analysis of these links between macro and micro levels of racism is crucial for our understanding of ethnic prejudice and discrimination in the daily interethnic encounters of multiethnic societies.

Obviously, the task just sketched is exceedingly complex. It would require a whole series of books, not just a single book, to unravel the many details of such an intricate problem. Therefore, the focus is on a few main lines of inquiry, sketching its theoretical outlines, and reporting results from empirical (field) studies carried out in the Netherlands and the United States.

Thus, the first step must be a clarification of the cognitive dimensions of racism. That is, we must make explicit the ways ethnic attitudes in general, and prejudice in particular, are represented and strategically used in memory, and how such representations and strategies affect intergroup perceptions, evaluations, and interactions.

Second, we analyze how ethnic prejudice becomes manifest in discourse. How does what in-group members think and feel about out-group members influence what they say about such "others," and how is such talk organized at various levels of analysis?

Third, talk is not just an expression of underlying beliefs or opinions but is also interpersonally and socially constrained in the communicative context. Therefore, we also examine how discourse about ethnic minority groups is monitored by interaction strategies (e.g., those of positive self-presentation and persuasion), as well as by social goals, norms, and values. These constraints may well be conflicting and demand that negative opinions about ethnic minority groups be formulated in terms of ethnic or racial tolerance, or dissimulated in other, strategically effective, ways.

Fourth, we analyze how prejudiced discourse is understood, evaluated, and represented by in-group recipients who participate in such talk. This step is essential for our understanding of the persuasive dimension of the communication of ethnic attitudes, and for our insight into the processes of their diffusion and sharing throughout the dominant group as a whole. Here, we also examine which beliefs or opinions people attribute to other sources, such as the media or personal conversations.

And finally, we want to know how the communication and diffusion of prejudiced group attitudes transcend the level of single, isolated, interpersonal conversations. Talk is embedded in more complex, higher-level systems of social information processing within groups, which also involve institutional discourses such as that of the media, politics, or education. Social members routinely invoke such other discourses, or the inferences based on them, to develop and sustain their own attitudes, and to warrant argumentatively such attitudes in talk, for instance, as public, if not as shared, social opinions.

The Discourse Analytical Approach

It is through these steps of this inquiry that we hope to establish a crucial, and hitherto missing, link between the cognitive and the social dimensions of racism. Our perspective on this link is the role of discourse and communication. That is, we do not study patterns of discrimination. Neither do we study the ways majority group members talk *to* ethnic minority group members. The inquiry is limited to the analysis of informal discourse *about* ethnic minorities and the reproduction of racism within the White majority group. Each step of this analysis can be made through a detailed analysis of the ways the communication process is exhibited in the various structures of conversation. Cognitive representation and strategies of ethnic attitudes are analyzed through their formulation in discourse, and the same holds for the role of interpersonal strategies of self-presentation and persuasion. Similarly, the role of the sociocultural context, of institutional discourses, and of general norms and values, is also studied through members' interpretation and expression in talk. Thus, discourse represents both the object as well as the method and data of this analysis.

The Interdisciplinary Perspective

Despite the emphasis on the discourse analytical perspective in this study, it goes without saying that its theoretical foundation must be interdisciplinary. This is not only because discourse analysis itself, as it has developed in the past two decades, emerged from several disciplines in the humanities and the social sciences, such as linguistics, rhetoric, literary scholarship, speech and communication studies, psychology, anthropology, and sociology (van Dijk, 1985a); rather, each of the dimensions of this inquiry is traditionally located and studied in related but autonomous fields of academic scholarship, each with its own goals, methods, theories, and terminology. Thus, conversation has been an important subject of research in many disciplines, first in microsociology and ethnography, later in sociolinguistics, philosophy, and speech communication (Atkinson & Heritage, 1984; Schenkein, 1978; van Dijk, 1985a, vol. 3).

The analysis of cognitive representations, understanding and planning discourse, has been the major goal of recent psychology and Artificial Intelligence (AI) (Schank & Abelson, 1977; van Dijk & Kintsch, 1983). The persuasive communication of attitudes has been a classic object of attention in both social psychology and the study of speech communication (Petty & Cacioppo, 1981; Petty, Ostrom, & Brock, 1981). Because ethnic attitudes and their reproduction are inherently social phenomena, these approaches need be extended toward a study of social cognition (Forgas, 1981; Higgins, Herman, & Zanna, 1981; Wyer & Srull, 1984). In particular, we are interested in the ways social cognitions of in-group members about ethnic out-groups are formed and communicated (Berger & Bradac, 1982; Roloff & Berger, 1982). That is, we are not interested in personal opinions but in social representations of groups and the processes of their reproduction (Bourdieu & Passeron, 1977; Farr & Moscovici, 1984).

More specifically, the study of ethnic intergroup perception and stereotypes has been a prominent topic of inquiry in the new field of social cognition at the boundaries of social and cognitive sociology (Hamilton, 1981; A.G. Miller, 1982; Tajfel, 1981). And, finally, the study of prejudice, discrimination, and racism has occupied researchers in several of the social sciences, especially in social psychology and sociology (Apostle et al., 1983; Ehrlich, 1973; Essed, 1984; Jones, 1972; Katz, 1976; Pettigrew, 1987; Wellman, 1977). Although I cannot possibly refer to, let alone survey, all of this research, I try to integrate as much as possible from the most relevant advances in these fields into this approach.

Although there are increasing mutual influences and dependencies among these various disciplines, their methods and theorizing are still rather diverse. It will, therefore, not be easy to integrate these various perspectives on social cognition, discourse, and persuasive communication, on one hand, and on prejudice and racism, on the other hand, into one coherent and unified framework. However, from a methodological and theoretical point of view, social cognitions and their expression in socially relevant talk require such an interdisciplinary framework. Indeed, they may be an ideal illustration of the necessity and the possibility of the integration of the cognitive, communicative, and social sciences. A complex problem such as the reproduction of ethnic prejudice in society can be adequately studied only through such an interdisciplinary approach.

Antiracist Goals

This study is not just motivated by its attractive theoretical or interdisciplinary perspectives, as sketched above. The fundamental reason and ultimate goal is to contribute to a more profound and effective understanding of a major social problem of our "Northwestern" societies: racism. Hitherto, linguistics, discourse analysis, speech communication, and cognitive psychology have contributed little to the study of racism. Social psychology often limited its focus to individual prejudices or stereotypes, thereby often ignoring the essential group-based and social dimensions of ethnic cognition and interaction. It is striking that the term *racism* is seldom used, if not implicitly denied, in that research. Similar reductionism characterizes much of the (White) sociological analysis of race relations and racism (for critique of White sociology, see, e.g., Bourne, 1980; Centre for Contemporary Cultural Studies [CCCS], 1982; Ladner, 1973; Lawrence, 1982).

At the same time, the ethnic situation in most countries of Western Europe and North America is such that racism should (still or even increasingly) be taken as a serious sociocultural and political problem (Bowser & Hunt, 1981; Castles, 1984; Miles, 1982; Pettigrew, 1987). That is, it is the problem of White, dominant groups, and *not* the problem of (or caused by) the many ethnic minority groups that have come to live in our societies as migrant laborers or as expatriates of our former or actual colonies. Most White scholars in the humanities and social sciences have conveniently ignored this social problem, if not in their everyday life, then mostly in their academic work.

Indeed, they are members of the dominant White group, and even belong to the "ideological elite" of this group. Some members of this elite have in the past, and occasionally even in the present, formulated the "scientific" underpinnings of racism and thus have legitimated prejudice, discrimination, and exploitation against millions of people (Chase, 1975; Unesco, 1983).

Much more subtly and indirectly today, racist presuppositions and goals still inspire much (White) academic work on ethnic groups and race relations, for instance, in the denial of the structural nature of racism in our societies (Bourne, 1980; CCCS, 1982; Essed, 1986). This research ignores and thereby confirms and reproduces the fact that both blatant and very subtle racism permeates *all* social and personal levels of our societies: from the decisions, actions, and discourses of the government or the legislative bodies, through those of the various institutions, such as education, research, the media, health, the police, the courts, and social agencies, all the way down to everyday interaction, thought, and talk.

Aside from the direct experiences in the everyday lives of ethnic minority group members (Essed, 1984)—one of the fields of research conveniently ignored, or deemed "too subjective," by White social scientists—there is ample research to document this state of affairs. As (White) scholars, we are involved and even more responsible than others because we have the instruments to study and criticize. Against this background of shared responsibility for the existence and perpetuation of racism, this study contributes to the fundamental insight that racism is, indeed, *our* problem, in the sense that we are part of the problem. It does so by analyzing *our* talk, and *our* informal communication, and by studying how *we* (re)produce racism in society. And *we* here not only means *we, White people*, but also, if not in particular, *we, members of the White elite*, or *we, White scholars*. Whereas most of this book will be about everyday talk and communication, attention is focused also, especially in the last chapter, on the elite and media sources of ethnic prejudice and its reproduction throughout the White in-group.

2. Data and methods

This study reports results of various projects on the reproduction of racism in discourse carried out at the University of Amsterdam and at the University of California, San Diego, between 1980 and 1985. These projects all deal with the problem of prejudice and racism in various types of discourse. Aside from studies of the representation of ethnic minority groups in textbooks (van Dijk, 1986a), and especially in the media (van Dijk, 1983a), the major empirical data have been collected in field studies on the everyday talk of White majority group members in the Netherlands (van Dijk, 1982b, 1983b, 1984). Additional interview data have also been collected in Southern California, especially with the aim of finding out whether the results of the research in Amsterdam not only hold for the Netherlands or Western Europe but are also relevant in the United States. Therefore, results of work by others about prejudice and racism in Western Europe are briefly discussed.

The Interviews

With the assistance of research associates and students, about 180 free interviews were held, recorded, and transcribed in detail, and then analyzed at several levels of discourse organization (see the Appendix and below for details and some discussion of the method of interviewing and interviewee selection). The interviews in Amsterdam were held in three different groups and in various periods during the years 1980 to 1984. The California interviews were held in the fall of 1985. In the examples, these interviews are identified by code numbers preceded by an "A."

The interviews held in Amsterdam (overtly or covertly) topicalized the respondents' experiences and opinions regarding the ethnic minority groups in the Netherlands. Most salient of these groups are the immigrant citizens from the "East Indies," now Indonesia (250,000), especially the group of Moluccans (35,000), and, further, Turkish (156,000) and Moroccan (107,000) migrant workers, Black expatriates of the former Dutch colony of Surinam (adjacent to Guyana at the Caribbean border of South America; 185,000), as well as immigrants from the Dutch Antilles (42,000) (data according to the Central Bureau of Statistics, 1983/1984). Aside from these relatively large groups, there are smaller groups of immigrant workers from other Mediterranean countries, as well as Chinese political refugees and the group of Jews who survived the holocaust. These various groups are usually referred to as "foreigners" (*buitenlanders*) in everyday conversation, even when they have Dutch nationality, as do most immigrants coming from Surinam. Together, these minority groups form an estimated 6% minority, that is, more than 800,000 citizens of a total population of 14 million. Immigrant workers and Surinamese are concentrated primarily in the larger cities, such as Amsterdam, Rotterdam, the Hague, and Utrecht. Thus, 12% of the 800,000 citizens of Amsterdam belong to ethnic minority groups.

The interviews held in San Diego, California, focus on several minority groups in the United States, especially Blacks, Mexican Americans (or other Latinos), and Asian Americans (most notably Filipinos), who account for 77,700, 130,610, and 57,207, respectively, of a total city population of 875,504 citizens (according to the 1980 census).

Data from other research about prejudice and racism in Western European countries involve mostly immigrant workers from several Mediterranean or (North) African countries in, for example, West Germany, Sweden, Switzerland, Belgium, and France, or various Black immigrant groups from the West Indies, South Asia, or East Africa in Great Britain. The main focus, however, will be on the interviews collected in the Netherlands, with occasional examples drawn from the California interviews.

In order to trace the mechanisms of prejudice reproduction, special attention was paid in the interviews and their analysis to references to and interpretations of sources of information and opinions about minority groups. People were informally asked about talk with family members, friends, neighbors, or shopkeepers, as well as about the information they attributed to the media. A fourth group of interviews were conducted with the specific aim of asking people about the sources and targets of their talk and opinions about ethnic minority groups, but these interviews are not analyzed in this book.

Other Data

Additional information and results were drawn from both experimental and field studies, including work by others, of ethnic prejudice in the Netherlands, Europe, and the United States, for instance, from content analysis of the media. Attempts to collect personal diaries in which people recorded their daily communications and information about ethnic minority groups were not very successful. Survey data about ethnic prejudice were used only as supplementary (quantitative) background information, because the main aim of the data collection and analysis was qualitative. We want to know how people talk (or write) in texts and contexts that are as little constrained as possible and how they acknowledge talk and text from other sources about the same topic.

Obviously, each of these discourse and communication types needs analysis in its own right because the structures, as well as the relationships with the cognitive and social embeddings, are rather diverse. Yet, at the same time, each discourse type has also been considered as an expression and reproduction of the same underlying attitudinal, ideological, and social reality, namely, that of the ethnic situation and of racism in our Northwestern countries in the 1980s.

Methodological Issues

From this brief listing of various types of data, it may already be clear that methodologically also, this study is complex and interdisciplinary. Although it is certainly possible to examine some aspects of ethnic prejudice in the laboratory, we have found that experimental approaches impose restrictions that do not allow an adequate study of the problem. To study everyday talk from people (and not just psychology students) in various neighborhoods, with different opinions and experiences, we obviously need methods that yield more naturalistic data. Although these methods hardly allow control of specific variables (of speakers or talk), we have found that informal, in-depth interviews yield rich data for a qualitative analysis of discourse structures and their underlying ethnic opinions and attitudes. This is also one of the reasons that we did not have recourse to questionnaires with highly prestructured or otherwise controlled interview questions and settings (Hyman, 1975).

Recording everyday conversations is one thing (see Chapter 2, section 10), but collecting "real" conversations about ethnic minority members is quite another. Especially in what we called *high-contact,* that is, mixed, neighborhoods, people talk about "foreigners," a great deal, but it would still be a very inefficient way of collecting data when we would record hundreds of hours of talk in order to get perhaps a few hours of talk about ethnic groups. This is why we had to resort to interviews that were as natural and informal as possible but that allowed us partially to control the "ethnic topics" we wanted to analyze. The discourse properties of such interviews are attended to in the next chapter, but we have reason to assume that they are sufficiently similar to spontaneous conversations to warrant conclusions about the nature of everyday talk about ethnic minority groups. Thus, we shall see that, of course, people sometimes give socially desirable answers to questions even in informal interviews. Yet, they also do so in ordinary talk, especially with strangers, about a "delicate" issue such as "foreigners." Indeed, we are specifically interested in the strategies of such "socially desirable" ways of self-presentation.

The same holds for other methods that try to assess the personal and public communication of ethnic beliefs. Thus, we have neither direct access to natural media usage situations nor access to other natural communicative events that have ethnic groups or relations as the main topic. Therefore, we had to work with accounts about such communicative events as they were, often spontaneously, given in the interviews. This also allows us to examine how communicative events in general, and sources, information, or beliefs in particular, are interpreted and reproduced by the interviewees.

The Relevance of Self-Reports as Data

In the social sciences, such data were traditionally considered incomplete, biased, or unreliable. More recently, however, informal interviewing, self-reports, and protocols have received renewed interest and positive appraisal (Ericsson & Simon, 1984).

Another reason for the traditional skepticism toward natural data is that most researchers were primarily interested in the phenomena such reports are about, or in the "objective truth" of reported events. Our aim is quite different, however. For our purposes, self-reports in (informal) interviews may provide precisely what we want to know, namely, insight into the contents, strategies, and structures of "foreigner talk," and insight into the ways people subjectively recall, transform, and reproduce information from previous personal experiences or from other sources, even when such transformations are "biased" or "unreliable." We are not merely interested in what people have actually heard or read, but rather in the ways they have interpreted and further processed that information and how they convey it in conversations with others. Reproduction of talk and opinions is necessarily biased by many cognitive and social constraints, which is a well-known factor of social information processing (see the early work by Bartlett, 1932). That is, we are primarily interested in the self-reports for their own sake, but through their systematic analysis we, at the same time, hope to be able to make inferences about cognitive, interactional, and social processes that constrain such talk. Our discourse analytical methods allow rather subtle assessment of such communicative constraints and transformations.

These methodological considerations also have a firm theoretical basis. From a discourse analytical point of view, interviews are a form of discourse that require and allow analysis that is not fundamentally different from that of other forms of talk (Erickson & Shultz, 1982). Despite the systematic skepticism, in modern experimental psychology, about introspection and hence about self-reports (see, e.g., Nisbett & Wilson, 1977), interviews provide perhaps the most interesting and rich data about the subjective processes at work in the representation, retrieval, recall, and reproduction of information, although such methods and data have not yet been used very often. Current cognitive psychology of discourse production and understanding, however, provides insight into the relationships between cognition and talk that may also contribute to enhanced reliability of the inferences involved (van Dijk & Kintsch, 1983).

In social psychology, increasing attention is being paid to the relevance of personal "accounts" as the method and data of research (Harré, 1979; Harré & Secord, 1972). And despite its prevailing experimental approach, attribution theory and its interest in "naive" interpretations of action may provide a theoretical basis for the examination of natural talk, for example, stories of the "ordinary explanations" people give about their own and other's actions (Antaki, 1981) or about the language used for such explanations (Hewstone, 1983). The possible "biases" (Nisbett & Wilson, 1977) in such explanations, as suggested above, are precisely the elements in which we are interested.

In qualitative sociology, interviews and other forms of talk have been analyzed for many years as relevant data about social members' shared, commonsense interpretations of social life. Such talk may exhibit the strategies or rules people apply in their reconstruction of social episodes and how these are relevant for ongoing interactions (Cicourel, 1964, 1973; Schwartz & Jacobs, 1979). We may assume that the current developments in the integration of cognitive sociology and cognitive social psychology in the study of social cognition (cf., e.g., Fiske & Taylor, 1984; Forgas, 1981) may lead to further interest in the role of discourse and discourse analysis for the study of social interpretations, interactions, and situations.

Discourse Analysis of Interviews

Similar methodological remarks may be made for the methods of data analysis. Although we do report some quantitative results, our descriptions are predominantly qualitative. This means that, in this stage of research, it is more important to know how people talk about ethnic groups and how they reproduce ethnic beliefs than to show how variation in such talk is a quantitatively assessable dependent variable of a number of context characteristics, such as neighborhood, gender, age, or various sources, such as the media, family members, or neighbors. The same holds for the properties of talk itself: We want to know, for instance, how people tell stories or argue rather than how often they do so. This means that we systematically analyze the respective levels of (interview) talk, such as overall thematic (macro) structures, narrative or argumentative schemata, local semantic strategies, lexical style, rhetorical operations, and more specific conversational properties of talk.

This is done against the background of earlier work on the structures and strategies of discourse (van Dijk, 1972, 1977, 1980a, 1981a) as well as on that of other work in discourse analysis (see van Dijk, 1985a, for introductions, surveys, and methods).

Finally, it should be stressed that our application of discourse analysis in this book is not autonomous. Rather, we try to interpret features of the structures just mentioned as expressions or signals of cognitive representations and strategies and of interactional processes, such as those of persuasion or self-presentation. In the following chapters, we return to the methodological and theoretical problems of such analyses in more detail.

3. The structure of the problem

Before we go into more detail with the various dimensions of the problem of communicating prejudice and racism in everyday talk, we must further analyze the nature and the structure of this problem. In the first section, there was a general characterization of the goals of this study, as well as a brief summary of the disciplines and notions involved. Exactly how these are mutually related, and, therefore, how the chapters of this book cohere, require further explanation. This is accomplished by discussing and relating the key notions used in the analysis of the interpersonal communication of ethnic attitudes. Details and references about such notions are provided in the respective chapters.

Discourse and Discourse Analysis

The main object, the data and the method of analysis, are forms of discourse. We focus attention on how people talk about ethnic groups in society, and how they express, convey, or form ethnic beliefs or attitudes in such everyday conversations. Because discourse plays such a central role in this study, the first task must be a systematic analysis of such talk. This alone would represent a respectable goal for a vast research project, so we must confine ourselves here to the general outlines of such an analysis (for detail, see, e.g., van Dijk, 1982b, 1983b, 1983c, 1984, 1986c).

Following earlier work in discourse analysis, we first distinguish between a global, macro level, and a local, micro level of talk. At the global level, there are the various "themes" or topics, that is, the semantic macrostructures of conversation. If people talk about foreigners, what kind of topics are discussed, whether spontaneously or prompted by questions of the interviewer? At this global level, we also distinguish various sorts of "schematic" organization, such as argumentation structures, or the narrative structures of stories. At the local level, we deal with the structures of individual turns, moves, sentences, and speech acts, and their mutual relationships. Thus, we focus on semantic moves that are accomplished within overall strategies of discourse and interaction, as well as the expression of meaning in style, rhetorical operations, and conversational formulation. Chapter 2 is devoted to the systematic analyses of these various discourse structures of prejudiced talk.

Initially, this systematic discourse analysis has a "structural" bias. That is, we take talk about ethnic groups simply in its own right and survey its major properties as we would do for other discourse forms. Especially within a social science perspective, however, such an approach is incomplete. Discourse is not just a form of language use but is also a cognitive and social accomplishment within a communicative context. Talk is itself a form of interaction, and many of its properties can be understood and analyzed only when their interactional relevance is taken into account. It will become clear, for example, that at several levels of analysis, talk about ethnic groups involves complex strategies and moves aiming at positive self-presentation within the overall goal of negative other-description. Especially when delicate topics are discussed, and when social norms are rather strict, face-saving is essential: The expression of even the most racist opinions tends to be embedded in moves that are intended to prevent the inference that the speaker is a racist. In our discourse analysis, then, we already pay attention to this interactional dimension of everyday talk about foreigners.

The same holds for the further social dimensions of discourse. Although we focus on interpersonal communication, talk about other ethnic groups is not merely an "individual expression of individual emotions," as the Romanticists claimed about literature. Rather, people are talking as members of a White, dominant group about other people as specific outgroup members. In this way, they enact, at the same time, various forms of intergroup conflict, dominance and power, and other macro social dimensions of racism. The topics of talk, for instance, reflect the social position of the speaker as a group member and, conversely, the social dimension enables us to understand why people discuss certain topics, such as competition, and not others.

Discourse structures as well as their interpersonal and social functions are cognitively interpreted, programmed, planned, monitored, and executed. From its overall topics, narrative or argumentative organization, to its local moves and lexical style, talk expresses cognitive representations of knowledge, beliefs, and attitudes, as well as the mental operations or strategies that are applied in their retrieval, storage, and usage in discourse production. In other words, we also pay attention to the cognitive relevance of such discourse characteristics. Because we have no direct access to mental structures and strategies, discourse structures are the only empirical data that may reveal what people think about ethnic groups. In other words, discourse analysis also allows us to account for the structures of ethnic prejudice and, conversely, shows us how ethnic attitudes are expressed and formulated in talk and interaction. It now becomes clear why, in our view, discourse plays such a central role in this study: It not only represents an important social phenomenon by itself, but it also enables us to link the cognitive dimensions of ethnic prejudice with its interactional and societal functions.

Reproduction

When White majority group members talk about ethnic out-groups, they do not merely express their personal beliefs and attitudes. In different senses of the term, they *reproduce* ethnic opinions of their in-group as a whole, such as shared stereotypes or prejudices and information they have heard or read from other sources. These processes of communicative reproduction are very complex and involve an interaction of personal experiences and beliefs, representations of information from a variety of discourse types (both public and interpersonal), and more general, socially shared, belief and opinion structures about ethnic minority groups. This means that people seldom act as passive reproducers of personal or social information derived from previous communicative events. As we indicate, below, for the analysis of cognitive processes, recipients apply a number of discourse comprehension strategies resulting in mental representations that may be rather distant transformations of the original source messages. Similarly, people may also have biased memory for the very communicative events themselves and, for example, attribute beliefs or opinions to plausible rather than to the true sources of their information. In fact, after longer delays, recipients often no longer remember concrete communicative events and their messages but tend to abstract and generalize and thus form decontextualized meanings, beliefs, or opinions.

An empirically adequate analysis of such reproduction processes, however, is rather difficult. We seldom have access to the original discourses, so that it is not always possible to study the various transformations involved in reproduction. But again, discourse analysis does enable us to describe what people say and to infer from even vague references to other sources how people subjectively construct their own version of events or input opinions. In Chapter 3, we analyze how people refer to and interpret such communicative events and source messages about ethnic groups.

Reproduction is not just the active transformation and expression of concrete input messages and their meanings. As social members of the dominant group, people also reproduce the dominant ideologies of this group. Analysis and comparison of a large number of interviews allow us to assess not only the obviously shared beliefs and attitudes about ethnic groups but also how each individual social member—or various subgroups—use such social cognitions in their own personal context and in the actual communicative situation. In this sense, reproduction is also an instance of the sociocultural reproduction of the in-group as a group.

Aside from shared beliefs and opinions about other ethnic groups, reproduction also involves the cognitive basis for consensual social action and interaction. Discursive reproduction in that case is both a contribution to the diffusion and confirmation of ethnic prejudice and a form of communicative preparation for discriminatory acts. People formulate "acceptable" shared norms and goals for in-group members in their dealings with out-group members. It is in this complex sense that we take prejudiced talk about ethnic minority groups both as an instance and as a form of reproduction of racism. Here, the structural, macro notion of racism meets with its individual and interpersonal enactment by dominant group members at the micro level of social organization. Chapter 6 focuses in particular on these various social functions of ethnic prejudice and examines, for instance, the special role of elite groups and the media in the (re)production processes of ethnic prejudice.

Interpersonal Communication and Persuasion

Whereas the notion of reproduction, so to speak, conceptualizes how people discursively and cognitively face "backward" toward their personal or public information sources, the interpersonal communication of ethnic prejudice, of course, also has a "forward" dimension. People are not just passive recipients, but actively and persuasively convey their interpretations and representations to others in new communicative events. They not only express previously acquired and transformed ethnic beliefs and opinions, but also interactively engage in communications that are intended to "influence" other members of their own group. They have recourse to persuasive discourse strategies, such as those of positive self-presentation and of social group competence and affiliation display, and thus tell stories or formulate arguments that are moves in an effective realization of communication goals.

The interviews yield interesting data that illustrate such strategies. Also, in informal interview talk, interviewers are unknown others who are perceived as in-group members who need to be persuaded of the relevance and the truth of personal experiences, as well as of the defensibility of both personal and shared social opinions about ethnic minority groups. Discourse analysis and comparisons of interviews thus allow us to assess such persuasive strategies and, at the same time, may suggest at which point these are not just individual tactics but rather socially shared—or even stereotypical—maneuvers of the communicative reproduction of ethnic prejudice. Indeed, people may not only tell very similar stories or use the same arguments and thus convey stereotypical prejudices, but also may do this in very similar, persuasive ways. Besides prejudiced in-group attitudes, there may be a shared rhetoric of racism. In Chapter 5, we deal with the various topics of the communicative and persuasive dimension of ethnic attitude reproduction.

Cognitive Structures and Strategies of Prejudice

Discursive expression and persuasive communication of ethnic prejudice are programmed and controlled at the cognitive level. Few discourse characteristics or interpersonal communication properties can be fully understood without an explanation of their cognitive dimension. Therefore, in Chapters 4 and 5, extensive attention is paid to the mental nature of ethnic prejudice and to the processes that guide its expression in talk and communicative interaction.

This means, first, that cognitive contents and structures, that is, the representation of ethnic beliefs and opinions in memory, must be made explicit. Against the background of earlier work in psychology and AI on the cognitive representation of knowledge and beliefs, we analyze prejudice as a complex interaction of (a) negative (ethnic) group attitudes organized by schematic categories, (b) negative (biased) models of personal experiences, also involving previous communicative events, and (c) a set of cognitive strategies that connect these attitudes and models and also determine how ethnic encounters or talk about them are attended to, interpreted, represented, retrieved, and expressed. It is argued that such structures and strategies are not simply cognitive in the individual or personal sense but are rather forms of social cognition. This socio-cognitive perspective also allows us to connect explicitly ethnic prejudice with social interaction (and hence with conversation) and with social structures of discrimination and racism.

Second, cognitive analysis allows us to show how people use ethnic beliefs and opinions in concrete discourse production. Speakers try to control what they say, and what they prefer to be silent about, especially when a delicate topic such as foreigners is concerned. We want to know which strategies are involved in these controlled processes of "expression" and "production" in conversational interaction. We also want to know exactly how people cognitively manage ongoing conversational interaction, how self-presentation is monitored, and how persuasive tactics are programmed and executed. In other words, the strategies of talk and persuasion must correspond to cognitive strategies for the manipulation of ethnic information in memory.

Third, for both the actual recipient of ongoing talk, as well as the actual speaker participating as a recipient in previous communications, we must know exactly how media or personal communications are being interpreted and represented in memory. That is, the process of persuasion cannot be fully understood if we ignore its detailed cognitive nature. Because transformations of social beliefs and attitudes are involved, we should know exactly how discourse information is processed, stored, and used in the formation or change of such ethnic beliefs.

Social Context and Social Structure

Because we focus attention on the micro-level reproduction of racism, notions such as discourse, interpersonal communication and persuasion, and (social) cognition play an important role in our theory and analysis. We also stress, however, that prejudice and racism are not characteristics of individual persons but involve people as group members. Discourse and communication about ethnic minority groups can be understood only in this double social perspective: They are social events at the interpersonal (micro) level but, at the same time, they are instances of a particular form of intragroup and intergroup relationships, that is, of higher-level social, cultural, and historical processes. This means that prejudiced talk is multiply integrated into and indicative of both its immediate social context and its embedding within broader societal structures.

Against this background, Chapter 6 shows which other social goals and functions may be distinguished for such prejudiced talk. Speakers actively reproduce, and thus diffuse, group-based cognitions. They express, confirm, and show allegiance to group goals, values, and norms, and may thus evaluate group actions toward ethnic out-groups. They express group attitudes that are assumed to be held by other group members and thus may or may not display conformity with their own group. At the same time, they may show acceptance of group-based beliefs about the perceived competition from or threats posed by ethnic out-groups. In other words, we also must analyze the proper social embedding of the social cognitions analyzed in mental frameworks.

Aside from this account of talk about ethnic minorities as an instance of intergroup relationships, social analysis also involves the more "structural" dimensions of reproducing racism. It was suggested earlier, for instance, that institutions, such as the media, education, the government, and other authorities, play a decisive role in the control of racist discourse. People show how the media are used as a permanent source of information and opinions about minorities and may point to the role of authorities when validating their own opinions. Although it is not a major aim of this book, there is a brief analysis of the way interpersonal talk and communication about minorities mesh with these various components of the immediate and global social contexts.

Further Clarification of Key Notions: Prejudice and Racism

We now have briefly defined the key notions to be dealt with in the following chapters. However, a few further terminological remarks are in order, especially as we use some terms with a different meaning than in other work. First, the notion of *ethnic prejudice* itself. It was suggested above that ethnic prejudice will be theoretically analyzed as a specific type of negative ethnic attitude shared by the members of a (dominant) in-group. This fragment of a definition, which, of course, is to be fully spelled out in a theory, already suggests (a) that the analysis of prejudice is framed primarily in cognitive terms, but also (b) that it is a social concept in the sense that it is a form of social cognition about other groups and is shared by in-group members. In other words, for us there is no inherent distinction between the *cognitive* and the *social,* as the very notion of *social cognition* suggests. Of course, this does not mean that groups have minds or mental structures of their own (as is suggested by traditional notions such as "group consciousness"), but that the members of such groups share cognitions they acquire, use, convey, and change as group members in group-based interactions and communicative events.

To allow for some stylistic variation and simplicity, we usually abbreviate *ethnic prejudice* to *prejudice*. Because this book does not deal with prejudices about other social groups, this will not lead to confusion. Sometimes we also use the more general term *ethnic attitude,* which, of course, need not imply a negative orientation but, from the context, it will be clear when this generic term denotes ethnic prejudice. In Chapter 4, we show why a distinction should be made between (ethnic or other) *opinions* on the one hand and *attitudes* on the other. We do not use these terms as synonyms. The term *attitude* always denotes a complex, schematic structure of general opinions stored in long-term memory, whereas opinions are single evaluative beliefs, whether particular (context bound) or general.

We generally use the general term *ethnic* relative to social groups that are identified in ethnic or racial terms. This means that their members are perceived to be different in physical appearance and/or sociocultural properties (origin, language, norms, and so on) with respect to dominant majority groups. Although we follow everyday usage here, there is also a theoretical reason. Prejudice and racism, both in Western

Europe and in the United States, are not limited to what are traditionally called different *racial* groups. Especially in Western Europe, in particular in the countries that have immigrant workers from several Mediterranean countries, the discourse of race and racism has gradually taken a more sophisticated form by focusing primarily on "ethnic" properties of minority groups, and by emphasizing "cultural" differences. Hence, racism needs a more general, sociocultural correlate, namely, *ethnicism* (Mullard, 1985), to account for prejudice and discrimination against ethnic minority groups in general. Our usage of the term *racism* follows the traditional terminology, but it is intended to cover also the notion of *ethnicism*. In this perspective, we sometimes use the term as an adjective, for instance, in combinations such as *racist attitude,* which in that case is synonymous with *ethnic prejudice* (because of the negative implications of the term *racist*). The term *minority* is used here only as an abbreviation for *ethnic minority group* and implies that such a group is economically, socially, and culturally dominated by a majority group, in our case White "Northwestern" caucasians (such as Dutch and Anglos).

Finally, racism or ethnicism are taken as notions that denote complex social phenomena both at the abstract, macro levels of societal structures, and at the micro levels of social cognition, discourse, communication, and interaction. In fact, the distinction between macro and micro analysis becomes blurred as soon as we talk about group ideologies (which we describe as social cognitions, but that are traditionally studied as typical macro phenomena), or when we study institutional actions (see Knorr-Cetina & Cicourel, 1981, for a more general and detailed study of the relations between macro and micro analysis). Hence, we do not simply take ethnic prejudice as a micro notion, and racism as a macro notion. Racism is an abstract property of social structures at all levels of society that manifests itself in ethnic prejudices as shared group cognitions, in discriminatory actions of persons as dominant group members, as well as in the actions, discourses, organization, or relationships within and among groups, institutions, classes, or other social formations.

Schema for This Book

We have briefly discussed some major notions and analytical frameworks that need to be worked out in a sound theory of the interpersonal reproduction of racism through everyday discourse. Each of them is, of course, associated with many other notions, as well as with much theoretical and empirical work, to be detailed and discussed in the succeeding chapters of this book. It has become obvious that our problem is as complex as it is fascinating, both academically and sociopolitically. Its vast interdisciplinary ramifications cannot be explored in one book and by one author. I can only provide a first sketch, work out some partial problems, and suggest the interdisciplinary framework for a study of the discourse dimension of racism.

The beginning is an analysis of the discourse structures of prejudiced talk. Theoretically, this is, of course, arbitrary because the beginning could just as well have been an analysis of the cognitive structures of prejudice or the social functions and contexts of such talk. However, for practical reasons, attention is paid to prejudiced talk first because it will provide the crucial empirical data on which further theorizing about prejudiced cognitive, interpersonal, and social structures and processes will be based. Prejudiced discourse is not only the central phenomenon in the communication of ethnic prejudices and the reproduction of racism; it also provides a rich data base that shows or signals the cognitive and interactive work of speakers and hearers, as well as the relevant properties of the social context. Once we have assessed the contents and organization of such discourse, we can move to their underlying cognitive representations and strategies, both as origins in the production of discourse, and as targets in persuasive communication. Similarly, we need this cognitive analysis first in order to be able to account for the processes of interpersonal communication.

Again, this ordering of the chapters is inspired mainly by practical reason of presentation. In reality, the processes of discursive reproduction of social cognitions are, of course, integrated and none of its major elements have either priority or a fully autonomous status. Indeed, social members strategically do it all at the same time: They think, speak, and (inter)act. Therefore, the following chapters will contain multiple cross-references to other chapters. We may need to refer to cognitive structures or interactional strategies in order to analyze and explain certain discourse structures. And, conversely, we need discourse structures both as empirical evidence for and as concrete manifestation or enactment of these other processes.

2

Structures of
Prejudiced Discourse

1. Introduction

One major thesis of this book is that prejudice is socially reproduced through discourse. If we want to understand this important property of the social communication of ethnic attitudes, we must examine the structures of such discourse in detail, that is, both its forms and contents. Such an analysis allows us to assess the way underlying attitudes are strategically expressed in discourse in various social and communicative contexts. And, conversely, the structural analysis may give us clues about the cognitive organization and strategies of prejudice. Finally, discourse analysis allows us to examine how prejudiced talk also depends on constraints of the communicative interaction, and how recipients of such talk interpret such talk. In other words, discourse is in many respects the central element in the processes of the interpersonal communication of prejudice, and discourse analysis is a key method for the study of the cognitive and social structures and strategies that characterize these processes.

Our analysis is limited to everyday conversation, that is, to face-to-face verbal interaction, among members of the White, autochthonous population. Obviously, such talk is only one instance of the many discourse types that communicate ethnic attitudes of and to majority group members. Other major channels involve the print and broadcast media, such as newspapers, weeklies, radio and TV programs, and educational discourse, such as lessons and textbooks, as well as novels, film, comics, public speeches, meetings, announcements, advertisements, institutional texts, and dialogues, such as parliamentary debates, job interviews, or interviews in social welfare agencies. These few examples show that the variety of discourse types that express and convey ethnic beliefs and opinions is impressive. Only a few of these discourse types, notably the media and textbooks, have been systematically analyzed for their expression of ethnic beliefs and attitudes. If data are available and relevant for the study of everyday talk about ethnic groups, we take them into account, but we cannot possibly include all research results about these other genres and communicative contexts.

It is relevant, though, to stress that everyday conversations about ethnic groups form an integral part of the full communicative and discursive "environment" of social members. Talk, indeed, often reproduces what is interpreted from the various media or institutional texts mentioned above. In this chapter, though, we study conversation in its own right. In Chapter 3, we then focus on the possible communicative contexts and "sources" of the beliefs and opinions expressed in conversation.

Our discourse approach to the reproduction of racism does neither implies that majority group members acquire their beliefs and opinions through discourse only, nor that they always or only show their ethnic cognitions in talk. For people who have regular contacts with ethnic minority group members, part of the information may also be drawn from personal experiences, that is, from perception of action of and participation in interaction with minority group members. And similarly, they also exhibit their beliefs and opinions through nonverbal discrimination against minority group members. We maintain, however, that for most majority members, the information sources about ethnic groups are predominantly discursive. Even for people who have daily contacts with ethnic minority members, a large part of their information comes from the various discourse types we have enumerated above. Similarly, the consequences of previous verbal or nonverbal experiences with minority groups will be predominantly discursive, which, for most people, means everyday talk rather than letters, media texts, or institutional dialogue. In everyday life, people usually formulate, reproduce, and thus socially share their experiences through talk, and this also holds for the evaluations, norms, and attitudes that underlie the interpretation of such experiences. In other words, social cognitions, in general, and ethnic attitudes, in particular, are acquired, shared, validated, normalized, and communicated primarily through talk (and the media) rather than through perception and interaction. In Chapter 6, we pay special attention to these various functions of talk about ethnic minority groups.

2. Some principles of discourse analysis

Discourse analysis has become a vast and burgeoning new field, and, therefore, it is imperative to introduce briefly some of its major principles and further explain our own approach. The theoretical framework of our analysis is based on earlier work on discourse (e.g., van Dijk, 1972, 1977, 1980a, 1981a). Yet, as suggested in the previous section, for a number of additional theoretical notions, especially those that account for the local organization of everyday talk, we borrow from other approaches, such as discourse linguistics, psychology, conversational analysis, ethnography of speaking, sociolinguistics, and microsociology (Brown & Yule, 1983; Coulthard, 1977; de Beaugrande & Dressler, 1981; Tannen, 1981; van Dijk, 1985a).

To illustrate this interdisciplinary approach to discourse analysis, some of its basic assumptions and principles are summarized. More detailed explanations are given at the beginning of each of the next sections of this chapter. Although this summary is primarily intended for those who are unfamiliar with modern linguistics and discourse analysis, it also features some choices and assumptions that are less obvious or less widely accepted in discourse analysis.

Discourse as Social Interaction

First, a rather obvious, if not trivial, assumption: Discourse is primarily taken as a specific form of social interaction, and not just as an "abstracted" or "produced" result of such interaction. That is, social members "participate" in discourse in a similar way as they participate in other types of social interaction. This is particularly obvious in face-to-face verbal interaction but, derivatively, it also holds for the production of written discourse forms, which are usually also produced for a recipient. Because notions such as *text* or *discourse* are often also used to denote the (abstracted) linguistic product of monological or dialogical verbal acts, we shall add the term *interaction* when ambiguity may arise. The terms *talk* and *conversation* are only used in this interactional sense: They denote what people do when speaking in face-to-face encounters (Atkinson & Heritage, 1984; Goffman, 1967; McLaughlin, 1984; Schenkein, 1978; Sudnow, 1972).

I stress this rather obvious interactional nature of discourse because it allows us to integrate a social and sociocognitive dimension into its theoretical and analytical study. If we abstract from what people actually do, both socially and mentally, we cannot account for many of the contents, forms, or strategies of talk, nor are we able to integrate the analysis into wider frameworks of communication, social interaction, and social structure. That is, the discursive reproduction of ethnic prejudice is neither merely some type of text, nor the individual or solitary activity of speakers or writers, but a form of social interaction between social members, taking place in social contexts that are constrained by (interpreted) social structures and cultural frameworks (Bauman & Sherzer, 1974; Cicourel, 1980; Duranti, 1985).

This implies that talk assumes the usual properties of (inter)action, for instance, that it is planned (intended), goal-directed, controlled, ongoing, and sequential activity, coordinated by at least two participants. This summarizing characterization of (inter)action suggests that it features both *observables* (Sacks, 1985), namely, utterance or activity fragments that may be produced, heard, or seen, and *nonobservables,* such as intentions, plans, goals, strategies, beliefs, and interpretations.

It is, however, a sound methodological principle to take into account only those nonobservables that, sometimes very indirectly, show or exhibit themselves in observables and, conversely, to analyze only those observables that are expressions of, interpreted as, or functions of mental and social representations or processes. In other words, *overt* activities are integrated with *covert* cognitive and social processes. We stress the cognitive dimension because some sociological analyses of conversation tend to have a somewhat "behavioristic" bias and neglect the important cognitive correlates of talk (but see Cicourel, 1973). A full-fledged discourse analysis is not just interested in what is actually observable or "shown." That position would, when taken seriously, reduce our account to the visual or acoustic level, which is obviously not what discourse and social interaction are about. And if we talk about *meaning, belief, intention, interpretation,* or *common sense,* we talk about mental objects, even when they are socially shared.

Dimensions and Levels of Analysis

Whereas the interactional assumption about the nature of discourse stresses the "integral" account of cognitive, social, and textual aspects of talk, all serious analysis proceeds through a number of divisions and abstractions. Thus, even for the analysis of ongoing discursive activity, we isolate structural units that are theoretically assigned "object" nature, that is, forms, functions, meanings, categorial values, or boundaries, for example: words, phrases, clauses, or sentences at one level of analysis, concepts, propositions, or topics at another level, or turns, moves, speech acts, interactions, or strategies at a third level of analysis. That is, properties of discursive interaction are defined as objects of different theoretical "type," and for each type a different theoretical account may be needed. The same holds for the relations between objects of different types, as is the case between sentences and propositions, or between propositions and moves, or for units that require characterization at several levels at the same time, such as repetition, repair, side sequence, or story. Without such systematic distinctions, the analysis becomes vague, confused, and unsystematic.

Linguistic Structure

We recognize, here, the familiar levels, units, and categories of phonology, morphology, syntax, and semantics of structural sentence and discourse grammars, as well as those of speech act theory (pragmatics), conversational analysis, or rhetoric (see the various contributions in van Dijk, 1985a, vol. 2). The theoretical operations that make such levels or units "discrete" properties of discursive interaction do not imply that they do not have a "dynamic," processlike nature. This holds both for small units such as words, as well as for larger units such as stories in conversation. Both are "segments" in otherwise continuous verbal activity. Just as in a physical theory of light, the properties of discourse may be studied as ongoing, dynamic operations or processes (waves) or as discrete units (particles).

Much in the same way as such segments may need analysis of their structures and functions at several levels, they may be studied along different dimensions or from different perspectives. Traditional linguistics, for instance, studies its levels or units of utterances as properties of static, structured objects, such as sentences. The same is true for the additional units studied in discourse linguistics, namely, discourses (texts, dialogues). In both cases, the abstractions may pertain to observables such as sounds, words, phrases, clauses, sentences, or sentence sequences or to nonobservables such as meanings, associated to the observables by abstract relationships, such as interpretation. The account of physical continuities of speech, both in terms of articulation or in terms of acoustics, is then left to phonetics.

Beyond Grammatical Structures: Style, Rhetoric, Schemata

Linguistic analysis is often identified with grammatical analysis. However, verbal utterances may be characterized in structural terms that go beyond the levels and units of grammar. First, discourse exhibits style, that is, a characteristic form of language variation, typically at the surface levels of pronunciation, syntax, and lexicon. Such variation is usually defined in terms of alternative ways to formulate the "same" meaning, namely, as a function of variable factors of the communicative context, such as mood or evaluation of the speaker, or the position, status, gender, age, or social relationships of the speech participants. Discourse style thus may be viewed as the signaling trace of the context in the text. In this sense, a "formal" style may be globally associated with a "formal" communicative event or social situation (Norton, 1983; Sandell, 1977; Scherer & Giles, 1979).

Rhetorical structures are a step further removed from grammar. Unlike style, they are not inherent properties of discourse, but optional, "extra" structures at all levels of grammatical analysis. Basically, they can be defined in terms of specific transformations of grammatical structure, such as additions, deletions, permutations, or substitutions, as is the case in alliterations, rhymes, or parallelisms at the morphosyntactic level, and metaphors, irony, or understatements at the semantic level. Basically, such rhetorical operations have a communicative function. They may be used to enhance the effectiveness of discourse, for instance, by making an expression or meaning more salient (Kahane, 1971; Plett, 1977).

As a specific case of the kind of discourse organization also accounted for in classical rhetoric, we may distinguish higher-level forms of a "schematic" nature, namely, superstructures (van Dijk, 1980a). Thus, many discourse types, such as stories, news reports, conversations, or psychological reports, may exhibit a conventionalized (and hence culturally variable) overall structure, defined in terms of hierarchically ordered categories. For instance, several discourse types have a *Setting* or a *Summary* category, and in dialogues we often find various *Opening* or *Closing* categories. The superstructures organized by these categories are filled with variable (macro) semantic content. Schemata or superstructures organize the higher discourse levels in a way that is reminiscent of the syntactic structure of sentences. They provide the overall "form" of the overall semantic "content" (macrostructures) we introduce below. Generally, as we shall see later in this chapter, such schemata are described in specific "genre" theories, such as a theory of narrative or a theory of argumentation.

Acts and Speech Acts

The traditional linguistic isolation of sentences and their elements from ongoing speech activity not only led to a neglect of the dynamic or processual nature of talk, it also meant an abstraction from the action and interaction properties of language use. This dimension was partly restored by the analysis of utterances as *speech acts,* by which an abstract account is given of what speakers "do" when they talk, that is, of the social act being accomplished through or beside the meaningful production of sounds. That is, sentences of a given form, and with a given interpretation, when uttered by a speaker in a specific context may also be interpreted as assertions, promises, or threats (Austin, 1962; Searle, 1969).

Note that the description of such speech acts should encompass also the other, for instance, the grammatical levels of analysis, mentioned above, such as those of sentences or propositions. The additional dimension, that is, the "illocutionary" function (or meaning), thus becomes the specific task of another type of theory, namely, pragmatics (Leech, 1983; Levinson, 1983; van Dijk, 1981a). This theory specifies, among other things, under which grammatical and contextual conditions an utterance may be produced and interpreted as a given speech act type. In other words, a pragmatic theory relates grammar with an (abstract) account of social action. This also means, as suggested earlier, that a cognitive dimension becomes involved: Action also needs analysis in terms of intentions and goals (or their interpretations). Also, for each speech act, other cognitive "states" such as knowledge, beliefs, wishes, or opinions of speakers, may be relevant. Thus, in a request, we wish the hearer to do something that we believe he or she can accomplish. Besides these cognitive dimensions of speech acts, we may require specific social constraints on speakers who accomplish such acts, such as institutional functions, or social relationships of familiarity or power, for instance, in the description of the speech acts of commanding, threatening, or acquitting somebody.

Traditional speech act theory has one limitation it shares with traditional grammars: In practice it is usually limited to the analysis of isolated, single speech acts, performed by the utterance of single sentences. Obviously, in language use, speech acts seldom come alone, and a serious pragmatics of discourse, therefore, also must account for sequences of speech acts. Conditions of connection and coherence at the local level must be formulated for such sequences, as well as rules or conditions for the performance of global or macro speech acts. A news report thus may globally function as a higher-level assertion and a ransom note as a macro threat. Such pragmatic macrostructures also need their own proposition content, namely, in terms of semantic macrostructures.

Obviously, this additional account of verbal interaction in terms of speech acts merely provides a very specific perspective on the nature of interaction. That is, further social analysis may be needed. For instance, by making an assertion, issuing a command, or lodging a complaint, social members may "do" many other things, often at the same time. Indeed, they may defend themselves, attack others, enhance their self-esteem, "save face," show concern or solidarity, or negotiate or cooperate with other social members. In fact, the major goals of talk are often just the accomplishment of such actions or interactions, or their component moves and strategies, through the accomplishment of speech acts, themselves accomplished by the utterance of sentences or discourse fragments. Aside from an additional dimension of analysis, this sociological account of interaction also shows the hierarchy of verbal (inter)action, namely, from the plans and goals of word and sentence production (locutionary acts) via those of proposition formation (semantic acts: those of "meaning" and "referring"), and via the plans and goals of illocutionary acts, to the plans and goals of social acts.

The Cognitive Dimension

In the semantics of a linguistic approach already, and certainly in the account of discourse in terms of speech acts and social interaction, we cannot do without an analysis of the cognitive dimension of discourse. Although grammar deals with meanings and interpretation in abstract terms, it should be emphasized that, empirically, meanings and interpretations of utterances or activities are to be accounted for in cognitive terms. No serious account of discourse meaning, coherence, or other semantic properties is possible without notions such as concepts, knowledge and beliefs, frames, scripts, or models, that is, in terms of mental representations and cognitive processes of various kinds. The same is true for the analysis of action and interaction: Notions such as plans, intentions, goals, strategies, control, and monitoring are essential in both the theoretical and empirical description of speech acts and social action. The same holds, at all levels, for the representations of the communicative context, including speakers, communicative goals and the social properties of the participants and the situation.

Local Versus Global Analysis

The next set of principles of discourse analysis pertains to the "scope" of our description and theory formation. At several levels, especially those of semantics, pragmatics, and action theory, it makes sense to distinguish between a "local" and a "global" range of phenomena, that is, between microstructures and macrostructures (van Dijk, 1980a). Local structures of discourse are partly accounted for in terms of the usual grammatical levels: words, phrases, clauses, sentences, and immediate sentence connections. The same is true for the analysis of isolated speech acts or speech act pairs, or for the local analysis of turn taking in conversation. It is, however, characteristic of discourse that global levels of analysis are also involved, for instance, meanings of larger discourse segments, or global (speech) acts (Ferrara, 1985; van Dijk, 1980a, 1981a). That is, we deal with sequences of sentences, propositions, (speech) acts, turns, or moves, and these may exhibit specific forms of organization.

Some of the special notions that have been introduced in discourse analysis, such as topic or theme, moves and strategies, narrative and argumentative structure, or other schematic forms (superstructures) of text and talk, cannot be explained without such global units, categories, or representations, both in structural terms and in cognitive and social analysis. Obviously, local and global structures are closely related, for instance, in hierarchical networks, by rules or strategies of interpretation and inference, or by other mapping rules. Many local phenomena can only be properly explained in terms of their functions in global structures.

In cognitive terms, this distinction implies the usual complementarity of bottom-up and top-down processing. Many cognitive operations, such as storage, retrieval, instantiation, and application cannot work without the distinction between micro- and macrostructures. Most discursive interaction is sequentially and hierarchically complex, and plans and goals usually operate both locally and globally. Relations between utterance and situation may hold again at both levels, and characterizations of genres or whole communicative events are impossible without analyses at the global, overall level. At this point, we find another basic distinction between traditional sentence grammars or speech act theories, on one hand, and discourse analysis, on the other.

To avoid possible misunderstanding, it should be added, finally, that the micro/macro distinction recalls a similar distinction in the social sciences, but should not be confused with it. In sociological terms, discourse analysis of text or talk in social situations takes place at the micro level of social analysis. This does not mean that typical sociological macro (or structural) notions do not impinge at this level: Social formations, institutions, norms, and ideologies are also relevant at the micro level of social analysis. In fact, it is at this micro level that such macro phenomena are actually occurring or being enacted (Knorr-Cetina & Cicourel, 1981). We show this in detail for the typical macro notion of "racism." This structural property of dominant groups or society finds its actual instantiations at the micro level through (discriminatory) interaction, the communication of ethnic prejudice, and the social cognitions of individual social members as majority group members. The macro analysis of racism generalizes and abstracts from such micro-level cognitions, interactions, and situations, and introduces higher-level notions, such as the role of institutions (government, the police, the media, and so on), of class formations, of ethnic groups, and their complex mutual relationships and processes, such as socialization, education, exploitation, or discrimination. Obviously, this brief statement about the macro versus micro levels of social analysis is short for a complex theoretical account that cannot be elaborated here.

Integration

We have briefly summarized a few basic principles of modern discourse analysis. In many respects, discourse analysis may be seen as a necessary and relevant extension of contemporary grammars, in particular, and of linguistics, in general. Discourse analysis takes into account units or categories of larger scope than the sentence and, at the same time, sets out to study the many complex forms of language use. In its characterization of sentence structures, it, of course, embodies grammar. Yet, it also accounts for relations between sentences or propositions, for instance, in the study of coherence. Classical speech act theories are extended to full-fledged discourse pragmatics. Discourse analysis takes into account many additional, such as stylistic, rhetorical, or schematic, properties of language use, and does so both at the local and global levels of analysis. Its extension toward more natural forms of language use, toward cognition, (inter)action, and communication, suggests that discourse analysis aims at a full characterization of communicative events, as it was advocated by Hymes (1962) more than two decades ago for the ethnography of speaking.

These various levels, dimensions, and approaches of discourse analysis have, often independently, been developed in several disciplines in the past 20 years. One of the main aims of discourse analysis in the coming years is a theoretically adequate integration of these orientations. The boundaries between abstract grammars of language "systems," on one hand, and the various theories of "language use," on the other, have been crossed and blurred, for example, by the necessary introduction of properties of action, cognition, and communication as direct determinants of the structures of verbal utterances. In our analysis of everyday conversations about minorities, we have tried to integrate the various approaches into a coherent framework. Even when we systematically analyze structures at different levels, it should be kept in mind that both empirically and theoretically, all these levels and dimensions are closely related.

3. The discourse environment of prejudiced talk

Before we start with our analysis of prejudiced conversations, we must briefly point out that talk is not the only discourse channel for the expression, reproduction, and diffusion of racism in society. Informal, interpersonal interaction is certainly at the heart of the individual participation and interaction within overall racist societies, but its conditions and consequences should be located at more embracing or higher levels of discursive communication. The news media, magazines, educational materials, novels, comics, movies, advertising, propaganda, political speeches, laws and regulations, institutional documentation (of national or local government, the police, the judiciary, business, and so on) provide the public discourse in which everyday conversations are coherently embedded. Reproduction relations are mutual here: The mass media reproduce and reconstruct the ethnic attitudes and discourses of social members and groups, and, conversely, everyday talk presupposes and refers to the many forms of public discourse that are produced by the many institutions of society.

Unfortunately, we have as yet little systematic insight into the precise structures and functions of these many types of possibly prejudiced discourses. Most work is limited to the mass media, film, literature, and educational materials, such as textbooks. These discourse types are often of a representational and narrative kind: They are about people, actions, events, and situations. That is, they express models of fragments of real or constructed social reality. Analyses in that case often pertain to the contents of these models or to the style of expression. They study how Blacks, immigrants, foreigners, or minority groups are represented.

The general finding is that this representation or portrayal is biased: Ethnic minority group members (or women, or other dominated groups), are shown in stereotypical roles and situations, with prevailing negative evaluations, and from a dominant perspective, if they are represented at all. They also have minority status in discourse, or in discourse-producing institutions. They are portrayed in passive roles, except when attributed negative actions, such as crime, riots, or many forms of deviance. In this respect, public discourse both models and persuasively communicates the position of minority groups in society. That is, it is neither a passive reflection of dominant group attitudes, nor a routine account of social structure. Public discourse both models and forms the dominant consensus. We shall later show (in Chapter 6) that various elite groups, such as politicians (Reeves, 1983) or academics, play a central role in the production and reproduction of these forms of prejudiced public discourse.

3.1. THE NEWS MEDIA

A primary role in this construction of the dominant consensus is played by the news media, such as the newspaper, radio, and TV. This role is not only defined in terms of its vast, mass-mediated scope, or by the assumed representational goals of the print or broadcast media in the reporting of social events; the media also play an intermediary role in the reproduction of other types of public discourse. Much of the news is not so much about happenings or events, but about what other people, typically the powerful and the elite, say or write (Galtung & Ruge, 1965; Gans, 1979; van Dijk, 1983d, 1985f, 1987a). Most people read or hear about the discourses of institutions, government, politicians, business people, professionals, groups, parties, unions, churches, or other groups and institutions through the media. And news production is organized to access such source discourses routinely in the most effective way (Fishman, 1980; Tuchman, 1979).

The active processing of these source texts and talk in news production is the major contribution of the media in the reproduction and transformation of public discourse (van Dijk, 1987). These news production strategies involve ideologically shared values and routines of attention allocation, institutional access, selection, summarization, relevance assignment, stylistic (re)formulation, and exclusion. This holds *a fortiori* for socially and ideologically prominent topics such as various minority groups and ethnic relations (Cohen & Young, 1981; Hall et al., 1978). And because the media provide the daily discourse input for most adult citizens, their role as a prevailing discourse and attitude context for thought and talk about ethnic groups is probably unsurpassed by any other institutional or public source of communication.

Hartmann and Husband (1974), in their seminal study of racism and the mass media, have explicitly paid attention to these information sources for what people know and find out about ethnic groups. In standard interviews and written questionnaires, they asked children and adults from which sources they got their ethnic beliefs or opinions. As expected, the media score high in areas with no or few ethnic minority groups, followed by personal experiences and what they heard from other people. Yet, in high-contact areas, both adults and children attribute most of their beliefs to personal experiences. In general, the media are especially given credit for information about national issues such as immigration, the numbers of immigrants, violent conflicts (riots), and the occurrence of discrimination. Personal experiences are espcially mentioned for information about cultural differences, both in the high- and in the low-contact areas.

These findings partially agree with our interview results but should be interpreted with care, additionally because the research method was of the well-known survey type. For instance, the relatively low score on media information in low-contact areas does not necessarily mean that people have actually had much less information from the media in such areas as opposed to high-contact areas, but only that many kinds of beliefs are rather attributed to more reliable or more concrete personal experiences. The same is true for the relatively low scoring on hearsay information. For most categories, it is highly unlikely that people have acquired information by personal experience only. It is probable that personal experiences often also include things they have heard "from other people." For instance, the fact that many people say they know about "resentment" or "prejudice" against minorities suggests that they heard about this from others, or from the media. We return to this role of the media, hearsay, and personal experiences in later chapters.

Hartmann and Husband (1974) not only surveyed the information sources and opinions of children and adults in various areas, but also conducted a (mostly thematic) content analysis of a number of newspapers (*Times, Guardian, Daily Express,* and *Daily Mirror*) over a period of seven years (1963-1970). The major themes the newspaper reports on are, for example, housing, education, health, employment, numbers (of immigrants), White hostility, Black hostility, discrimination, police, crime, disturbances, and cultural differences. A dominant topic during these years was the immigration of Commonwealth subjects from East Africa, the Caribbean, and India. In this as well as in the other topics, minority groups are primarily portrayed as a threat and as causing "problems." These may be the very "numbers" that were seen to "invade" the country, the perceived competition for houses, work, education, and social welfare, as well as the frequent associations with crime, riots, or other "disturbances." In other words, immigration and social problems are redefined as a "race" problem. The press did pay attention to conflicts, tensions, and resentment against the new citizens, but hardly discussed the underlying causes and consequences of this resentment, such as ethnic prejudice and racism, or discrimination against Black people. On the whole, minority groups were not represented as being part of British society, but as outsiders who preferably should be "kept out." Racist statements of someone such as Powell received wide coverage in these years. The authors conclude that the media have not just expressed general opinions and feelings, but have themselves significantly contributed to such negative feelings.

Other British studies confirm these conclusions. Critcher, Parker, and Sondhi (1977), and Troyna (1981), in their analyses of the British regional press (Birmingham and Manchester), found that most items are about crime and human interest, followed by the national issues of immigration and the debate about legislation against such immigration. The actions of the neofascist National Front receive much attention, and although there is space devoted to the "White" side of the "problem," namely, discrimination, this is typically portrayed as incidental, as the act of extremist individuals, and not as a structural manifestation of British racism. Hall et al. (1978) in their extensive study of the political, legal, social, and media reactions to the "mugging crisis" also found that young Black West Indians tend to be associated with crimes in general and with mugging in particular. Downing (1980), who summarizes his findings from an analysis of TV programs, stresses that Blacks, both in Britain and in African countries, are seldom allowed to give their opinions. The media rather invite a (male) White "minority specialist" to give his views. Immigration is the main theme, and violence against Blacks is treated as regrettable incidents.

Most other studies on the portrayal of ethnic groups in the press that have been carried out in the United States and in various countries in Europe have come to similar conclusions. Yet, there are few in-depth content analyses of the news media. De Mott and Roberts (1979) in their bibliography list 138 items in English, including British studies, but most of the items are brief and anecdotal. There is not a single full-fledged study of the portrayal of minorities (or of any minority group) in the American press until the more general monograph by Wilson and Gutiérrez (1985). Fischer and Lowenstein (1967) feature a number of articles by journalists, but do not report results of systematic research. The 1960 "riots" are widely covered, and it is concluded that here too the negative, sensational, violent dimensions of racial conflict are stressed. The Black perspective is seldom represented, and the same holds for police brutality (see also Schary, 1969). Knopf (1975), in her study on "rumors and riots" in earlier decades, also finds that, generally, Blacks are portrayed negatively, and that the White dominant perspective is always given in press accounts. Also, Greenberg and Atkin (1978) and Roberts (1975) conclude that Blacks are mostly present only in "nonspeaking" roles, even for events that directly involve them. This is true not only for their role in press stories, but also for their participation in the news media themselves: Especially in higher positions, there are virtually no Black journalists (Greenberg & Mazingo, 1976).

Gutiérrez (1978), in his study of the California media, concludes that Chicanos tend to be portrayed negatively when conflicts arise, and that police versions or other Anglo sources of such conflicts are usually preferred over those of Chicano representatives. Chicanos are routinely defined as "illegals" so that they can be treated as a "problem of justice" (see also Wilson and Gutiérrez, 1985).

Our own studies of the Dutch press (van Dijk, 1983a, 1987b, 1987d), which were both quantitative and qualitative, found that the picture is similar to the one found for the American and British media of the 1960s and 1970s: Ethnic minority groups (immigrant workers from different Mediterranean countries and the Surinamese) are sometimes subtly associated with social and economic problems. In the early 1980s, the immigration topic itself became somewhat less prominent, but socioeconomic and cultural themes are discussed and indirectly associated with threat, ten-

sion, conflict, problems, and other difficulties. Crime and deviance are
the most frequent topics, "even" in the quality press. Much like the
mugging problem studied by Hall et al. (1978), the Dutch press continues to be fascinated by the Amsterdam drug scene, which is also preferably redefined as at least in part a "Black" problem. Discrimination is
reported, but more easily when it affects Jewish people and institutions
than when individual Black or ethnically different immigrants are
involved. Similarly, acts of discrimination are reported as incidents
rather than as expressions of widespread racism. Racism is a taboo
notion, and when Blacks have experienced racism, for instance, by the
authorities (notably the police), such events will go unreported or are
reported with the usual distance markers, such as quotes, modalities,
and other doubt-implying particles. Research findings that show the systematic occurrence of ethnic prejudice and racism are either ignored or
tend to be marginalized or discredited by much of the press. The traditional myth of Dutch tolerance is not challenged.

The emergence of right-wing racist parties also received substantial
attention, especially when one of these parties obtained a seat in Parliament in 1982. Yet only the spectacular actions and conflicts created by
this party are focused on, not the background, ideas, history, or the systematic links with people and ideologies within the established parties.
Thus, racism in politics is treated just as incidental as racism in general. It is simply attributed to a small right-wing party, and—with more
understanding—to poor people in urban neighborhoods where this party
collected up to 10% of the votes. Prejudice and discrimination elsewhere, such as in national or local government, the police, the courts,
education, or the media, is never extensively reported or analyzed. We
discuss the implications of this tendency in the mass media for the reproduction of ethnic prejudice in everyday talk in later chapters.

Summary

Despite the obvious differences be-
tween newspapers, countries, regions, and the periods examined in the
(few) substantial studies about the representation of race in the press,
there seem to be a number of prevailing and persisting commonalities:
(a) Ethnic minorities are also minorities in the press—they are less
employed and less represented. (b) Many of the dominant topics are
directly or more subtly associated with problems, difficulties, or threats
to the dominant values, interests, goals, or culture. (c) Ethnic events are
consistently described from a White, majority point of view, in which
the authorities are given more space and credibility than minority spokespersons. (d) Topics that are relevant for the ordinary daily life of ethnic

groups, such as work, housing, health, education, political life, and culture, as well as discrimination in these areas, are hardly discussed in the press, unless they lead to "problems" for society as a whole or when they are spectacular. (e) Racism is systematically underreported, reduced to incidents of individual discrimination, or attributed to small right-wing parties and located in poor city areas. Racism of the elite or the various institutions is seldom discussed.

Conclusions

It goes without saying that against this background, the media have been reluctant, to say the least, to discuss publicly their own role in the reproduction of racism in society. Critical analysis is censored, and my own experiences with the Dutch press suggest that critics are often personally discredited or prevented from collecting data in fieldwork.

For the discussion in this book, the role of the media is highly relevant. They provide the main "data" and the issues people may use for everyday conversation, especially for those topics of talk that cannot be inferred from personal experiences or contacts with other people: immigration and national immigration policies, the numbers of immigrants, unemployment statistics, the role of ethnic groups in housing and education, discrimination, and crime statistics.

This does not mean that most newspapers explicitly formulate racist opinions. Many editors and journalists will maintain that they are against racism, and generally loathe extremist racist parties. Their role, indeed, is more subtle and indirect. Partly, but only partly, is negative reporting a consequence of routine conditions of news production and news values: Negative, spectacular events tend to get more attention, and any group without power, influence, and organized spokespersons will have less access to the news media.

On the other hand, many properties of content or style can only be explained as expressions of the dominant ideologies of class and ethnic group to which the journalist belongs—hence, the White perspective, the special attention to the actions and opinions of the authorities, the location of racism in "poor" areas, and the reluctance to cover racism of elites or institutions. Similarly, the focus on "problems" associated with the presence of immigrants of color (because other immigrants are not so discussed), is not just the consequence of the general media bias that favors coverage of negative issues and problems.

The many "neutral" topics that are present for the White majority (such as political organization, culture, the arts) are not there when they are about minority groups. And the problems for the majority (economic recession, unemployment, lack of housing, crime) are not paralleled by those problems that are relevant for the minority. On the contrary, the majority problems are often subtly attributed to the very presence of minority groups. Deeper social causes, contexts, and consequences, such as the role of discrimination in housing, everyday contacts, education, and employment, are seldom discussed.

Even when the media do not formulate negative opinions themselves, they provide a definition of the ethnic situation that makes such negative inferences not only possible but also plausible. In this way, they both preformulate prejudice and reinforce the partial models of the ethnic situation that are acquired by personal experiences, hearsay, and socialization.

3.2. TEXTBOOKS AND CHILDREN'S BOOKS

Where the mass media are the primary information source about ethnic groups for adults, textbooks and children's books (including comics) play a similar role for children, probably surpassed only by television. Indeed, many of the initial prejudices we bring to bear on present minority groups may find their origin in this important textual dimension of socialization and education (Katz, 1976; Milner, 1983).

It comes as no surprise, then, that analyses of children's books and school textbooks yield results that are rather similar to those of the media. The studies that examine history, geography, or social science textbooks in various countries consistently find variable degrees of ethnocentrism, prejudice, and racism (Dixon, 1977; Ferro, 1981; Pearson, 1976; Redmond, 1979; Stinton, 1980; van den Berg & Reinsch, 1983; van Dijk, 1986a; World Council of Churches, 1979; Zimet, 1976).

Briefly summarizing the major results of these studies, we find, first, that the home country, and then other Western countries or Western civilization, are systematically portrayed more extensively, more favorably, and as superior to the colonized, Third World, or "Black" countries and civilizations of the southern hemisphere, notably in Asia and Africa. Second, immigrants from those countries in the home country are often treated in similar ways, if at all. As in the press, the White dominant perspective prevails. In U.S. textbooks, American Indians, Blacks, Chicanos, Puerto Ricans, or other groups are systematically underrepresented.

In Dutch textbooks of the mid-1980s, we find the same systematic exclusion of minority groups from high school textbooks (van Dijk, 1986a). Descriptions are often stereotypical, ahistorical, and, as usual, neglect the problem of discrimination and racism. Colonial history, as is the case for most textbooks in most ex-colonial countries, is described in terms of adventures, explorations, heroic feats, or the diffusion of "civilization," rather than in terms of exploitation, slavery, or brutalities. Colonized people are still characterized as "primitive," and their histories of before and after the colonial period neglected.

The dominant picture of different ethnic groups and of other peoples that arises from such textbooks is an important contribution to the ethnocentric socialization of knowledge and beliefs in adolescents. The biased definitions of such groups, even when very incomplete and sketchy, contribute to a negative overall framework in which such groups are associated with cruelty, crime, (self-inflicted) poverty, primitivism, stupidity, and "strange" or, at best, exotic behavior. As soon as immigrants from such countries, often former colonies, actually become prominent in our present-day societies, such early definitions may be used as the basis for the further extension of stereotypes and prejudices. The striking similarity between the contents of stereotypes or associations in everyday talk, the media, textbooks, and literature suggests that present-day attitudes about minority groups are not just formed on the basis of everyday experiences, hearsay, or media inferences. There is a systematic, historical foundation to the current cultural definitions of foreigners.

3.3. CONCLUSIONS

Although we summarized systematic research findings mainly on the representation of ethnic groups in the news media and books for children, these are by no means the only forms of discourse that form the ideological environment for prejudiced talk. TV programs, movies, and advertising also play an important role in which the function of images is also relevant for the formation of ethnic stereotypes (see Bogle, 1973; Greenberg & Mazingo, 1976; Maynard, 1974; Pierce et al., 1978; Wilson & Gutiérrez, 1985; and many other studies).

The results of these studies suggest that prejudice in talk is not spontaneous, "invented" on the spot, or simply a consequence of ethnic encounters. Rather, through socialization, education, and the many forms of mass communication and the media, majority group members have been constantly confronted with repeated negative stereotypes and ethnocentrism. Even, or maybe because of, their most "innocent" or subtle forms, such stereotypes provide dominant models of the ethnic situation and its participants. The mass communication of these models explains why they can become a dominant consensus. And as we shall see in the next sections and chapters, the content of everyday talk is in many ways coherent with the models conveyed by the media as preformulated by journalists, teachers, advertisers, politicians, scholars, and other elite groups. Indeed, most prejudice may not be expressed on the street but behind the typewriter or word processor.

---

4. Topics of conversation

4.1. TOPICS AS SEMANTIC MACROSTRUCTURES

We start our analysis of everyday talk about ethnic groups with a description of the topics or themes that are expressed in such discourse. Theoretically, topics are defined in what we have called *semantic macrostructures* (see, e.g., van Dijk, 1980a, for details). Thus, topics are properties of the global meaning of discourse. They represent what a fragment of text or talk is about, globally speaking. They also may be considered as the "gist" or most important information of such a fragment. When we summarize a discourse, we essentially express its underlying semantic macrostructure, or thematic structure. Topics organize the local meanings of a discourse and, therefore, also define its overall coherence. Speakers in conversation are expected to follow or keep to the topic once introduced, or must strategically change the topic. If not, incoherence is the result and such incoherence will often be negatively evaluated by the other speech partner. Topic elicitation, introduction, maintenance, or change are complex strategies of conversational interaction (Button & Casey, 1984; McLaughlin, 1984).

Semantic macrostructures are derived from local meanings of words and sentences by macro rules, such as deletion, generalization, and construction. Such rules leave out the irrelevant details, combine similar meanings to higher-level abstract meanings, or construct different meaning constituents in higher-level event or action concepts. Thus, the details of actions such as going to the airport, checking in, going to the gate, boarding, and so forth may be constructed as contributing to the overall discourse topic of "traveling by plane to . . . ." This means that macro rules reduce the complexity of lower-level meanings to simpler, more abstract, higher-level meanings. Because they are also meaning constructs, topics are represented as propositions and not, for instance, as isolated concepts, such as "travel." The concept of travel would in this case be a component part of the thematic proposition "A travels by plane to B," which could be the overall topic of a concrete story. Of course, several of such stories may be classified under the common conceptual denominator or theme (in the traditional sense) of travel.

Topics can be derived from sequences of local meanings (propositional sequences, or "episodes," see van Dijk, 1982a), only on the basis of world knowledge: The inference of "air travel" from information such as going to the airport and checking in can be made only by discourse participants who have world knowledge about air travel, such as scripts of such routine episodes of our culture (Schank & Abelson, 1977). And because all interpretation is subjective, based on personally and socially variable cognitive representations, the inference of topics may also be subjective. What one participant finds "important" or "topical" in a fragment of discourse may not be found important by other participants, for example, because there are different models of the situation, different opinions, or different attitudes. These differences in topic structure may also affect the course of conversation. Speakers, therefore, often need to negotiate about a common topic, or may speak in related but different topic control sets, which may lead to misunderstanding and conflict.

Cognitive Macrostrategies

Actual topic production and understanding is strategic (van Dijk & Kintsch, 1983). Speakers do not form or infer a topic "after the (f)act" of propositional sequences. In production, they first need to have at least some vague topical plan within which the individual propositions are locally planned and expressed. In conversation, local information in turns of the next speaker may then lead to a revision of the initially planned topic. Similarly, in comprehension, a recipient tries to find out as soon as possible what the discourse "is about," that is, forms a provisional topic. This may already be accomplished from knowledge inferred from the context of communication, obvious goals or characteristics of speakers, and/or from first sentences. Once a topic has been construed, it is a powerful, while top-down conceptual structure in the memory Control System of the recipient. It monitors and facilitates the local understanding of the individual words and sentences of ongoing discourse, shows where incoherence is produced, and allows the recipient to continue current topics coherently, or change them. Much like other strategies, these cognitive macrostrategies are flexible, multilevel, and effective ways of handling very complex information. Yet, they are also "hypothetical." Unlike rules, they are only a form of guessing, and they, therefore, may lead to error. A wrong assumption about an actual topic may, therefore, have to be modified by subsequent information from later sentences or turns.

Semantic macrostructures dominate the textual representations in memory. That is, in processes of retrieval they are easily and effectively found, and experiments have shown that in general they are much better and can be recalled after a longer time than local meanings. This is in accordance with our intuitions: We remember best the main topics or most important information of a text or conversation (Kintsch & van

Dijk, 1978; Kieras, 1982; van Dijk & Kintsch, 1982). For other reasons, only striking details are remembered well in specific circumstances, such as details that are associated with strong emotions (Martins, 1982), very concrete imagery, personal experiences, or prominent attitudes.

Similarly, macropropositions also dominate so-called *situation models* constructed from the interpreted text and from previous personal and general knowledge. These models are what a text is about in the referential (and not in the meaning, intentional) sense. But our representations of complex events or scenes also need to be organized and, therefore, are "headed" by an overall macroproposition. Thus, the event of taking a trip by airplane, whether actually participated in or read about, is pictured in a model of this event, and this model is also dominated by an overall "definition of the situation," that is, by a macroproposition such as "A flying to . . . ." This means that macropropositions in discourse may activate both previous discourses and "previous" models.

4.2. TOPICS IN PREJUDICED DISCOURSE

Obviously, topics play a crucial role in the meaning and the actual production or comprehension of discourse. Indeed, without the overall control of a topic, we would be unable to accomplish a conversation of more than a few turns, because we would not have an idea what the conversation was about at a particular moment. Also, we would be unable to remember previous conversations. This role of themes or topics is, therefore, also crucial in talk about ethnic minorities. Whatever the length or complexity of such talk, speech participants not only must be able to talk about a mutually negotiable topic but also must draw general inferences from such talk for later use, for example, in action or in other conversations. And only if they have been able to assign topics to news reports in the media (often signaled by headlines), or to discourses from other sources referred to, are they able to use such information in actual conversations.

As we discuss in more detail in Chapters 4 and 5, the assignment of topics to text or talk fragments about ethnic minority groups is, however, a socially controlled subjective accomplishment. Speakers may have topical intentions that may be significantly different from the topical assumptions of recipients. A news report about unemployment among young minority group members may be assigned the topic "They cause unemployment" instead of the topic "They suffer from unemployment." The same is true in everyday conversations. Local meanings may be subjected to a number of specific strategic operations (such as negative associations, transfer and attribution, selective attention, and so on) that may form the basis of different macroproposition formation by the recipient.

Similarly, the listener may also "upgrade" local meanings to higher-level macropropositions, by taking a detail as the organizing conceptual framework of a discourse fragment. Making sense of talk, thus, essentially involves making sense of the overall intentions, meanings, or topics of talk, and for prejudiced participants, such overall meanings may be biased. This process will be described in more detail later. Here, we focus primarily on what conversational participants themselves say about ethnic minority groups. That is, they carry the major responsibility of "executing" a topic, even if that topic is vaguely or indirectly suggested by the participant/interviewer. Yet, even then their topics are formed and executed locally within the overall definition of the communicative context, including its goals and possibly its overall topic, for example, "contacts in the neighborhood" or "foreigners in town."

A full-fledged analysis of all main topics and secondary topics of some 180 interviews is a very cumbersome enterprise, especially if we want to show explicitly how such topics can be derived from local propositions expressed in talk. Therefore, we use a more intuitive method of inferring main themes from a number of relevant fragments, namely, summarization. We have seen that summaries may be taken as expressions of underlying macropropositions, and although our summaries may also be subjective, we have no other practical method than this to establish the main themes as they organize talk about ethnic groups.

The first group of interviews (N = 49, with 53 interviewees because some interviews were held with more than one person), held in various neighborhoods in Amsterdam, express topics that can be further categorized in various fields of experiences, opinions, or attitude dimensions. These topics are not necessarily "prejudiced," but they stereotypically tend to "come up" as soon as "foreigners" are discussed, whether associated with negative or more neutral evaluations. In our simple listing of topics, we summarize for the group as a whole and do not study possible correlations between topics in general or within individual interviews in particular.

(a) Contacts and information sources.
The first set of topics is particularly important for our discussion because they concern contacts and acquisition of information about ethnic groups. We order the topics in this category by their frequency of occurrence (some topics occur several times in the same interview). We use the pronoun *them* to refer to ethnic minority groups, sometimes different ones, as is it done by the speakers. We comment upon this use of the pronoun later.

	N
(1) I have/want no contact with them	50
(2) I have heard that from others	37

(3) I have seen that myself	30
(4) I know about that from a relative	17
(5) You read about that in the newspaper	15
(6) I know them from my work	12
(7) I have seen that on TV	9
(8) I have had contacts with them in the shop/market	9
(9) I have heard that on the radio	2

These are, as such, mostly rather local topics, which are discussed briefly as "evidence," or lack of knowledge, about the more substantial topics. Their frequency of occurrence, however, suggests that contacts or (purported) lack of contacts, as well as the information sources about the beliefs and opinions, are important for speakers. Prevailing is the topic that denies contacts with foreigners, but this denial often has a strategic function in conversations: It allows the speaker to "opt out" when a delicate subject is introduced, especially in the beginning of an interview. It may literally mean that people have no or few direct contacts, for example, of friendship, but later in the interviews it usually appears that people do have contacts after all. Denial of contact, then, is an effective move to avoid speaking about possibly incriminating opinions, a move we shall later discuss in more detail as an element of the strategy of positive self-presentation. Avoidance, both of topic and of talk, is a general move that has been often found in studies of conversational interaction, for example, in therapeutic interviews (Kreckel, 1981; Labov & Fanshel, 1977).

The other topics in this category are directly relevant to the main issue of this book. We see that personal experiences are referred to as a major source of beliefs and opinions about ethnic groups, especially in high-contact areas of Amsterdam. This finding is in agreement with the survey results of Hartmann and Husband (1974), discussed above. Yet, according to our data, people even more often topicalize the information they have from others, especially from relatives. Next, the different media, especially the newspaper, are mentioned as main sources of knowledge about minority groups. Direct personal contacts, for instances, at work and in shops or in the market, are somewhat less topics of talk, and most of these contacts are "passive," that is, perceptual rather than interactional: People say that they have "seen" what has happened.

(b) National policies. A major category of the structure of ethnic prejudice is the "origin" of immigrants. This means that people have specific opinions about how the foreigners came here in the first place. These opinions also may be topical in conversation, for instance, when people talk about general policies toward immigrants or ethnic minority groups. In order to allow a first comparison with the interviews in San Diego, we have starred the topics (usually opinion statements) that were also brought up in the United States:

(1) They have been invited to come to Holland (10)
(2) They should be sent back (5)
(3) *Immigration policies should be stricter (5)

Compared to many other beliefs and opinions, the explicit topic of "sending them back," which is a political slogan of the right-wing racist party, is not discussed very frequently. In more implicit ways, however, many negative opinions do seem to have this implication. The same holds for tightening immigration, which is a general policy of conservative parties and the actual policy of the Dutch government. Many people correctly recall that immigrant workers were invited to come to work in the Netherlands, a policy that is now often regretted, instead of having come to work on their own initiative.

(c) Social problems. The next set of topics, typically those featured in stories, are about various social "problems" with which ethnic groups are associated. Many of these topics have a prejudiced nature.

(1) *I feel unsafe (I do not dare to go out anymore) (29)
(2) *They are involved in crime (15)
(3) *They cause the decay of Amsterdam/the neighborhood (11)
(4) *They are involved in (other) negative acts (9)

These are the stereotypical topics of majority members who feel threatened by the presence of ethnic groups. Elderly women especially feel unsafe, and often this lack of safety is attributed to (male) "foreigners" in the neighborhood or in the inner city. Sometimes this attribution is made more specific by attributing minority groups with crime, aggression, or violence. Aside from the safety topics, it is the topic of urban decay especially that comes up frequently, and here again the run-down neighborhood is directly associated with the presence of foreigners. From the very choice, ordering, and structuring of topics in discourse, we may infer contents and organization of dominant macropropositions in situation models and ethnic schemata. Thus, the attributions are consequences of the general strategy of trying to establish causes or causing actors in the representation of events and actions. And, as we shall see later, it is a typical "biasing" strategy to attribute negative states of affairs (lack of safety, decay, or lack of housing) to ethnic minority groups.

(d) Work and (un)employment. One of the more specific social topics associated with the presence of immigrants is based on the beliefs about the kind of work ethnic minorities do. These opinions are mostly stereotypical, and show that ethnic and class attitudes may be related:

(1) *They (immigrant workers) work hard (20)
(2) They have unpleasant (dirty, heavy, monotonous) jobs (18)
(3) *They do not want to work (11)
(4) Dutch people do not want to work (either) (8)
(5) They do all sorts of cleaning jobs (7)
(6) *They do the kind of work our people do not want (6)
(7) They work in factories (5)
(8) They want to work, but have no jobs (5)

From these topics, we first may conclude that there is a dominant belief that holds that the immigrant workers work hard and do the dirty jobs, such as cleaning and work in factories. On the other hand, we also find the frequent topic that they do not want to work. It is interesting to note that such conflicting beliefs may sometimes be held by the same individual, that is, on one hand that they do not (want to) work—and abuse the social welfare system, see below—and on the other hand, "that they take our jobs." Obviously, such apparent inconsistencies must be accounted for in an adequate cognitive theory of the organization and the uses of ethnic prejudice.

(e) **Rights and duties.** Many topics deal with the general rights and duties to which the ethnic minority groups are subjected. Again, there seems to be conflict between general normative statements about tolerance and rights, and on the other hand, the opinion that ethnic minority members abuse the social welfare system:

(1) *They have various rights (to live here, have education, to have a house, and so on) (20)
(2) *They take our houses (13)
(3) *They abuse our social security system, are on welfare (10)
(4) *They think our country is a social paradise (10)

(f) **Norms and cultural differences.** A major topic is the assumed deviance from Dutch norms and cultural differences in general. Some of these topics may be very general and may be hierarchically superior to more specific social and cultural topics. Topics 3 and 4 might be classified also as a separate, highest-level category, signaling the overall negative evaluation dominating ethnic prejudice.

(1) *They have to adapt to our norms and rules (17)
(2) *They have different life-styles/habits/traditions (12)
(3) You have good and bad ones among them (9)
(4) *Other people do not like them (8)
(5) *They treat their women differently (worse) (8)
(6) *They have (too) many children (6)

In these opinions, cultural differences dominate as a topic, mostly with the conclusion that "they" should adapt to the Dutch norms and rules. Differences in life-style are perceived to emerge especially in different family structure, such as the number of children and the "backward" treatment of women, mostly by Muslim men. If "tolerance" is formulated at all, then it is often conditional: I do not mind them if they adapt to our ways. This means, in fact, that the assumed tradition of tolerance in the Netherlands—with respect to groups with a different religion or social philosophy—no longer seems to hold for ethnic minority groups. Indeed, many people resent the introduction of Islam into the Netherlands and ignore the many similarities with religious beliefs and practices of the various Christian religions in our Northwestern countries. The frequent reference (also made by men) to the inferior treatment of women is interesting for many reasons, especially when we realize that, in several respects, women in our culture are hardly treated better. Later we try to provide an explanation for this and other prejudiced opinions and their topical relevance in talk.

(g) **Education.** Education is a less prominent topic of discussion. Yet, not only through the media, but also through information from their children, people have rather clear ideas about whether or not there should be a policy of special (e.g., remedial) education or language teaching:

(1) *Education should be only in our own language (11)
(2) *The presence of minority children causes problems at school (10)
(3) *There are cultural differences between their and our children (7)
(4) *They should have lessons in their own culture (5)
(5) *They should not have lessons in their own culture/language (5)

The view that in the domain of education, the foreigners cause problems, seems to dominate here, and it is concluded that education should be in Dutch only, even when some speakers find that ethnic groups should be allowed to have education in their own language and culture. It should be added, however, that people may well oppose equal rights or affirmative action in other domains without objecting to special forms of education. Indeed, in the traditional list of prejudiced complaints, people spontaneously mention work, housing, and welfare, but seldom education, even when they have children—which would make the opinion and the topic relevant for them. Education is also one of the few domains in the Netherlands and elsewhere in which the authorities have implemented a systematic policy (intended to be) in favor of minority children, within the framework of multicultural education. Although these policies are not exactly antiracist (see, e.g., Mullard, 1985, for a similar situation in the U.K.), they might suggest to the public that the authorities "give a good example" as far as education is concerned, which may be a prejudice-reducing factor.

Prejudiced Topics in the Netherlands and California

In the previous section, we have simply taken the major topics that were discussed in a series of interviews. Many of these topics may be qualified as "prejudiced," in the sense that they are based on negative ethnic group attitudes or negative generalized models. To be able to compare, we have made the same analysis for the second group of interviews (N = 37, held with 44 people), all taken in one of the poor neighborhoods. This time we focus only on prejudiced topics, although, of course, tolerant topics were also realized in that neighborhood. The list of the most frequent topics is as follows (again, items that also occur in the California interviews are starred):

    (1) *They have a different mentality (20)
    (2) *They do not respect women (15)
    (3) *They are dirty, cause dirtiness and decay (13)
    (4) *They are a closed group; they keep to themselves (13)
    (5) *They must adapt to our norms, integrate into our society (12)
    (6) *They are aggressive (11)
    (7) *They profit from our social services (11)
    (8) *The town/neighborhood has changed (negatively) because of them (10)
    (9) *They have (too) many children (9)
    (10) *They are threatening, criminal (8)
    (11) They take our houses (are favored in housing) (5)

These 11 major topics taken from the talk in a high-contact area overlap significantly with the negative opinions we found in other neighborhoods, which we discussed above. We see that most prejudiced topics also occur in the California interviews, except that the topic of favorable treatment in housing is not a relevant topic in San Diego, that is, because there is no city-controlled housing and because housing is less difficult than in Amsterdam.

To show further differences between California and the Netherlands, we also made a list of the topics that were expressed most often in the interviews conducted in San Diego (by at least 5 interviewees out of 25):

    (1) They don't want to learn, take opportunities, are lazy (17)
    (2) They are threatening, aggressive (16)
    (3) They (immigrants) should learn (do not want to learn) English (11)
    (4) They live on, or abuse welfare (9)

(5) They steal, are dishonest (7)
(6) They complain too much (7)
(7) They are favored (e.g., in jobs) (5)
(8) They are criminal (5)
(9) They take "our" jobs (5)

Most of these prejudiced topics refer to Blacks or minorities in general. A frequent topic applying to various types of immigrants, such as Mexicans and Asians, is that they do not want to learn or use English (e.g., demand bilingual education or voting in Spanish) or that they take our jobs. We see that, as in the Netherlands, classical prejudices prevail: Minorities are involved in crime, abuse welfare, do not adapt to our ways (e.g., language), take our jobs, or are treated favorably by the authorities. Also, minorities, especially Blacks and Latinos, are perceived as making too many complaints or demands. People seldom explicitly say that minorities are "lazy," but this old stereotype, applied especially to Blacks, is now usually formulated in terms related to education and job opportunities, in which minorities are said to take too little advantage of the possibilities.

Characteristic of the American interviews is that in addition to these prejudices, there is frequent mention of various types of affirmative action, such as busing or setting quotas in jobs and schools. Most people find that there should be equal opportunities for minorities, but that busing and quotas should not be forced. This topical opinion is in agreement with the general findings of survey research about racial attitudes in the United States (Shuman, Steeh, & Bobo, 1985): The majority of Americans now favor the general principles of equal opportunity but, at the same time, oppose the government controlled and enforced implementation of such a policy. This topic is related to the more general topic of (perceived) favorable treatment, which is also featured in the Dutch interviews.

A topic that is typical of mixed neighborhoods in Amsterdam, but that we have hardly found in the California interviews, is that of neighborly nuisance and harassment: There are fewer "complaints" about noise, smells, or other culturally based conflicts. The main reason for this difference is probably the much more crowded, typically urban, housing situation in Amsterdam, where apartment houses prevail, whereas in California most people we interviewed lived in independent houses. More generally it seemed that, due to the generally acknowledged nature of the United States, and especially California, as a land of immigrants, cultural differences are less resented than in the Netherlands. Yet, at the same time, in both countries, we find the general opinion that immigrants should adapt to the ways and learn the language of their new country.

Finally, the more liberal interviewees also mention topics that are critical of the White majority: Anglo-Americans are often said to be prejudiced or to discriminate against minorities. Specifically in Southern California, people often resent the exploitation of "illegal aliens," that is, primarily, undocumented workers from Mexico, by the farmers or ranchers. Different from the actual situation in the Netherlands, though, is the widespread opinion that such workers are welcome to do the jobs that White Americans do not want to do (for the low pay offered). This opinion is similar to the one about immigrant workers from Mediterranean countries that prevailed in Western Europe in the 1960s.

Topics and the Prejudice Schema

To show that many of the prejudiced opinions that are topical in talk are based on ethnic attitudes, we may try to fit them in the main categories of an attitude schema, of which the structures will be discussed in more detail in Chapter 4. The assumption underlying such an attitude schema is that people do not have very different attitude structures for each out-group. On the contrary, it is plausible that they have learned to develop a similar schema for the storage and uses of beliefs and opinions about a social group. This schema consists of a number of basic categories that are crucial for social information processing about out-groups and are central in monitoring perception of and interaction with ethnic minority groups. Somewhat simplified and abbreviated, the main prejudiced topics can be inserted into the categories of such an attitude schema (see Table 2.1).

This attitudinal organization of the major topics may even be further simplified and generalized. That is, throughout the various categories, we also find similarities along other dimensions. Thematically, talk about ethnic groups in the Netherlands and the United States focuses on a few central notions, such as *difference, deviance,* and *threat.* The few topic classes we thus obtain are as follows:

(A) THEY ARE DIFFERENT (IN CULTURE, MENTALITY, NORMS)
(B) THEY DO NOT ADAPT
(C) THEY ARE INVOLVED IN NEGATIVE ACTS (NUISANCE, CRIME)
(D) THEY THREATEN OUR SOCIOECONOMIC INTERESTS

Obviously, topic class B can be collapsed further with A, because A is presupposed by B, and B usually taken as a conclusion of A. So, A/B can be interpreted as a perceived threat to our norms, rules, habits, and cultural order. Class C can be interpreted as a threat to our safety or well-being or in general a threat to our social order (laws, respect, and so on),

TABLE 2.1:   Prejudiced Attitude Schema

---

0. *General*
   0.1. I do not like them
   0.2. Others do not like them

1. *Origin and appearance*
   1.1. We should not have invited them
   1.2. They should be sent back
   1.3. Immigration policies should be stricter
   1.4. They look different (color, clothing)

2. *Socioeconomic goals/status*
   2.1. They take our jobs
   2.2. They do the dirty jobs
   2.3. They take our houses
   2.4. They abuse our social system

3. *Sociocultural differences*
   3.1. They have a different life-style
   3.1.1. They should adapt
   3.2. They treat women badly
   3.3. They have too many children
   3.4. They do not speak our language
   3.5. They are dirty (cause urban decay)
   3.6. Their children cause problems at school

4. *Personal characteristics*
   4.1. They are aggressive (violent)
   4.2. They are criminal
   4.3. They are dirty
   4.4. They are lazy (don't want to work)
   4.5. They are noisy

---

and D is a perceived threat to our interests. At this level, the basic attitude elements are the same in the Netherlands and the United States. Only the socioeconomic interest dimension is instantiated by different opinions in the two countries: Whereas in the Netherlands, perceived competition in jobs and especially housing are prominent topics and opinions, Americans more often resent the implementation of equal opportunity policies, such as neighborhood desegregation, busing, or affirmative action on the job, policies that have as yet hardly been developed and enforced in Holland.

These operations of abstraction show various things about the underlying cognitive organization of prejudice. First, these further generalizations also seem to organize around some of the central categories of attitude schemata: socioeconomic goals, sociocultural differences, and personality, with the sole difference that "personality characteristics" are marked negatively as threats to our social order and norms (e.g., safety, diligence, cleanliness, respect for the law). In other words, the "traits" are not assigned to persons, but to out-group members, and hence to the group as a whole. Second, cultural difference and social deviance are not just resented but subjectively construed as a "threat" to the culture, society, country, town, or neighborhood. That is, the ethnic outgroup, unlike other social groups, is typically put in the perspective of an "opposing" out-group, as an enemy, of which "we," the in-group, may be seen as "victim."

Finally, it should be added that organizing attitude dimensions such as "difference," "deviance" and "threat," may be further organized by the well-known dimension of "superiority": The perceived difference or competition involved are not taken to divide equal groups. On the contrary, the minority group is seen as inferior in its various properties and, therefore, denied the same socioeconomic privileges. We here touch on the social and economic functions of prejudice schemata and prejudiced talk, which we return to in later chapters.

The simplest prejudiced—thematic and cognitive—representation of ethnic groups both in the Netherlands and in the United States, therefore, may be rendered as in Figure 2.1.

Experimental Confirmation

In order to examine whether the major topics as they are expressed in the interviews are not just "personal beliefs," but "known," largely shared attitudinal opinions, an experiment was carried out in which students had to list what they thought prejudiced people would typically think about ethnic minority groups (Sprangers, 1983). She first found that it was much easier for the students to list possible negative opinions than positive ones. Then, it was found that the list of prejudices mentioned most frequently was very similar to the one we obtained by analysis of the actual interview topics. There are also a few differences, however. The students also listed a number of racist beliefs that were not directly topical in the interviews, such as those about the "inherent" characteristics of foreigners: "they are lazy," "they are stupid," and especially, "they are sexually perverted." The latter assumed opinion never occurred in our interviews. Yet, research among ethnic minority groups into their experiences of everyday racism has shown that these prejudiced opinions also appear to underlie many of the verbal and nonverbal interactions of White majority members with minority group members (Essed, 1984). This means that the overall positive self-presentation strategy of the speakers excludes topicalization of those opinions and feelings that may be taken as fundamentally racist, namely, the attribution of inherent negative personal properties. The other negative characteristics assigned to ethnic groups seem to be

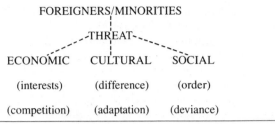

Figure 2.1: Simplest Schema for the Thematic and Cognitive Organization of Ethnic Prejudice

more acceptably topicalized, because they can be constructed as over-all group differences and threat. That is, arguments may be found that make resentment or resistance against these economic, cultural, and social threats a defensible position, that is, as a defense of the "rights" of the in-group.

Conclusion

Our analysis of the major topics of talk in two sets of interviews has shown first that many of these topics are stereotypical. What people say about ethnic minorities is seldom based on unique, personal experiences or opinions. Rather, the topics as well as the ethnic models or attitudes they are based on are socially shared and stereotypical. An experiment has shown that whether or not people share such prejudices, they are well known, even when there are also stereotypes about stereotypes. If the concept of "foreigner" is intro-duced in conversation, it tends to act as a retrieval cue for a limited num-ber of standard experiences or opinions. These appear to be organized under the constituent categories of ethnic prejudice and can be summa-rized in topic classes under the general label of (perceived) "threat": threat to our social identity (autonomy, norms, or rules), to social order (safety, well-being), and to our interests.

Topics, it should be recalled, organize talk and, therefore, also depend on the social constraints of interaction. This means that they are subject to the usual strategies of positive self-presentation. This form of socially induced self-control in topicalization suggests that some racist opinions are expressed only indirectly, such as the various topics related to inher-ent personal characteristics of ethnic group members. Research about the daily experiences of racism, however, shows that feelings of superi-ority that underlie these "forbidden" topics are nevertheless an important organizing feature of prejudice. This is also confirmed by an analysis of the presuppositions or other implications of the explicit topics in our interviews. In other words, for speakers, it is most expedient to organize their topics around the notion of "threat," which is a concept that allows positive self-presentation ("we are allowed to defend ourselves against such threats"), rather than around the concept of "superiority," which would be against the official norms and might lead to loss of face. It follows that an analysis of topics is an important method of assessing the contents of dominant prejudiced opinions, but that transformations due to the strategic management of the communicative context should be applied when inferring thought from talk. These transformations will be discussed in Chapters 4 and 5.

It should be noted finally that we have analyzed topics only at the level of abstract semantic (and cognitive) macrostructures. We have ignored the local moves of the elicitation, introduction, elaboration, maintenance, or change of topics in talk. Part of these moves will be discussed in the subsequent sections of this chapter in which we analyze the local organization of conversation.

5. Stories about minorities

Especially in high-contact areas, there is much story telling about ethnic minority groups. Unlike many other types of conversational narrative, such stories usually have an argumentative function. They are not primarily aimed at diverting the audience; neither do storytellers tell about their experiences to brag of heroic feats. Much like other forms of informal talk about minorities, they are primarily performed as complaints, in which the storyteller (a family member or friend) is portrayed as a victim of the presence of foreigners in the neighborhood. The narration of such experiences thus serves as factual "evidence," that is, as premises for evaluative conclusions. They are a macromove within an argumentative strategy of negative other-presentation and positive self-presentation. Negative stories make negative conclusions credible and defensible, so that the general norm of ethnic tolerance is, apparently, not violated.

5.1. STORY STRUCTURE

Conversational stories theoretically display general characteristics of both narrative and conversational structures. Interactionally, they come about not just within a single turn of a single speaker. Rather, they tend to be constructed dialogically in such a way that one speaker, the primary storyteller, tells about personal experiences in a sequence of narrative moves, and the recipient may routinely interrupt to ask questions, to show surprise, to challenge the interestingness or relevance of the story, or to interpolate fragments of a story about his or her own experiences. Indeed, the narratability of a conversational story is usually locally negotiated, and the storyteller cannot take or maintain the floor unless the recipients agree that the story is worth telling. And unlike monological stories, such as those in letters or novels, they may run astray and remain incompleted. The general narrative "plan" may not be executed in a straightforward manner and may need permanent local modifications and adaptations to the ongoing communicative context. (For details, see, e.g., Ehlich, 1980; Polanyi, 1985; Quasthoff, 1980.)

Story Schemata

Also, conversational stories display an overall narrative pattern that identifies them as stories. Such narrative structures have been discussed in a vast amount of literature in several disciplines, starting with and inspired by early anthropological work on Russian folktales (Propp, 1928/1958); first, in French Structuralism in semiotics and poetics (Chabrol, 1973; Communications, 1966; Todorov, 1969; van Dijk, 1985b); second, in sociolinguistic and ethnographic work on natural stories (Chafe, 1980; Labov, 1972; Labov & Waletzky, 1967); and finally in psychology and AI, around a sometimes fierce debate on the nature of "story schemata" or "story grammars" (Black & Wilensky, 1979; Mandler, 1984; Mandler & Johnson, 1978; Rumelhart, 1975; Kintsch & van Dijk, 1975; see van Dijk, 1980c, for a collection of papers). We cannot discuss the merits and weaknesses of the recent approaches to story structure here (see van Dijk, 1980b, 1980c, for details), but will merely summarize our own theory of story structure, which combines elements from the theory of action (van Dijk, 1976) with some structuralist and sociolinguistic notions, as well as cognitive dimensions (van Dijk & Kintsch, 1983).

Stories are a class of related discourse types that have an overall narrative "form" in common. This abstract, underlying formal structure can be made explicit in terms of narrative superstructures. These are described, just like macrostructures, at a global level of analysis: They characterize sequences of sentences (propositions), and not isolated ones. And much like the "formal" structure of a sentence, narrative superstructures or story schemata, are accounted for by means of typical categories and rules. Categories involve, for example, Summary, Setting, Orientation, Complication, Resolution, Evaluation, and Coda (or Conclusion) (Labov, 1972; Labov & Waletzky, 1967).

These categories are ordered hierarchically, so that several of the categories just mentioned are organized in higher-level, more abstract categories. For instance, Complication and Resolution together function as the event core, or "happening" of the story, and the Setting, of course, extends its "scope" to this entire happening. The Complication usually contains events that are contrary to the goals, wishes, or expectations of the protagonist or storyteller, and the Resolution the actions performed in such a predicament, with or without success. The Evaluation, which may appear discontinuously throughout the whole story, is the category that collects information about the personal opinions or emotions of the storyteller about the events, in expressions such as "That was really dangerous," or "I was really afraid." The Coda or Conclusion, finally, provides information about the actual relevance of the story for the present communicative or interactional context. In our interviews, for instance, the Conclusion may tie in with the argumentative schema in which the story was embedded, and that aimed at strategically conveying a negative opinion about foreigners.

To provide readers or listeners an important clue about the relevance or interestingness of the story, it is often prefaced by a Summary, which may also locally connect the story to the ongoing conversation. Such a Summary is even obligatory in news stories in the press (van Dijk, 1983d, 1985e, 1985f, 1987a). Whereas the Setting specifies location, time, and participants, the Orientation of the story provides the special circumstances that led to the Complication.

In actual stories, some of these categories may remain implicit, for instance, when they are presupposed by the storyteller to be known to the hearer. Also, especially in rhetorically or literarily effective storytelling, stories may show various transformations of the canonical schema informally outlined above, and represented in Figure 2.2.

Different cultures may have different story categories and constraints (Chafe, 1980; Kintsch & Greene, 1978), as we may also find in different story types in our own culture (such as news stories, conversational stories, literary stories, and children's stories).

Story Schemata and Topics

Because narrative structures are only an overall schema or form of a story, they also need an overall "content" to fill the terminal nodes of the story schema. This content is precisely provided by the semantic macropropositions or topics we have discussed in the previous section of this chapter. In other words, we may expect that the prejudiced topics we have found earlier are the typical contents of stories about minorities. Each narrative category has typical constraints on the macroproposition by which it defines the overall narrative function. For instance, Settings require place and time descriptions, and Complications must involve interesting, interfering events and actions.

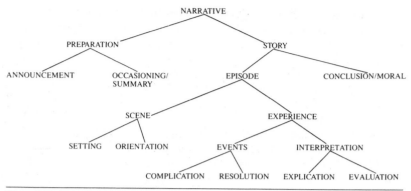

Figure 2.2: Narrative Schema of Story

The Cognitive Basis of Stories

Cognitively, stories may be treated as partial expressions of situation models, that is, of episodic representations of personal experiences. We shall discuss the nature of such models in more detail later, but it is important to note here that the actual production and understanding of stories is cognitively monitored by a strategic application of story schema rules and categories on the memory representation of some event the storyteller has experienced (lived, or read about). For an adequate analysis of the role of storytelling in the diffusion of ethnic prejudice and the reproduction of racism, this cognitive basis is crucial (van Dijk, 1985d). It shows most directly how people have interpreted and stored an ethnic encounter, including possible "biases" in the representation of ethnic minority actors and actions.

Stories rather faithfully express how people deal with ethnic minority groups in their immediate social environment, and especially how social members of the in-group place themselves within this environment. In other words, stories—much like gossip and rumor (Shibutani, 1966)—are rich data bases for guided inferences about ethnic relations and their cognitive modeling by social members.

5.2. STORIES ABOUT "FOREIGNERS"

To illustrate the general theoretical notions introduced above, let us start our discussion about "ethnic" stories with a concrete example. The story is told by a woman who lives in a new suburb that is known in Amsterdam for its relatively high percentage of Surinamese. In the same interview, she had already told other stories of negative experiences with "foreigners" (Spanish people who clean fish just above the fresh laundry of her mother, and Moroccan kids who urinate down on the laundry of one of her colleagues). The story that follows is prefaced with some more specific experiences of her own that she has when she goes shopping in her own neighborhood, during which she claims to be harassed by young Black Surinamese boys (interview and transcription by Nico Hergaarden; approximate—and far from ideal—English translation of spoken Amsterdam Dutch is ours; "I" stands for the interviewer and "W" for the woman). Narrative categories are placed in the right margin on the line where the category begins. In this trancript we do not follow specific transcription conventions, except three points to mark pauses and capitals to mark special stress).

(1) (E1)

W: But a . . . a long time ago, a Surinamese lady   SETTING
    came uhh to the supermarket, which at that time
    was still on B-square
I: Oh yes, that was . . . yes
W: That was in the beginning
I: Yes
W: and what was it, I believe that it was still the
    Spar [supermarket chain] and that lady bought   ORIENTATION
    bread. She leaves the store and comes back and
    says "I don't WANT that bread."   COMPLICATION
I: Hmm
W: Then the manager very POLITELY . . .:
    "Madam, we do   RESOLUTION
    not exCHANGE bread."
    NO, in Holland one doesn't   EVALUATION/CONCLUSION
    exchange bread, do we, and no meat products
    either. Well after that
    the lady took on TERRIBLY,   COMPLICATION
    and the manager you know he tried to explain it   RESOLUTION
    to her, that bread cannot be exchanged here and
    in a very polite manner, after which that woman COMPLICATION
    started to SHOUT, like, Don't touch me.
I: . . . hmmm
W: She throws the man that bread into his face,   COMPLICATION
    walks to the cash register and grabs two packets of Pall
    Mall.
I: Yes.
W: I still remember that very well.   EVALUATION/CODA

This rather characteristic story about the assumed cultural differences between Surinamese and Dutch, and indirectly about the perceived negative behavior of the Black woman and the polite behavior of the (White) Dutch manager, shows the major narrative categories we have discussed above. There is no need for a special introduction or summary because the conversation is already oriented toward her experiences with Surinamese in the area. In fact, the woman had just asked, "Do you want details?," which is—of course—affirmed by the interviewer. So, she directly starts with a description of the Setting, including both location and time ("long ago," which will prove functional at the end, because it shows that the event was important enough to her to be remembered so many years). The Orientation, as we interpret that category, is the description of a usually trivial daily situation, which already may prefigure the "difficulties" to be told in the Complication, as is also the case here. The Complication, in this case, has various "installments," which we encounter more often in conversational narrative: Bringing back the bread, taking on, shouting, and finally stealing packets of cigarettes (revenge for not being given her money back for the bread?). The Resolution also has two installments, and consists in the reaction of the supermarket manager.

At this point, the storyteller interpolates her own explicit evaluation and conclusion about the events: One does not exchange bread in the Netherlands, which at least implies the stereotypical opinion, "They are different." At other points, her evaluation of the events shows in the emphasis on the rhetorically contrasted concepts predicated on the Black woman and the White manager, respectively: to take on terribly and to shout versus politeness and trying to explain.

The illustration of the main opinion, "They are different," or "They have a different mentality," has other dimensions in this story, however. That out-group members are depicted in negative terms and in-group members are portrayed as reacting positively, even after the perceived "unreasonable" or unacceptable acts of the out-group member, are the usual moves of the main strategies in such talk, namely, negative other-presentation and positive self-presentation (where self here refers to we Dutch people, because the woman does not tell the story as an individual but as a member of the dominant group). But at the same time, "bringing back bread" is not just an act the woman disapproved of or found strange and in conflict with explicitly invoked Dutch shopping norms (which may themselves be "invented" locally to make the story more convincing). Also, the storyteller implicitly conveys that Black women might not be as clean as White Dutch people supposedly are, and that they are impolite, aggressive, and thieves. That is, in a few words, the storyteller sketches a very clear vignette of a stereotypical ethnic "conflict" in which the in-group member remains tolerant and understanding and in which the out-group member not only breaks the rules but also displays other deviant behavior and characteristics.

Although, as such, this incident may be rather "innocent," it goes without saying that its narrative reproduction persuasively argues for a number of prejudiced opinions (foreigners are dirty, aggressive, and criminal). Even if the event took place more or less as told by the woman, the story selects precisely this event for further communication, and this selective attention for negative experiences may contribute to the informal communication of such prejudiced opinions. The story is, of course, told from a White, dominant perspective, in which the woman story-teller rather chooses the side of the manager (her possible opponent in shopping conflicts). Also, rather significantly, it is not told *why* the Black woman brought back the bread (was there something wrong with it?), and whether the bread was packaged, or not (which would be essential in judging about the "cleanliness" angle of the story). Packaged items can usually be brought back according to implicit Dutch supermarket rules, and it is rather unlikely that a Surinamese woman would bring back unpackaged, and hence touched, bread given the strict rules of hygiene in tropical Surinam. Finally, we are not told either why the Black woman took the packets of cigarettes from the cash register.

From these few observations we conclude, first, that such stories are subjectively biased, incomplete expressions of ethnic encounters, in which the perspective is that of the storyteller and the in-group, and in which a selection seems to be made of those acts and events that are positive for the in-group and negative for the out-group. This means that such a story is not merely an account of personal experiences, but rather an expression of our "social experiences" as members of the in-group. They are not *I*-stories, but *we*-stories, and that makes them particularly effective in informal communication and diffusion. Indeed, the story may relevantly be further told in the community by any of the recipients ("My neighbor told me yesterday that . . ."), which is not the case for all personal stories. Negative opinions are not always explicitly expressed but left to the inferences of the recipient. It is sufficient to describe the negative acts and to invoke the general norms, rules, or habits that are broken. Nonverbal clues such as pitch, intonation, angered face, and some specific particles that express anger may be sufficient to convey the appropriate evaluation of the storyteller about the events in particular and about the ethnic out-group in general.

Story Categories

From the brief and informal analysis of one example, we may have gleaned how "foreigner stories" are organized and what they may be about. The individual categories play a functional role within the overall strategic goals of the storytellers. Thus, reasons, introductions, or summaries provide the motivation and relevance of the story that is to follow and, in our case, usually reveal how some general questions or statements about ethnic minority groups can be illustrated or backed up. Sometimes such introductory or bridging story fragments also express a clear evaluation, so as to make the story more effective and therefore interesting:

(2) Well, that is not what I call pleasant living. And it so happens that my daughter . . .
(3) I'll tell you something funny. . . . This sheep slaughtering that is really terrible . . .

We already observed that Orientations may express rather mundane situations and actions, such as shopping, walking on the street, taking a streetcar, and doing the laundry. Again, these trivial circumstances may have specific functions for the difficulties that are to follow later in the story. First, they show that what did happen, can happen, any day, to any one of "us," and in most ordinary circumstances. That is, the events need not be highly exceptional and are portrayed as part of everyday life. Second, the triviality of the Orientations also shows the "innocence" of the storyteller: She was just doing her everyday things, minding her own business, and then suddenly. . . . Without such an implicit guarantee of innocence, the recipient might infer that the storyteller was also part of the "problem," such as by having provoked the minority actor or by having started the conflict herself. Third, the triviality of the mundane activities rhetorically contrasts with the nonmundane, deviant behavior of the minority actor. Fourth, for everyday situations and activities, the usual norms, rules, and habits apply, so that their breach is all the more conspicuous. That is, the storytellers construe situations in such a way that the occurrences in their stories become more salient or *prägnant* (van der Wurff, 1983).

Evaluations, Explications, and Conclusions are the categories or dimensions of our stories in which the opinions and attitudes, and the norms and rules on which they are based, become most clearly visible. The formal antidiscrimination norm does not allow too open or direct racist evaluations and conclusions, so that these either remain implicit, indirect, or vague, or are toned down through various mitigation moves, which we shall discuss in detail later. Thus, many stories abound with generalities, such as, "That is the way they are," "We don't do that here," "You see, they don't know how to . . .," "They have a different mentality," "A normal Dutch guy wouldn't do that . . .," or more specific expressions, such as, "We do not exchange bread (slaughter sheep at home) in Holland."

The obvious argumentative function is to establish a general, and, therefore, "acceptable," opinion about cultural difference and conflict. This topic alone engenders many stories about strange, funny, or curious events and acts, but mostly more is involved. The acts of the minority members are not merely portrayed as different, but as negative and inferior, and so are the rules and norms on which such acts are based. So, evaluative explications of this type provide evidence about the general framework in which in-group members interpret narrated events.

Conclusions in that case are barely necessary. In only a few cases, storytellers say what they have learned from the events (e.g., not to go out at night, not live in the inner city, or not go shopping here or there, anymore). And only occasionally will a storyteller conclude generally by saying, "So, therefore I don't like these guys," as one of our storytellers does. For these stories, one could say that the point or conclusion coincides with the evaluation: The main goal of the story is to provide evidence for a negative opinion about the minority group. Narrative event evaluations thus function metonymically as (negative) group evaluations.

Complications and Resolutions: Story Topics

The kernel of a story is formed by the combination of a Complication and a Resolution. Unlike the other categories, these are obligatory in storytelling. Without a Complication there is no story, and without a Resolution a story would be typically incomplete and be met with questions such as "What happened (then)," or "What did you do?" Thus, the Complication is the category that dominates topics about what went wrong, which goal was frustrated, or what other undesired or unexpected events or acts took place. The Resolution classically should feature what the story protagonist (for instance, the storyteller herself) did, how she reacted to this predicament or surprising event, and, therefore, how the problem was solved (or not), or what the relevant consequences were.

It is interesting to find, however, that in many of the "ethnic" stories we have analyzed, such a Resolution is absent. In Table 2.2, we see that more than half of the stories do not have a clear Resolution.

There may be several functional explanations for that structural feature. First, as we already indicated earlier, the stories are "complaint" stories, and, therefore, they *should* not feature (re)solutions. The storytellers want to communicate precisely the opinion that there is a minority problem, and it would not be very effective if they had personally "solved" it in their daily life. Therefore, the storyteller or in-group members are often portrayed in a victim role and the foreigner in the role of villain.

Second, if some tentative resolving actions are mentioned, they are mostly followed by failure, which suggests the powerlessness of the storyteller as an in-group member: The minority actors will invariably

TABLE 2.2: Narrative Categories and Their Frequencies in Stories About Minorities (stories in interviews of Group II were explicitly elicited)

Interviews	N storytellers	N stories	Occasioning	Summary	Setting	Orientation	Complication	Resolution	Evaluation	Explication	Conclusion	Stories/ Teller	N of categories/story
Group I	20	50	22(44%)	6(12%)	50(100%)	21(42%)	50(100%)	24(48%)	33(66%)	13(26%)	17(34%)	$2^{1}/_{2}$	4.7
Group II	30	83	22(27%)	9(11%)	81(98%)	45(54%)	81(98%)	48(58%)	49(59%)	20(24%)	27(32%)	$2^{3}/_{4}$	4.6
Total	50	133	44 (33%)	15 (11.3%)	131 (98.5%)	66 (49.6%)	131 (98.5%)	72 (54.1%)	82 (61.6%)	33 (24.8%)	44 (33.0%)	$2^{2}/_{3}$	4.7

react aggressively, as is the case in the bread exchange story. Third, the unsolved predicament is also functional in enhancing the argument that "the authorities don't do anything against it either," which we find in many stories. According to competition-frame analysis, in which two parties in conflict represent two angles of a triangle and a judging or distributing authority a third angle (Schank & Carbonell, 1978), impartial authority is needed in the resolution of conflicts. However, in stories about minorities, the local or national authorities are often portrayed as favoring the minority group, so that the majority members feel discriminated against (Bovenkerk et al., 1985; den Uyl & van der Wurff, 1984). Of course, aside from a breach of in-group solidarity, this "discrimination" by the authorities also represents an instance of real class conflict. Thus, the narrative consequence of the complicating events is that "we (ordinary) Dutch people" have to suffer, which is both narratively and argumentatively very effective in conveying the opinion that the presence of "foreigners" leads to unresolved problems.

Rather characteristic is the fact that in most of the stories in which the storyteller did take initiative to solve a problem successfully, she appeared much more tolerant about the presence of foreigners. The message in that case seems to be: There might be difficulties once in a while, but with some tact and ingenuity they may be solved as mine was. Of course, the tolerance dimension implied in that case is a functional move in avoiding negative self-presentation ("I am not a racist," "I am tolerant"), as well as a form of self-enhancement, as is usual in "heroic" storytelling ("Look how smart I was"). In some of these stories, we also find examples of people who took the side of the foreigner in a conflict, while at the same time denouncing the discriminating acts of their own in-group members. This does not happen very often, however. In most cases in which in-group members display tolerance and problem solving, ethnic minority groups are treated in a rather patronizing way.

The Complications of the story are usually about negative acts of ethnic group members. Of the stories, nearly 70% picture such negative acts by Surinamese and immigrant workers (Turks and Moroccans) alike (each appearing in about 45% of the stories, the other stories being about other groups, which also shows how prominent only a few groups in Amsterdam are for storytelling). As may be seen from Table 2.3, in which the various topics included in the Complication category are listed, the major topic is "violent conflict" (aggression, violence, fights, and so on), followed by that of "crime" (theft, mugging, hold ups, and so on), and various forms of personal harassment and other forms of neighborly "nuisance" (smells, loud music, and so on).

These topics alone account for half of the 131 complicating story events. They indeed make "good" and, therefore, effective storytelling,

TABLE 2.3:   Topics in the Complications of Stories About Minorities

 1. Aggression, violence, menacing behavior, and fights (27)
 2. Holdups, theft, and mugging (13)
 3. "Abnormal" behavior (due to cultural differences) (9)
 4. Nuisance, bothering, harassment (9)
 5. Being dirty, unhygienic behavior (7)
 6. Noise, loud music (7)
 7. Avoidance of contact (6)
 8. Leakages and similar neighbor conflicts (3)
 9. They ruin their apartments (2)
10. Home slaughtering (2)
11. Independent behavior of women (2)
12. Abuse social benefits (1)
13. They dance differently (1)
14. They do not want to work (1)
15. They are favored in housing (1)
16. They take our jobs (1)
17. They do not adapt (1)
18. They are stupid/backward (1)

because they clearly show the others in a negative light: All these topics embody deviance and threat as perceived by the storytellers. The other topics are less directly focused on deviance, but may be about cultural differences, and the "abnormal" or "different" behavior of the minority group member (dress, ruining apartments, slaughtering at home, and so on).

These story complications show in particular how the prejudiced topics analyzed in the previous section are structured in talk. They also show about which topics people tend to tell "foreigner stories" and about which topics people have no personal experiences to report. Thus, general prejudiced opinions, such as "they do not want to work," "they abuse the social services," or "they are favored in housing," appear often in the interviews, but seldom in the stories. This suggests, as shall be shown in more detail later, that they do not originate, cognitively, from models of personal experiences, but directly from more general prejudiced attitudes, as formed from hearsay or interpreted media stories. Storytelling, therefore, also distinguishes talk about ethnic minority groups in high-contact areas from such talk in no- or low-contact areas, where more general arguments tend to be used. Similarly, many of the stories more generally exhibit the problem topics on which people in poor inner-city neighborhoods tend to focus: decay, crime, lack of safety, bad quality of the houses, or noise. These are the more general social problems that in our stories tend to be attributed very concretely, namely, by personal experience and, therefore, credible evidence, to the presence and the actions of the "foreigners."

An American Story

By way of comparison, let us finally give an example of one of the stories from our interviews held in San Diego. Just as in Amsterdam, such stories are told primarily in ethnically "mixed" neighborhoods, where people have more daily experiences with ethnic minority group members than in the nearly exclusively White and more affluent neighborhoods. The following story is told by an elderly couple who had immigrated from Canada to the United States some 30 years before. They are preoccupied by crime and burglaries in their neighborhood and give an example of a burglary next door ("M"—Man; "W"—Woman; "I"—Interviewer):

(4) (A-TD-1a,b)

> I: And the people who, who, do you have an idea about the people who do the burglaries about here. I mean, what kind of people would they be?
> W: Well, one day . . . Yeah tell him about
> M: . . . A lot are Mexicans. I was home (?) one time I had the flu, and uh I came out to the kitchen to get myself a cup of tea, just in my pyjamas, and I happen to look out of the window, and I see them breaking in into the house next door. At first I thought they were doing some work, that he had hired somebody to work at the windows and then I realized they are breaking in. So I came to the garage door here, and I got a real good description. I was terribly sick at the time, and I got a real good description, at least one of them.
> I: There were two?
> M: There were three altogether.
> I: Three!
> M: And uh, people were in the yard there, and one was out here, and I got a good description of him. He must have heard me, cause he took off, and I thought well, uhh, I can grab that one, so I went out of the door, but he was so fast, he was gone, he was down about there by the time I get out of the door, and he ran around the block, and over the church lot behind us. And uhh, so anyway, I called the police and gave them a description, and it wasn't ten minutes, they had a car in the area apparently, he picked them up.
> I: Really?
> M: They were illegal aliens, Mexican.
> W: They came over on the bus, didn't they?
> M: Came over on the bus, and they had shopping bags, and they had uh I don't know how many shopping bags stashed in the bushes.
> W: . . . They had twenty shopping bags stashed in the bushes.
> M: . . . Was it twenty?
> W: . . . Twenty.
> M: In the church lot, near the church, behind the bushes. They had broken into how many places was it?

W: I don't remember.

M: I think they said forty homes, up the hill and in the college area, all the way down to here, and they were working their way down here.

W: You wouldn't believe it.

M: And so they brought them back, and uh identified them, this one feller, and uh the police took him away, took him to jail and I was contacted by the police department, by the attorney uhh

W: . . . prosecutor

M: . . . prosecuting attorney, and he said that they were holding him for a trial, and they would be, trial coming up such and such a date. Anyway, uh it wasn't long after that, we got a letter, forget all about it, we send him back to Mexico.

I: They wouldn't go through the hassle of doing, of trying him and uh

W: . . . No

M: . . . No

I: They just sent him back?

M: They just sent him back. Trying to (???) to the people, and just send them back [laughs]. So this is what's done, they slap their wrist, and tell'em "naughty, naughty," and "go home now."

This story, which reflects much of the ethnic situation and the prejudices in Southern California, features the usual narrative categories: a Setting (one day, house of neighbor), Participants (Mexicans), a mundane Orientation (being at home with flu and looking out of the window), and a Complication that instantiates a general prejudiced opinion (Mexicans, and especially illegal aliens, are criminal), namely, breaking in next door. In this case, however, there is at least part of a Resolution. The man emphasizes, by rhetorical repetition, that he got a "good description" of one of them, and that one of the burglars was quickly arrested by the police. That would be a classical resolution for a crime story, but in this case, this result is not the real Resolution. After a narrative section that emphasizes the criminal acts of the burglars, also by rhetorical means (the number game: 20 bags, 40 homes), it turns out that the burglars were sent back to Mexico. In other words, there is no real punishment, and hence no (moral) resolution. And, much like in other "minority stories," the authorities are held responsible for this lack of firmness. After the apparent Resolution, as we might call it, the storyteller identifies—after undeniable, because official, "identification" by the police—the burglars as illegal aliens from Mexico, thereby indicating the relevance of the story for his arguments that much crime in the city is committed by aliens. Finally, the Conclusion of the story features a generalization about the treatment of criminals ("So this is what's done . . .").

Whereas this conclusion is sufficient to stress the victimization of law-abiding American citizens (as the couple describes itself), there are some further aspects that contribute to such an interpretation, such as the man being "terribly sick," which may also be taken as a good reason why he didn't catch the burglar. Note also that the repeated reference to the "good description" the man was able to get implies that he was doing his duty as a good citizen, that is, by helping the police identify one of the burglars. This is one of the elements in the story that may be seen as a move that is a functional part of positive self-presentation.

The story section that explains what other crimes the burglars had committed in the neighborhood may be read as part of the Complication, for example, by stressing the seriousness of their crime (it was not an isolated burglary), but also as a form of Evaluation, putting the burglary into a more serious perspective. Indeed, it is at this point that the woman expresses an explicit evaluation ("You wouldn't believe it") following the typical rhetorical emphasis obtained by mentioning the numbers of burglaries and bags of loot.

Concluding this section, we have found that stories about minorities tend to be told as "evidence" in an argument to demonstrate that minorities are somehow deviant, criminal, or otherwise problematic, mostly by breaking the law or the customs of "our" society, and that "we" are the victims of such acts. Whereas the Complication typically features such a deviant act, there is often no (real) solution, for which, often, the authorities are blamed. In later sections, we shall see how such stories are made more persuasive by various semantic moves and rhetorical devices.

6. Argumentation

The expression of delicate or controversial social opinions in conversation is routinely expected to be backed up with arguments. It is not surprising, therefore, that interview talk abounds with argumentative sequences. This is also because the interviewer generally is a relative stranger, whose opinions and speaker-judgments are not known to the speaker. Within the combined strategies of positive self-presentation and negative other-presentation, such arguments have the fundamental function of protecting the speaker against unwanted inferences about his or her ethnic attitudes. Negative evaluations, taken as conclusions, must be sustained by defensible premises, that is, by shared beliefs, rules, laws, principles, norms, or values, and by demonstrably true "facts." Such facts may, for instance, be taken from personal experiences, and stories may function precisely as descriptions of such experience-based facts.

Argumentation Schemata

These elements of acceptable argumentation may become conventionalized in a fixed schematic form in a way that recalls the narrative schema we have discussed in the previous section (Toulmin, 1958; van Eemeren & Grootendorst, 1983; van Eemeren, Grootendorst, & Kruiger, 1984). And just as for stories, there are differences between abstract, formal reasoning, and informal everyday argumentation, and between written forms of argumentation and argumentation in talk (Schiffrin, 1985). Despite these differences, we assume that in talk also, people generally follow an elementary schema of argumentation, which may be specified as follows for our interviews (where X is a [negative] property or action, and Y is an ethnic minority group; Y1 is an instance, that is, an example, of Y, and X1 an example of X):

(A) Position statement (opinion): "I do not like X of group Y"
(B) Inference principle (mostly implicit): "If Y has/does X, then Y is bad" (here based on value)
(C) General fact: "Y always have/do X"
(D) Particular fact: "I have experienced that X1 did/had Y1"
(E) Supporting ("objective") evidence for truth of C or D.

Position statement A, expressing an opinion that must be supported by arguments, usually comes first in conversational argumentation, unlike conclusions in formal argumentations. Sometimes this opinion is expressed only indirectly or remains implicit. In that case, the general negative fact (C) may simply be mentioned. The negative opinion, which presupposes an evaluation, requires an implicit inference principle (B), which must be based on a social value, norm, or other general principle. To apply the principle so that (by informal *modus ponens*) the conclusion is valid, a general "fact" must hold (C). Sometimes this general fact is itself stated explicitly, as is the case for direct expressions of prejudiced opinions, such as, "They always steal." However, for reasons of positive self-presentation and antiracist norms, such general statements are usually not strong enough as evidence, so that sustaining "proof" must be given for the plausibility of C. Typically, such proof may be provided by giving examples or telling about personal experiences. Of course, such experiences must in principle be "verifiable," and we sometimes also find expressions of their nonsubjective (unbiased) nature, as in "You can ask her yourself," or "Other people reacted in the same way" (E).

Transformations and Realizations

This abstract argumentation schema of informal, conversational argumentation may, of course, be realized in different ways in different communicative contexts. Some speakers give no reasons (arguments) for opinion positions, so that there is no argumentation at all (the zero case). Others only mention a generalized fact, usually a prejudiced opinion, as a basis for their particular evaluation of a group, or just a particular fact in the form of an example or story. Whereas usually general norms and values remain implicit in argumentation, they play an important role in the prejudiced judgments of ethnic minority groups, who are precisely perceived as threatening these norms or rules. This is why in talk, a general norm is often explicitly stated, even when the speaker may assume that the (in-group) interviewer knows and/ or shares this norm. In our bread exchange story in the previous section, we saw that the storyteller explicitly states the norm that "one does not exchange bread in Holland." The stereotypical and more general form of this norm invocation is the expression "We are not used to that here," which occurs frequently in prejudiced talk.

The simple schema we have outlined above may also show different forms of expansion and other transformations. The "particular fact" category may be filled by a lengthy story, which itself may contain subordinate argumentation sequences, statements of general facts, or invocations of norms and values. This also shows that argumentation structures are not just a local, but rather a global phenomenon. They organize complex sequences of propositions (or speech acts), for which they define special functions and, therefore, can be characterized in terms of superstructures, in the same way as for narrative schemata. Also, for argumentative schemata, we find that there are some core categories that are obligatory, and a few "supporting" categories that are optional. Most of the categories are recursive, in the sense that they may occur several times within an argument. This recursion may also be analyzed in terms of complex, discontinuous categories, as we also found for certain narrative categories.

Conversational Constraints

Although the schema presented above is specifically designed to capture conversational argumentation, it does not capture many other properties of informal "arguing." It still has the flavor of a monological structure, whereas argumentation is, at least implicitly, inherently dialogical. The various strategies that may be used locally to perform the respective argumentative "steps," may involve questions, (dis)agreements (Pomerantz, 1984), objections, and, hence, counterarguments from the recipient. In fact, the categories are "recipient-designed" in the sense of anticipating such counterarguments. Similarly, initial opinion positions need not be fixed and well defined but may undergo strategic modifications, especially if the speaker progressively understands that the original position as it stands is no longer defensible. The same may hold for each move in the argumentative sequence, and each of the factual or evaluative propositions used in the defense of the highest-level (main) position may be challenged and in need of independent subargumentation. Hence, apart from being a hierarchical form or schema, an actual conversational argument also has many local, strategic, and interactional features. We shall, however, examine these, as well as those of stories, at the local levels of analysis we deal with in the subsequent sections. The same holds for our analysis of an example we must turn to now: We limit ourselves to the overall, global argumentation structure.

An Example

The following argumentative moves have been taken from an interview with a 36-year-old woman, a musician in a well-known Dutch orchestra, who lives in a rich, no-contact area of Amsterdam. In the beginning of the interview, she volunteered: "It depends in what neighborhood you are interviewing. If you take somebody from De Jordaan [a well-known old popular area of Amsterdam, which however, contrary to her assumptions, does not have a large percentage of minority groups], you will of course get big stories about foreigners, and that you will of course *not* hear if you come and talk with people in this neighborhood." She stresses the fact, however, that one can still have opinions about "foreigners" wherever you live in the city. The interview then features the following (macro)moves (we ignore the literal wording here):

(5) (RL2)
(1) I know people [in De Jordaan] who first had nice Amsterdamese neighbors, and who now got Turkish and Moroccan neighbors, who make a lot of noise.
(2) I can very well imagine that therefore it is not easy for them to stay friendly with these new neighbors who have large families.
(3) So, I am glad I live here. They cannot afford living here.
(4) What people would object to here are the large families and especially the noise.

(4.1) These people have another life-style than we have.
    (4.1.1) We are used to living indoors, whereas they are used to living outdoors.
        (4.1.1.1) They come from a warm country.
    (4.1.2) A certain noise is normal in their way of living.
        (4.1.2.1) In Turkey or Morocco in the street you have these bustling crowds.
            (4.1.2.1.1) That is very nice and pleasant.
    (4.1.3) But they also do that here.
(4.2) And we are not used to that.
(4.3) It would be strange if we would have to adapt to that.
    (4.3.1) If you want to sit down quietly, you hear the noise of these children.
(4.4) Tolerance is fine, but if life-styles are really different, then it may bother me.
    (4.4.1) Because they have another national character.
    (4.4.2) Dutch large families make a different kind of noise.
        (4.4.2.1) At least you can talk to them.
(4.5) But the foreigners have a different mentality ($= 4.1.$).

This woman basically defends the position that she can understand that people have "opinions" (read—*negative opinions*) about the presence of foreigners. The first major step in her argumentative support for this more or less implicit position is an example: the resentment of her friends against being "sandwiched" between "noisy" foreigners with large families. The implication of her position is that the woman would not like to live among foreigners, mainly because they are supposed to be noisy, and the explicit question by the interviewer about the hypothetical presence of foreigners in this neighborhood is reacted to in a complex series of moves, including the argument that "they" would not be able to afford that, and, if they could, it would depend on the size of the family.

Yet, her main objection remains the assumed noise, and for that position she sets up an elaborate series of arguments. The basis for the argumentative steps is her statement that there is a fundamental difference in life-styles. Foreigners are used to noise, which in turn is "explained" by their outdoor living, briefly supported by a reference to the "warm" countries from which they come. Importantly, the woman stresses that, "as such," foreigners and their noise do not bother her (she even likes the bustling life in these countries), but that their life-style clashes with the quieter life-style of the Dutch. Upon the interviewer's question, whether a large Dutch family is not just as noisy, she provides counterarguments such as the assumption that their noise would be different, that one could communicate (and ask them to be quiet), and there would be mutual respect. A basic position thus being defended is that it would be unacceptable ("strange") if we had to adapt to their life-style, which is a dominant prejudiced opinion in many of the interviews.

As usual in this type of talk, this woman dissimulates her dislike of foreigners behind a potentially defensible point of view, namely, the common assumption about cultural differences, in this case, mainly focusing on noise. This is a rather "safe" strategy if one shares the stereotype that indeed foreigners are "noisy," and if it is legitimate to object to noisy neighbors. The general arguments about cultural or national differences and life-styles protect her against questions or inferences about her personal opinions.

When the interviewer poses a hypothetical question about foreigners moving into that neighborhood, she first states the very impossibility of the hypothesis: They cannot afford that (presupposing that all foreigners are poor), and then a hesitating conditional acceptance (if the family would not be too big). But then she comes back to the general topic of noise and cultural differences, which clearly conveys her dislike for close association with foreigners. In fact, she even states explicitly that she is glad to live in that neighborhood. When the interviewer, somewhat later, explicitly asks her about this connection (does she live here because foreigners have a different life-style, and so on), she indignantly rejects that inference, however, "No, not that, oh no, no that is, that would carry us too far, what we what we are talking about now. . . . No, therefore of course I don't live here because of that. That would be ridiculous . . . I live here because I like to live close to my work." We see that as soon as the interviewer makes an explicit inference that could seriously harm her tolerant self, her reaction is very defensive and emotional, even when somewhat more indirectly she has earlier stated that she is glad not to live "there" (where foreigners bother her friends). We see how argumentation is closely linked with the strategies of positive self-presentation, that is, with the ways people defend their opinions in a normatively acceptable way.

In terms of our argumentation schema, we thus end up with the following basic argumentative steps in our example:

(1) Main position (implicit): I do not like (the noise of) foreigners.
(2) Inference principle: If people make noise, I do not like them.
(3) General statement: Foreigners are noisy.
(4) Particular fact (example): Friends of mine had noisy, large families of foreigners as neighbors, and didn't like it.
(5) Support (for 3): They have different life-style, large families, come from warm countries.

This is the highest-level structure of her argumentation, but at several points further important arguments are used to back up each step. Thus, both the inference principle, and the support of the general opinion that foreigners are noisy and have different life-styles, need to be founded on a general norm or principle, lest she may be found intolerant by the recipient. Therefore, she resorts to the general principle that "we," the Dutch, need not adapt to their different life-style in our "own" country. This is indeed one of the stereotypical moves made in argumentative strategies of many prejudiced majority members: In our own country we have the right to maintain our own life-style (norms, values, habits, and so on), which implies the other major opinion we find in our data: They must adapt to us.

Notice also that this woman's emphasis on the "noise" dimension of the cultural difference category of ethnic attitudes is perhaps in line with her basic personal and professional interests as a musician. In other words, as soon as ethnic groups are perceived as a threat to fundamental interests of a group, it is the relevant prejudice category that will become most salient. For a musician, this may be a "quiet" environment (ignoring for a moment that a musician's neighbors may in turn have little appreciation of practice sessions). Based on the goals derived from this interest, she then must design her argumentative strategy so that there are "good reasons" for her to resent the presence of "noisy foreigners." She does *not* do this, however, by simply saying that she is a musician, and that, therefore, she needs quiet, because in that case the argument would be too personal and too obviously linked to her own interests. On the contrary, she comes up with the example of friends, and more generally argues at the abstract level of cultural differences, life-styles, and adaptation.

We have found this kind of argumentation, this abstractness and these generalizations, more often in the talk of (upper-) middle-class people and the (intellectual, political, and financial) elite in no-contact areas. Such talk has few concrete stories about personal experiences but tends to formulate general principles, usually based on information from the media or on occasional examples from hearsay (friends or acquaintances, typically maids, who *do* have personal experiences).

"They Have to Learn English"

This also holds for the argumentations we find in the California interviews. Instead of stories about concrete experiences, people in the low-contact neighborhoods in San Diego typically give sometimes lengthy arguments about such well-publicized issues as illegal immigration, affirmative action, or learning English. The last issue was particularly relevant during our field-work, and part of our interviews were clearly held against the background of an extended media discussion about bilingual education and voting and amidst protests against billboards in Asian languages (mostly Chinese) in some neighborhoods of Los Angeles. So let us summarize some of the premises used in argumentations that conclude that immigrants should all learn English, an argument supported by many of the people we interviewed, whatever their opinions about other issues.

(6) (A-LG-3)
1. If you choose to be American, you ought to learn English.
2. If I go to Italy, I wouldn't expect the Italians to learn my language.
3. It is not sensible to encourage differences.
    3.1. If you expect everybody to live in a society peacefully.

(7) (A-TD-1a, b)
1. You should learn the ways of the country you come to.
    1.1. Too many people demand that we adapt to their ways.
2. The United States is a melting pot, with people from many nations.
3. If you would go to Holland, and if people wouldn't speak English there, you would be in bad shape.
4. Children at school learn under an English teacher, they learn American laws, and about governing the American people.
5. If they didn't speak English in the working world, they would not know that two and two makes four in America (and, We would not educate them to take their place in the world).
6. We lost a whole generation (due to education in Spanish).
7. People must respect the country they are in, like we would do if we went to Mexico or other countries.
8. People from Northwestern Europe do adapt here, but people from Southern countries they always demand their rights.

(8) (A-LG-2)
1. If they (Mexicans) learn English, it is easier for them to make their way.
2. Their kids must be immersed in it.
3. This is an English-speaking society.
4. It is for their own benefit.
5. It would do the kids a disservice not to learn English at school.

From these argument summaries, it appears that similar reasons are given to support the statement that immigrants must learn English. The general conditional underlying the argumentation is that if you (want to) live in an English-speaking country such as the United States, you have to learn English. This conditional may be further supported by more general if-statements about cultural adaptation, as well as by frequent (mostly hypothetical) comparisons. Just like the people in Amsterdam, the people in California also tend to say that immigrants should learn the ways (and hence the language) of the new country, just like we would have to adapt and learn the language in another country (we ignore at this point the arguable assumption that most Americans would learn the languages of the countries they are visiting or in which they are living). Typical for the United States is, of course, further support from the argument that "this is a country of immigrants, a melting pot, where everybody should learn the common language," and hence the argument that presupposes that a different language would also favor other differences and would hence be a possible threat to peace (in example 6). Note that the interviewee in A-TD-1 goes much further than that and surmises, as elsewhere in that interview, that people from Northwestern Europe (the man was born in Sweden himself before emigrating to Canada as a boy) adapt themselves more easily than "southern" people—who also are perceived to be more "protesting" and claim their "rights." In other words, we see how prejudices against "southern" people, and hence people with a different appearance and culture, may support assumptions used in argumentations for adapting and learning the language.

The next set of arguments is well known in "ethnic arguing," that is, the altruistic type of arguments: It is for their own good. In the case of language learning, indeed, it is argued that people will do less well in society if they don't know the language. In line with these arguments, most people also oppose voting in minority languages, notably Spanish, or street signs in Chinese. One argument, given in a newspaper interview, is that people feel excluded and hence threatened when they are unable to read public messages or understand public conversations. One of our interviewees holds that he thinks people speaking another language to each other in his presence might be making fun of him. We have found similar opinions and anxieties in our Amsterdam interviews.

Generally, we may conclude that argumentation types and styles in this kind of talk are rather similar in California and the Netherlands. People may use the same arguments, the same implicit conditionals, and the same strategies to make statements or opinions (more) plausible. Learning the language is found to be a very important condition of (purported) acceptance of immigrants in both countries. It should be added, though, that in both countries people usually emphasize that they have "no problem" when immigrants speak their own language at home or when they keep other aspects of their own culture, especially, in private contexts. The implicit condition, of course, is that, publicly, immigrants should not be "bothering" us: They are welcome if they completely adapt to our ways. It is this conditional that is perhaps the most general, widespread, and most accepted opinion of the "ethnic consensus" both in the United States and in the Netherlands. It is the opinion that is most typical also for the self-defense of dominant group identity. Of course, the argument is only partly valid: Speaking the language may be a necessary but, of course, far from a sufficient condition for "acceptance," as is obvious from the position of Blacks, both in the United States and in the Netherlands, whose language and culture is not radically different from the dominant one, and who know the dominant culture very well, both as participants and as outside observers.

Conclusions

Argumentative structure is the routine schematic form for the support of delicate opinions, and people who volunteer opinions about ethnic minorities will, therefore, implicitly or explicitly, state such opinions, preferably with several types of supporting evidence. Such arguments may involve general principles and general facts, as well as particular facts, such as personal experiences. As a general constraint, no arguments may be used that could be heard as expressing a racist opinion about foreigners. Therefore, supporting evidence and evaluations must be in accordance with accepted norms and principles, must avoid references to personal interests, and generally must be embedded in strategies of positive self-presentation. At the level of particular supportive facts, concrete stories have an important persuasive function because they are in principle "true" and not just "opinions." If such stories and their general conclusions show what kind of ethnic conflict exists, or why it is difficult to live with or accept foreigners, they yield intersubjectively defensible support for overall negative opinions about ethnic minorities.

Another frequent move in such argumentation is to emphasize cultural differences (they are "used to" making more noise, being livelier, or having more children), which may be used as a form of pseudoexplanation for the perceived cultural conflict. Such explanations presuppose, first, that the foreigners indeed have the cultural properties as stated and then attribute such cultural behavior (and hence the conflict) to such cultural differences. Thus, the others are blamed and, at the same time, the speaker contributes to positive self-presentation by showing explanatory "understanding" for such cultural differences. Similarly, pseudoaltruistic arguments are provided that claim that some action would be in favor of the foreigners (e.g., going back to their own country, "where they can help build up the economy"), where in reality the argument is self-serving.

Because many of the arguments are, at first sight, rather plausible, they can be very persuasive. The experiences people tell about seem real and the conclusions they draw are based on principles of reasonableness and generally accepted norms. Presupposed are the premises "we all know are true" (e.g., "they are noisy"), and the norms and values used for judgments are also defensible ("making noise is unpleasant for other people"). It, therefore, is often difficult for recipients of such arguments to produce counterarguments. First, because they often lack the counterinformation to challenge the wrong (prejudiced) presuppositions, and second, because they are not aware that the application of specific norms may sometimes violate higher norms (even if foreigners were noisier, then this is no reason for discriminating against them). We shall see later that such counterargumentation must be socially acquired, just as prejudices are acquired, and that the media, official discourse, and everyday talk of people provide few instances of such forms of persuasive (and hence equally acceptable) counterarguments against prejudiced opinions. Within a racist consensus, prejudices and their argumentative support are routine and, therefore, easy to formulate and more easily accepted.

7. Semantic moves

In each turn of a conversation, a speaker is accomplishing a variety of acts at several levels. One or more speech acts may be performed, each with several interactional and social functions within different local and global goals (Kreckel, 1981; Labov & Fanshel, 1977; McLaughlin, 1984). We have repeatedly shown in this chapter that prejudiced talk about minorities, among other things, has the overall goal of negative other-presentation, while at the same time preserving a positive self-impression (or avoiding the loss of face). These goals are sometimes in conflict, for instance, when social norms do not allow uninhibited negative talk about minority groups. Therefore, expedient strategies are in order to reconcile these real or apparent inconsistencies. These strategies are accomplished by sequences of moves that try to realize both goals as effectively as possible, for instance, with a maximum of negative other-presentation and a minimum of negative self-presentation. In other words, speakers persistently try to manage or control the social inferences the recipient is bound to make about them on the basis of what they say (Arkin, 1981; Goffman, 1959; Hass, 1981; Schneider, 1981; Tedeschi, 1981). In Chapter 5, we shall analyze in more detail the persuasive and interactional dimensions of these forms of self-presentation. Here, we only pay attention to the discursive "implementation" of such strategies.

Global and Local Strategies

Whereas part of these moves are pragmatic and rhetorical, an improtant set of them may be called *semantic* because they may be defined as strategically managed relations between propositions, that is, in terms of the "content" of speech act sequences. Conversation content allows inferences by the recipient about speaker beliefs and opinions, and within the overall goal of establishing or preserving a positive social face, these inferences need to be managed carefully. The speaker, therefore, must take special care of what is said and how it is said. Thus, within the overall goal of negative other-presentation, the speaker may simply say "They always steal," but such an assertion may also be interpreted as an expression of a racist opinion. At the global level of conversation, therefore, the speaker will make sure to provide arguments and stories that are subjectively taken as "evidence" for such an opinion. In that case, the proposition would no longer be a subjective, prejudiced opinion but a statement of fact, a socially warranted judgment.

At the local level, there are other strategic moves that may inhibit negative inferences about the opinions or personality of the speaker. For instance, after saying "They always make a terrible noise," the speaker may add "But the Dutch families do the same," or "You hear everything in these bad apartments." That is, by extending the negative characterization to Dutch neighbors, the speaker cannot be accused of ethnic prejudice, and by adding an explanation that specifies one of the causes of the noise as heard, a possible excuse is formulated: Not their noise, but bad apartments cause the speaker to be annoyed. Similarly, instead of expressing the negative general opinion that "they always make a lot of noise," the speaker may also say "I do not like it very much when they play music in the middle of the night," which reduces the negative opinion to a matter of personal taste or preference, and downgrades the statement about (loud) music to a presupposition ("That they play music in the middle of the night"). In this way, the negative statement may be toned down or mitigated, and mitigation, thus, is one of the moves of presenting negative opinions that do not "sound" very negative.

There are a large variety of moves that mitigate negative propositions because they are often essential in polite interaction (Brown & Levinson, 1978; Goody, 1978; Leech, 1983). Mitigation, at the same time, is a move characteristic of "indirect" language use in general (Stubbs, 1983). In our case, however, politeness and indirectness are not so much a feature of concern for the status or respect of the recipient but rather part of the overall strategy of positive presentation of the social self. By being less extreme, and by moderating negative opinions about others, the speaker presents him- or herself as more or less tolerant. The same impression management may be performed by the examples of "extension" and of "explanation," given above.

Definition of Moves

Theoretically, these semantic moves can be defined as functional relationships between (sequences of) propositions (van Dijk, 1977, 1981b). That is, the strategic function of an (expressed) proposition is determined by the nature of its link with another, previous or following, proposition. Thus, the expression of B is a mitigation move, if B is less negative than a previous proposition A. And B is a generalization move, if B is more general than A. In formal terms, this means that A entails B. And conversely, B may also be an instance or example of A, and in that case B entails A. Similarly, B is a contrast or contradiction move if B entails not-A. In this way, the other strategic moves also may be defined in terms of abstract relationships between propositions, and that is why we call them *semantic* in the first place.

As soon as relationships between speech acts, as such, are involved, we would qualify them as pragmatic moves, as is the case, for instance, when an accusation is followed by a defense, or when a request is followed by a justification. Often we find a combination of such moves at several levels. That is, not only is the proposition itself strategically "chosen," but, of course, also its actual use—that is, its expression within the accomplishment of a speech act, for instance, an assertion. Similarly, mitigation or contrast may also have been conventionalized as effective moves, for instance, within a rhetorical framework, where they may be known as fixed operations such as litotes, understatement, and rhetorical contrast. Although these various levels of analysis are in reality often intertwined, we keep them apart for theoretical reasons. That is, moves defined in terms of propositional relations are called *semantic,* and the same holds for moves that involve referential links. Thus, providing causes or reasons for an event or act is a referential-semantic move, which, at the same time, may have the functional-semantic role of giving an explanation and the pragmatic function of making excuses to justify a previous (speech) act. Although the theoretical framework is much more complicated than this brief explanation, it will do for our purposes (see Kreckel, 1981, for a taxonomy and further analysis of such sets of communicative acts).

Moves as Functional Units of Strategies

Also the notion of *move* itself needs some comment. Although it has been used often in the analysis of conversation and other forms of dialogue and interaction (see, e.g., Coulthard, 1977; Sinclair & Coulthard, 1975), there is no explicit definition of the concept. We simply define a *move* as a functional unit in a strategic interaction sequence. Whereas the overall strategy may be to reach a goal in an action sequence optimally and effectively, a move is each component act that is intended (consciously or not) to contribute to the realization of that goal (van Dijk & Kintsch, 1983). Note that although the concept of move is a functional category, it does not specify the act itself, but the function the act has in a strategically controlled (and hence goal-directed) sequence of acts. Thus, justifications, motivations, explanations, challenges, confirmations, or disagreements are moves that have specific (pragmatic) links with previous speech acts, but they are not speech acts themselves: They may each be accomplished by many different speech acts. In conversation, such moves may also be defined in terms of relations to the acts of a previous speaker. We may not only correct what we have just said, but also what was said by the previous speaker, for instance, when what was said by that speaker shows a possible negative inference of what the actual speaker had said before.

Our notion of *semantic move,* defined in terms of propositional links, therefore, should be understood as a functional unit in semantic act sequences. Propositions, however, are not usually taken to be "acts," and, therefore, we should be more precise and talk about the interactional "use" (or "production" or "expression") of propositions, that is, in terms of propositional acts or semantic (intentional or extentional) acts. That is, we talk about "meaning" neither as an abstract concept nor as a cognitive construct, but as an interactional and social act. This is important, because if we simply have the sequence [A, B], where B is partly equivalent with, but also partly different from A, B may functionally be a "correction" of A only when actually used in a conversation and actually meant as a correction of the act of meaning A, that is as an act of canceling or substituting what was meant by uttering A. The conceptual meaning of A does not change in that case, of course, but a speaker may very well cancel, that is, change the present validity, of what was meant by a previous semantic act. Conversationally, such self-corrections may appear as various types of repair, to which we return briefly in section 10 below (see also Heritage, 1984; Schegloff, 1979; Schegloff, Jefferson, & Sacks, 1977).

Socially speaking, this may mean that the speaker considers him- or herself no longer "responsible" for the earlier meaning act, nor for its possible consequences, such as—and this is most important for our discussion—the inferences the recipient may draw from the earlier meaning act (which does not mean that recipients always refrain from making such inferences, or that all corrections are socially acceptable).

Analysis of Examples

After this theoretical introduction, a number of concrete examples and analyses are in order. We discuss the major semantic moves as we have repeatedly found them in talk about minorities. This does not mean, by the way, that they are exclusive to such talk. We do not have special discourse rules or strategies that apply only for a specific topic of talk. Yet, a specific topic and the interactional strategies associated with it may require a specific choice or combination of such moves. We limit our examples to utterances of people who are interviewed, although there are also examples in the questions of the interviewers themselves (interviewer turns are marked with "I" in our quotations):

Example. In the interview with the woman (the musician living in a rich neighborhood), from whom we also characterized an argumentation fragment, we also find a number of characteristic moves. One of the first is the move of providing examples when "evidence" is needed to back up a general statement, as in:

(9) (III-Rl-2)
     One can have an opinion about those people, irrespective of where you live, and I happen to know friends who live in De Jordaan who (. . .)

This Example move explains why the woman feels entitled to have opinions about foreigners even when these do not live in her part of town. The example that follows is taken from reliable hearsay, and the general (negative) opinion is illustrated by the opinion her friends have about foreigners in their neighborhood. Thus, the Example (or Illustration) move is a typical argumentative move: It provides proof, evidence, or concrete facts that support a general opinion, in our case, often a prejudiced one. In high-contact areas, the Example move is typically introduced with a general statement, often negative, followed by a narrative illustration. The following woman, 62 years old, from such a neighborhood, first says that the neighborhood has changed, that it was a nice neighborhood, but that it has become "terrible," because of the many foreigners now living there:

(10) (II-MA-6)
      Many strangers and uh, well that is not very nice. For instance, next door second floor, of course, it is none of my business, but when I am in the kitchen, I can see it all right. I think they live there three years, and never there has been a sponge or leather on those windows. In the kitchen, you see, well you see all kinds of open bins with rubbish and uhh that is always like that. Well, we are not used to that.

Generalization. The complementary move of giving instantiating examples, is, of course, Generalization. After a particular statement or after a story or example, the speaker generalizes to the whole group of Dutch or ethnic minorities. After stories, this is essential for the argumentation because otherwise the recipient may take the events as an incident or a personal experience only. Therefore, people typically will add sentences such as "This happens all the time," or "This also happens to other people here." Thus, the following statement is made by a 40-year-old woman who lives in a high-contact neighborhood:

(11) (II-MA-1)
      I no longer dare to go out alone at night. But that is the same for the whole neighborhood here.

The generalization used by a California woman in the next example may also be interpreted as a form of mitigation: New immigrants may not want to learn English, but you may find such people "anywhere":

(12) (A-TD-4)
     None of those who are newly arrived, uhh they're . . . uh just like anywhere, there are certain personality types that say the hell to you (?) that I am gonna learn English.

Apparent denial and negation. One of the most stereotypical moves used in prejudiced talk is Apparent Denial, which usually contains a general denial of (one's own) negative opinions about ethnic groups, followed by a negative opinion: "I am not a racist, but . . .," or "I have nothing against foreigners, but . . . ." In the interview with the musician we have met before, we find an interesting example of such a denial, here in a concessive format:

(13) (III-RL-2)
     And then YOU have to keep talking friendly about those people. They hardly manage that anymore, you know, even when they are of good will, and anti uhh or not uhh anti . . . discriminatory and so.

That her friends (and by association the speaker herself because she agrees with her friends) have a negative opinion about foreigners in their neighborhood may be heard as an instance of a prejudiced opinion, and, therefore, the speaker closes her story with a denial of such a possible inference. We call this an Apparent Denial because it is not a real denial of what was said, but only a denial of possible inferences the recipient may make, as well as a statement that is inconsistent with what is actually stated in previous or next assertions.

A more direct form of denial is accomplished by simple negation. This interactional move is relevant as soon as the interviewer states or suggests that a person might have negative opinions, which at the same time would be inconsistent with dominant norms. In this same interview, for instance, the woman is confronted with an expressed inference of the interviewer and indignantly rejects that inference, after having just stated that these people have a different mentality:

(14) (III-RL-2)
    I: Is that also one of the reasons why you live in this neighborhood?
    W: No, oh no, not at all, no by the way that is that carries us too far you
        know what we are talking about now . . . No . . . of course not,
        that is not why I live here, that would be ridiculous . . .

The directness of the interviewer is met with repeated and insistent
denial, even when the woman has said earlier that she is glad to live in
this neighborhood so that she does not have foreign neighbors. Yet, when
made explicit, the inference of the interviewer would clearly be inconsistent with a nonprejudiced attitude, so that the woman is obliged to deny
that inference for the sake of positive self-presentation. Interestingly, the
woman also makes an avoidance move when she says that such a conclusion and, in fact, the very topic, would carry the discussion "too far,"
which could be read as a polite attempt to say "that is none of your damn
business." It is at this point of the talk that the delicacy of the topic and
especially the somewhat provocative strategy of the interviewer have
become too "close" to the real attitudes of the speaker.

That such moves are very general may be concluded also from the
frequent examples in our California interviews, as in the following:

(15) (A-LG-3)
    I would put up one HECK of a battle if my daughter decided to marry
    Black (. . .) and it doesn't have to do with superiority or anything
    else, it's just too vast a difference for me to be able to cross over.

(16) (A-LA-1)
    And then this one Black family moved in a few years ago [and it unset-
    tled the other people], not that they were prejudiced, but just from
    whatever subconscious attit . . .

(17) (A-TD-4)
    I don't think they [in the office] have any aversion to them [Blacks].

So, denial is a move typically used to dispel a possible interpretation
that prejudice or racism is involved.

                    Explanation. Statements about deli-
cate topics or controversial opinions usually need various forms of explanation. Above, we gave the example about noise ethnic groups in the
neighborhood are said to cause, and giving an explanation of such a
negative characteristic may somewhat mitigate the straighforward negative statement. This is exactly what the woman does, as follows:

(18) (III-RL-2)
    W: Noise, mainly noise
    I: . . . only noise?

W: Yes, it is the the l uhm . . . people have a different LIfe-style than
we have . . . Look, we are just Dutch people, we live indoors, we
are used to the climate, and well, those people come from a warm
country, they have always used have always been used to living
OUTdoors to . . . YES uhh a certain kind of noisiness in their
behavior is NORmal, you see, you only have to go and walk in the
streets in Turkey or Morocco, that is a bustling of people, that is
very NICE, that is very pleasant, but they also will they ALSO do
that here and we are not used to that (. . .)

This fragment shows a move to explain (and partly excuse) why immigrants are so noisy. In fact, the explanation takes the form of a complex
argumentation. It is not simply asserted that the immigrants have a different life-style, but also the reason for such a difference is further explained
by a quasi-ethnographic description of daily life in their home countries.
The assertion that their behavior there is "normal" is again a move that
is intended to eliminate the possible inference that the woman thinks
being noisy is deviant in general.

Explanations, also in California, tend to be framed in terms of cultural differences. Consider, for instance, the explanation given for the
lack of knowledge of English of Mexican women in San Diego:

(19) (A-TD-4)
The husband is the only one who speaks English. And they have a
little boy who speaks English, cause he goes to school now. But the
mother . . . the Mexican gentlemen always seem to keep their wives
incommunicado. I suppose they have good reason.

Apparent Concession. In the next move
of example 18, the woman goes one step further by making a positive
statement about the pleasantness of this bustling life in southern streets.
We may call such moves Apparent Concessions: The speaker apparently
conceeds that there is also something neutral (normal) or even positive.
The stereotypical form of such Apparent Concessions is "I like them a
lot, but (NEGATIVE PROPOSITION)." Another form of the same move
is "Dutch people also do that, but . . .," as we find in the following
fragment of a 40-year-old woman living in a poor high-contact neighborhood. This passage also features an explanatory move: The woman
rather exceptionally mentions a possible cause of the deviant behavior of
foreigners:— discrimination. She tells about an old lady who had been
mugged:

(20) (II-MA1)
And that was also, well I am sorry, but they were foreigners, they were
apparently Moroccans who did that. But God, all young people are
aggressive, whether it is Turkish youth, or Dutch youth, or Surinamese
youth, are aggressive. Particularly because of discrimination uhh that
we have here . . .

Somewhat later in the interview, the woman musician counters the
interviewer's suggestion that sometimes people are also intolerant when
they have no direct experiences with ethnic minority groups at all. The
woman then begins to explain (which is a move) that there are several
kinds of tolerance, such as tolerance of foreigners "as such":

(21) (III-RL-2)
uhh . . . how they are and that is mostly just fine, people have their
own religion have their own way of life, and I have absoLUTELY nothing against that, BUT, it IS a fact that if their way of life begins to differ
from mine to an EXTENT that . . .

Invariably, Apparent Denials and Apparent Concessions are combined
with statements of negative opinions about ethnic groups. They are the
standard moves to prevent negative inferences about the speaker by
accomplishing the semantic act of meaning "Even when I say something
negative, this does not mean I am prejudiced," or "Although I say something negative about them, they also have positive characteristics (or,
Dutch people also have negative characteristics)." Apparent Concessions and Denials typically introduce negative statements and thus "prepare" the recipient by establishing a correct interpretation scheme or
inference base for the next statements. A clear example is the following
fragment of an interview with a 77-year-old retired construction worker
living in a somewhat run-down middle-class neighborhood. He resents
the changing character of Amsterdam (things getting "dirtier") and
says that some of his acquaintances no longer dare go out at night. The
interviewer then asks what they might be afraid of and the man answers
as follows:

(22) (III-AB-4X)
Yeah, . . . what could they be afraid of? They are of course afraid,
uhh you can of course not point to somebody in particular, there are of
course VERY sweet Surinamese, those I also know, you know, and I
am sure there are also very sweet Turks and Moroccans, but the
whole package of what is now going on, like that uhh that economic
collapse . . .

Clearly, the association of lack of safety with the presence of ethnic
minority groups comes to mind with the speaker, but instead of directly

saying that he thinks people are afraid of foreigners, he starts with a stereotypical "positive" move of concession: There are also very nice ones
among them. And then he does not continue to say something negative
about foreigners, but rather explains in vague terms the conditions (economic recession, protest of the people, people are "kind of forced into
something") that might be interpreted as causing fear of and resentment
against foreigners. Thus, in this case, the apparent concession is combined with what could be called a move of Vagueness, which is one among
a series of indirectness moves, which also include Association, Implication, Presupposition, Avoidance, and similar moves that are aimed at
suggesting things without expressing them explicitly.

Sometimes liberal people provide a quasi-admission of their own
prejudice, especially when the following statement can hardly be interpreted in that way, thus, implicitly provoking a reaction such as "but that
is not prejudiced," which also implies a denial of their prejudice. The
following example occurs nearly literally twice in the same California
interview:

(23) (A-LG-1)
It sounds prejudiced, but I think if students only use English . . .

Mitigation. A more direct way of im-
pression management is avoiding altogether saying (very) negative things.
Interviews, therefore, abound with various types of semantic mitigations,
which, however, may also be analyzed in rhetorical terms, namely, as
understatements or litotes (which stress exactly the opposite of what is
said). The musician in example 21 continued:

(24) (III-RL-2)
And if you happen to want to sit down quietly for a moment, and there
are stamping children and a a and a a kind of kasbah on the street at the
same time, then that is a matter to which WE happen to have to adapt
ourselves, and that situation is a LITTLE bit strange, isn't it . . .

From the way she tells the story, the obvious conclusion is that she
finds it *very* "strange" (unacceptable) that *we* should adapt to *their* way
of life, but the use of "a little bit" mitigates this very negative opinion.
Apart from rhetorical understatement, there is often also a trace of irony
or cynicism in these frequent mitigations. Similarly, when one interviewer concludes from a story by a California woman "that Blacks don't
want to learn," the interviewee mitigates her implied statement by reducing the scope of quantification: "some of it, some of it" (A-LG-3); similarly, in moves such as "You can't say that of all Blacks, but . . ."
(A-MS-2). Sometimes, mitigations may also take the form of correc-

tions, which are interview features that are typical for the spontaneous nature of "delicate" talk, as in "maybe 'civilized' isn't the right word" (A-LG-2).

Contrast. If social conflict is perceived and expressed in talk, we may expect moves that emphasize contrast between the two groups involved. In our interviews, there is a standard move that points to the assumed favorable treatment by the authorities of ethnic groups and the neglect of "our own" people. Thus the 77-year-old man we have quoted before resents that 50 million guilders are spent to restore a housing project in a new suburb in which many Surinamese live, while at the same time there are not 7 million to pay for a machine for people who have a kidney condition:

(25) (III-AB-4X)
You read that? That goddam G. [housing project in suburb], and that is how it starts, you know, (???), hate, 50 million, you know, and there is no 7 million for that uhh machine for kidney functions or other things . . .

Similarly, when making comparisons, people tend to focus on the perceived differences in treatment. The following elderly couple (who have an Indonesian son-in-law), after a few very positive remarks about a Surinamese couple who lived downstairs and who left, regrettably "because you never know who will come next," also make a comparison between "us" and "them":

(26) (II-TK-4)
[Woman:]   Like at this moment. I know, in those years we needed people, but these last years no, and they still come in by the dozen, no I think that is . . .

[Man:]   and then I think that our children must give in so much for all those who do not want to work. If they work here, OK, but if they do not work here, they should rather go back. Abroad they do not take our children either when they do not work, and THAT is OUR opinion. . . . When our eldest son went to Australia, well you had to know so many trades and show your diplomas because otherwise they wouldn't let you in, while here they can come in like that, and the first thing they are able to say is GAK [abbreviation for the city administration bureau which registers unemployment benefits].

This passage is a rather characteristic example of poor people who, on the one hand, have friendly contacts with their foreign neighbors, and who help them when they can, but who, on the other hand, resent what they perceive as favorable treatment. This resentment is based on a number of stereotypes such as "It is easy to come into our country," "They live on unemployment money," "We have to work hard for it," and "They take away our jobs." Note that several of these stereotypes are of a general nature, based on media reports and hearsay, and not on direct observation in the neighborhood. In this way, the speaker's model of the situation need not conflict with their more general negative attitude schemata. Semantic contrast moves, thus, may be based on perceived competition (contrastive goals) as represented in actual experiences as well as those stored in general prejudices.

Again, the same principles underlie sometimes virtually identical examples in our California data, as in the interview with the couple who had immigrated from Canada and resented the undocumented immigration of Mexicans:

(27) (A-TD-1)
It took us one year [to get our papers], as I said we had to have so much money per head, we had to have a job guaranteed, someone to vouch for us here, and yeah these people can run across the border, on the south of us here, and uhh nothing is really done about it.

Generally, contrastive comparisons are used to emphasize the differences between in-group and out-group, where the in-group is seen to have a victim role or a more negative position. Typical examples may be found in passages that express resentment against the assumed "richness" of (supposedly poor) minority groups: "They are driving new cars, and my father didn't" (A-MS-2). One American interviewee made a long contrastive comparison between the position of immigrants in Europe and the United States, arguing that in the United States the officials should be just as strict as in Europe in keeping immigrants out.

Other Moves

The moves we have discussed are rather typical in prejudiced discourse. Yet, there are also other moves and further semantic properties of such talk. We already mentioned the set of indirect or implicit statements, in which the intended proposition is not expressed but left to the inferences of the recipient. The same holds for various forms of vagueness, in which very general terms (such as *all those things, that stuff,* or pronouns such as *they*) are used for more specific terms. One type of vagueness move is related to more general forms of semantic, pragmatic, or conversational "avoidance," in which people emphasize that they have no experiences or contacts with minorities. We might call this the *ignorance move* that precedes or follows statements that apparently contradict that ignorance, as in "I don't understand the way the Mexican people think, but . . . maybe it's education or uhh I don't know, I don't know, I don't know what it is" (A-TD-1). Thus, ignorance is often expressed when people provide possibly prejudiced explanations.

Aside from the usual form of mitigation and understatement, we also find exaggerations in which a minor event or action of foreigners is described in very dramatic or negative terms (*terrible* is a word often used in such a case). Then, it is often the case that negative opinions are not so much formulated as personal opinions, but attributed to others, as in the stereotypical expression: "I do not mind very much, but the other people here hate them/that." Similarly, the reason for bad contacts may be attributed to the foreign group, instead of to one's own lack of initiative. Because talk about minorities is a delicate topic, many people at least at first react with avoidance moves, such as "I don't know," "I have no contact with them," "I keep on my own," "I mind my own business," even when the rest of the conversation turns out to show many experiences and opinions related to foreigners.

Negative presuppositions are, of course, common in interviews about minorities, and it is fairly standard that when minorities or a minority neighborhood is brought up in talk, people will spontaneously say that they "have no problems" or that they are "surprised how friendly and nonthreatening" (A-LG-1) the people are.

There is a class of moves that seem to have metastatus: They are *about* previous or following propositions or speech acts in the conversation. Thus, a specific form of Example is the emphasis placed on personal experiences, as in "I have seen that with my own eyes," or on specific truth claims: "And that is a fact," "It is true, really." There are various forms of showing empathy, either with ethnic groups, or with members of the in-group: "I can understand that very well," mostly referring to negative attitudes as a result of perceived negative experiences with the other group.

Then, within the strategy of positive self-presentation, speakers will tend to emphasize their own positive behavior and usually focus on their own helping behavior (which then may be frustrated by negative actions of the foreigners): "And we used to bring them soup now and then." Along the same line, speakers repeatedly recall that whatever the negative circumstances, they are "reasonable" people. And within a strategy of saying negative things about the other group, concessive differentiation between subgroups, that is, exceptions, are made, such as "One cannot generalize of course, but . . .," "You have of course various kinds of them," or "A Turk is different from a Surinamese in that respect . . . ."

Pragmatic Moves

Some of the semantic moves also have a pragmatic dimension. Avoidance, for instance, is not merely a negation of having information but also a refusal to make specific assertions. Denial usually involves a negation, but it also has the pragmatic property of asserting the opposite of an expected or presupposed statement. Similarly, Contradiction is also pragmatically relevant because it involves an assertion that attacks a previous assertion. And finally, speakers often make Appeals to the recipient, especially when they check the opinions of the hearer or rhetorically emphasize the shared nature of norms and rules: "They can't do that, don't you think?" or "Tell me, what I should have done."

Cognitive and Social Functions

The moves and operations we have discussed in this section have several cognitive and social functions and we have emphasized those of positive self-presentation and negative other-presentation. Cognitively, the various moves may show how people maintain coherence among often contradictory ethnic opinions. In interaction, the major goal of prejudiced people may well be the negative portrayal of ethnic groups or emphasis on their own predicament. For many speakers, however, the moves mentioned above serve to present these negative opinions and experiences in the most acceptable way. Thus, they manage the possibly negative inferences the recipient might make about the social characteristics of the speaker. We have the impression that high socioeconomic status (including education, class, and occupation) is positively correlated with the amount of such presentation moves. We examine these social embeddings of self-presentation moves later.

8. Style

The same underlying opinions can be expressed in different ways. One speaker may say "I hate foreigners," whereas another might say "Well, I am not particularly fond of them." Thus, propositions have variable lexical and syntactic expression, which we identify as *style*. Stylistic variation in discourse is usually a function of contextual properties such as (in)formality of the social situation, social dimensions (power, status, position, gender) of the speech participants, and also personal features, such as emotions (anger, fear) (Norton, 1983; Sandell, 1977; Scherer & Giles, 1979; Sebeok, 1960). A full stylistic analysis of some 180 interviews is, of course, impossible, so we focus on a few characteristics of prejudiced talk only.

The Style of Moderation

In our interviews, we may expect that interactional constraints, such as politeness and—again—self-presentation, also play a role in stylistic variation. We have found, for instance, that the direct forms of negative affect are seldom used—however strong the emotions against ethnic groups, we seldom find forms such as "I hate them." Neither do we find explicit racial slurs to denote or describe such groups, their presence, or properties. On the contrary, the general tendency is to express negative feelings in rather "soft" language, as we have also observed in the use of semantic moves such as mitigation and vagueness.

Aside from the obvious goal of positive self-presentation, there is also the fact that the interviewer, even when he or she is a younger student, is seen as a (relative) stranger, maybe even as a representative of the "institutions" (government, media, education, research). That is, in rather informal interviews, people may very well tell what they feel but the presentation style will probably be rather different from the one employed among close friends. Degree of familiarity is a potent style factor, and when delicate topics are discussed, differences between language use among trusted friends or family, and language use in talk with vague acquaintances, or with strangers on the street or in public, may be considerable. Because of strong official norms in the Netherlands against fascism and racism, the very notion of "racism" itself seems to have become taboo, which also influences talk that might be interpreted as racist. Hence, in many conversational situations, people will try to formulate their "honest" opinion in various stylistic forms of downtoning, mitigation, or understatement, as in the following fragment of the beginning of an interview with a 62-year-old woman (W):

```
(28) (II-MA-6)
    I:  Well, how do you like living here?
    W:  Well, unfortunately the neighborhood has changed very much.
    I:  In those 26 years
    W:  Yes, unfortunately, it used to be a VERY nice neighborhood, but it
        has become terrible.
    I:  In what sense terrible?
    W:  Uhh, many strangers.
```

I: Is it, yes yes, I saw that on the street.
W: Many many strangers, and uuh well that is not so nice.

Consider how this woman tries to find a lexical balance between the negative "terrible" on the one hand, the clearly distanced, neutral, and semiformal uses of "unfortunately," and the understatement (litotes) "that is not so nice," which we have found many times in talk about foreigners.

The stylistic effect of semantic moves in interview contexts is often such that indirectness and vagueness are preferred over direct value expressions, designations, and even proper names. After the standard opening questions about the neighborhood, a 66-year-old man (M) chooses his words as follows, after having stressed that he wouldn't want to move from this neighborhood:

(29) I: But a lot has changed in all these years.
      M: Yes, people (pause)
      I: How, people?
      M: Well, it uhh there are a lot of yes outsiders, you know, strangers.

Rather characteristically, he uses the word *outsiders* (*buitenstaanders*), although he might have meant *foreigners* (*buitenlanders*), which is phonetically rather close, and then corrects himself and uses the word *strangers* (*vreemdelingen*, which might also be translated as *aliens*). So, the change in the neighborhood is first of all attributed to the different "people" who have come "from outside," or even from other countries, that is, strangers.

"Foreigners," "Strangers," or Other "Ethnic Minorities"?

This latter passage is interesting also because it is one of the few in which ethnic minority groups are not directly called *foreigners* (*buitenlanders*), which has become the standard colloquial expression in Dutch, even when it literally denotes anybody from abroad. Technically, many Turks and Moroccans still have their own nationality and, therefore, could be described as "foreigners." Yet, whether or not minority group members already have Dutch citizenship, as is the case for Surinamese and Antillians, many autochthonous White people still call them *foreigners* (*buitenlanders*), and sometimes *strangers* or *aliens* (*vreemdelingen*). The latter term also appears in the name of the immigration police (*vreemdelingenpolitie*) from which immigrants get their residence permits, but in that case it denotes again anybody from abroad.

The terms (*ethnic*) *minority* or *cultural minority* are seldom used in everyday conversation outside of formal, political, or academic contexts. People are, however, aware of it through the media and sometimes use it in rather formal passages or, ironically, when they refer to perceived favorable treatment (and hence also to the "favorable naming") of ethnic groups:

(30) (II-PD-5)
There were not yet so many minorities as they call it, because of course you may not say foreigners.

(31) (II-PD-5)
(In a story about a mugging of an old couple):
Man: I saw two of them, on their back. I saw that they were dark uh things
Woman: Yes, MINORITIES you should call them.

In general, though, the notion of "foreigners" now has acquired the specific meaning of *ethnic minority* in informal talk, and because of prevailing negative prejudices, it sometimes has a slight negative association by itself. To make ourselves understood, we also had to use it in informal talk with people in popular neighborhoods, as is also the case for ethnic minority groups themselves, who sometimes use the term in a more neutral sense of denoting all nonautochthonous groups in the Netherlands.

In California, stylistic variation in denoting ethnic minority groups also shows constraints from positive self-presentation and terminological confusion. Thus, in San Diego, people who are from Mexico, whether they have become American citizens or not, tend to be called *Mexicans*, whereas *Mexican Americans* is a more academic term or a term used by Mexican Americans themselves, besides *Chicanos,* and *Latinos* for people from Latin America in general. White officials also use *Hispanics,* which, however, is less used, or even criticized by Latin American immigrants. And whereas the current usage to denote immigrants from Asian countries is *Asians,* some of our interviewees also use *Orientals.* More than in the Netherlands, where the equivalent of *Negro* is still widely used by White people, also in the press and by intellectuals, Afro-Americans generally are described as *Black.* Only once, by a Californian who came from Louisiana and appeared to be very racist, was the term *nigger* used, which we didn't find in our Dutch interviews. We have reason to believe that generally more negative terms may sometimes be used by racist speakers, but only in familiar contexts, that is, when they speak to family members or close friends of whom they know the ethnic opinions. This suggests that interviews, indeed, are not examples of such casual talk but should rather be seen as exemplary of conversations with acquaintances, colleagues, or unknown others.

The Taboo of "Racism"

In the Netherlands, words such as *race* or *racial group* do not occur very often, neither in academic nor in everyday talk in which they are mostly replaced by the more general term *ethnic*. One reason for this discrepancy with British and American usage may be the culturally shared resentment against the Nazi occupation of the Netherlands, and the frequent mention of *races* in fascist ideologies.

However, this antifascist tradition may also be one of the reasons that many Dutch people strongly resent the use of the words *racism* and *racist,* which they reserve for extremist right-wing parties that are against the presence of ethnic minority groups (immigrants) in the Netherlands. Similarly, many people emphasized that, even when they did not like many characteristics of the foreigners in their town or neighborhood, they explicitly reject "racism," or "racial discrimination," "and those things." In other words, they not only say this as moves in self-presentation strategies, but also because they do have a different conceptual representation associated with words such as *racism*.

The same is true for most journalists and many minority researchers in the Netherlands. We surmise that it is through these restricted, elite definitions of *racism* that the term still has its narrow (taboo) sense in everyday usage. Actions in the 1980s by ethnic groups are slowly changing the acceptable range of meanings of the term *racism,* especially when used in combinations such as *everyday racism,* the *new racism, subtle racism* (Essed, 1984). There is no general understanding of the fact that negative feelings, opinions, talk, and action (even when subtle or indirect) against ethnically and racially different people in the Netherlands are not just "xenophobia" or "resentment" that can simply be attributed to economic recession or frustration, but phenomena that are functional components in a complex racist society.

Against this background of subtle elite racism, it is, of course, hardly surprising that people in everyday talk do not adopt a terminology that may express an overall threat to the face of the in-group. And it should come as no surprise either that the term *racism* is seldom used to describe the elite itself, that is, the intellectuals, politicians, journalists, educators, researchers, professionals, the police, and the courts. Instead racism, or rather xenophobia, is attributed to poor people, popular neighborhoods, and all those who have to suffer from the economic recession. This attribution is simply given the "scientific" explanation of "scapegoating" and it is easy to quote talk that would confirm such an analysis: "They take away our houses, jobs, etc." In this way, the elite are able to transfer their own racism, which they have helped to reproduce and sustain through the various institutions (state, education, media) in the first place, to the working class, the unemployed, or the poor. We discuss this social dimension of prejudice, racism, and their formulation in talk in Chapter 6.

We have made this brief excursion into the sociopolitical context of the uses of words such as *foreigner, ethnic minority,* and *racism* in the Netherlands because these uses and their contexts also heavily determine the style and descriptions in our conversations. It explains why people may use the term *ethnic minority* or *so-called ethnic minorities* in an ironic sense. They see it as part of the terminology of all those others (government, authorities, intellectuals, media, and, of course, all those who are not poor and not living "here") who do not have to "live among them." The nice and academic term, thus, is considered as part of the language variant used by those who are seen as "friends of foreigners."

The Pronouns of Ethnic Distance and Prejudice

More than one-quarter of a century ago, Brown and Gilman (1960) wrote their famous article about the pronouns of "power and solidarity." They were able to show how the use of pronouns such as *tu* and *vous* in French, and similar second person pronouns in other languages, are associated with power and group relationships among speech participants. Deictic terms, in general, may be used to indicate spatial, temporal, and especially social distance from the speaker. In that sense, V-forms signal more social distance (at the same level, or from low to high level) than T-forms (Brown & Fraser, 1979).

In conversations about ethnic groups, there are uses of pronouns and demonstratives that recall this use of deictics as forms of social distance marking. Typically, ethnic groups such as Turks, Moroccans, or Surinamese are often not called by their name, or by the term *foreigners,* but denoted by pronouns such as *they* and *them.* Indeed, the pronominal contrast between *us* and *them* has even become stereotypical in its own right.

Similarly, we find the equally "distanced" expression, *those people.* Naming taboos are well known: We avoid naming (at least by given name) people we do not like. We say "that man" or "that woman" or simply use "she" or "he." Also, we may preface the family name with a distancing demonstrative, as in "that Johnson is a creep."

The same happens with ethnic groups. In our interviews, we find long passages where people only make use of sometimes vague and confusing pronouns simply to avoid naming the relevant ethnic group. Part of this may be due to the rules of conversational style and contextual disambiguation, which allow less explicit designations (see Marslen-Wilson, Levy, & Tyler, 1982). And some of it may be related to social class and education (according to the traditional "restricted code" characteristics as described by Bernstein, 1971). Yet, we interpret these uses of pronouns and demonstratives here as expressions of attitudinal distance and, hence, as signals of prejudice. We thus have a scale of designations running from "Surinamese people (man/men, woman/women)," and "those Surinamese people," to "those Surinamese," "those foreigners," "those people," "those Blacks," to specific (not coreferential) "them." Degrees of what may be called *attitudinal depersonalization* apparently also show in pronominal expression, just like power and (lack of) solidarity. Here is a typical example in which ethnic groups or foreigners are not actually mentioned, yet referred to:

(32) (II-PD-5)
   BUT, you also have those here who have never worked. And when you see of what they live . . .

Thus, if the overall topic contains the concept of "foreigners," many speakers tend to use simple pronouns to avoid using more specific names. One other reason is that Turks and Moroccans, together denoted as guest workers (*gastarbeiders*), are sometimes difficult for Dutch people to distinguish. In that case a "vague" or "sloppy" pronoun or demonstrative is easier to use. Slightly less negative, but with paternalistic undertone, is the use of "those people." Generally, however, ethnic groups are referred to by expressions that imply that they form another group and, as such, they are systematically differentiated from "us" (autochthonous, White) Dutch people. At this point, language use may be interpreted as a rather direct signal of the structure of underlying ethnic attitudes.

9. Rhetorical operations

The expression of ethnic opinions in everyday talk is part of persuasive communicative interaction. At several levels, speakers try to verbalize these opinions not only in an acceptable but also in a convincing way. Topic construction, storytelling, argumentation, semantic moves, and appropriate style are all attempts to convey the truth of assertions and the reasonableness of ethnic opinions. Special effects, however, may be obtained by the use of various rhetorical operations. Thus, traditional "figures of style," as described in classical rhetoric, may focus the attention of the recipient on the opinion or the arguments given for it (Corbett, 1971; Lausberg, 1960; Plett, 1975, 1977). They may make expressions more memorable, such as through enhancing their degree of cognitive organization (Kintsch & Yarbrough, 1982).

The operations can most economically be described in terms of a few basic transformations, namely, deletion, addition (repetition), substitution, and permutation, applied to morphonological, syntactic, and semantic structures. Surface structure operations, such as sound repetition (rhyme, assonance) and intended syntactic transformations, are rare in our conversations. At that level, nonarbitrary repetition or parallelism of syntactic structure is most obvious:

(33) (II-MdV-3)
    I: Uhh, do you have contacts with foreigners who live here?
    W: Oh no, I always mind my own business. Oh no, not at all, with nobody. (. . .) Well, I'll tell you honestly, I tell you . . .[renting a room to Surinamese](. . .) No, that uhh I wouldn't do that again. I have done it then, but I wouldn't do it again.

(34) (II-RA-2)
    (They make a lot of children) Well, YOU pay for that, and I pay for that.

Semantic Operations

More conspicuous are the rhetorical operations at the semantic level, such as comparison, metaphor, irony, contrast, hyperbole, litotes, or understatement. Some of these have already been described as specific semantic moves that link propositions, for instance, the use of subsequent mitigations or contrast for different goals or favors of the in-group and out-group. Sometimes these moves have a clearly rhetorical function, such as when such oppositions are construed within one sentence, when they are formulated with specific contrastive stress, and when the lexical formulation also shows opposition (use of antonyms).

Comparisons are mostly used with the obvious goal of comparing properties or actions of *us* and *them*. Pervasive, for instance, is the argumentative comparison between what foreigners do (not do) here, and what Dutch people abroad would do. The following fragment is taken from a very long (several transcript pages) comparison made by a 62-

year-old man between his position in a provincial village and the position of ethnic groups in the Netherlands:

(35) (II-AC-3)
These people [foreigners] have another attitude, another mentality than we have. And yes, we have to get used to that and in a certain sense we have to adapt to it. Look, I don't mean that, look I think these people should integrate here, more than we should, that is logical, isn't it. Because when I am in Drenthe [a Dutch province in the Northeast] in uh on my little farm ehh which I have in Drenthe, you know, then I adapt to those people there. I can hardly expect that that whole village community will adapt itself to someone from Amsterdam . . . [They have to adapt to us] You know, we also had to do that when we emigrated to uhh, to uhh to uhh Australia, then I know that you do not have Dutch communities who together, who speak Dutch, and uhh maintain all kinds of traditions from Holland, but have to integrate to the Australian or wherever they are, also South Africa.

We found earlier that in California very similar comparisons are used as part of argumentations that conclude that immigrants should learn English, the "same as if I went to Italy, and . . . ."

Metaphors may be used to highlight, implicitly, such comparisons between in-group and out-group, but are mostly used to describe properties and actions of minority group members, for instance, when direct, literal description would threaten face-saving, or conversely, when descriptions of everyday affairs must be made livelier:

(36) (New Moroccan family upstairs; children go to bed late) And then they had a lot of visitors of uhh just like a pilgrimage of all those families who live here, and those of course wanted to know something, what happened in Morocco.

Yet, creative, new metaphors are used relatively little in the interviews we have recorded, and racist descriptive metaphors (such as *stovepipe* for Blacks) occur only occasionally.

Other Rhetorical Operations

Here are a few other examples of rather typical rhetorical operations:

Rhetorical question.

(37) (II-MdU-3)
These are large apartments, you can see that. But they are also occupied by foreigners. Don't we have enough Dutch people who need housing? Am I right or not? Why should the foreigners have all those beautiful big apartments?

In one of the California interviews, a story is told by a cabdriver about an immigrant who is said to have caused an accident. The point of the story, however, is that the other driver doesn't speak English. This point is underscored by repeated rhetorical questions such as "What's he doing driving a car?" (A-LG4). Because rhetorical questions need not be answered, they presuppose obvious or preferred answers without having to spell out such statements explicitly, for instance, people who do not know the language should not drive a car (because they cannot read road signs).

Contrast. Contrast is one of the most pervasive rhetorical operations in our data, and may be used to signal the conflicting values, goals, and interests of the in-group and out-group:

(38) (A-TD-1)
It took us one year (to get our papers), as I said we had to have so much money per head, we had to have a job guaranteed, someone to vouch for us here, and yeah these people can run across the border.

(39) (II-RA-2)
It is a big scandal, when you see those young Turkish women, 18 years old, with an old man of 50.

(40) (II-SM-4)
Listen, they always say that foreigners are being discriminated against here. No, WE are being discriminated. It is exactly the reverse.

(Hyperbole(?):)
(41) (II-SM-2b)
They have stolen a complete bicycle store from me, here in front of the house. [A story about a bicycle being stolen on the market.] (. . .) In all that time about 30 bicycles have been pinched from me. And then I do not exaggerate, you know, I honestly do not exaggerate.

Conclusion

From these examples we may conclude that most rhetorical operations have both an interactional and a cognitive function. The use of special figures draws attention to formulations and may contribute to better organization in memory. Thus, contrast may be used to express and convey special organization in situation models of participating in-group and out-group members. In the next chapters, we shall find examples of people who explicitly refer to the persuasiveness of "well-told" ethnic stories.

In interaction, not only persuasion, but also strategies of self-presentation, may be made more effective by rhetorical operations. Thus, *contrast* both expresses and emphasizes the differences and conflicts between in-group and out-group, and so does *comparison*. Hyperbole and other forms of exaggeration also focus on the seriousness of the predicament or the truth of a story, although various forms of mitigation, such as litotes or understatement, are used more often, mostly with the goal of keeping control over possibly negative inferences of the recipient.

Together with the semantic and pragmatic moves analyzed earlier, and with an adequate stylistic formulation of underlying opinions, thus, rhetorical operations may further enhance the effectiveness of conversational interaction. This is particularly important, because for a delicate topic such as "foreigners," effective persuasion, as well as avoiding misunderstanding or negative social evaluation, are crucial. A delicate balance must be chosen between the rhetorical operations: A story may be told with the usual forms of exaggeration, but the ethnically relevant evaluations and conclusions may need downtoning and mitigation. In other words, this ambivalent choice of rhetorical operations is also a function of the overall strategic goals of positive self-presentation and negative other-presentation.

---

10. Prejudiced talk as conversation

The main focus of this book is on the diffusion of ethnic attitudes through everyday conversation. Although our data are informal interviews, we still hope to get insight into the ways people express prejudices in their everyday talk. Because we are, of course, primarily interested in what people say, and how they say it, we have somewhat neglected the proper interactional constraints on their contributions to conversations. Thus, we ignored the, rather brief, questions, replies, encouragements, or other contributions of the interviewer. Also, we hardly paid attention to the unplanned, spontaneous dimensions of talk as spoken discourse, such as the organization of turns, pauses, hesitations, repairs, repetitions, and intonation. Yet, we may assume that these also may signal important cognitive, interactional, and social functions. After the seminal work of Sacks, Schegloff, and Jefferson (1974), conversational analysis in the past decade has studied in detail many of these properties of dialogue (Atkinson & Heritage, 1984; Labov & Fanshel, 1977; Schenkein, 1978; Sudnow, 1972; van Dijk, 1985a, vol. 3). Little work, however, has as yet been done on the role of conversation in the reproduction of social beliefs and attitudes (see, however, Pomerantz, 1984, who analyzes how people indicate their knowledge sources in talk).

Unfortunate for our Dutch interviews, many of these properties of talk are so much tied to the colloquial style of the Dutch language (or the Amsterdam urban dialect) that we can only make a few observations on features that allow approximate translation into English.

An Example

To get an idea of a more realistic conversation, we give fragments of an example in which three women talk with the (female) interviewer. W1 is a hairdresser, W2 a client and W3 is W1's assistant. The conversation was recorded in a high-contact area in East Amsterdam. The women knew that an interview would be recorded, but during this passage they thought the recorder had not yet been turned on. Because of the overlap, several turns are incomprehensible. As usual, the pronoun *they* refers to ethnic minority groups. Transcript conventions are minimal and follow the usual spelling and notation.

(42) (I-D-1)

W1: They have been brought in like that, a beautiful house and they have it so good here, and really they are going to profit from it, I have an acquaintance, a foreigner . . . you don't put that thing on, do you [laughing]

5   I: Nooo

W1: I have a friend myself, a foreigner, but he is a crook, really, he exploits the lot and h . . . it is really a darling, but he is a foreigner, honestly because he uhh he is really nice but OK he shouts and he does, he really wants, when he leaves he wants to have it

10   made, that is the way it is . . .

I: But why, do you think, because of what?

W1: uhh ehh . . . just as I said, they come to the Netherlands, because they say about the Netherlands in the Netherlands you can get rich, that is the clue, but yes it it is no longer the case that one can

15   get rich here, seems to me. I I already work 10 years on my own and I am still not rich [laughs]

I: . . . Yes . . .

W2: Well, like that Surinamese lady uhm well then she came to live in that apartment, well uh she presented herself very decently, it is a

20   nice little lady and so on, and uh well she had gotten money from welfare to buy things and uh a carpet well that was not enough, she had to have more money because she had to buy a bed as well, so she easily went back to welfare to ask, and yes somewhat later a beautiful bed, OK via W* and uh N* or so [cheap direct order

25   chains], and those they also cheated because they had uhh a hifi and I don't know what, but (???)

W3: They come to the Netherlands to uhh spoil the lot . . .

W1: Well not to uhh but simply to profit of "Dutch people have it made, we also want to have it made"

30 W3: They can do what they like here, I think they can do more than us because they get a new house under their ass just like that, and uhh when you want a house then you get nothing

    W2: Yes, and when you intimidate a bit, I believe you can get what you want, and well we aren't like that

35 W1: . . . well . . . no we aren't like that

    W2: That's it

      I: Hmm, but

    W3: (????) they get it from, God knows, because they all do not work, each of them, that's what I think

40   I: . . . Oh yes?

    W1: . . . Well (??) or there are women from Yugosla . . . no not Yugoslavia, Portugal, and you know

    W3: Turks are again rather different from Surinamese . . .

    W1: Well those are real nice, really, because we hardly get uhh Suri-
45 namese or uuh client and no uhh Moroccans, they hardly come they do a lot themselves, but Portuguese women and that kind of (???) they work very hard, really, I can't say otherwise (?????)

    W2: Oh but you have that also among Surinamese, you can't avoid that, you have people who like to work everywhere, there are also peo-
50 ple uhh

    W3: No, no I mean that those people all work, but you can see that most Surinamese do NOT work . . .

 W1/2: . . . Yes

    W3: And they say that they are being dismi discri discriminated
55 W2: yes but by . . . discriminated, yes but

    W3: That is not true (???)

    W2: It only attracts more attention because of their skin color, look we have more hobbies we have perhaps more hobbies than those who are brown and we better know how to have fun than those who only
60 walk the streets doing nothing

      I: . . . Hmm

    W1: Well, I keep saying it that they really come here come to the Netherlands to become rich on the expense of everybody and everything
65 W2: Yes, OK but social services are good here, aren't they, yes, it is much too easy for them here

    W3: . . . They get everything here

    W1: (???) and soon we'll have war here, between the brown foreigners and the Dutch
70   I: . . . you think so?

    W1: They SAY so, I do not THINK so, because I am still young to uh to that all uhh I don't understand those things but I get people of 50 years old and who really uhh . . . know life

    W2: They really see a lot of disadvantages
75 W3: Because since they are here there is uhh nothing but fights well according to me that is true, because since those guys are here there is nothing but fights always, that's what I think, OK I am

      I: Yes?

    W3: only 16 but uh

This conversation between three young women and the interviewer is interesting for several reasons. It has a clear, coherent topic: "Foreigners abuse our social services." This topic is illustrated by both W1 and W2, who give brief stories about Black people they know who abuse the social services in the Netherlands. Within this topic, there is much local repetition, and mutual confirmation. The persuasive character in the respective contributions is, however, not only realized by such examples, but also by the frequent use of "really," "honestly," and the (untranslatable) Dutch particle *hoor,* which has a similar function of reassuring the recipient of the truthfulness of the speaker. At several points, the women balance the negative assertions with the usual positive concessions ("He is really nice, but . . ."), which apparently are also used among speakers who have similar opinions, and not only to make a good impression on the interviewer.

At several places in the conversation, the women display functional hesitations, such as when they start to say something negative about the foreigners:

(1) But yes uhh he shouts and does
(2) They come to the Netherlands to uhh spoil the lot

Hesitations in the conversations are typical in positions in which an ethnic group must be named:

(3) because we hardly get uhh Surinamese or uh clients and no uhh Moroccan

Repetitions are also used in contexts where there is hesitation to apply negative predicates to foreigners:

(4) he he exploits the lot

In the second turn of W1 (lines 6-10), there are several repairs or false starts, in which a sentence that apparently will be about a negative characteristic of the friend is broken off for a positive move:

(5) he he exploits the lot and h . . . it is really a darling, but it is a foreigner, and really because he uhh it is a nice boy but yes he uhh he shouts . . .
(6) and she presented herself nicely, it is a nice little lady and so on and everything, and uhh well she had gotten money from welfare.

False starts, hesitations, and repairs are not just an expression of production strategies, such as model activation and search, lexicalization, and general semantic monitoring (Levelt, 1983), they also may have interactional functions (Polanyi, 1978; Schegloff, 1979; Schegloff, Jefferson, & Sacks, 1977). In our case, both cognitive and interactional strategies are at work in the highly controlled description of ethnic groups and their assumed properties. Planned conversational contributions within the goal of negative other-presentation may be broken off during execution, and repairs or other corrections may signal to the recipient that the ongoing description needs to be modified. Such modifications usually involve the well-known apparent denials, concessions, or mitigations.

Overlap takes place at several points. First, at the end of the story told by W2 about the Surinamese lady who is thought to abuse welfare money, after line 26, where all start to talk at the same time.

Further Examples

Similar observations may be made for talk in the other interviews. Consider, for instance, some fragments of interviews held in a well-known minority neighborhood in Amsterdam (De Bijlmer). First with a woman, 40 years old, who also told the story about the bread-exchange:

(43) (I-E-1)
I, I do not like Surinamese people. And they stand . . . I have also experienced that also a group of Surinamese were standing in front of the butcher's . . . and then [I am?] coming along . . . I found it sheer provocation what they did (. . .) You know . . . and then . . . then provoke you, you see, and k k k eep standing in that doorway.

Also, in this passage, we find several signals of emotional states, hesitation, and interactional impression formation, such as repetition or hesitations ("I, I," "then then," and "k k keep") that are close to emotionally conditioned stuttering. The false start in the first line seems to suggest that she planned first to express the event she has experienced ("they stand in the doorway . . ."), but she reformulates the event by prefacing the important "source" of the information: her own experiences. Instead of giving the full details of the story (e.g., "when I was coming along and approached the door of the butcher shop"), she hurriedly gives her evaluative impression (story Evaluation) of that episode ("provocation"), repeated again in the next sentence. Strategically, it is important for the speaker that the negative evaluation precedes the description of the event, because "standing in (or before) the doorway" may be interpreted as a rather innocent act. Only when the situation is previously defined as "provocation" does the fragmentary story have a point in her conversation (Polanyi, 1979). This is also the reason why the clause "I have experienced" must be inserted: It signals that a (true) story of own experiences is now being told, and not just a subjective impression is given about young Black men.

The same woman tells a brief story about what Spanish immigrants (about whom, in our data, practically no stories are told) are claimed to have done to her mother, elsewhere in Amsterdam:

(44) and they manage above my mothers laundry to clean fish scales . . . to clean fish . . . .

Because the (dirty) fish scales are, of course, in focus as those things that were falling on her mother's clean laundry hanging outside, this noun phrase is "erroneously" chosen first, but then the sentence is corrected at least partially, "to clean fish," but it is not necessary, in that case, to further add something like "so that the fish scales were falling on my mother's laundry."

In the same neighborhood, a woman of 50 was interviewed. Her major topic is that "those people" do not feel at home here, a stereotypical move of false empathy used in arguments that imply that "they'd better go back to their own country." The interviewer, in this case, reacts with a rather pointed question, which audibly and visibly confuses the woman:

(45) (I-E-2)
    W: . . . I personally believe that those people also do not feel at home here among us.
    I: Did you ever ask them?
    W: Uhhm . . . no . . . but I uh NO I have never asked that . . . but I don't . . . I wouldn't ever do no trouble for that . . . but I would politely say good morning good afternoon . . . also hold the door open for them . . . but I won't take up contact easily with them.

The reply to the question of the interviewer is a good example of interactional problem solving and impression management. Obviously, the interviewer's question is interpreted by the woman as an expression of the interviewer's doubts about the justification of her opinion: If the woman expresses an opinion about the assumed feelings of foreigners, without ever having asked her foreign neighbors themselves, it may be interpreted as a prejudiced opinion. So the first steps of her reply are hesitations ("Uhhm") and pauses, followed by a first hesitant denial, which is taken up more forcefully a second later. Yet, directly after the first "no," the woman starts with a corrective move initiated by "but," followed again by hesitations and pauses. The countermove is apparently intended to deny that she ever has (conversational) contacts with her foreign neighbors, so that she couldn't have asked them their opinion about the issue. Yet, obviously that move is hardly satisfactory, because it could also be interpreted as an expression of her lack of interest in her neighbors. Therefore, she corrects that move again, starting with "but" followed by reference to positive acts (polite greetings, holding open the door) of good neighborship. The last sentence of the turn then reaffirms the reason why she has not asked the foreigners, but she does so in a slightly less direct manner, adding "easily" (in Dutch she says *niet zo gauw,* "not so soon," which implies that she might do it, but that she is not readily inclined to do it). In other words, the face-threatening question of the interviewer has now been answered by a mitigated denial embedded in a description of positive acts of the speaker. The pauses, hesitations, and false starts, however, show traces of how cognitively and socially this problem is solved.

Next is a fragment of an interview with a 66-year-old man living in the same neighborhood, de Bijlmer. At many points the man seems fairly tolerant, but then again there are issues related to the presence of minorities in the neighborhood, especially the Surinamese, which he resents. It is especially dirt and the lack of neatness in garbage disposal that he does not like (he says that he had seen that somebody threw a bag of garbage down from the apartment building). The following turn of the man is spoken with a lot of emotion, which also shows in his repeated stuttering (only partly rendered in the English version):

(46) (I-E-5)
uh I mean that's what you get of course, that's what you get you ge that irritated atmosphere which that you don't see that you are anti but uhh and that you think . . . but if it comes down to it and that's how it is with me if you have mixed these people you run the risk that you have more CONFLICT, because their life pattern is DIFFERENT.

It is not easy to reconstruct exactly what the man wants to say or to convey (which is a general recovery problem in the analysis of false starts, repairs, and hesitations), but apparently he wants to say that the behavior of the foreigners (throwing away their garbage like that) will lead to irritation with the (our) people. However, within this general strategy of blaming the victim, which emphasizes negative consequences of the presence of foreigners and attributes all problems to their own behavior, the man seems to realize also that such an opinion may be heard as prejudiced. Like many other speakers, therefore, he interpolates fragments of an apparent denial ("you don't see that you are anti, but . . ."), which seems to suggest that he has this opinion not because he is "antiforeigner" (prejudiced), but that living with them leads to conflicts because of differences in life-style. In other words, demographic and cultural reasons are given, in an explanatory move, for the inevitability of conflict.

In one of the California interviews, a young man formulates many rather blatant racist opinions, and favors immigration being stopped. When the interviewer then asks whether he would be willing to pay more taxes to enforce such a decision, his answer begins with conflicting replies (yeah no), usual fillers (really, you know), false starts, repairs, and corrections of various types (note that in the rest of his interview he is not hesitant at all about his opinions):

(47) (A-LG-4)
Yeah no, see, really, you see, I'm not so much, you know stopping immigration, they should let, they should all be, anyone that wants to come into this country, come in, fine, they shouldn't get any welfare, they can't get any unemployment, for a specified number of years.

Conclusions

These few examples show that spontaneous talk about ethnic minority groups features the usual properties of unplanned conversational contributions, such as hesitations, pauses, repairs, false starts, or corrections. Yet, these are not placed arbitrarily, and, hence, are not just consequences of cognitive formulation difficulties. They typically occur where the cognitive and interactional monitoring is crucial, namely, before or in the middle of sentence fragments that express (negative) opinions about foreigners. Local plans for the execution of such fragments are apparently suspended to reformulate them within the major strategic goal of avoiding negative self-presentation: Mitigation, concession, or denial are often inserted before the planned negative opinion is actually expressed. The same is true for the very identification or naming of ethnic minority groups. In this respect, the conversational markers of hesitation and control are intimately linked with the use of distancing deictics, semantic moves of negative social inference management, and rhetorical operations (such as contrast, understatement, and repetition) that effectively control possibly negative interpretations.

In the long example of "free" talk among the three women, we have seen that such cognitive and interactional control also takes place when the women hardly have to bother about mutually negative interpretations (they all seem to agree about the negative consequences of the presence of foreigners). This implies that delicate topics generally may be formulated with more self-control, manifested as frequent semantic, rhetorical, and conversational moves of correction and mitigation.

The interactionally functional formulation features of talk about foreigners are not merely cognitively controlled, but also may be used as evidence for the very cognitive strategies used to activate, search, and apply relevant knowledge and beliefs about foreigners. Thus, if a negative predicate seems to be planned first, this suggests that this predicate is more available in memory (Kahneman & Tversky, 1973). As we shall see in more detail in Chapter 4, this means that the structures of ethnic situation models and attitude schemata in memory are organized in such a way that negative properties of ethnic minorities are easier to find and to retrieve, for instance, due to higher-level occurrence in such structures. Once such properties have been retrieved, a local production plan is being designed (or completed) featuring such belief propositions. This production plan, however, must also be compared with the various goals of the communicative context. During on-line production, this may mean that strategies of positive self-presentation may block the expression of opinions that are "too negative," and, in spontaneous speech, this will lead to hesitations, pauses, repairs, or other corrections.

A delicate topic, hence, requires delicate formulations, and self-control thus shows in a rather hesitant style of speech production. Interestingly, speakers thus exert control over the semantic content of talk, but are hardly able to control consciously, at the meta level, the very conversational signals of such control (avoiding hesitations, repairs, pauses, and so on). Hence, analysis of such features provides a fairly reliable measure of actual cognitive monitoring and strategic processing. There, probably, are few empirical measures that are as sensitive to cognitive processing and interactional controls as these properties of speech production.

11. Conclusions

In this chapter, we have made the first step in our analysis of the everyday conversational reproduction of racism. We have tried to show that systematic discourse analysis, as it has been developed in the past 20 years, is in principle a valuable instrument for the assessment of some major dimensions of this process of reproduction.

We have found that at all levels of discourse analysis, speakers show how they plan, execute, and formulate the global and local meanings that adequately express and communicate their attitudes about ethnic minority groups. They display their cognitive representations and strategies of handling ethnic experiences, beliefs, and opinions. At the same time, though, the interview goal of "giving opinions" or "telling about experiences" is paired with more general interactional goals. Speakers do not just give opinions or tell about experiences but will try to do so in a credible, justifiable, defensible, and socially acceptable way. Blatantly negative opinions may be in conflict with general norms of moderation and tolerance, and their expression may be face-threatening. Therefore, the main goal of negative other-description is permanently monitored by the interactional goal of avoiding negative self-presentation.

Topic choice and ordering, story structure, argumentation strategies, semantic moves, style, rhetoric, and signals of conversational production monitoring, all contribute to the most effective realization of these combined goals. Hence, our discourse analysis not only allows us to examine what people say and think about foreigners, but also which cognitive and social strategies characterize the reproduction of racism in talk. Whereas we now have a first analysis of the discursive implementation of these cognitive and social strategies, the next chapters must provide the further and independent analysis of these underlying structures and strategies of conversational reproduction processes.

3

Sources of Prejudiced Talk

1. Methodological preliminaries

In this chapter, we must make the next step in the analysis of the interpersonal communication of ethnic attitudes and examine the various sources people use in the formation or transformation of their ethnic beliefs. This is probably the most intricate empirical problem within the overall question of how ethnic prejudice is reproduced in society. The methodological complications are practically insurmountable. For instance, there is no obvious way to access the multiple communication sources for social beliefs in experiments in the laboratory. Neither can we simply go into the field and observe how, when, where, and with whom people talk with others about ethnic groups. We would need hundreds of researchers and thousands of situations to record enough relevant data, simply because people talk about so many other topics as well. Also, researchers (with recorders!) usually have no unobtrusive access to natural communicative events, such as family conversations, talk during parties, or to other dialogues in a large variety of interpersonal situations. Finding data, in such a case, would amount to a search for the proverbial needle in the haystack. The only exception to such a wild-goose chase would be a focused observation of specific communicative events in which the topic "foreigners" would be likely, such as public discussions in community centers, for example, when ethnic "events," and especially conflicts, are salient. To a limited degree, it would also be feasible to place observers in public places for some time where community talk is likely, and where such talk may be "overheard," such as in shops, at the market, or in doctors' waiting rooms.

Interviews as Sources of Information About Sources

Although we have some data from such natural conversational events in which ethnic opinions are persuasively formulated and reacted to by speech partners, we have for several reasons again followed the principle: "Why not ask them?" (Harré & Secord, 1972). During our informal interviews about ethnic groups, people often spontaneously volunteer information about where and from whom they obtained information or opinions about ethnic groups. In other cases, they respond to questions such as "How do you know?" or "Who told you that?" in a rather natural way (Pomerantz, 1984).

Therefore, we reanalyzed all our interviews with the special purpose of examining each passage in which explicit or implicit mention is made of information sources for beliefs about ethnic groups. Most people we interviewed indeed refer to such sources, if only to substantiate their opinions argumentatively: Mentioning sources is a well-known move in a strategy of persuasive credibility construction, not only by the press, but also in everyday talk. The results of this analysis are some 200 passages in which, sometimes very briefly, sometimes very elaborately, speakers show that their beliefs are not just private beliefs, but borrowed from reliable sources, or shared with other in-group members.

Types of Sources

As may be expected, there are two main source types: the media and personal conversations with other people, sometimes in combination. Of course, these sources do not account for all beliefs people have. Especially in high-contact areas, people derive much of what they know or believe from direct observation and participation in interethnic interaction (Hartmann & Husband, 1974). And we have outlined in Chapter 2 which other discourse types are relevant for the formation of ethnic beliefs in the communicative environment of people, such as parent-child talk during socialization, textbooks, stories, movies, advertisements, among many others. We focus, however, on the two sources that seem most relevant for most adults, namely, the news media and everyday talk. Also, both for communicative and for observational sources, the information obtained is, of course, processed cognitively, so that a large part of the actual beliefs of people are actively (re)constructed by their own thought processes, such as inference, combination, instantiation, model building, and so on. Hence, reproduction is always at the same time production.

Special Source-Tracking Interviews

To complement these data, we conducted an additional 19 interviews in another high-contact neighborhood. These interviews were specifically aimed at eliciting particular information about the various sources people use for their information about ethnic groups. Again, within rather informal, conversational-style interviews, people were asked about newspaper reading or TV watching, and about talk with other family members, friends, neighbors, colleagues, or just people in the neighborhood, focusing on the topic of foreigners. Such interviews may be more systematic in getting to know the information and communication context for in-group citizens. However, we found that such interviews do not yield much more information about sources than we found in the other interviews, in which we focused on the opinions of the people themselves, and in which references to sources were often more spontaneous and functional.

Reliability

Both for the opinion interviews and for the more focused information source interviews, we have, of course, the general problem of reliability. We have found in the previous chapter that, after decades of often well-motivated suspicion of verbal reports and especially of introspection as data, some research traditions in psychology and communication studies have taken a fresh look at both the cognitive and social relevance of such reports (see, e.g., Ericsson & Simon, 1984; Harré & Secord, 1972). Still, in addition to, but also through, systematic analysis of self-reports or accounts, we like to know how original communication contents and contexts map into their verbal reproduction in interviews. From daily experience and experimental research we know that people forget practically all surface structures and most of the detailed contents of written or spoken discourse, especially after longer delays (van Dijk & Kintsch, 1983, many references and further evidence given there). For only very salient and relevant communications still have access on the same day to significant portions of text or talk.

For general social information about ethnic groups, this is, of course, seldom the case. Except perhaps for recently told, concrete stories, people usually do not even remember from whom and when they got information. Furthermore, even if they do remember contents and contexts of communication, they may transform these heavily, for example, under the influence of the various biasing strategies of ethnic information processing and conversational self-presentation that are discussed in the next chapters.

We also tried to get information about the use of different sources by having people fill out a personal daily diary, in which they were asked to write down with whom they had talked that day about ethnic minorities or whether they had read or seen anything about that topic in the media. It turned out, however, that this method needs to be further refined, because it is not easy to get people to follow the instructions and really attend to their diaries at the end of the same day—when they may be tired and the last thing they want to do is write in a diary. We did collect some useful data from high school, though, but these were, unfortunately, too little to be useful for our analysis. So, in general, we shall again rely on what people provide in the interviews for information about different sources and contents.

Conclusion

From this brief discussion of our chief methodological predicaments, it may be concluded that, on the whole, we follow several routes that we hope will lead to the same goal, namely, the reconstruction of communicative events and persuasion processes in the reproduction of ethnic beliefs through everyday discourse. The well-known, although in prevailing social psychology still controversial, method of gathering accounts of people is followed, but rather fundamentally extended by systematic discourse analyses. Also, the analysis of interviews allows a double view at reproductive communication: In this chapter it focuses on sources and how contents of communications are recalled and represented, whereas in other chapters we take the interviews themselves as "sources" of ethnic opinion production, and analyze their own strategies of persuasion and self-presentation.

Communicatively, cognitively, and socially, we take the various discourse types that represent such accounts at face value and as genuine social expressions of social experiences, beliefs, or attitudes. Whether "true" or "false" accounts, whether incomplete or biased, these accounts are (close or identical to) how people "tell it to others," and that is precisely what we want to know. At the same time, though, we have cognitive and social models that explain how and why such discourses have the properties we observe. This means, for instance, that we can also assess in what respect such discourses may be incomplete, biased, or otherwise transformed with respect to the "real" cognitive or social events of which they are reproductions.

2. Analysis of source types

Information sources may be as varied as the communication events they are part of, and so are the multiple ways such sources or events may be categorized or classified. Information about ethnic groups in society may be exchanged in virtually any communicative event, but there are, nevertheless, constraints on possible topics of text and talk. That is, it is more likely that people hear about other ethnic groups through informal talk with others or through news reports than from mathematics textbooks, dictionaries, or during doctor's visits. And if ethnic groups are topical in parliamentary debates, administrative regulations, political propaganda, or social research reports, most social members will read about it through news reports. This suggests at least a distinction between direct and indirect sources. The same distinction holds for informal talk: We may hear about somebody's own personal experiences, or about what they have heard from others' experiences, or about what others have heard or read.

There is also a set of communicative events or discourse types that may be relevant, but that are so only occasionally or during a restricted period of time. Socialization talk between parents and children, to start with, is crucial for initial ethnic information, and so is peer group talk, and joking and play for children and adolescents (P. Katz, 1976; Milner, 1983). The same holds for children's books, (TV) movies and programs, and textbooks or lessons at school. In societies in which Whites are a dominant majority, it may be the case that for most people this initial information is the only information they have before being confronted with members of other ethnic groups. We have seen before that much of such initial information may be incomplete, stereotypical, and racist. The same is true for mass-mediated information we acquire in later life, such as from movies, novels, or advertisements. Thus, for most people in Europe, this means that they had acquired a very indirect, vague, confused, and highly biased picture of Black people before they ever actually met Black people in daily life, and before Blacks became a relevant topic of everyday talk and daily news reports about their own country or city. It should be borne in mind that even when we do not further analyze all these sources of information in this book or in this chapter, they also have, of course, contributed to the formation of ethnic beliefs and thus provide elements in all "current" information about ethnic minorities.

Talk and the Media

The major portion of our daily information about ethnic groups comes from (a) the mass media, especially

TV programs and newspaper and magazine articles, and (b) everyday talk with other people, primarily "known people," such as family members, friends, acquaintances, neighbors, colleagues, or shopkeepers (see Katz & Lazarsfeld, 1955, for general discussion, and Beinstein, 1975, for talk in public places). Part of the topics of informal conversations are, however, again based on media information (Atwood, Sohn, & Sohn, 1978). These two sources account for more than 90% of the actually acknowledged sources of information in our interviews. In a few cases, people indicate that they obtained information from leaflets, advertisements, books, textbooks, classroom discussions, or movies. Therefore, we focus our further analysis on the news media and on everyday talk. According to self-reports about these source types, nearly 40% of all source indications in the interviews are about TV, the press, and (much less) the radio, whereas nearly 70% of such passages refer to conversational sources (which means that for about 10% of the passages, several sources are indicated for the same fact or opinion).

Similar percentages hold not only for the amount of passages but also for the number of interviewed people. Especially in low-contact areas, a considerable part of people's knowledge and beliefs about ethnic groups is based on media and talk. Personal experiences are rare in this case or limited to distanced observation of foreigners in the (shopping) streets of the city or in the market. Our interviews conducted in the typical low-contact areas of Amsterdam featured few concrete stories about personal experiences, but many more references to what people heard from others or what they had seen on TV or read in the paper. But also in high-contact neighborhoods, observation and occasional interaction with members of minority groups is insufficient as a source for knowledge and beliefs about such groups. Many general opinions, and sometimes even concrete stories, cannot possibly have been derived from personal observation or interaction. Practically all stereotypical opinions, for instance, about the assumed favorable treatment of ethnic groups, their profiting from the social services, or their criminal acts, must come from hearsay and/or the media, simply because such events hardly occur or cannot simply be witnessed as a general rule.

Very important, also, is the talk of prejudiced individuals interviewed by the media: They provide a form of media-mediated informal mass communication that diffuses hearsay "evidence" for millions of readers or viewers. Interviewees regularly comment on such personal opinions made public by the media.

The Role of Personal Experiences

From direct observation and from talk with neighbors in high-contact areas mainly, people acquire beliefs about such topics as noises, smells, family structure, and "strange" behavior. Yet, the fact that such beliefs are also widely known in low-contact areas again shows that such prejudices must have been partly distributed through the media as well. It would be highly unlikely that the personal networks of acquaintances of people in low-contact areas were such that they all got so much and such similar information about what "was going on" in the high-contact neighborhoods (Emler, 1982, 1983; Fine, 1985). We have already mentioned, in Chapter 2, the experimental finding of Sprangers (1983), who showed that what experimental subjects (psychology students) think people's ethnic opinions are is very similar to the actual opinions we found in our fieldwork. In other words, there is a consensus about what the stereotypes are, and such stereotypes again form the general basis for much talk and are thus reproduced in everyday interaction between majority group members.

Note also that of 143 people interviewed, 105 (73%) mention no or just a single occasion in which they talked with others about ethnic groups or ethnic events. This, of course, does not mean that many events have not been known through such talk, but only that such talk is not mentioned in the interview. When asked about personal communications, people often say that they do not talk about foreigners very often, and, at the same time, the interviews suggest that people hear about it "all the time." This seems to mean that concrete conversations are perhaps not well remembered, but that on the other hand, each conversation that is being processed is specifically selected for special attention and contributes to the overall impression that "you hear about *it* all the time."

Direct Contacts with Ethnic Minority Group Members

Direct contacts with members of ethnic groups are relatively rare. Of 143 people (in the first three interview groups in Amsterdam), only 28 reported having contacts with ethnic group members and, even then, it was often just one person or one family. In high-contact areas, the interpersonal relationships with ethnic group members are reduced to those of distanced neighborship. Only a few people report that they engage in regular interaction with such foreign neighbors. According to some theoretical predictions (for discussion about this so-called "contact hypothesis" see, e.g., Amir, 1976; Gurwitz & Dodge, 1977; Rose, 1981; Stephan, 1977), it appears that the higher the real contacts with ethnic group members, the lower our estimated prejudice score (3.7 for people with no or a single contact, down to 2.2 for people with regular contacts, measured on a qualitatively based seven-point scale), which we discuss shortly. This does not mean that people who have such personal contacts have no prejudices, but only that their opinions can at least be tested daily by experiences with ethnic group members, which may tend to lead to a reduction in the assumption of obviously wrong generalizations about such groups (see, also, Chapter 6).

Assumptions

Against the background of the situation sketched above, we may now formulate a number of more specific assumptions, which we shall further elaborate below in our analysis of interview data:

(1) In the ethnic situation of countries such as the Netherlands (and this holds for most of Western Europe, and for much of the United States and Canada), most information about ethnic minority groups is formulated by or transmitted through the mass media, primarily TV and the newspaper. Evidence for this assumption is that people have much common "knowledge"—often stereotypical—about ethnic minorities even when they hardly ever have direct experiences with minority group members or know people who have. In part, this is even true for high-contact areas (mostly in the inner cities) when the immigrant groups have only marginal contacts with autochthonous groups. This also holds for the 25 people we interviewed in California, who often said they had few close contacts with minority group members, although the higher percentage of minorities in San Diego, of course, leads to more encounters and interaction with minority group members in public places, such as shops or on the job. This is probably also one of the reasons that the interviewees in California rarely refer to the media or talk with other people for their information about minorities. A few interviewees refer to talk about "ethnic topics" with family members or friends, and only occasionally is a reference made to an event that they learned about from the media. In this chapter, we shall, therefore, limit our analysis to the data gathered in the Netherlands. More, and more extensive, interviews in the United States are necessary to trace the sources of ethnic information, but we have reason to believe that our results will hold at least partially for social information processing in that country. One of the differences between the American and the Dutch interviewees was that Americans more often attributed information or beliefs to their socialization: Several people said that they were influenced in their thinking about minorities, both positively and negatively, by the way they were raised.

(2) The media are especially involved in the diffusion of information about the following topics (see, also, Hartmann & Husband, 1974):

(a) (new) immigration of foreign groups;
(b) the political and social situation of the home countries of such groups and, hence, about possible motivations for immigration;
(c) the policies of government or government bodies regarding (mostly: against) such immigration;
(d) general "problems" that are described as being the actual or possible consequence of immigration, such as housing, (un)employment, social services, and education;
(e) first reactions of "locals" and others directly involved in contacts with the (new) immigrants (public officers, police, or people living in the same neighborhood);
(f) prejudice and discrimination among the majority against the new immigrants, or against an already established minority group, often in the form of stories about personal experiences;
(g) crime and deviance associated with minority groups;
(h) conflicts with or among minority groups, especially violent conflicts, such as riots;
(i) typically "ethnic" culture: family relationships, religion, or language, especially those aspects that are perceived as problematic for the majority; and
(j) the reactions of the local and national government, and of authorities such as in debates, political programs, and laws related to the previous points.

In accordance with research into media contents (see Chapter 2) about the portrayal of ethnic affairs, we may conclude from these points that media information is usually of a general and negative nature and, therefore, highly conducive to the development of ethnic prejudices.

(3) Everyday talk primarily reproduces this form of public, and, hence, a priori "shared," information and beliefs transmitted through the media. Experiences of individuals recounted through the media not only reach millions, but also seem to be "general," and, hence, true and legitimate, while broadcasted (see the contributions in E. Katz & Szecskö, 1981, for discussion). Whatever the personal experiences of people, these "common" beliefs may be used as a point of departure for everyday talk, even if individual recipients may doubt such opinions or be against them. A popular theory in mass communication suggests that the media at least set the "agenda" for talk about minorities (McCombs & Shaw, 1972; but see Becker, 1982). In Chapter 7, we further examine the role of specific social formations, such as the elite, in this mass-mediated preformulation of ethnic topics.

(4) In low-contact areas, personal communication about ethnic minorities largely consists of this mass-mediated body of consensus opinions. Occasional contacts with minority group members, or people living in high-contact areas, may add some further information about

ethnic groups. Yet, this information tends to be selectively attended to and memorized under the influence of stereotypes people already know or share. For many others in such areas, even such direct or indirect personal contact or experience information is not available. They either accept the general stereotypes or more tolerantly suspend their opinion "because they have no experience about that." This all suggests that topics of talk in such neighborhoods tend to be rather general, and the mode of presentation rather argumentative than narrative.

(5) In high-contact areas, direct communication forms are much more frequent, and partly based on personal observations and experiences. Aside from the reproduction of "new facts" obtained from the media, everyday talk among family members, neighbors, or in public places will be about the latest developments in the neighborhood or about occasional personal experiences. Typical topics in such neighborhood talk would be, for example:

(a) incidents, accidents, and conflicts in the neighborhood perceived to be caused by ethnic group members (e.g., fights, police calls);
(b) local crime (mostly mugging, burglary, and theft);
(c) interaction conflicts, harassment, and so forth among direct neighbors, such as being bothered by noise, food smells, different forms of hygiene ("dirt"), and other small conflicts mostly due to cultural differences; and
(d) observational "facts," such as "witnessing" people who don't work, who live on welfare, cheat welfare agencies, or are favored in housing, men who treat women in a different way, and clothing differences.

Note that even such topics, based on more or less direct observation, experience, interaction, or hearsay from direct participants (family, friends, neighbors), are largely reproducing the general stereotypes and prejudices: crime, aggression, harassment, cheating on welfare, being favored in housing, and other negative things ascribed to ethnic minority groups. In other words, everyday talk also selects those topics that "confirm" general attitude schema opinions. Even particular stories with unique details tend to have such general prejudiced opinions, as we have shown in the previous chapter. In Chapter 4, we show in more detail what the cognitive processes are that underlie this specific attention for and selection of stereotype-confirming topics.

Positive Talk

Not all people engage in negative talk about ethnic groups. Across areas, about 25% of the people appear positive about the presence of ethnic groups or explicitly resent discrimination and prejudice, whereas about half of the people do not formulate predominantly negative opinions about minority groups. Characteristically, the positive stories, especially in high-contact areas, cannot possibly be instantiations of general stereotypes or prejudices. They must be either instantiations of general (positive) norms or they are based on direct evidence and on experiences of family members or friends. Other expressions of positive evaluations or experiences are of the "exception to the rule" type, and may occur among otherwise negative or stereotyped stories or arguments: People talk about one foreign neighbor or acquaintance who is particularly nice and friendly, and with whom they never have "problems."

More extensive positive stories in overall positively formulated talk are usually about mutual help, for instance, in sickness, mutual visits, participation in parties, and the specifics of how it is to take part in events, such as a Turkish wedding. There are, however, few of such stories. Most tolerant talk is of a more general nature, especially in the low-contact areas: People are against discrimination, against racist parties, or display empathy for the problems with which the minority groups have to cope. Several people reported that they resent other people's racist talk but that they did not react to that "because you only get into trouble."

Moderation

From the prevailing social norm that prohibits explicit racist talk, and from the uncertainty people may have about the opinions of unknown others, even those in the same neighborhood, we may further infer that, generally, talk with strangers will often be "cautious." People may resort to the common stereotypes borrowed from mass-mediated hearsay, which are semilegitimate forms of negative talk and, hence, not against the prevailing norm. Or they may tell authentic personal experiences that cannot be challenged as false. But in both cases, they at the same time will first "test out" others as to their opinions about foreigners. We surmise that "really racist" talk, therefore, only takes place among close friends and family members, which also explains why we have few instances of it in our interviews (27 of 143 interviewed persons in Amsterdam, and 3 out of 25 people in California), which, however, are mostly formulated in still rather polite terms and seldom in harsh terms of abuse. This would suggest that prejudices formulated in much semipublic talk (e.g., in shops, with neighbors, or in public transport) are of the "moderate" kind, which is also the type that may be expressed in press interviews or in TV programs. This seems to be in accordance with the general distribution of the prejudice scores among the interviewed, which will be discussed later.

The close interaction between everyday talk and media topics about ethnic groups confirms this overall picture of "moderate prejudice" in most interpersonal conversations among people. This kind of ethnic attitude involves such opinions as "Dutch people are tolerant," "We do (too) much for those foreigners," "They should at least partly adapt to our norms, rules, and habits," "They must learn our language," "They live out of our pocket," and "They should not be favored in jobs or housing." This form of moderate prejudice also rejects racism, does not want to send them back "because we have invited them to come and work for us," acknowledges that also among Dutch people there are bad individuals, that we should not generalize, that they may keep part of their own culture, such as religion, or that their children should be able to learn their own language at school. This moderate form of prejudice agrees with implicit government policies and many of the media accounts that associate ethnic groups with "problems," at least in the social and economic domains.

Conclusion

We conclude this section by generally assuming that everyday talk about ethnic groups across high- and low-contact areas first of all reproduces the "public discussion" topics and opinions formulated by the media. Second, local stories about personal experiences of the storyteller (or family or friends), may be added as new information or as evidence, but in most cases only as instantiations of general prejudices that are known—and often shared—in the public discussion. Indeed, such stories may again be recorded and published by the media, which accounts for the circular nature of the reproduction of prejudice in informal and formal mass communication. Third, explicitly antiracist talk or protests against negative opinions about minorities may be rare and restricted to small groups of people of similar opinions. Indeed, because the dominant media are not antiracist, there is no "model" for such talk, no standard phrases or counterarguments, and no dominant public discussion fed, sustained, or monitored by the authorities, the institutions, and (therefore) the media.

Finally, especially those who have access to alternative forms of talk and text, such as children at school, students, social workers, and, generally, the better educated—who also get explicit lessons, use occasional critical textbooks, read results of research, reports, or have access to specialized publications—and people who have more experiences with ethnic group members themselves, might (but do not always) develop different topics of talk and, hence, different opinions and different preju-

dices. We will pay more attention to these societal determinants of prejudiced talk in Chapter 6.

3. Description of source reproduction

To test and explore further the
assumptions formulated above, an analysis was made of all passages in
the opinion interviews in which implicit or explicit reference was made
to interpersonal or mass-media communication. We first give some simple descriptive statistics, and then proceed to a qualitative analysis of the
topics reproduced through these communicative contacts. The figures
given in this section should merely be seen as rough indications of the
nature of sources and source information to which people refer. Without
the rigorously controlled conditions of sampling or other features of traditional survey research, a more sophisticated statistical analysis would
falsely suggest "hard facts" our method was not intended to offer.

Of 143 people interviewed (from the three groups we initially interviewed in Amsterdam), two-thirds (94) made 198 references to other
sources, that is, somewhat more than two such references each. Most of
these references (138 or 70%) were made to personal communications,
whereas 79 references (40%) pertained to the media, which means that
some passages mentioned both a personal and a media source.

We counted as "personal communication" each reference in which
the speaker explicitly mentioned a source, such as "husband," "friend,"
or "neighbor," for some belief about ethnic groups or ethnic relationships in the Netherlands. Yet we also counted the reproduction of those
events or opinions for which a personal source must have been used, for
instance, concrete events that happened to others without the presence
of the speaker.

The Prejudice Scale

In our quantitative account of commu-
nication sources, as well as in the subsequent chapters, we also include
an approximate estimate of the "prejudice level" of the interviewees.
This estimate is based on a seven-point scale, running from no prejudice
(P1) to very high prejudice or blatant racism (P7). Scoring on this scale
is derived from qualitative analyses of the interviews. Each point of the
scale is defined as a characteristic profile of ethnic opinions. Thus, at
level P1, people not only formulate no ethnic prejudices but, in fact,

are generally positive about the presence of ethnic minorities, explicitly reject prejudice and racism in Dutch society, and concretely show how they have acted in an antiracist manner. At level P2, formulation is more neutral, without negative statements about ethnic groups, and only more general statements against prejudice and racism. P3 represents a profile that is generally neutral, with an occasional and incidental negative statement limited to a special domain or special persons, often based on personal experiences. Generally, people at this level hold that foreigners "should adapt somewhat to Dutch norms and society." In this profile, no statements that explicitly reject racism are made. From P4 upward, an increasing amount and diversity of negative stereotypes are expressed. At the highest level, these negative stereotypes are also accompanied by statements that "they should be sent back" or other statements about negative (sometimes violent) actions to be undertaken against minority groups. At this level, we also find accounts of direct abuse against foreigners.

Obviously, this scale is merely an approximation and an abstraction and cannot replace true qualitative analysis. It ignores individual variations of a more subtle kind, differences of prejudices against various ethnic groups, and situational as well as conversational variation. It merely represents an indicative summary of the kind or level of ethnic attitudes people express. In this sense, it is more a typological than a purely quantitative scale. We use scorings (and later also means for special social groups) mostly to suggest the nature of the ethnic opinions that individuals and groups have. The scale is *not* intended to suggest any kind of quantitative precision beyond shorthand characterization of ethnic attitudes types. Although our interviews and the scale based on them are certainly more sensitive than the usual prejudice scales used in the literature, the measurements are still derived from explicit and implicit statements. As we shall see in more detail later, this will undoubtedly favor respondents who are better able to dissimulate "true opinions" with words, even in informal interviews. This also partly explains why better-educated interviewees usually score lower on this scale. In order to infer their actual ethnic attitudes, other approaches are necessary, such as an examination of the experiences of minority group members in interaction with such elite majority group members (Essed, 1984) or an analysis of the sometimes subtle forms of racism in special elite discourse types (van Dijk, 1987d).

Personal Communication

Both for the media and for personal communication, references could be very general, such as "one hears everyday" or "one reads everyday," and we also included these general statements that were thus vaguely attributed to others. Yet, such general references differ from the more concrete ones made to statements made by identified others. Therefore, we established a scale of closeness of interpersonal communication contacts, as follows:

(1) Family members
(2) Friends
(3) Acquaintances, colleagues
(4) Identified neighbors
(5) Neighbors in general
(6) People in general
(7) Authorities, institutions

This scale represents not only an approximate measure of social distance for the speakers, but (therefore) also a measure of the amount and familiarity of interpersonal communication. The same remarks hold as those made for the prejudice scale: It is merely an abstraction and a practical approximation—some people may actually have more or more intimate contacts with friends or colleagues than with family members. The figures used below, therefore, are not more than first impressions of the possible generality of our qualitative results, as well as possible suggestions for further discourse analysis and comparisons.

With these caveats in mind, we may tentatively give some figures that relate closeness of personal sources with types of prejudice. The average score for the closeness of communication sources on this scale is 2.8, which suggests that the majority of the references are to rather close others. The prejudice level for the people who refer to other people as a source is 3.7, which is somewhat higher than the overall prejudice mean of 3.4. Interestingly, the prejudice score of people who use their own family members as a source is markedly higher (4.8) than the prejudice level for those who refer to more distant sources (which is around the mean of 3.4). More source references are made by women (they account for 62% of the references), than by men (38%), whereas the proportion of men and women interviewed is 45% to 55%. As for all interviewed, there is no difference between the prejudice levels of men and women who mention other sources, although, as we shall see below, young women have a lower prejudice score than young men, and older women have a slightly higher score than older men.

The area in which the references are made does seem to matter, however. People in the low-contact areas usually refer to closer sources (2.6) than those in high-contact areas (3.0). This might be explained by the fact that in the high-contact areas, people may more often refer to sources such as neighbors and the neighborhood, whereas in the low-contact areas, sources referred to are family members or friends, because there the relevance of talk about ethnic groups among neighbors or people in the street is much lower (in fact, many interviewees say this explicitly). In the high-contact areas, the prejudice level of those who refer to other sources is 4.4, whereas it is only 3.1 for the low-contact areas. These figures are higher than the overall prejudice means for those areas, especially in the high-contact areas (where it is 3.9 for all interviewed persons). This difference suggests that people in high-contact areas tend to have recourse for their negative opinions to stories and opinions of others, or that people who are more prejudiced give more accounts of interpersonal communications about ethnic groups. Apparently, prejudiced people tend to mention others for evidence for their opinions, which also suggests that they are more engaged in the everyday reproduction of racism.

The Media

The mean prejudice score for people who mention the media is somewhat lower (3.3) than for those who mention personal communication (3.7). However, this may be an area effect: In low-contact areas people must draw their beliefs more often from the media. The calculated prejudice scores for people who mention the media are lower in low-contact areas (2.9) than for those reporting media sources in high-contact areas (4.6). Although the differences are small, there seems to be a reverse media-area interaction: People who mention the media in low-contact areas are below the mean of 3.1 for all who mention sources in that area, whereas those who mention the media in high-contact areas are 0.2 above the mean of 4.4 in that area. The reverse is true for interpersonal contact: In high-contact areas people who refer to others are slightly less prejudiced (4.2) than the mean of their neighborhood (4.4), and those in low-contact areas people who mention personal sources are somewhat more prejudiced (3.2) than the others in the area (3.1).

Interestingly, prejudice seems to be lower for people who refer to the newspaper as a source (3.1), than for those who mention television (3.7). This suggests that the paper must be used more often for moderately prejudiced opinions, or that low-prejudice people use the paper relatively more often to substantiate their opinion. There may also be an area or education effect here: Because (in this kind of superficial analysis) low-contact areas overall score lower on prejudice, and because people in these areas have better jobs and more education, the general reliance on TV in the poorer high-contact areas may account for more references to TV as a source. It is strange that the radio is little mentioned as a source, despite its frequent ethnic programs, and despite the fact that during the daytime (when there is little television in the Netherlands) people at home often listen to the radio. The communication relationships, thus, may be very complex, and it is certainly not the case that from this difference we should conclude that television is more prejudice-inducing than the press. On the contrary, in the Netherlands there is an impression that TV programs generally are somewhat more positive about ethnic groups than at least the widely read popular press. As a public broadcasting organization, television must remain closer to official norms. Generally, we have the impression (but no statistical data), that television programs more often than the press feature ethnic minority speakers.

Reported Facts

As a crude measure of the kind of "facts" attributed to sources, we first associated each passage with a measure for implied attitude toward ethnic groups or ethnic relations as it emerges in the account of such a fact: 1 for a positive, 0 for a neutral, and -1 for a negative event told about ethnic groups. In some cases, such facts also pertain to events or acts involving Dutch people in relation to ethnic groups. For instance, an act of discrimination, when mentioned, is here simply counted as evidence in favor of ethnic groups, as are also, of course, any acts that directly favor ethnic group members.

The vast majority (103 or 52%) of all references are made to negative facts about ethnic groups, whereas in only 14 cases (7%) are positive facts reported about ethnic group members. The rest of the cases are neutral (or no specific facts mentioned). It is striking, however, that the prejudice level of people who do report negative facts is lower (3.4) than those who report positive facts, neutral facts, or no facts at all. This suggests that people do not use others primarily as a source for confirming their own opinion, but merely as a source for topics, which may be evaluated independently. Indeed, people often mention that others or the media say negative things about ethnic groups, and then state that they resent that. Note, though, that this may also be an obvious move in the well-known strategy of positive self-presentation. The converse may also be true: People may mention that others say something positive about foreigners, and then tell the interviewer that they do not agree with that evaluation.

Reactions

Apparently, in addition to the reproduction of facts, we also need a measure for the reaction people display to such facts. As a positive (negative) reaction, we counted each reaction (whether commenting on a positive, neutral, or negative fact attributed to a source) that implies a positive (negative) attitude toward ethnic minority groups. We found that the neutral and absent cases dominate (114 or 56%), followed by the negative reactions (56 or 28%). Only 28 reactions are positive. In this case, there is a clear difference in prejudice level: People who react positively are at the 2.6 level and people who react negatively are at the 4.2 level. This suggests that most positive reactions tend to be against the negative attitude that is associated with negative "facts" (mostly stereotypes about ethnic groups). However, in this case, we only have a general measure of how people react to reproduced facts.

More enlightening is how people react to positive or negative facts as reported. This shows that, indeed, most negative reactions (52) are reactions that are in line with the negative facts. In a few cases (10), people show a reaction that is in accordance with a positive fact (and the mean prejudice level for people who do this is 3.4). In only two cases do people mention a positive fact to which they react negatively (and this happens for people with a high [5.5] prejudice level). In 18 cases people react positively to a negative fact, that is, they seem to contradict what sources tell them. As expected, such active counterarguments tend to be formulated by people with a low prejudice level (2.1).

Despite the few positive reactions, however, we see that, overall, people either tend to avoid reaction, give a neutral reaction, or their negative reaction concurs with the negative direction of the facts they reproduce. At the same time, reported facts are markedly more negative (their mean is −0.4) than the mean of the reactions, which is −0.1. In other words, although there is a general tendency toward negativity in both reported facts and reactions, people represent their own reactions more positively than the facts reported through others or the media.

Opinions

From the passages about sources, that is, from reported facts and people's own reactions to such facts, we may also infer the ethnic opinions people attribute to such sources (or people speaking through such sources, such as people quoted in the press or appearing on television). If we compare such an opinion attribution with explicit personal opinions or explicit opinions of the interviewees, we obtain a measure of agreement. Again, we did so only in a very rough and approximate way. Subtle discourse analysis is needed to assess in detail exactly how people (dis)agree with others in their ethnic opinions. Note that this agreement need not be identical with the kind of reaction: Such a reaction may be focused on a single fact reported about a source.

Personal and attributed opinions have a more general nature. People may have an overall negative attitude about ethnic minority groups but display a single and specific positive reaction on some point in their interview. This is one of the reasons that, in the next chapter, we shall make a clear distinction between particular opinions and general ethnic attitudes or prejudices.

Our analysis of the passages showed that it is again the neutral (or unexpressed) opinion that occurs most often: 98 (49%) of the passages scored 0, 79 (40%) expressed a negative opinion attributed to a source, whereas only 21 (11%) reproduced a positive attitude toward ethnic groups in such passages. The tendency here seems to be that sources are more often credited with negative opinions, although in most cases there is no or just a neutral opinion attributed to the source. Again, it is interesting to note that the prejudice level of people who refer to positive opinions is slightly higher (3.7) than that of people who mention negative opinions (3.5). This is probably a result of the fact we encountered earlier: There are many low-prejudiced people who (negatively) comment upon negative reporting or talk of sources.

How do such references compare to the personal opinions people formulate about the facts, events, or opinions they report? In agreement with the general prejudice scores of the people interviewed, we find that 111 (56%) of the passages express no or a neutral opinion, 50 (26%) a negative one, and only 36 (19%) a positive one. Comparing this distribution with the proportions of people scoring at the respective prejudice levels, we see that, for instance, the number of overall low-prejudiced people, that is, people who score P1 or P2, is 36 (25%), which is somewhat more than those who display positive opinions in the passages that mention other sources. This may mean that people may simply report negative facts or opinions borrowed from others, without expressing their own opinion, or that more people incidentally agree with a negative point, while overall displaying low prejudice. This might suggest that communication has a negative effect on the prejudice level of people: They tend to agree more often with negative facts or opinions than their own opinions would suggest. Overall, the average agreement score is 0.0, however, which suggests that personal positive or negative opinions and those opinions attributed to others seem to balance each other. As may be expected, the overall score for reactions and personal opinions is more or less the same, and slightly negative, namely, –0.1 in both cases.

Personal Contact or Media?

Finally, the facts and opinions borrowed from other sources may be attributed to the media or to other people. For the 14 positive facts, 7 are attributed to the media and the other 7 to other people. The negative facts are drawn relatively more often from personal communications: 76 of 103 facts are attributed to talk. Generally, then, the media are referred to less often as a source of negative facts. This agrees with the observation made above, that the average prejudice level for people who mention the media is lower than for people who mention personal sources. In our case, this might partly be a sampling effect because relatively more interviews and source-denoting passages were recorded in low-contact areas (121 of 198 or 61%), where people happen to score lower on prejudice and at the same time must rely more on media information about ethnic groups and ethnic relations.

Also, we saw that the prejudice level for people referring to other people as a source is higher than for those who mention the media, although, this difference may have several explanations. For instance, it might suggest that (negative) personal communication is more effective than media communication, that the media generally are less negative about ethnic groups, or that the media are less often used (and mentioned in talk) for information that supports negative opinions, or, again, that more prejudiced people make less use of media information in general. Such alternatives may be decided only by further investigation of the content of the media, the facts or opinions attributed to the media, and, of course, by a full-scale analysis of media usage, which cannot be the task of this book.

It was mentioned earlier that there is a recipient difference between newspaper and television source mention: People who refer to TV have a higher prejudice score (3.7) than people who refer to the press (3.1), a difference we attributed to a well-known area/education effect for media usage (see, e.g., Robinson & Levy, 1986, for analysis). Similarly, there are also source differences: People do not just mention the media but also different kinds of people who speak in/through the media. Therefore, we distinguished between a general voice, in which no particular media-actor attribution is made, a particular (autochthonous) voice, and a particular minority voice, such as when members of some ethnic group are mentioned as media actors. Finally, there is the official voice of the institutions, such as the local or national government. Generally, people react negatively to the official voice (overall reaction mean is −0.5, and agreement level −0.8), whereas the few references to ethnic representatives tend to be positive. The absolute numbers in these cases are too low, however, to draw conclusions from these differences. It emerges from our qualitative analyses, however, that the official policies, whether for or against ethnic groups, tend to be judged negatively. The authorities are usually blamed for "letting them come," for "favoring them," and for "not doing anything against all this."

Age and Gender

A well-known factor traditionally used in the explanation of measured prejudice is age: Older people tend to be more prejudiced for a complex structure of reasons, such as their assumed lack of flexibility, the difficulties they have in adapting to new social situations, higher fear of assumed dangers in the city or on the streets, and so on. These tendencies, indeed, appear in our data. The mean age for people who refer to other sources is relatively high, namely, 49, which suggests that we have interviewed a somewhat larger number of people of higher age (and few people under 20). The analysis of the passages also showed that most of them were expressed by women (124), than by men (74), which is higher (62%) than the percentage of women interviewed (55%).

The prejudice level of the 103 people 50 and older is 4.1, which is higher than the overall mean of 3.6, and the level of the 31 people under 30 is 2.5, which is far below the mean. Interestingly, the women over 50 were slightly more prejudiced (4.2) than the men (4.0), whereas the young women were markedly less prejudiced (2.1) than the young men (2.8). There is also an area effect here, as may be expected: The older people in high-contact areas scored much higher (4.5) than those in low-contact areas (3.8). However, in the high-contact areas, it is more or less the same as the overall prejudice score (4.4) in such areas, whereas in the low-contact areas, older people score markedly higher than the mean of 3.1. Similarly, for young people there is also an area effect: In the low-contact neighborhoods it is 2.4 and in the high-contact neighborhoods people under 30 score 2.8, on average. For the in-between age of 30-50, the overall mean prejudice is lower than the mean for all interviewed people, namely, 3.2, and there is hardly any difference between men and women in this case.

The somewhat higher prejudice level of older women may be related to their often-expressed fear of going out, and their association of such fear with (young, male) foreigners. Conversely, although younger people as a group seem to express less prejudice in their reports about sources, there are a few cases of young highly prejudiced males, which also can be noted in the predominantly male adherence to racist or fascist youth groups, also in the Netherlands. Below, we shall further investigate what topics people of different age or gender groups typically mention when they indicate communication sources. From such an analysis, we also might infer the cognitive basis of the differences in ethnic attitude.

Conclusion

We now have a first (quantitative) impression of which people in which neighborhoods mention which sources, and which ethnic facts or opinions are attributed to such sources by people of different ethnic opinions. Tentatively, a few social constraints (such as area, education, age, and gender) might be detected in the description of the groups that mention such sources. More important for our analysis, though, is to see in which respect the media and/or personal communication are mentioned more often, and how or for what reasons. Crucially, we find that most (assumed) facts attributed to other sources, whether one agrees or not, are negative. People often react to this neutrally, but if they do show an opinion, then it tends to agree with the predominantly negative facts as reported. Yet, antiprejudiced people also mention such negative facts, mostly in order to show disagreement or to emphasize that many (other) people are prejudiced. Although we assumed that television is generally less negative than the press (for instance, because it does not report ethnic crime news on a regular basis), people referring to TV as a source tend to score somewhat higher than those who refer to the printed media (which may be a combined area-occupation-education effect). Personal communications more often serve as a negative source than the media, however. Indeed, these are the sources for the highly persuasive stories about (negative) personal experiences. The media are rather used for reference to more general information about ethnic groups (immigration, official policies, or unemployment, but also discrimination).

4. Topics of talk

W hat do people hear and read about? Now that we have some general facts about the source types and reactions by different groups to communications about ethnic groups, it is, of course, crucial to know about the contents attributed to these communications. For the opinion interviews, we only have what people tell us as evidence about source contents, and such reports are usually highly fragmentary, incomplete, and biased. However, we suggested, it is exactly the summarized and subjectively transformed nature of such reports that gives us clues about the ways people have actually interpreted such source contents and about how they communicate them to others. Also, differences between people's accounts of the same events allow us to compare source information and reported information. And finally, people are sometimes rather accurate in reporting source information, and then may add their own, independent, opinion to the facts as reported.

In this section, then, we focus on the overall contents, that is, on the topics of the passages in which interviewed people refer to other sources.

Again, we approach these data from several points of view. We examine them in a nearly raw state, with a qualitative design, as well as more systematically by categorizing topics in a few clusters. We also give some descriptive quantitative data about the uses of various topics in different neighborhoods and by different people.

Personal Communication: Examples

To start our analysis, we first give a few characteristic examples of the different ways people may refer to sources of information about ethnic groups. Some of the passages in which this happens are very long and occupy pages of transcript, whereas in (many) other cases people just say things like "You read about that in the papers" or "Oh, yes I saw that on TV." For a topical analysis, this also means that the actual content of what is drawn from other sources is not always explicit, or it may be mingled with contents of the rest of the interview, and, hence, integrated with personal opinions, experiences, or other memories, as well as with the contents expressed by turns of the interviewer.

For each example we have added, after the code number identifying an individual interviewee, some data about that person: age, gender, occupation (if known), high- or low-contact area, and the overall prejudice score we have assigned on the basis of our qualitative analysis of the whole interview. Some passages are from interviews with two people, mostly family members or friends. The English version is merely an approximation and often markedly less natural and colloquial than the Dutch original. For the (macro)analysis of topics, this is, however, less of a problem. Because many of the passages are very long, or contain irrelevant information for this stage of analysis, we have sometimes summarized them in our own words. In that case, a passage (or turn) is preceded by (S). Literal quotes in summaries have been signaled by double quotes. Summaries enclosed in parentheses are summaries of parts that have preceded, that follow a passage, or summarize what an interviewer said. We give them only as necessary context for better understanding of the passage referring to other sources. Passages that are (translated) literal quotes from interviews are also given to show some of the interesting local details of reported talk, media contents, or communication processes about ethnic groups.

To organize our discussion of the examples, we have provisionally categorized them in four classes: (a) the general nature of talk about foreigners, (b) denial or avoidance of such talk, (c) references to general stereotypes in such talk, and (d) mention of concrete events experienced by known people. Some examples are given in the different categories.

(a) The nature of talk about foreigners.
Speakers have the ability to describe and evaluate general talk about foreigners, and may use such semitechnical expressions as *stereotype* quite often. Some of them are also aware of the opinion and prejudice-inducing nature of negative conversations. Thus, especially the better educated, instead of talking about their own opinion, tend to talk about those of others, or about the mechanisms of opinion formation. In the following abstracts, we find a few of such general comments on foreigner talk:

(1)   I-G-1 (Boy, 16, low-con, P2)
I: If you talk with your friends about Turks, Surinamese or Moroccans, what kind of things do you hear?
B: When we really talk about it then they are really negative conversations (. . .) But I do not bother with that . . .

(2)   I-Z-1/2 (Woman/Woman, 45/45, housemaid/clerk, low-con, P3/P3)
I: What do you think about foreigners coming to live in Amsterdam?
W1:   I have little to do with that, but uhh I thought that it . . . uhhm . . . one quickly takes over the opinion of others . . .

(3)   I-Z-1/2 (Woman/Woman, 45/45, housemaid/clerk, low-con, P3/P3)
W2:   No, I mean we can't really have an opinion about that. I do have an opinion, I could form an opinion, after all that talk you hear in the streetcar.
W1:   Just as I say! You hear so much from others.
W2:   Two or three times a week, you are sitting in the streetcar, I had it twice last week. This old lady sitting beside me, a decent old lady, begins to tell stories like that about foreigners, that she doesn't accept them . . . I can see that from all her talk. She simply says that in the streetcar, where everybody can hear her. Did she have it from herself, or did she hear it from others?
W1:   Well, I didn't react to that, because it was a woman of over 60 years old.

(4)   II-AC-3 (Man, 63, bookseller and librarian, high-con, P3)
      (About a foreign family) M: You can't blame the foreigner for that, but the neighbors do that, the people who the do the people in this neighborhood, they tend to blame it on the
I: That is, that is what you hear
M: Oh yes, yes, they come to me in the library and they go like "they did this and that or this happened and I don't dare to do anything about it," because when when it hadn't been a colored erson, if it hadn't been a Surinamese, if it hadn't been a Moroccan, or hadn't it been a Turk, then they surely would have spoken up, because I had them here as clients, people like you would say one shouldn't have an argument with them, because if she would open her mouth, you know, then you were finished.
I: But what kind of stories did they tell, for instance, what happened to those people?
M: (S) Story about Surinamese family with a lot of children, who make a lot of noise, leave open the front door, etc., and the old [Dutch]

downstairs neighbor is not used to that and is complaining all the time.

(5)   III-CB-1x (Man, 34, sociologist, low-con, P2)
(S) Sometimes you hear from people who live there about rags hanging before the windows, and toilet bowls being removed. And when I lived in one of those neighborhoods "you could often hear from people that they resented that, and that was discussed, I mean people all the time were busy forming their opinions about that, say, and testing what . . . you thought about that yourself, and what your own experiences were with others" so that you knew whether people were for or against foreigners, and for what reasons. In that sense people knew more about each other than in this neighborhood.

(6)   III-ET-1 (Man, 37, university teacher, low-con, P1)
(Story in newspaper) (S) M: Yes, those stories you read all the time like slaughtering sheep and blood streaming from the walls, type of stories you hear on each point where people have unfounded opinions. You are sitting in the train and somebody starts to talk to you about all those people on unemployment allowances, and then they start telling a story "I KNOW SOMEBODY, a family of 5 persons of which 4 have an allowance, they together make twice as much as we make." Such stories are told a hundred times, until they legitimitize the conclusion that the allowances may well go down, because people live nicely on them and couldn't care less about a job (. . .) Apparently it is allowed and interesting for people to tell and hear those stories, especially when they are never contradicted. It is important to react to this, for instance, when in the papers or as I saw recently on TV, people do as if those stories are normal, and that the media just register them so that people are getting used to them and a normal way of storytelling.

(7)   III-MR-3 (Man, 36, low-con, P3)
(S) You hear those stories, things that are salient, like how Turks treat their women, or about slaughtering, usually not very positive things. I don't know what to believe of those stories (. . .) There is a lot of bullshit among it.

(8)   III-AB-4x (Man, 77, retired construction worker, low-con, P5)
(S) If foreigners stay here for too long, it will lead to chaos, then you get those racist situations, that people start to say, What are they doing here, we already have so many people, that is what people talk about in their daily conversations (. . .) I hear both old and young people say sometimes, OK let us have this Centrum Party. [Racist party that at the time of this interview had just obtained one seat in parliament. This CP party is discussed often in all interviews of group III, recorded in a typical noncontact area.]

These examples first suggest that people have the impression that most talk about foreigners is negative (see, e.g., example 1). This is so often said in the interviews that it has nearly become a stereotype itself. It suggests that people do not talk positively very often about ethnic groups. The experiment by Sprangers (1983), discussed before, already found that people are able to (re)produce negative stereotypes much more often than positive ones. Indeed, other examples show that people have no consensual stereotypes about positive or at least neutral talk. Exceptions are the more positively intended media messages, especially TV programs, which, in fact, are often commented upon negatively by people (see below).

One woman (in example 2) states that—probably negative—opinions emerging in everyday talk tend to be taken over rather quickly, and (in example 3) she mentions an interesting event from a typical streetcar situation, which is one of the few public situations in which people talk to each other about things of common interest. The old lady is described as expressing plain negative opinions about foreigners, and the comment of the woman who tells this story is relevant for several reasons: First, she apparently felt embarrassed that one should talk so negatively about foreigners in a public place (which suggests a strong norm against prejudiced talk), and, second, she wonders whether, in fact, the old lady has the opinions on the basis of personal experience or hearsay. In other words, people do differentiate between opinions based on experiences and those based on just talk. Third, the woman indicates that she did not react to this kind of talk, which is a kind of reaction reported more often: Only a few people openly contradict the racist talk of others, even when they seem to disagree. In studies about the nature of racism, this kind of "silence" has been called a form of "passive racism" (Essed, 1984). Finally, she also gives a reason for not talking back: It is an old lady. This may mean that one does not start a fight with elderly people (out of respect), that the elderly cannot be held responsible for what they say, or that the elderly (elderly women?) only have such prejudices, which would be in line with our earlier finding that there is a correlation between higher prejudice and higher age.

The other examples show various additional instances of communication situations, such as the train, the public community library, or just the neighborhood in general. The speakers in these three other examples are all men who apparently have experienced or thought about such events more often. They actually analyze them and venture generalizations or hypotheses about prejudice formation. The librarian (in example 4) observes that people make complaints about foreigners to him, but that they do not dare to speak up to the foreigners themselves, a topic we have found in several other interviews. The sociologist analyzes the situation in his own previous (high-contact) neighborhood, and observes that people in such neighborhoods, in general, have more mutual knowledge about each other, including knowledge about what the opinions are about foreigners. Talk about foreigners, in that sense, is seen as an "opinion test" for the recipient and as a device to measure agreement. The university teacher (in example 6) gives examples of the stereotypes you may hear on the train and adds the observation that the very fact that they are not contradicted may contribute to their legitimation. He gives the reproduction of negative stories in the media as an example of how such prejudices may be further reproduced and made acceptable. Although only theoretically (he does not say that he did so himself), he is one of the few speakers who suggests that recipients (and the media) should actively react against such negative talk.

Others, like the interviewee in example 7, show how most people report their reactions: They have doubts about what they hear, do not react at all, or react neutrally or noncommitally. The man in example 8 also observes that there is much racist talk, but attributes it to the presence of ("too many") foreigners, thus, blaming the victim.

           (b) Denial and avoidance. In Chapter 2, we found that people often have recourse to an avoidance strategy when delicate topics are involved. They say that they have no contact with foreigners, don't know anything about them, and so on. Something similar happens when questions are asked about talk about foreigners. Several people, in low- but also in high-contact areas, say that there *is* not much talk about foreigners, although the rest of the interviews or even the same passage show that "people don't talk about much else anymore." Of course, such a denial may mean that people do not want to talk about such conversations, that they don't remember concrete examples, or else that they deny that *they* talk (negatively) about foreigners, because typically *any* talk about foreigners is understood as being negative talk.

    (9) I-D-4 (Woman, 35, high-con, P5)
     I: Do you ever talk with friends and acquaintances about foreigners in Amsterdam?
    W: Well, if it uhh happens in this staircase [in this house] or in the neighborhood, but for the rest not really, because you don't hear anything but that.
     I: But can you tell me anything about that, what people talk about?
    W: Yes, you . . . well the same things I already told you, I mean uhh it is something everybody uhh thinks is unbearable uhh like that they profit from uhh yes our social services and all that and and uhh hanging out and show off and uhh . . .

    (10) I-D-5 (Woman, 25, social worker, high-con, P2)
     I: What do people talk about in that community center?
    W: Uhh, yes, that they . . . well (???) there ISn't much talk about them. Yes, they take our our uhh jobs and . . . they all live on welfare, they get better houses than we are offered . . . that is we Dutch, uhh let me think . . . I believe that that was the biggest list of complaints.

    (11) II-MA-2 (Woman, 30, artist, high-con, P2)
     (S) I never heard concrete stories, only abuse and stereotypical things like, "They stink," and "When you start talking about it, or when you want to defend them, then it stops."

Although these three women all mention that there is not much talk or that they do not hear stories, they are very well able to mention the major topics of foreigner talk. Whether as a generalization from communicative events or from general social knowledge about stereotypes, all three mention some frequently formulated negative attitudes. The difference between the highly prejudiced woman in example 9 and the other two women is that the woman in example 9 first maintains that everybody has the same (negative) opinion about the facts she mentions, whereas the other women mark a more critical distance, for example, by using the notion of stereotype, or by ironically referring to a "list of complaints." The woman in example 11 further suggests it is her experience that when you react critically to such talk, people stop saying such things.

(c) General stereotypes. People not only may have stereotypes, they also know that others have them and may talk about them. Especially in the low-contact areas, frequent mention was made of stereotypes being repeated in the newspaper or in everyday conversational stories. In the following characteristic examples, we find instances of reports of such stereotypical stories. These may be told as evidence for personal opinions, or as evidence for the negative attitudes of other people in the neighborhood or the city.

(12) II-TK-2 (Woman, 65, high-contact, P3)
   (She doesn't dare to go out at night anymore)
   I: Do you know why you don't dare to go out?
   W: I really don't know. You hear those strange stories.
   I: They are stories you hear from others or things you read in the paper?
   W: Nothing has happened to me.
   I: No
   W: Oh no, I myself haven't, nobody told me anything . . .

(13) II-PD-5 (Woman/man, 60/65, high-contact, P6/P5)
   W: The average people here hate the uhh what shall we call it, the foreigner, like the pest. But you know, most of them don't dare to talk about it (???)
   I: Are they afraid for revenge or so?
   W: Yes
   I: That the people would do something back.
   W: I think that that would happen . . .

(14) (= 9) I-D-4 (Woman, 35, high-con, P5)
   I: Do you ever talk with friends and acquaintances about foreigners in Amsterdam?
   W: Well, if it uhh happens in this staircase [in this house] or in the neighborhood, but for the rest not really, because you don't hear anything but that.
   I: But can you tell me anything about that, what people talk about?
   W: Yes, you . . . well the same things I already told you, I mean uhh it is

something everybody uhh thinks is unbearable uhh like that they profit from uhh yes our social services and all that and and uhh hanging out and show off and uhh . . .

---

(15) (= 10) I-D-5 (Woman, 25, social worker, high-con, P2)
   I: What do people talk about in that community center?
   W: Uhh, yes, that they . . . well (???) there ISn't much talk about them. Yes, they take our our uhh jobs and . . . they all live on welfare, they get better houses than we are offered . . . that is we Dutch, uhh let me think . . . I believe that that was the biggest list of complaints.

---

(16) I-C-4 (Woman, 69, high-con, P2) What I hear, what I hear from other people, is that they make a lot of music at night and all that. We don't know about that.

---

(17) II-RA-2 (Woman/man, 62/65, retired, high-con, P4)
   (S) There is growing antipathy in the neighborhood against foreigners. That is easy to feel. Mainly because of the unemployment.
   I: How do you notice that in the street?
   W: Well, in the conversations in the street, then they start, you know
   I: When you talk with people in the shops, or what?
   W: No, like the general opinion in the street can you can, if you know people a bit, you can read it from their faces.

---

(18) III-SV-2x (Woman, 37, low-con, P2) (Divorced from Moroccan)
   I: (S) What do they say in your family?
   W: (S) Everybody has to look at himself. I don't notice those things. They say that foreigners profit [from the social services] And my brother-in-law has those prejudices. So I don't go there anymore. I feel that they discriminate against me, also because I'm on welfare.

---

(19) III-AB-1x (Man, 79, teacher, low-con, P1)
   (S) Many people I talk with blame the economic crisis on the presence of foreigners. They are not all fascists. I know a learned Jewish lawyer who also says the same thing.

---

(20) III-MR-3 (Man, 36, low-con, P3)
   (S) You hear those stories, things that are salient, like how Turks treat their women, or about slaughtering, usually not very positive things. I don't know what to believe of those stories (. . .) There is a lot of bull-shit among it.

The woman in example 12 makes a rather stereotypical reference to "stories you hear" as a reason for her not going out anymore, a reason given by many elderly ladies. Yet, she does not specify what kind of stories, nor that these are related to foreigners, although that is clearly implied by the context of this passage. This is also an example of an avoidance strategy, because she redirects the conversation to the danger topic, and also denies that people have actually told her personal experiences (as we found in category b above). Example 13 is more explicitly negative about foreigners and suggests that the stories being told must be negative, expressing very negative opinions of the people in the neighborhood. This woman also addresses the well-known topic of retaliation: autochthonous people don't dare to complain openly for fear of revenge by the foreigners (see also the story of the librarian in example 4). This means that negative talk is experienced as difficult for many people: On the one hand it is censored by the overall norm of tolerance and on the other hand the victims of such talk may strike back. This, of course, enhances the self-portrayal of prejudiced people as being victims themselves of the presence of ethnic groups. One of the main tenets in the propaganda of racist parties (such as Centrum Party) is, indeed, that they plead for an "open discussion about the problem of foreigners," whereas they and others (for instance, journalists) also maintain that it must be possible to express one's attitudes freely in a democratic society: Talk (i.e., negative talk) about foreigners should not be taboo. Apparently such views appeal to the widespread feeling that it is (unjustly) forbidden to say negative things about foreigners.

The actual stereotypes are given in examples 14 through 20. The woman in example 14, whom we have met in the same example 9 before as first denying the occurrence of such stories, mentions that foreigners profit from the social services, which is one of the prevalent stereotypes in the interviews. The other opinions are less stereotypical and seem to be a more personal evaluation: Showing off and hanging out patently refers to Blacks, who are sometimes said to dress (too) well and to behave too immodestly.

The next examples add to the stereotype about welfare cheating, about taking jobs and houses, and making too much noise (especially loud music). The woman in example 16 adds that she doesn't experience such negative facts, whereas the woman in example 18 says that she doesn't react to such stereotypes anymore but simply stays away from her family. Interestingly, she establishes a link between these stereotypes and her own position both as being divorced from a Moroccan and as being on welfare herself. This suggests that she sees a coherent pattern in the prejudices of her family, whether against foreigners or against people who are dependent on welfare.

The woman in example 17 mentions and agrees with the general opinion that foreigners cause unemployment and, at the same time, denies that she knows of concrete talk: She can infer opinions from people's nonverbal interaction. This again suggests that there might be a general reluctance to talk about such things, but that people make indirect references or make faces when the topic comes up.

The two men in examples 19 and 20 also refer to general stories, and add stereotypes such as blaming the economic recession on foreigners and the usual list of cultural differences, such as assumed sheep slaughtering at home and the bad treatment of Turkish or Moroccan women. The man in example 20 hesitates about whether he should believe such stories but supposes much of it must be untrue. This suggests that people seem to make a distinction between general opinions, which one might hold or not, and between concrete stories, which may be true or false, and, hence, fall under criteria of credibility.

The old man in example 19, himself a Jewish historian with strong antiracist opinions, expresses the widely held opinion that even when people vote a racist party like CP, they need not all be racists themselves: They may vote for the party just because of frustration about the economic recession. He sustains that argument with a concrete example of an acquaintance (also Jewish, "so therefore not racist," and a lawyer, and "therefore, an intelligent person"), who also has the opinion that foreigners cause unemployment.

Although far from all stereotypes have been discussed here, the examples show how they come up, are evaluated, and commented on in and after talk about ethnic groups. Some people simply reject them as racist opinions or as just talk, others are hesitant and have doubts, whereas others again accept the stereotypes as general and accepted facts, that is, as things "everybody knows around here."

(d) Concrete stories. Of course, many of the general opinions are not isolated negative stereotypes but are sustained by concrete experiences and stories about them. In the following examples, we find a few instances of references to talk between the interviewee and others about concrete experiences they have had. These examples also show how people hear and select experiences of others as illustrations of their own opinions:

(21) III-TM-1 (Woman, 76, physiotherapist, low-con, P4)
   (What if more Surinamese would come and live in this neighborhood. What would people say?)
   W: I think they wouldn't like it. It is quite a life-style, isn't it. From a city council member I know—he lives there on J-street (. . .) but in a simple little apartment, downstairs. Upstairs lives a Turkish family. That lady is used to throw a pail of water on the floor and scrub it. And then it leaks down (. . .) And then the food, you know, you smell the onions a couple of houses further down the street (. . .) Yes foreigners have to adapt, that Turkish lady also did that there on J-street. Because later I asked Mrs. D. "How is it going How is life," "No, she has accommodated herself." So she has adapted herself.

(22) III-RL-1x (Woman, 55, German teacher, low-con, P3)
   (S) Can imagine that people discriminate. My maid comes from such a neighborhood and has Turkish and Moroccan neighbors, and the things that happen there explain why Dutch families get mad once in a while, like using a loose bath, without a tiled floor so that there is leakage.

(23) I-C-6 (Woman, 60, low-con, P6)
   (Daughter is not impressed by charm of foreign men) She says, they look at you [on the bus] as if they want to undress you with their eyes.

They are used to that there, that women and girls are not allowed to go out of the house. DO WE HAVE TO STAY INDOORS BECAUSE THEY ARE NOT USED TO THAT?

---

(24) I-D-4 (Woman, 35, high-con, P5)
(Turk gave his apartment to another Turkish family) Yes, maybe it is just talk, I don't know [hesitating].

---

(25) I-E-1 (Woman, 40, office, high-con, P6)
(S) My mother gets fish scales on her laundry when Spaniards upstairs clean their fish above it.

---

(26) I-E-1 (Woman, 40, office, high-con, P6)
(S) And with a colleague of mine, Moroccans live upstairs and they pee over her laundry.

---

(27) I-E-5 (Man, 66, retired fireman, high-contact, P4)
(S) The old lady next door was mugged by three young Surinamese kids.

---

(28) II-PA-1 (Woman, 27, secretary, high-con, P3)
(Greengrocer assaulted by a foreigner because he didn't want to sell after closing time. People standing around while the policeman took away the foreigner with force) (S) People were aggressive. But the opinions were divided. Some thought it was a scandal that the greengrocer was beaten up, and so found it natural that the policeman was rough with him. Others, "colored people quote unquote," had doubts about it (. . .)
I: Are these the kind of stories you hear more often here in the street?
W: (S) I don't hear much because I work the whole day. "The only things I hear is at the greengrocer's and well a bit through my contacts with the people next door." And I notice also that when elections are coming up I get leaflets of the CPN [Dutch Communist Party], but at the same time from the Centrum Party [anti-foreigner party], and that same evening a letter from the community center against that and "I read then this and that and that many colored people live here . . ." But I don't notice that and I don't care.

In these examples we find concrete stories but, at the same time, they illustrate stereotypes. Apparently, it is especially those events that confirm general prejudices—or what are known as such—that are paid attention to and reproduced in stories. In examples 21 and 22 we find two typical "leakage" stories, which are usually told to illustrate the kind of neighborly trouble autochthonous people claim to experience from ethnic minority groups that are not used "to our way of doing things." Apart from being stories about harassment, they also show, sometimes rather patronizingly, how stupid or backward "those people" still are. "They don't know how to . . ." is a typical introduction for such concrete stories. Notice that both stories are told by women in a low-contact area, attributed to an acquaintance and the maid, respectively, who live in "such a neighborhood."

In example 24, brief reference is made to the well-known (assumed) fact that foreigners take houses or are favored in housing by the city authorities. In this case, however, the woman who tells the story adds that maybe it is "just talk," which shows that people may be aware of the fact that even concrete stories may be made up. The following stories are more concrete and intended to illustrate how "dirty" foreigners can be. Sources this time are the mother and a colleague of the interviewed woman. To emphasize the truth of the first story, the woman adds that the interviewer "can go there herself and ask," giving the address. Similarly, the woman in example 23 gives an example of the traditional stereotype that foreigners are sexually aggressive—which does not occur often in our data. In retelling the experience of her daughter, as well as emphasizing the negative opinion of her daughter about such events (the story would, of course, be pointless if the daughter would happen to like such attention), she also adds an explanation of the behavior of the foreign men: Their women have to stay at home. Finally, the interviewee gives an indignant, rhetorically formulated, moral judgement: "We" Dutch women cannot be expected to do likewise and stay at home, just to avoid foreign men. One other aspect in this topic is the "right to our own territory" principle, which can be found in many concrete stories and stereotypes in which ethnic groups are assumed to infringe on the privacy, space, or rights of autochthonous people.

The brief example summarized in example 27 implicitly denotes a neighbor story about a mugging, which we have quoted because of its stereotypical nature in high-contact areas. Many elderly people refer to such stories, although most of them also add that until now they have not yet experienced such violence themselves. Yet, because such events take place, one or a few stories may be sufficient to influence many neighbors, and this is especially the case if they are being broadcast by the media. Indeed, most people refer to the media for such instances of crime rather than to concrete stories from known people.

Finally, the last example (28) is a nice reconstruction of an informal communication situation apparently being participated in by the interviewee. After the assault on the greengrocer by a foreign customer who reacted against the refusal of the greengrocer to help him after closing time, the policeman arrives and "firmly" takes the foreigner into custody. People watch and talk. The woman has understood that in such talk different perspectives are possible; about the assault itself, people may agree. But then, the treatment of the foreigner by the police is open to discussion. Rather unusually the woman also mentions the point of view of the Black bystanders. In most other examples in which ethnic group members (mostly Surinamese) are mentioned as sources of talk, they are quoted as saying negative things about other Surinamese, thereby functioning as the ultimate confirmation of own opinions: "They say so themselves." In the same example, this woman also adds some information about other information sources in the high-contact neighborhood: propaganda, political party leaflets, and even a letter from the community center protesting against the racist propaganda of the Centrum Party. Apart from the public media and everyday talk, there is apparently at least an important third source for both racist and antiracist opinions: pamphlets, leaflets, flyers, or public letters. Racist pamphlets generally confirm and emphasize in more explicit ways the negative stereotypes many people already have against foreigners, whereas the party letter may argumentatively try to defuse such racist writing, either by giving counterarguments, facts instead of prejudices, or simply by disqualifying it as racist. Unfortunately, we have very few further data beyond a few of these examples about the possible role of leaflets on everyday talk about ethnic groups. Further studies on racism in discourse that focus on this form of communication are necessary.

Conclusion

From the examples given in this section, we have been able to reconstruct at least in part what people (say they) hear from others about ethnic groups. We have observed first that there may be a general reluctance or even fear to engage in such talk, either because of strong norms prohibiting racist talk or because of possible retaliation from the others. Second, people sometimes even avoid reference to such talk or don't remember instances of it by claiming that there *is* not much talk about foreigners at all, whereas at the same time it is conveyed that you hear "those stories all the time." Third, the vast majority of references to talk by others is in general terms: Neighbors or just "other people" tell stories or say general negative things about ethnic minority members.

The topics of such talk are the well-known stereotypes we also discuss in Chapters 2 and 4: They live on welfare, cause unemployment (two stereotypes of which the inconsistency is rarely noticed by the speakers), have strange habits such as sheep slaughtering, mistreat their women, make loud music, cause leakages, are dirty, and, above all, they are aggressive and criminal. These stereotypes may be marked as such and resented by the speakers, they may be doubted or may be accepted as true generalizations. Yet, independent of the speaker, the stereotypes are frequently identical, which, of course, is exactly what stereotypes are all about. Thus, even if they are not generally endorsed, they are at least generally known. Whatever the direction of the actual attitude, the stereotypes about foreigners thus have become consensual.

Finally, concrete stories told by family members, friends, or neighbors also pertain to events that illustrate these general negative opinions. This suggests that not any odd, even negative, story will do when persuasive talk is engaged in. Impressive stories in this case should neither be unique nor specific, nor illustrate a nontypical negative characteristic of ethnic groups (their lack of tactics in soccer, for instance), but must confirm "what we all know already." In other words, personal communications hardly seem to add anything new to what people know and believe about ethnic groups, at least in a stage in which these have been living in the country for several years already. Talk about foreigners, thus, is often a replay, an exercise, and a confirmation of the dominant ethnic consensus.

5. The media

On many occasions, people refer to the media as a source of information or as a source of ethnic opinions with which they may agree or disagree. Newspaper articles or TV programs may be read or watched by millions of people, and also form a source of topics and beliefs for everyday talk and comment. Although this book does not specifically examine the role of the media in the expression or reproduction of ethnic prejudice, it is obvious that interpersonal communication about ethnic groups, especially in the low-contact areas, is heavily dependent on media information. A striking example during our field work in a low-contact area was the frequent reference to a well-known talk show (Sonja Barend) on Dutch television, in which people who had voted the racist Centrum Party were allowed to explain why they had done so. Reactions to this program were divided and show how media information may be interpreted and represented in different ways by different viewers.

To limit a potentially vast list of topics of passages in which people refer to the media as a source, we have selected those that are rather typical and that fit into the following practical content categories: (a) General negative, (b) Concrete negative, (c) Resentment of negative reporting, (d) Positive, and (e) Racist party propaganda.

a. General Negative: Crime Reporting

In this category, we find passages in which people mention the media in general, or the press in particular, for "evidence" about the negative characteristics of ethnic groups. Crime is the major topic in this case, although sometimes also other themes are mentioned, such as cultural differences or favorable treatment. Some of these topics are also discussed in racist party propaganda, which we deal with below. Passages in which people mention negative reporting specifically as a reason for their resentment against bad media treatment of ethnic groups are also treated separately below, as are more concrete, particular stories with a negative topic.

(29) I-G-8 (Woman, 60, works in laundromat, hi-con, P4)
(S) A lot of crime in the city, drugs, but no bad experiences, but you read about it in the paper . . .

(30) I-G-7 (Man, 45, market vendor, hi-con, P6)
(Decay of Amsterdam, crime) It is very dangerous. You have to look nowadays at the people, you read about it in the paper everyday, is that necessary but you also see, a while ago it was in the paper, that 80% of those foreigners are in jail, against 20% of Dutch.

(31) III-RL-3 (Woman, 40, low-con, P5)
(S) Crime of foreigners is much bigger, and that is not only in the most widely read morning paper [Telegraaf], but also in other newspapers. In nine out of ten cases, it is a foreigner . . .

(32) III-TM-3x (Woman, 58, secretary, low-con, P3)
People are TERRibly afraid and that is fed with everything you read in the paper, what you see on TV, what the radio tells you. That is a big factor. That people are afraid.

(33) III-AB-4x (Man, 77, retired construction worker, low-con, P5)
(S) Too many foreigners, and some of them are criminal, and now you sometimes think, again somebody murdered, you only have to open the newspaper sometimes three per day, and then people think primarily of those foreigners, and they quickly suppose, Oh, it must have been a Turk, or a Moroccan, and that is nonsense of course . . .

(34) I-Z-13 (Boy, 12, no-con, P5)
B: (It is getting much worse with all those foreigners, especially the Turks)
I: Why?
B: They stab you!
I: Do they?
B: That's what I mostly read in the paper . . .

(35) II-RA-2 (Woman/man, 62/65, retired, high-con, P4)
W: (S) Young Turkish women marry old men, have a lot of children.
I: Did you ever talk to those foreign women, what they think about that themselves?
W: No, you don't get any contact with them. They are not allowed to have contact with Dutch people.
I: Sometimes there is a language barrier.
W: Yes, but Madam you have to see it like this, they are not alLOWed to have contact with Dutch people, no.
I: How do you know, or
W: THAT, I have I have once uhh uhh read here and there, yes, in the paper, that well yes, that a WOman must stay INdoors, period . . .

The first five examples all refer to the media as a general source of reports about crime, and at the same time as the basis for feelings of insecurity and fear. People also mention the media as a source for their statistics, as in example 30, or calculate the incidence of minority crime by the estimated proportion of articles about crimes committed by ethnic minority group members. Of course, selective and biased memory plays an important role in this case: Even a few reports about minority crime are salient, and confirming negative attitudes are better recalled or generalized (see Chapter 4 for details about such biases in ethnic information processing).

The largest Dutch newspaper (*Telegraaf*), selling more than 750,000 copies read by probably two or three times as many people, pays a lot of attention to crime and is one of the few national newspapers that still mentions the ethnic background of defendants. As our other examples show, people are well aware of this, and many resent it. This conservative newspaper, which, it is remembered, chose the side of the occupying Nazis during the war, mentions ethnic backgrounds as a deliberate policy, and actions against it have been met by plain refusal by the editor and by the reluctance of the union of journalists to demand a change of that policy. Also, the constitutional freedom of the press as well as the difficulty of proving deliberate racist intent as required by the discrimination article of the law have up to the present continued to frustrate legal action against this practice.

Our data suggest that such ethnically biased crime reporting has a pernicious influence on the beliefs and, hence, on the ethnic attitudes of many readers. Because most people have no immediate personal knowledge about or experiences with (ethnic or other) serious crime, much information is borrowed from the press. In principle, it should be possible to show with these data that deliberate policies to mention the ethnic background of crime may indeed contribute to legally prohibited inciting of racial hatred against minority groups.

Some people are aware of the specific consequences of such reporting, as we see in example 33, in which a prejudiced man explicitly states that it is "of course, nonsense" that all or most crime is committed by foreigners. Despite these rational reactions, many people, also in our examples (see, e.g., example 32), at the same time have fears that may be partly based on this kind of crime reporting. Many interviewees, especially women, refer to the media for reasons for this fear and for their hesitation to go out at night or to visit the inner city. Compared to other cities in the world, Amsterdam is one of the safest. This suggests that fear, and in particular fear of "ethnic crime," is largely the result of crime construction by the authorities (the police) and the media, because it is also reproduced in everyday talk (Chibnall, 1977; Fishman, 1980; Hall et al., 1978). In a brief study about crime reporting in the Netherlands, Coenen and J.J.M. van Dijk (1976) suggest that the general score of "crime concern" among readers is directly correlated with the amount of crime news in the press: Readers of *Telegraaf* have the highest score. Conversely, once people have more fear of crime, they also tend to attend more than others to crime stories in the press. Thus, source or message characteristics are interactively related with the cognitions or emotions they help construct in the first place.

Example 35 is an instance of a different kind of information attributed to the media, namely, cultural differences in the treatment of women, a well-known stereotype in the Netherlands. The example is particularly instructive because the (female) interviewer is pressing the woman to specify how she knows "what everybody knows." The woman then resorts to the strategy of vaguely referring to a printed source, and although she probably doesn't remember a specific article, the topic comes up regularly in the press, and, therefore, has become common knowledge. Typically, however, it is not usually brought up in talk as a concern about women's rights, but rather as an example of the "backward" culture of "those foreigners." At most, the women are pitied, or the foreign men blamed, which may lead to well-known problems of substituting racism for antisexism (Essed, 1982). We mention this topic because it is also a typical media issue: Although in high-contact areas people actually see that many Turkish or Moroccan women are treated differently or have less freedom according to (present-day) Dutch norms, most people know about this from the press. The woman in example 35 indeed refers to the press rather than to her own experiences in the high-contact neighborhood where she lives.

Thus, not only crime reporting in the right wing popular press, but also ethnic reporting in other media, may often have negative associations or implications even when it is not overtly racist (see van Dijk, 1983a, 1987b). It is this overall picture that is relevant for judging the long-term impact of media influence. And the indirect and subtle forms of prejudice and discrimination especially may not be detected as such by many readers. In fact, in our examples we only found resentment against blatantly negative portrayals, as in crime reporting or racist party propaganda. This resentment is mostly passive, however. People generally do not react against racist discourse or portrayal whether by the media or in personal communication, for instance, by active protests or other forms of action. In our passages, the interviewees do not explicitly resent either the general tendency of the news media to represent minorities as a problem in most areas of social life, or against the under-representation of minority members as neutral or positive actors and spokespersons. Such findings of academic research are not common knowledge because they are not reported in the press. As we shall see in somewhat more detail in Chapter 6, antiracist research results about the media and other elite groups are in fact either ignored or ridiculed by the press.

b. Concrete Negative

Although both high- and low-preju-
diced people may refer to negative reporting in the media in a general
way, high-prejudiced people especially mention concrete examples of
events that show how criminal ethnic group members may be. In our
next two examples, we find retellings of such press stories, and especially the embedding of such stories in argumentation and reactions
make them interesting for our analysis of the reproduction of racism.

(36) I-C-6 (Woman, 60, low-con, P6)
We saw a program on television with a Dutch woman who was married
to such a, such a uhh Turk, and that that didn't work out at all, and that
wasn't even a small girl, but a school teacher . . .

(37) I-C-6 (Woman, 60, low-con, P6)
No, but that is true with those foreigners (???), and then you only have
to read the paper . . . How many of those cases that you read the
paper, it is practically always a Moroccan or a Turk or such who have
been involved in stabbing or shooting. Yes, and I think they could do
something about that, because the other day that uh uh uh . . . market
gardener, whom they have say uhh who a former employee, such a
Moroccan, such an illegal, knocked his brains out with a hammer, was
in the paper last week, and his wife was lucky, she was called too, she
thought God why is my husband staying out so late, and she also went
to that hothouse, and she calls him, and then somebody tells her: Come
here, because your husband is not well, but she thinks: WELL, there is
something wrong, I am going to get the dog, and he ran away, otherwise she would have been dead as well, and only because you helped
illegal Moroccans with a job. Yes, they have exploited them, that's what
they say at least, you know, but well I don't believe that either . . .

Both stories are told by the same highly prejudiced woman, living
in an elegant low-contact neighborhood of Amsterdam. It is the same
woman who, in our previous section, tells of the experiences told by her
daughter about foreign men "undressing her with their eyes," as well as
many other negative stories. In the first example, she mentions a TV
documentary in which a marriage between a Dutch woman and a foreigner went wrong. The example is, of course, used to argue that such
marriages, and in general "living with" foreigners, are impossible. She
mentions the fact that the woman was a teacher, and thereby suggests
that she was not just a "dumb kid" fooled by a foreigner, but an intelligent woman who must have made a deliberate decision (and who might
be supposed to have less prejudice against foreigners). This is again a
nice example showing how a single instance of a TV story may be interpreted negatively and then be generalized by viewers.

The second story has been discussed before (in Chapter 2) as a characteristic story about foreigners. The events as recalled from the press

report are retold in detail, as well as the woman's own very negative evaluation of the situation. Interestingly, she also briefly mentions (press?) information that might be interpreted as a reason for the murder (exploitation), but that information is simply rejected, whereas the positive evaluation of the "helping" victim is stressed. In other words, whatever the precise situation description of the press, the woman may very well reconstruct this situation according to her own opinions and attitudes.

c. Resentment of Negative Reporting

Several people resent negative reporting about ethnic minority groups and say so in our interviews. In the following examples, we see how people argue against this form of discrimination and how they see the media as a possible source for prejudices. It might be interesting to add that these kind of reactions are seldom published in the press, whether liberal or conservative. From our own studies of news and news production, and in particular from our investigations of the representation of ethnic groups in the media, it has appeared that the press in general is highly reluctant to publish (self-)critical articles or letters. And we suggested, above, that this is especially true in the Netherlands when ethnic reporting and racism are involved.

(38) III-TM-2xa/b (Man/woman, 18/49, student/secretary, low-con, P3/P3)
(Foreigners are blamed for everything, for instance crimes) W: And then it is of course a pity that there is maybe some crime in which Surinamese are involved. And then ten times it has been in the paper that a Surinamese stabbed someone or has heroin. You are Surinamese, and then, yes. People think as simple as that, I think. I don't know whether I'm right, but I suspect it is like that . . .

(39) III-AB-2x (Woman, 15, low-con, P2)
(Fear in the inner city) W: Because when you read the newspaper and a Dutch man has raped somebody it says J.B.H. So-and-so has, but when it is a Turk, it says A 26-year-old Turk from Such-and-such, then you think gosh, then you really get scared, like this morning we saw a murder again, or in De Jordaan [popular neighborhood in Amsterdam] close to a Turkish coffeehouse somebody was stabbed, and again it is a Turk. And then you ask yourself, maybe this Turk has provoked it, and . . .

(40) III-CB-3x (Woman, 69, corrector, low-con, P3)
I: (S) Do you have the impression from the papers that foreigners are more criminal than Dutch?
W: I don't know. I really couldn't tell, I would have to see the statistics. I canNOT say that. (. . .) But it does bother me when they [the paper] write about a Surinamese so-and-so, but I believe that is diminishing, people have commented on that in letters to the editor. They don't write that it is a Dutchman who has done so-and-so.

Notice in these three passages by three women that there does not seem to be a firm, preconceived criticism of the press, but rather a hesitantly formulated doubt about negative crime reporting. People resent, however, that the ethnic background of defendants is often mentioned and have the impression that this may contribute to their own fears as well as to those of others.

d. Positive Reports

The media also feature articles or programs that might be understood as positive or in favor of ethnic minority groups. Different reactions are possible in that case. A few people pick up the positive message and use it as evidence for their own positive beliefs. Often, this positive message is negative, however, in the sense that it is negative about Dutch people who are racist or have been discriminating against ethnic groups. Also, according to the findings by Hartmann and Husband (1974) a decade ago for the English press, people get most information about discrimination against ethnic groups from the media. This seems likely and our data confirm this, because in everyday talk among majority group members there are, of course, very few negative stories about their own group. An external, official instance, such as (a few!) TV programs, is the only possibility to discuss such topics systematically. Yet, people are generally aware of them, as they show indirectly when they state that "we are not allowed to say negative things because then we are accused of discrimination."

Other people plainly resent media messages or even incidental actors who advocate antidiscrimination or a positive attitude toward ethnic groups. In this case, the media appearance of antiracist people is *not* generalized but individualized as the (questionable) opinion of one single person. Or else, the media are viewed as the channel for the "institutional voice," associated with the power institutions, such as the national or local government, as we see in example 42 below.

(41) II-PD-5 (Woman/man, 60/65, high-contact, P6/P5)
(Sometimes I am so mad) They simply get priority. Television too, minorities, minorities. When you wake up you hear minorities, minorities . . .

(42) I-G-7 (Man, 45, market vendor, P6)
A few months ago I saw on TV, there was a minister who tells a Turk, a Turkish girl it was I believe in Sonja Barend's show and she says yes but the Dutch they put us off, then that minister says, I don't remember his name, but he says but the DUTCH have to adapt to those foreigners. I ask you, where are we heading like this?

(43) III-GE-3 (Woman, 38, low-con, P2)
(S) I used to think that there is no discrimination in the Netherlands.

But I am changing my mind about that. Although I do not see it personally, I read about it in the paper and see it on TV, and therefore it is
probably true, like Blacks who are not allowed to go into some dance
clubs . . .

(44) III-ES-2 (Woman, 32, social worker, low-con, P2)
      (S) Dutch people haven't become more tolerant these years. Of course
      I don't know this from personal experience, but from what I read and
      hear. Even the government makes it more and more difficult for immi-
      grant workers, like the recent debate in Parliament about a law pro-
      posing special constraints on young foreigners who want to marry a
      foreigner who still lives in the original country.

The woman in example 41 expresses her general resentment against
ethnic minority groups, as well as talk and media reports about them.
Instead of using the term *foreigner,* she intentionally and repeatedly uses
the formal term of *minority,* both ironically and scornfully. Thus, she
expresses at the same time the favorable attitude toward ethnic groups by
the institutions. The man in example 42 mentions a specific program
(again Sonja Barend's TV talk show), and two particular advocates of
the foreigner's case: a Turkish girl and a cabinet minister. He focuses
especially on the controversial issue of adaptation, which we earlier found
to be one of the most frequent topics in our interviews. The dominant
view is that ethnic minorities should integrate into Dutch society, and,
therefore the reproduced statement of the minister is commented on very
negatively, namely, as a completely wrong policy for Dutch society.

The other two examples specifically deal with media sources for information about ethnic discrimination. The last one is particularly revealing because it shows that less prejudiced people do not associate the
authorities at all with the case of the ethnic groups. On the contrary, the
government is perceived as devising and enacting laws that keep foreigners out as much as possible. The law referred to in this example was
eventually repealed (in 1985) because it simply didn't work according to
a research report, and not because it discriminated against foreign youths
in the Netherlands. It should be recalled here that practically all government or institutional actions are known to the public specifically through
the media. Laws, parliamentary debates, and policies, as well as the general issues of talk they give rise to, are again reproduced by the media,
and do not emerge from personal experiences or everyday talk.

Because, in this case, very important issues are involved, such as
rights of ethnic groups or protection against discrimination and racism,
it is, of course, highly relevant how the media represent such official
acts: positively, neutrally, or critically. We have been able to show (van
Dijk, 1983a), that the majority of the national press represents the official policies and acts in a neutral and sometimes positive way when ethnic affairs are involved. There is little explicit criticism in the press of

government policies that are unfavorable to ethnic minority groups. This leaves the reading public again with a dominant view on ethnic relationships, and they are deprived of repeated critical arguments against such policies. Indeed, example 44 is the only example in all our interviews in which the government is actually criticized for negative policies against ethnic minority groups. In most other cases in which people are critical, this is directed against the racist CP party, and this criticism is also in line with the dominant view, namely, that racism is limited to a fringe of extremist people and such a racist party. Let us examine a few instances that are particularly relevant for the latter type of media references.

e. Racist Propaganda

In the 1982 national elections for the Dutch parliament, the incredible happened—a small racist party (Centrum Party) managed to get one seat. This led to much confusion, also in the press, because journalists didn't know how to handle such a representative: avoid writing about him and his party altogether, or write critically, with the risk of giving too much publicity or raising sentiments of compassion with the "lonely hero." What they eventually did was what the press routinely does anyway: It did not systematically or critically report the racist backgrounds and links of the party or party members, but focused on incidents, conflicts, or fights in which the party was involved. Also, the media featured a long discussion about whether or not such a party should be prohibited. The dominant view in that discussion was that prohibiting any party was against the basic principles of a democratic society. Whether the rights of minorities, as protected by the first article of the Constitution, were threatened by the official existence and parliamentary legitimization of a racist party, was a view that was much less defended. As usual, the minority point of view was barely represented in the press.

As an official political party, the CP also had the right to claim TV time to broadcast its ideas. Which it did, and also in this way its antiforeigner (but officially not racist) program was made known to millions of TV viewers. Yet, at the same time, CP ideas were taboo is the dominant ideology, which led to the overall confusion of many people who endorsed its xenophobic propositions. This confusion also emerges in many of our interviews, especially those in group III, which were taken just after the election and during the media debate about the CP. By this time, the small percentages at the national level appeared to grow to a serious 10% in municipal elections in the newly built town of Almere, 30 miles from Amsterdam, to which many people from the capital's inner-city neighborhoods had moved, often also to escape from the urban

decay and the foreigners. Sonja, in her TV talk show, invited CP voters
to explain why they adhered to that party, and newspapers interviewed
CP voters, sometimes with the well-meant assumption that the very
reproduction of CP ideas would be sufficient to disqualify the party.

The following passages refer to this confused media debate and the
appearance of racist propaganda on TV:

> (45) III-SV-2x (Woman, 37, low-con, P2) (Divorced from Moroccan)
> (The Centrum Party) W: I am against that. I have seen that program on
> what's its name on Sonja Barend that was on TV. I don't know much
> about politics, but of course I am against it, that is uhh, no that is noth-
> ing for me. (. . .) (And in that talk show) (S) A Surinamese lady was
> explaining all that, she did that very well. And everybody was talking
> about that and some had voted for that party and a man from Rotterdam
> told that he thought that his children were put back because of the for-
> eign children. "And he really showed that on TV, he says foreign chil-
> dren get more classes."

> (46) III-MS-1 (Woman, 48, low-con, P2)
> (S) I saw that program on TV with the Centrum Party, in Sonja Barend's
> show, and heard this guy telling about the old inner-city neighbor-
> hoods, and I can imagine that people who doubt might be persuaded
> by what he said. Especially younger people, because the older ones
> remember the war too well.

> (47) III-RH-3a (Man, 50, typographer, low-con, P1)
> (S) It makes me sick when I see on TV in Sonja Barend's show about
> the Centrum Party that intentionally the bad situation in the country is
> blamed on the foreigners and that they profit from the credulity or the
> stupidity of the people to mislead them . . .

> (48) III-MI-2x (Man, 42, personnel chief, low-con, P2)
> I don't know whether you read that story in Volkskrant [a liberal news-
> paper] about Almere, a very bad story, because it lets all those people
> speak without commentary, like he gets ten thousand guilders child
> allowance, and that kind of things, without putting various small com-
> ments that it was largely nonsense. And only a week later, they wrote
> something against it. But you get such stereotypes, and so everybody
> thinks, gosh what a rubbish, next time I vote Centrum Party . . .

Some of the interviewees appear to understand that such programs or
press articles may influence people actually to believe what the CP says
about foreigners, such as blaming the economic crisis on them and, especially, resenting the assumed favorable treatment of ethnic groups such
as in education. In example 47, we find an example of a person who
resents interviewing CP members without giving critical comment.

On the whole, then, low-prejudiced people are aware of the crucial
role of the media in the diffusion of racist beliefs. In our examples discussed above, we have seen that their misgivings may be well founded:
People do use the media as a source for "legitimate" complaints against

the presence of foreigners. Ironically, by thus focusing on the views of CP voters, such people also use the dominant strategy of identifying racism in society with a small extremist party.

For many of the other people we interviewed, there is another approach. If they recognize that some of their own opinions are close to those advocated by the CP, they explicitly state that the party is not racist but just wants to "redress the balance," as one man puts it, or to go against assumed favorable treatment of foreigners (which is not only resented by the majority, but as "positive action," is also unacceptable to many of those who appear to have less prejudice against ethnic groups). In the 1986 elections the CP lost its seat in parliament.

Conclusion

From these few typical examples drawn from a large body of references to the media as a source of information and discussion about issues regarding ethnic groups, we may first conclude that the media are credited or criticized for bringing up negative stories about such groups. "Ethnic crime" reporting in particular is sometimes resented, although other readers may use such stories as evidence for their fear of or prejudices against foreigners. Positive reports or programs are rarely mentioned, and, if so, it is done mostly critically by those who disagree with this kind of favorable treatment. Racist propaganda is normatively rejected by many of the people we interviewed but, at the same time, it may be mitigated by simply denying its racist nature or ignored by rejecting it as unacceptable. Even if some media users are conscious of the negative picture and impact of ethnic reporting in the media, it may be assumed that the more subtle forms of discrimination especially may be unwillingly adopted as an acceptable opinion by many people. Whether received positively or critically, media messages on many ethnic issues influence the topical agenda of everyday talk. This is especially the case for those people who have no daily contacts with ethnic groups and for those topics that cannot be based on personal observation or communication alone: crime and crime statistics, immigration, official policies, national politics and the role of racist parties, and discrimination.

It may also be assumed that whatever variance there may be in the reception of such messages by individual readers or viewers, the prevalence of the dominant views in the media will confirm an official "consensus view" by most of the public. At the same time, many other people pick up and selectively recall precisely those negative stories that are sometimes intentionally and mostly uncritically brought by the media as examples of officially unacceptable opinions. And because ethnic groups are also minorities in the media, as journalists, actors, or speakers, and the dominant view is not antiracist either, the public has no exemplary media models of the way to counter racism.

This also holds for the reproduction of media-based issues and topics in everyday talk. People know ethnic stereotypes very well and are able to tell many stories that portray ethnic groups negatively. In a rather general way, they also know about discrimination. Yet, there is neither widespread, media-based exercise in antiracist talk, nor a critical potential and consciousness for the analysis of everyday and subtle forms of racism in society as a whole. Racism is isolated and attributed to a few extremists or to "stupid people," as several of our interviewees (from a low-contact neighborhood) put it. Indeed, racism tends to be associated with poor people and poor neighborhoods. It is seldom covered as a systemic phenomenon in society, let alone as something that also characterizes elite groups and institututions. This is, of course, in line with the dominant view of the political and academic elites. Indeed, if there is one overall influence of the media, it is not just that their dominant picture of ethnic groups tends to be subtly, and sometimes even blatantly, negative, but rather that they do not support antiracism. We return to this issue in Chapter 6.

6. Further facts about sources and topics of talk

Our qualitative analyses of a number of passages in which people indicate which personal or public sources are used for their information and beliefs about ethnic affairs should finally be complemented with a somewhat more systematic account of the topics that occur in such references. We have found that a few (stereo)typical topics are attributed to the media or to talk with other people. Yet, we should give the complete list of all topics, and indicate which people from which areas mention which topics from which type of source.

Topic Categories

To do this, we subjected all 198 passages in which people refer to other sources to further topical analysis and isolated the few (macro)propositions that summarize such passages. Next, we classified these propositions (totaling 228) according to categories such as overall negative or positive opinions or facts about ethnic groups, crime, cultural differences, socioeconomic resentment, and perceived competition (such as "they take our jobs, houses, and live on welfare"), and topics such as discrimination and racism. Table 3.1 gives a list of such categories and their frequencies in the passages about communicative events.

The first obvious conclusion from the topic frequencies listed in Table 3.1 is that most topics are negative. According to the reports of people interviewed, based on what they recall or find most salient in talk or media reports about ethnic groups, most information consists of negative stereotypes.

This may mean that such sources are, in fact, mostly negative, or that people recall negative information more often. It may also be the case that talk about foreigners is itself stereotypically associated with negative topics. If that should be true, people recall that such conversations or media messages were (mostly) negative just because they know that people generally say negative things about ethnic groups. This would be possible for vague and general references to talk and the media, but hardly for specific communicative events or their contents. For all mentions of negative communication however, it is not likely that they would be the result of a prejudice against one's own in-group. Therefore, we may assume that such mentions may derive from generalizations based on experience. On the other hand, as "others" are very often attributed with negative opinions, some of the negative source evaluations may also be interpreted as a move of a positive self-presentation strategy.

Table 3.1 shows that the well-known prejudiced views about ethnic groups dominate. In fact, most topics are also featured on the list of stereotypical topics discussed in Chapter 2. In other words, there is convergence between overall topics of discourse and those attributed to other sources. Topics 4 to 6 (out of a total of 57) cover the resentment against assumed socioeconomic cheating and being favored in housing and employment, as well as the usual complaints about cultural differences and neighborly harassment. Together with crime and aggression, they constitute 102 (45%) of the 228 topics mentioned. Because the mean prejudice score for people who mention these topics is approximately the same as the overall prejudice means, these topics are apparently mentioned by various kinds of people, both in high- and in low-contact areas, including people who disagree with these stereotypes.

Most frequent as a single topic is that of the assumed crime, aggression, or threat attributed to foreigners. Many of the crime and aggression topics are attributed to the media, and we have commented on the role of the media in crime reporting in the previous section. Apparently, the crime topic is mentioned especially by people with a relatively high prejudice score. The same is true for people who mention various segre-

TABLE 3.1:   Topics of Talk and Media References and Their Frequencies
             (numbers between parentheses: mean prejudice score of people
             who mention this topic)

1. Generally negative about EM	33	(3.3)
2. Generally positive about EM	10	(3.3)
3. Crime, aggression, threat, and so on	45	(4.1)
4. They are on welfare, favored in housing	15	(3.7)
5. Cultural differences (religion, slaughtering, language, treatment of women	20	(3.4)
6. Make noise, loud music, cooking smells, leakages	22	(3.5)
7. Discrimination and racism	32	(2.9)
8. Denial of racism	6	(4.2)
9. Segregation: they must leave, stay on their own	9	(4.2)
10. They must/do adapt	4	(3.0)
11. They are cause of economic recession and problems	6	(1.8)
12. There are conflicts with or among EM	6	(3.3)
13. Other topics (N must adapt to EM, N don't dare to talk negatively about EM, and so on)	20	(4.8)
14. No topics mentioned	6	(4.3)

gation topics, such as "they should stay on their own," "they should leave the country," or "we don't want them as neighbors or in this area," as well as for people who deny or belittle racism in the country. Also, some of the other topics are typically mentioned by people with higher prejudice scores, such as the topic that Dutch people do not dare to speak up against ethnic groups.

The frequent negative stereotypes are partially balanced by the more positive topic of discrimination and racism, that is, a topic that expresses criticism of people in the in-group. This topic comes up especially in references to the media, mostly in low-contact areas. As may be expected, the prejudice score for people who mention this topic is lower than the mean (2.9). This is also the case for the "blaming the victim" topic that foreigners are the cause of the economic recession, but that topic is predominantly mentioned in a critical context. There are only a few topics that are generally positive about ethnic groups, but the mean prejudice score for people who mention these topics suggests that they are often reacted to negatively. Overall, the more positive or critical topics attributed to other people or the media constitute only about 20% of all topics.

Although the majority of the topics referred to are negative, people sometimes react to them critically, but we have seen earlier that this happens only in 18 of 198 passages. In only 37 passages do people have opinions that are not in agreement with the negative facts as reported (a figure that might be compared with the 38 people who score 1 or 2 on the prejudice scale). The majority of the passages show agreement (58), a neutral reaction, or no reaction (114).

Concluding this general analysis of topics mentioned in references to communicative events about ethnic minorities, we find that such attributed source topics are predominantly negative and stereotypical. Crime and perceived socioeconomic and cultural conflicts account for a large part of the topics, although the theme of discrimination is also mentioned often. We assumed that people either correctly generalize about such communications as being prejudiced and as portraying minorities negatively, or that they have a stereotypical picture (and, hence, selective memory) of such communications as being negative a priori. Positive and critical topics are mentioned much less, and it was assumed that they might be practically absent in everyday talk. Except for normative generalizations and the generally known occurrence of discrimination, there is no standard way of communicating more positively about ethnic groups or ethnic relations. Because many people either agree with the negative facts or opinions, or do not react to them critically, we may finally assume that in communications about ethnic groups, the negative points of view dominate, and this is also how most people represent and recall such communications.

Media or Personal Communication?

With a number of factors, it is interesting to investigate whether they correlate with topics mentioned in references to communication sources. A primary factor is, of course, the nature of the source itself: What topics tend to be reproduced from the media, and which ones are attributed to personal communication? Such an analysis may give us the necessary clues that might indicate the nature of the reproduction or persuasion process. Do some topics come up in media communications especially or rather in personal talk? We assumed earlier that conversations take many topics from the media, especially those that are not based on people's everyday experiences. This means that there is no unique source for topics. At most, we can hope to trace some tendencies, such as where certain topics come up first, where given topics dominate, or, even more importantly, where people themselves think certain topics and issues come from. In the analysis of our data, it is this last dimension of the reproduction process that is most relevant to us. For instance, if topics have been discussed specifically in everyday talk but people attribute them to the media, this must have a reason, which may not just be bad or biased memory, but may have to do with the social relevance, credibility, and presentability of topics and their reproduction in talk.

Table 3.2 shows whether some topics are attributed to the media or to personal sources. Among the media source, we differentiate between general references to "the media," the newspaper, or TV. The "other" media sources are the radio, books, magazines, textbooks, and leaflets. For the personal sources, we distinguish between different types of personal communication, depending on the (closeness of) participants. PC1 is "personal communication distance 1," which denotes talk with family members; PC2 refers to talk with friends; PC3 with acquaintances and colleagues; PC4 with neighbors; PC5 with unidentified people in the neighborhood and strangers; PC6 with just "other people" in general; and, PC7 with the authorities. In a few cases, people also mention ethnic minorities themselves as a source. We have grouped PC>4 together as "distant contacts," mostly represented by a vague reference to other people. As may be expected, there are few personal communication contacts with the authorities (as such, there are one or two references to talk with policemen), and in four cases people refer to communications with ethnic minority group members.

Although for many cells in Table 3.2, the absolute numbers are too small to make reliable conclusions, they nevertheless give us an impression about the sources of some major topics. The "general negative" topic apparently is attributed to the press, television, and to talk of unspecified others. Typical expressions are "you hear and read so many negative things about foreigners," or "they write terrible things about them in the paper." With this topic, apparently, the source indication is also general and vague. Crime and aggression are topics that are attributed mostly to the press (and much less to TV), and to talk in the family, the neighborhood, and with "others." It is thus both a general and distant topic of talk: It is attributed to the media but is also a topic that is discussed in everyday conversations with family members and neighbors. The mundane problems of everyday interethnic perception and contacts, represented by topics 4, 5, and 6, are apparently partially drawn from the press and television, but obviously are more often discussed in the family, with acquaintances, and in the neighborhood, as may be expected for such typical everyday conflicts, biased perceptions, and prejudices. Discrimination and racism, as we have argued before, are typical media topics. Indeed, in this case the notion of the media in general as a source indication is used relatively often. It is hardly a topic that comes up in everyday talk, that is, according to what people indicate. At most it is mentioned by people in general: "People (they) say that foreigners (they) are being discriminated against, (but)..."

A remarkable fact that might be concluded from Table 3.2 is that people hardly ever refer to friends as a source. This might be a terminological effect: The interviewed may simply refer to friends as "people they know," but, in general, we may assume that "ethnic affairs" is something talked about in the family or in the neighborhood, or what one hears from unspecified "others." This would also explain why several people

TABLE 3.2:   Topic Sources

Topic		Gen	Paper	TV	Other	PC1	PC2	PC3	PC4	PC > 4
		Media (N = 100)				*Personal Communication (N = 136)*				
1	General negative	0	8	7		0	3	2	4	13
5	Crime and aggression	3	13	3		6	2	4	8	9
4-6	Competition, conflict, and cultural differences	1	5	5		7	2	10	13	13
7	Discrimination and racism	7	8	12		1	2	2	3	7
	Other topics	3	5	7		6	1	3	3	12
	Total	14	39	35	12	20	10	21	31	54

indicate that they do not actually discuss the topic explicitly with friends (who may well live outside the neighborhood), but rather with (nuclear) family members and other people in the neighborhood.

The prejudice levels associated with the passages that yield the media references in Table 3.2 center on a mean of 3.3, again with a strong area effect: In high-contact areas, prejudice levels of people referring to the media is rather high (4.2 for the press and 5.3 for TV). The same holds for topics mentioned. Yet, reference to the crime topic (especially as reported in the press) is made generally by people with higher prejudice scores (a mean of 4.0), whereas for people who refer to the discrimination topic, it is generally low (below 3.0), especially for references to the media in general and to the press (there are somewhat more, or more, prejudiced people who resent discussion of discrimination on TV). Similar prejudice differences hold for people mentioning topics from personal communication: The highest score (4.3) is for people who refer to personal communications about crime, and the lowest score (3.2) is for references to personal communications about discrimination. Here, too, there are substantial differences between personal communication references in high- (4.2) and low-contact (3.2) areas. In general, the prejudice level drops with increasing communication distance: Most prejudiced are people who refer to (any topic from) talk in the family. Talk about crime in the family is mentioned by interviewees who score a mean of 5.2. This suggests that source, topic selection, and recall may be associated with ethnic attitude: As may be expected, people with high prejudice levels tend to mention the most negative characteristics of ethnic groups.

Clarification of the Different
Types of Figures Used

A brief clarification about the various figures used in the tables in this and other sections is in order. It may be recalled that data from 143 interviewed persons are given. From these interviews, 198 passages that contained references to communications about ethnic groups have been isolated. These passages together expressed 228 topics (the same topics several times, of course), which were classified in 20 categories, whereas in six cases, a source reference was just general and did not mention an identifiable topic. Associated with these topics, we now find 236 references to sources, which means that, in some cases, both personal sources and media are indicated for the same topic. Because the 100 references to the media were made in 78 passages, it may also be the case that people refer to several media at the same time, as we have seen in our examples of the previous section. In other words, our various counts pertain to (a) interviewed persons, (b) communication passages (often several for one person, sometimes none for one person), (c) topics mentioned in such passages, and (d) references to or indications of specific source types.

Prejudice scores are primarily associated with interviewees, of course, but in this section they also carry over to the passages in which communicative events are mentioned. That is, if one person refers to several communicative events, each of these passages is associated with the prejudice score of the speaker. It follows that higher prejudice averages may also be caused by the higher amounts of (negative) passages of highly prejudiced persons (and the converse for lower prejudice scores). In this way, we capture the general incidence of prejudice in communication: It may be based on the level of prejudice of the speakers and/or on the amount of prejudiced communications (reproductions) of those speakers.

Variations in Source References

Before we continue with the variations among people in their topic mentions, let us briefly analyze the overall differences between the various source types (media or personal communication) as they are related to some traditional demographic properties of the people interviewed (we return to these social backgrounds of prejudice in communication in Chapter 6). There might be age, gender, area, occupation, or education differences in source uses. It was already suggested that the combination of area and occupation may explain more reliance on the media (or on the press), for instance. Similarly, young and old people, men and women, may have different communication patterns, and these might also account for differences in their (reference to or reliance on) different communication sources when information about ethnic groups is involved.

In Table 3.3, we have listed some of the relevant figures for the respective source types. Again, some of the cells feature low absolute numbers, so that merely some hypothetical tendencies may be observed. (Recall that the same "source passage" may feature several references to specific sources.)

If we take area first, we find that in the low-contact areas, much less reference is made to the media than in high-contact areas. Personal communication is more frequent as a source in both high- and low-contact areas, but in high-contact areas, it forms 78% of all source references and in low-contact areas, it is 55% of all source references. This is, of course, hardly surprising because people in low-contact areas do not have many other sources than the media for their information about ethnic groups. Several interviews explicitly express this fact and indicate that people in the neighborhood do not talk about ethnic groups very much. For personal sources, there is a tendency in the high-contact areas toward sources such as family, acquaintances, neighbors, and others. In the low-contact areas, people tend to refer especially to information from friends.

There are not many striking differences in media uses between men and women. We had earlier found that women tend to talk about sources more often than men (women who are 55% of the interviewed provide 63% of the passages that refer to communication sources). Comparatively, men refer to TV somewhat more often. The differences appear rather in personal communications: Women more often refer to family sources (typically their husband or children), and somewhat more often to acquaintances, whereas men rely more on friends as a source.

As far as age differences are concerned, we must first recall that we have many more passages from people 50 years old and over than by young people under 30. In comparison, the younger people generally refer to the media more often, but hardly mention TV as a source. For personal contacts, the older people mostly refer to family members, to neighbors, and people in general. The younger people tend to favor friends as a source. This pattern is somewhat similar to the one observed above for men and women.

For the few data we have about job (and, hence, education) differences, the tendency is again that high-skill job people refer less to their own family, friends, or neighbors as sources than the people with low-skill jobs. They refer more often to acquaintances or colleagues or to people in general. These figures, however, are, of course, partly dependent

TABLE 3.3:   Differences in References to Media and Personal Communication
(N = number passages; M = number of passages about a specific source)

	N	M	Media Gen	Paper	TV	M	PC1	PC2	PC3	PC4	PC ≥ 5
low-contact areas	121	61	11	34	28	74	8	9	8	14	35
high-contact areas	77	17	3	5	7	62	12	1	13	17	19
men	74	33	4	18	17	51	3	6	6	15	21
women	124	45	10	21	18	85	17	4	15	16	33
age > 50	103	39	5	18	18	71	13	3	10	17	28
age < 30	31	16	6	10	2	30	2	5	4	4	5
high-skill jobs	40	16	3	9	9	28	1	1	5	6	15
low-skill jobs	48	20	1	11	10	32	4	3	2	12	11

on an area factor: Low-skill job people tend to live in the poorer high-contact neighborhoods, for which we witnessed similar distributions of source references.

The general pattern that emerges from these few figures is that low-contact (and, hence, also high-skill job) people—sometimes critically—depend on the media more often than people in high-contact areas, whereas in the high-contact areas, people have more information from family, neighbors, or unspecified people. Women and old people tend to refer to family sources more often than men and younger people, who prefer friends as a source of information about ethnic groups. Older people seem to depend more on TV than younger people and also have more information from their neighbors. And finally, high-skill job people tell us less about what their family members or friends told them but rather refer to acquaintances or people in general.

Topics in Different Areas

People may mention different topics in different areas, and there may also be variation among people of different age or gender. For a number of crucial topics, we have calculated these differences. Table 3.4 gives frequencies for mentions of some topics for both high- and low-contact areas (i.e., numbers of passages mentioned by people from these areas accompanied by the prejudice scores for the people who mention these passages).

TABLE 3.4:   Area Differences for Some Topics

Topic		High-Contact N = 77	Low-Contact N = 121
1	General negative about EM	10 (13%)	23 (19%)
2	Crime and aggression	22 (29%)	23 (19%)
4-6	Welfare, cultural differences, harassment	25 (33%)	27 (22%)
7	Discrimination and racism	6 (7%)	26 (21%)

We first notice that the classic stereotypical topics (crime, socioeco-nomic competition, and neighborly conflicts) are mentioned more often in the high-contact areas, as may be expected. In low-contact areas, there are more references to generally negative topics, but this is often the case in a general, that is, less concrete context: Speakers refer to what people in other neighborhoods say. Similarly, in high-contact areas there is not much talk about discrimination and racism, which, however, is a dominant topic in the low-contact areas. Indeed, our data strongly suggest that low-prejudice people and, in our case, also many people in low-contact areas, tend to talk about the discrimination and racism of other people and other neighborhoods. Obviously, these area differ-ences are closely associated with educational and occupational differ-ences between people, so that the amount of contact alone is not the only factor explaining these differences.

Age

One of the most conspicuous differ-ences in ethnic attitudes is related to age. We have suggested before that older people tend to have higher prejudice scores than young people. One of the reasons may be that younger people have more everyday and more natural contacts with ethnic peers, such as at school. Another fac-tor is, of course, education: Younger people are generally better edu-cated. Our interviews, for instance, those in which younger people were interviewed with one or both parents, also suggest that they resent the sometimes bigoted opinions of their parents. In their references to com-munications about ethnic groups, they may also attend to different top-ics, of course, simply because they will have different contacts than older people. Several school children mention discussions about racism at school, and such explicitly antiracist education probably provides dif-ferent topics of talk or different media interests.

Yet, generally, the differences are not dramatic: Overall, both younger and older people account for similar percentages of the various topics. Their differences in prejudice levels (indicated by P), however, suggest

TABLE 3.5:   Age Differences for Some Topics

Topic	< 30 N = 31	$\bar{P}$	≥ 50 N = 103	$\bar{P}$
1	General negative about EM	4 (13%)	2.5	16 (16%)	3.8
3	Crime and aggression	9 (29%)	3.0	26 (25%)	4.7
4-6	Welfare, cultural differences, and so on	6 (19%)	2.5	24 (23%)	4.1
7	Discrimination and racism	11 (35%)	2.2	13 (12%)	3.5

that younger people will often mention a negative stereotype in a more critical way, whereas older people will more often agree with the negative facts or opinions reported. And, in both cases, when crime or aggression are referred to, the prejudice level of the people who do so is higher than the mean for the group. The most conspicuous difference is the mention of discrimination and racism, which is the most frequent topic of young people and the least frequent for older people. And, for both groups, the people who do mention discrimination and racism have lower prejudice scores than the mean prejudice level of the group. Difference of interest and solidarity, daily interaction with ethnically different peers, and sometimes the beginnings of antiracist education at school may account for such a marked distinction between the old and young generations.

Gender

In general, there are no gender differences in ethnic prejudice, and for that reason, there is little reason to believe that there will be different ethnically related interests between men and women. We already found that there is an interaction with age in this case: Elderly women tend to be more prejudiced than elderly men, whereas younger women seem to score even lower than their male peers on the prejudice scale. Are there also differences in topics men or women tend to mention when referring to other communications? After all, there are significant social and cultural differences in interest and occupation, and we may expect that women talk more often with other women than with other men, whereas men will have more male communication input. Also, as we have seen above, women tend to refer more often to family talk. In Table 3.6, we do not detect large differences, however (also, the numbers are too low to make serious conclusions).

Women who refer to discrimination and racism tend to have lower prejudice scores than the men who do. On the other hand, references to socioeconomic competition, cultural differences, and neighborly conflicts are made more often by (more prejudiced) women. In our inter-

TABLE 3.6:   Gender Differences for Some Topics

Topic		Men N = 73	$\bar{P}$	Women N = 122	$\bar{P}$
1	General negative	14 (19%)	3.2	18 (15%)	3.3
3	Crime and aggression	16 (22%)	4.0	29 (24%)	4.1
4-6	Welfare, cultural differences, and so on	13 (18%)	3.3	38 (31%)	3.6
7	Discrimination and racism	14 (19%)	3.3	18 (15%)	2.7

views, as is probably the case generally, they are indeed the ones who most often tell the stories about conflicts with (ethnic) neighbors and about cultural differences such as living conditions, clothing, cooking, and so on. Although the communication references do not show this very clearly, they also seem to be more bothered, for obvious reasons, by crime and aggression, and we may assume that this will also be an important topic in their everyday talk with others. Recall that women, in general, tell us more often about talk with others. Of all interviewed, 45% were men and 55% were women, but the passages with references to communications with others are told relatively more often by women (62%) than by men (38%).

Occupation/Education

Finally, there are also occupation/ education effects in differences of topics mentioned. Unfortunately, however, our data about these demographic properties of the interviewed are incomplete (because initially we didn't want to mix strictly informal interviews with a standard questionnaire asking for such data; later, such a brief list of questions was filled out, after the interview). We have data about the occupations of 60 out of 143 people interviewed. Most of the other people are retired, jobless, or are housewives. In our occupation scale, most of them would score at the level of 1 (unskilled work). The highest level is 7 for jobs that require postgraduate specialization (medical specialists, university teachers, and so forth). Of all interviewed about whom we have data, 20 scored high (>4) on occupation, and 40 scored low (1 to 4). Generally, the high-skill occupation people scored lower on the prejudice scale (2.7) than the low-skill occupation people (4.1), a difference that is very similar to the age differences discussed above. It should be noticed, though, that this difference, of course, also embodies educational differences as well as area or degree of contact (with ethnic group) differences. Of the people with better jobs, of whom most also have a better education, nearly all lived in well-to-do low-contact areas.

TABLE 3.7:   Occupation Differences for Some Topics

Topic	High-Occupation N = 40	$\bar{P}$	Low-Occupation N = 48	$\bar{P}$
1 General negative	8	2.5	12	3.9
3 Crime and aggression	5	2.8	12	4.8
4-6 Welfare, cultural differences, and so on	11	3.0	8	4.2
7 Discrimination and racism	7	2.4	8	4.1

For the people who refer to communications, the mean occupation is at the intermediate (3.7.) level (for 88 passages of people whose occupational background was known). The few data we have only provisionally suggest that people with higher-skill jobs (and education) refer less to crime and aggression, which is indeed much less of an issue in their neighborhood. On the other hand, they seem to mention more often the economic and cultural stereotypes.

The Approximate Nature of Prejudice Levels

As a final word of caution, it should be stressed again that the differences in prejudice levels we have found, such as for age, area, and occupation, are differences in (interpreted) talk of people. That is, they have been calculated from what people actually say, which opinions are formulated, or which topics are talked about. We have assumed that informal interviews and a subtle discourse analysis are rather reliable methods for establishing prejudice schemata and contents for people. That is, the better educated especially are less likely to be able to dissimulate their opinions in the brief, socially desirable answers of preformatted questionnaires. We have seen in the previous chapter that there are too many unintended properties of conversations that may indicate some features of people's attitudes and the transformations these may undergo in the strategies of positive self-presentation.

On the other hand, also in informal interviews, the better educated may still have more control and social monitoring in their talk, especially when delicate topics such as ethnic minorities or discrimination are discussed. For them, and especially the liberals among them, the possible inference that they may be prejudiced or racist may even be more face-threatening than for other people. After all, they often consider themselves as the moral guardians of society. Also, due to a lack of daily experiences with crime, urban decay, socioeconomic competition, or neighborly conflicts about noises or smells, their prejudices have neither been "tested" yet nor forced to become more specific. As many people in the low-contact areas recognize themselves: It is easy for them to be "tolerant." Indeed, when people have less experiences, they probably also have less negative experiences that may be used to support ethnic prejudice. From other research, however, we may conclude that as soon as people with better education and better jobs have experiences with ethnic groups, their prejudices will develop along the lines of assumed superiority, social and economic competition, or threats perceived in their own contexts (Essed, 1984; Wellman, 1977). Just as in their talk, their forms of discrimination may appear more subtle, however. Yet, because these people have more power, the consequences are usually much more serious: They are the ones who control politics, the institutions, the job market, education, and social affairs. They are the ones who make the decisions that underlie the macroinequities of racism in society.

In this chapter, we have seen some effects of the actions of one such group, namely, journalists. What people report about the media, and what we have found in our earlier studies of media coverage of ethnic affairs, give us reason to believe that actual occupational practices may well exhibit ethnic prejudice. Maybe these prejudices are more subtle, maybe they are less stereotypical than those studied above, but they may well be more influential. We found that many beliefs about ethnic groups derive from the media, and even if not all these beliefs reflect the opinions of individual journalists, the uncritical media reproduction of prejudices of others may well be crucial in the formation and confirmation of ethnic prejudice in society. In Chapter 6, we continue this discussion about the role of the elite in the reproduction of racism in more detail.

Conclusions

In this chapter, we have examined in detail what people attribute to communication sources when they speak about ethnic minority groups. This question is important because it suggests what information or beliefs expressed by such sources tend to be used again by the "next" speakers as sources for new recipients. Within the complex discursive environment of talk about minorities, the mass media (the newspaper, radio, television) and personal communications appeared to be most relevant as sources for speakers, at least for the salient ethnic group in the present situation. Less explicit, but maybe no less influential, is the "hidden persuasion" (Packard, 1957) of advertising, movies, novels, comics, children's books, or textbooks in various stages of socialization or in different situations of everyday life.

We have found that in all passages in which people attribute information or beliefs to other sources, the negative topics are by far most prominent. Aside from generally negative opinions, we find frequent mention of such stereotypical topics as crime and aggression, perceived socioeconomic competition ("they take our houses and jobs, and they abuse our social services"), and the well-known cultural differences and conflicts. Such topics are predominantly attributed to personal communications, especially with family members and people in the neighborhood, and especially by people from high-contact areas. The media (mostly TV) are more often credited, mostly by people from low-contact areas, with information about discrimination and racism, although the press especially is mentioned (and criticized) for its crime reporting.

Overall, the use and attribution of topics to such sources is also influenced by various social factors. As may be expected, people from high-contact neighborhoods refer more often to the typical "experiential" stereotypes, such as crime, aggression, competition, and cultural differences, whereas people in low-contact neighborhoods refer more generally and abstractly to negative properties of minorities, on the one hand, and to discrimination and racism, on the other. Except for the topic of discrimination and racism, age does not seem to influence topic selection very much, despite the traditional finding that the elderly score generally higher on the prejudice scale. The same holds for gender differences, although there seems to be a tendency for women to refer more often to competition and especially to the usual complaints about cultural differences. Occupation and education are closely linked with the area factor: That people with lower-skill jobs (and education) focus more on crime and aggression is, of course, partly due to their less safe neighborhoods. And, conversely, lack of neighborhood experiences will often cause the better educated to pay more attention to general issues of socioeconomic competition and cultural differences.

The qualitative analysis of the interview passages showed that people reproduce from sources precisely those topics that confirm the dominant prejudices of a racist society. Even when they are doubtful or critical of negative opinions reported, people know them and talk about them. Although generally, negative facts mentioned about minorities also tend to be reacted to negatively, especially when attributed to personal communications. Thus, reproduction of prejudice mostly means agreement with a source. This suggests that sources are mostly referred to for evidence that may be used to bolster one's own prejudices or, that is, argumentatively used in persuasive communication. Few people counter negative talk with positive information or beliefs, often simply "to avoid trouble." On the other hand, it also appears that sometimes people avoid (very) negative talk, for instance, because of the official norm that prohibits racist utterances, for fear of retaliation (by ethnic minority group members), or because they might get into trouble with family members or friends.

Our analysis of attributed sources and their topics sketches further outlines of the process of communicative reproduction of ethnic attitudes within the in-group. It shows that people do talk very often about foreigners, especially when they have become salient in their neighborhood. Together with the public communications of the mass media, such conversations are said to be about precisely those (negative) topics people also deal with in their own statements. Thus, speakers suggest that they participate in a tacit (if not outspoken) consensus, according to which foreigners are a real problem for "us" in all relevant domains of social life. It has also become clear that people do not always agree with what they hear or read, but their reactions to racist talk tend to be neutral or passive. Both in their own statements, and in their references to the media or to personal talk with others, explicit and antiracist counterarguments are rare.

The lack of an antiracist consensus also shows in the lack of routine expressions or interactions that may challenge prejudiced talk in conversations. If not always persuasive, negative stories or statements are at least pervasive in society. They are about "what everybody knows" and the consensus thus also becomes rooted in commonsense representations and strategies for talk about foreigners. The individual actively reproduces the pervasive ethnic prejudices that charaterize the consensus and, at the same time, recognizes the legitimacy inferred from such a consensus. The conflict between the higher norm that prohibits racism, and the actual reproduction of racism through talk and action, is thus resolved: Our negative stories about foreigners are not prejudiced or racist, they are true and legitimate complaints, and everybody says so.

In the previous chapter, we have seen how people formulate such opinions and strategies in conversation. We have now seen how, and how much of, these may be reproduced from various sources within a broad consensus of acceptable talk about foreigners, both in private and in public. In the next chapter, we should finally go below this (socially relevant) surface of what is said. We need to investigate the underlying cognitive properties of such ethnic opinions and prejudiced attitudes, as well as the complex social information processes that determine their uses in our understanding and representation of discourses from communication sources and in our own contributions to conversational interaction. We can really explain what people tell and how they do so only with the help of such a cognitive framework embedded in an account of the social functions of prejudiced talk in society.

4

The Cognitive Dimension:

Structures and Strategies of Ethnic Prejudice

1. Cognitions and attitudes

1.1. ETHNIC PREJUDICE AS SOCIAL COGNITION

Communicating ethnic prejudice is a process that involves social attitudes of in-group members about out-groups. As we shall see in more detail in the next chapter, interpersonal communication and persuasion research is largely based on assumptions about attitudes and attitude change. Similarly, classical work on ethnic prejudice (e.g., Allport, 1954) also assumes that prejudice should be accounted for in terms of (negative) attitudes about ethnic or racial groups. In this respect, our approach runs parallel to the traditional conceptions of persuasive communication and prejudice.

However, on other points, we propose a different analysis of ethnic prejudice. The first step of such a new analysis is a more adequate conceptualization of the notion of attitude within the broader framework of a theory of social cognition. In this approach, attitudes are not taken as some unanalyzed intermediate variable, for example, mediating between persuasive messages (or other "stimuli") and "behavior," nor are they seen simply as "cognitive responses" to our environment (see e.g.,

180

Fishbein & Ajzen, 1975; Greenwald, 1968; Himmelfarb & Eagly, 1974; Insko, 1967; Lingle & Ostrom, 1981; Petty & Cacioppo, 1981; Petty, Ostrom, & Brock, 1981).

Attitudes require cognitive analysis in their own right. The same is true for other notions to which attitudes are systematically related, such as beliefs, opinions, ideologies, or (inter)actions and their intentions. Thus, attitudes are taken as complex, schematically organized, shared cognitions about social objects, such as persons, groups, and their actions (Abelson, 1976; Petty, Ostrom, & Brock, 1981).

Similar remarks hold for the analysis of ethnic prejudice. What we need is an explicit cognitive theory that accounts for the content, organization, and operation of ethnic prejudice in social contexts (Hamilton, 1981). Our discourse analysis in the previous chapters has yielded data that may be used to build part of this theory. Having established such a cognitive basis, we can later return to the interpersonal, persuasive communication processes involved in the reproduction of ethnic beliefs.

It should be recalled that, in our opinion, prejudice should not be characterized only in terms of negative ethnic attitudes of in-group members. What is also needed is a more active, dynamic dimension. Prejudice is not just a "mental state;" it not only involves the (trans)formation of ethnic attitudes, but actually operates through flexible strategies for the processing of group-based, ethnic or racial information. The representation and use of prejudice, then, is a specific form of what is now commonly called *social information processing* (see, e.g., the contributions in Wyer & Srull, 1984). Prejudiced memory "models" and schemata, on the one hand, and these "biasing" strategies, on the other hand, underlie the interpretation of discourse about foreigners and of ethnic encounters themselves. In other words, prejudice is not just "what" people think about ethnic out-groups, but also "how" they do so.

Finally, we have repeatedly stressed that attitudes and *a fortiori* ethnic prejudice are not (only) personal or individual opinions about other people. Their social nature goes beyond interpersonal perception and requires analysis in terms of group-based, shared cognitions within the framework of intra- and intergroup relationships and social representations (Billig, 1976; Deschamps, 1977; Doise, 1984; Farr & Moscovici, 1984; Jaspars & Fraser, 1984; Tajfel, 1978, 1981a, 1981b; Turner, 1981; Turner & Giles, 1981). Whereas the points made above imply that current theories of attitude and ethnic prejudice are not "cognitive" enough, we also suggest that they lack an important social dimension (R.A. Jones, 1982). Without this social component, it is not possible to link the cognitive notion of ethnic prejudice to macro social notions such as ethnic group conflict and racism. These further social dimensions of prejudice and its communication will be dealt with in more detail in the following chapters. Even more than the recent approaches to social cognition, then, we stress the need for further cognitive analysis of attitudes and prejudice (Fiske & Taylor, 1984; Forgas, 1981; Higgins, Herman & Zanna, 1981), and, at the same time, urge a more serious social analysis of these types of social cognitions.

1.2. THE COGNITIVE FRAMEWORK

This section briefly summarizes the major theoretical notions that define our cognitive framework (for details and further references, see van Dijk & Kintsch, 1983). The next chapter then elaborates in more detail on the role of this framework in discourse processing and interpersonal communication and persuasion, whereas the next sections show how relevant such a cognitive approach is in an explicit account of attitudes and prejudice.

Information Processing

Basically, the cognitive framework we propose is an extension of the information processing paradigm that has progressively influenced psychology since the early 1970s (Anderson, 1980; Kintsch, 1977; Lindsay & Norman, 1972). It represents people primarily as active information processors and no longer as passive mediators of or reactors to external stimuli, or as executors of conditioned "behavior," which was the dominant model of human beings in the behaviorist paradigm. In the information processing paradigm, thus, we find theoretical and experimental analysis of precisely the "intermediary" cognitive processes that characterize mental acts such as understanding, representation, retrieval, and recall of information, thinking and problem solving, or production and action.

Memories

The central location of these cognitive processes is memory. It has become standard to distinguish between different types (or functions) of memory: sensory memory that analyzes the external data (stimuli) that are perceived by our senses, short-term memory (STM) or working memory, which assigns structures and interpretations to such data, and long-term memory (LTM) that stores all information processed in STM. STM can only hold a few (between four and seven) chunks of information of various types at once, for instance, the words of a clause, or the clausal structure and the meanings of one or two subsequent sentences. After structural analysis and interpretation of such chunks, the resulting information is represented in LTM, from where it may be partially retrieved for future use. It is assumed that the structure assigned to the incoming information in STM also organizes the representation of that information in LTM. Generally speaking, the more such representations are structured—for instance, at several levels—the easier it will be to find them. This explains, for instance, why it is much easier to remember a meaningful sentence than an arbitrary sequence of words. The same is true for the understanding and memorization of sequences of events or action (episodes) or discourse about such episodes.

Episodic Memory and Social Memory

It also has proved useful to make a distinction within LTM between what is called *episodic memory* (EM) and *semantic memory* (SM) (Tulving, 1972, 1983). All incoming information that has been analyzed and interpreted in STM is provisionally stored, as "episodes," in EM. A text we have read, an interaction in which we have participated, or a scene we have witnessed are all represented in EM. Obviously, such mental episodes initially have a particular nature: They are about unique, personal experiences. They represent our subjective interpretations of real world episodes.

Semantic memory, on the other hand, has a more general and abstract nature. It contains our general and abstract knowledge of the world including all we know about language, discourse, interaction, people, and so on. Word (action, object, and so on) forms and meanings, rules, strategies, and structures we use to interpret discourse, images, scenes, or interactions in the multiple situations of our life are thus stored for recurrent use in semantic memory.

Much of this information is, of course, useful only when it is at least partially shared with other people. Language use and interaction, for instance, are possible only due to this socially shared nature of our word meanings, rules, and action concepts. Therefore, we tend to prefer the term *social memory* to refer to the collection of information represented in this semantic memory store (others, e.g., Hastie, Park, & Weber, 1984, use this term in a somewhat different sense, namely, as all memory about social affairs). After all, semantic memory does not only hold semantic information, but also structural or procedural information about images, action, or discourse. Episodic memory has a more ad hoc, personal (autobiographic) nature, even when this may also involve our personal interpretation and evaluation of social events we have witnessed. To use another comparison: Episodic memory is a personal diary, and social memory a dictionary, an encyclopedia, and a grammar.

Schemata: Frames and Scripts

Episodic memory and social memory are intimately related, otherwise we would not be able to learn from our individual experiences, neither would it be possible to use our general knowledge for the interpretation of concrete events. This suggests that there are a number of processes, such as generalization, abstraction, and decontextualization, that transform the information represented in EM into their more useful general correlates in social memory. Our experiences of the forms and functions of individual objects such as tables or cars, thus, result in general "frames" for the concepts of "table" and "car" (Minsky, 1975). Such a frame is a schematic cluster of knowledge that contains the general properties of such objects, leaving open—as "default values"—those properties (such as make or color) that may be variable in each situation. Also, such general knowledge may be represented in the form of *prototypes* (Rosch, 1978; Rosch & Lloyd, 1978). Prototypes represent a construction of the most "typical" member of a class, featuring the most typical properties, to which other elements of the class may be more or less similar. Below, we shall see that this notion is also important in the representation of ethnic groups and their members.

Similar organizational patterns are necessary for more complex chunks of knowledge in whole episodes such as "going to school," "having a party," or "shopping in the supermarket." We all "know how" to do this, and understand others doing this, on the basis of those shared, stereotypical, or prototypical, knowledge structures, which are often called *scripts* (Schank, 1982; Schank & Abelson, 1977). Much like other forms of knowledge in memory, frames and scripts are effectively organized because they must be quickly and frequently retrieved from memory for many cognitive tasks, and we have assumed that retrieval is easier when information is highly structured. Frames, prototypes, and scripts are specific types of *schemata,* that is, categorial networks that organize cognitive representations. The notion of *schema,* introduced and used half a century ago by Bartlett (1932), has now acquired a central position in both cognitive and social psychology (Brewer & Nakamura, 1984; Hastie, 1981; Norman & Rumelhart, 1975; Rumelhart, 1984). In social cognition, schemata are, for instance, assumed to organize our knowledge about other people and other groups and their actions. Unfortunately, the fashionable notion of schema has not often been made really explicit in much of this work such as by an explicit description of its internal contents and organizational principles. Besides these forms of knowledge, there are also other types of cognition represented in social memory—beliefs, opinions, attitudes, norms, and values, to which we turn below.

Whereas much is presently known about the structures and uses of knowledge in social memory, we know much less about the effective organization of episodic memory (Shoben, 1984; Tulving, 1983). Intuitively, we have assumed that this "recording" store represents all interpreted episodes we have experienced and also that these representations should have the structure assigned to them in STM. For linguistic objects, such as sentences and discourse, this would mean that their episodic traces can simply be represented in terms of the semantic meanings assigned to them by the analysis and interpretation processes working in STM. Our analytical machinery is, however, much less developed for the representation of action, interaction, people, objects, scenes, or images. Often, the sophisticated theoretical models of linguistic or logical analysis are used to represent part of the structures of these other information types. This presupposes a principle of cognitive economy that suggests that we do not have fully different analytical instruments for the understanding of discourse on the one hand, and of action or whole episodes, on the other.

Situation Models

For our analysis of attitudes and prejudice, however, it is important to introduce another crucial notion, that of *situation model*. This notion is intended as a theoretical correlate of more intuitive notions such as "episode" or "experience." That is, it is assumed that each time we represent an episode, for instance, a car accident, we form a "mental model" of such an episode (Johnson-Laird, 1983; van Dijk, 1985d, 1987c; van Dijk & Kintsch, 1983). It is further assumed that we do this each time in more or less the same way. After all, it is very effective if we would analyze real world scenes, events, or episodes in terms of more or less the same units and processes. In other words, it seems plausible that much in the same way as we assign similar structures to different sentence tokens, we also assign similar structures to unique events that occur in a given setting.

Therefore, it is plausible that we use a limited number of organized, fixed categories to do so. The hierarchical structure formed by such situation categories is a *situation model schema*. For instance, each event we witness, such as the car accident, may be characterized by a Setting (which) again may be analyzed in terms of Time and Location), by specific Circumstances (e.g., road conditions), Participants, and finally the Event or Action itself, each category possibly being accompanied by one or more Qualifiers. This kind of categorial analysis is familiar from several disciplines and recalls the semantic analysis of sentences (Dik, 1978), stories (Labov, 1972; Mandler, 1984; van Dijk, 1976, 1980c), and social situations (Argyle, Furnham, & Graham, 1981; Brown & Fraser, 1979). Thus, stories are expressions of our episodic representation of the (interesting) acts and events of past situations (Black, Galambos, & Read, 1984; van Dijk, 1985d). For our discussion, for instance, an encounter with a member of an ethnic minority group, or a story about such an encounter, may be represented as such a situation model. Among other things, prejudiced information processing involves specific biases in the models that represent such ethnic encounters.

Like the experiences they represent, models are in principle unique and individual. Yet, each day we experience many episodes of the same or of a similar kind. Going to a party tonight may recall our previous experiences of party going, and such particular party-models may, of course, be integrated, combined, and generalized. This also explains why people often tend to mix up what they remember of similar events in the past (Neisser, 1982). From particular models, thus, people form more general (but still personal) models of their experiences. Their "experience," in a more general sense, consists of these accumulated and then generalized models. Indeed, we hardly remember each shopping event of the last year, but have formed a generalized model of our shopping.

From Models to Socially Shared Schemata

Next, both particular and general models of our experiences may be compared with those of other people, typically so in observation, interaction, and especially through talk and text. We hear or read stories and thus are able to see in which respects the models of other people, expressed by their stories, also feature the typical structures and contents we have represented in our models of comparable experiences. In that case, we may abstract from our personal participation—our personal acts—from specific time, location, or circumstances and construct a more general, more abstract, and socially shared frame or script of shopping. When we tell a story about what happened yesterday when we went shopping, we *express* the specifics of our *model* of that particular event, but at the same time we *presuppose* the "shopping" *script* to be known to the hearer, because knowledge about the general properties of shopping episodes is shared by most members of our culture. This means, for instance, that we need not always tell that we went shopping to buy things at certain places, that such things cost money, or that once paid for, we own such things. In other words, to understand events or stories about them means that we "apply" our general knowledge in the construction of particular models of such events.

A large part of the processes operating in memory involve the (partial) activation, retrieval, and applications of knowledge representations like models or scripts. The major goal of *understanding* an individual episode or text is to construct a situation model of them on the basis of the meanings assigned to words, sentences, action units, or their sequences. Once we have constructed a coherent model of such an episode or text, we say that we have "understood" what happened. Understanding, thus, is model construction. And to do this, we need the help of previous models of similar episodes, as well as the abstract frames or scripts that represent the general, prototypical properties of such models.

Control

From this simplified picture of what is going on during various types of information processing, it may have become obvious that vast amounts of information are being analyzed, activated, and applied at each moment in different "parts" of our memory. Although sometimes things do get mixed up (we forget things, do not understand things, get confused, and so on), it is rather surprising that mostly things work smoothly and effectively. This is possible only when we assume that the whole process is adequately monitored. STM must be fed with specific chunks of models or scripts at the right time, information must be removed from STM and sent to LTM, models in EM must be activated, reanalyzed, and stored as provisional frames in social memory, and so on. The understanding of a simple piece of prose, thus, requires analysis and knowledge at many levels, from knowledge of words, clause structure, discourse or speech acts, on the one hand, to knowledge about communicative interaction, language users, people, goals, social situations, and the world knowledge embodied in the topics talked about, on the other hand. This process can be integrated only when an overall Control System takes care of the monitoring of the various processes going on at each level, registers which models or scripts are now active, which topic we are talking about, which situation we are now participating in, and so on. In other words, the Control System regulates the information flow between STM and LTM, as well as the various processes taking place within STM.

Strategies

Finally, we also assume that this kind of vastly complex cognitive processing is possible only when the very processes used to analyze, interpret, store, or retrieve information are flexible, fast, and effective. Therefore, they do not have a fixed, rulelike or algorithmic nature, but rather have a strategic character. Understanding discourse or action, then, takes place through the application of various types of strategies, each with its own specific goal. Unlike rules, such strategies operate on-line, and accept (even incomplete) information of various sorts, from several levels at the same time. This means also that strategies have a tentative, hypothetical nature. Stategic understanding is fast and effective but need not be perfect; further information may force us to revise initial assumptions.

For instance, we have important strategies that allow us to determine in an early stage what overall action people are engaged in (e.g., "having a party") or what "topic" people are talking about. We need not first hear or read the whole discourse, but will guess from the first words or sentences, as well as from the context, the participant, the social situation, and its goals, what kind of topic is most likely. While shopping, indeed, we expect neither a lecture from the shopkeeper about nuclear physics nor informal talk in a physics class about the taste of Italian strawberries. In other words, previous knowledge (models, scripts), allow us to apply "top-down" a strategy that construes plausible topics (or topic classes) as soon as we participate in communication. We shall detail this aspect of discourse understanding in the next chapter when we examine the implications of this cognitive framework for the analysis of interpersonal communication.

Conclusion

We now have an approximate map of the domain of memory in which we have located the various types of knowledge and the strategies applied to acquire and to use that knowledge in the processing of information. This framework is essential if we want to understand the structures of ethnic prejudice, their expression in discourse, as well their persuasive communication in everyday talk. In the rest of this chapter, we only go through one stage of this complex journey, namely, the analysis of the cognitive structures and strategies of ethnic attitudes. In the next chapter, we then turn to the strategies of their expression in talk, their reproduction from the talk of others, and to other properties of the social communication of prejudice.

1.3. ANALYZING ATTITUDE

Attitudes are usually defined in terms of evaluative beliefs, measured along various dimensions, such as positive-negative, pro-contra, or similar scales (Fishbein & Ajzen, 1975). According to the prevalent view, they are analyzed into three major components: cognitions, emotions, and conations (Breckler, 1984). This analysis reflects the intuitive assumption that attitudes involve beliefs about attitude objects (or targets), that such beliefs are evaluative and often based on affect (e.g., like or dislike), and that attitudes "predispose" people to specific behaviors (Rosenberg et al., 1960).

Unlike this classical approach, we only analyze attitudes in terms of socially relevant, schematic clusters of the evaluative beliefs that we call *opinions*. The central task of a theory of attitude is to describe the contents, the organization, and the strategic uses of such opinion structures in memory and interaction. These opinions may be associated with variable forms or degrees of "affect" or "emotion," but this affective dimension is context-bound, and not inherent in the definition of opinion per se. The same is true for conations: The "behavioral" component of attitudes requires separate analysis. Action and interaction are based on very complex, autonomous cognitive processes, which need attitudinal, motivational, and much other information for their planning, execution, and monitoring. This does not mean, however, that attitudes should not feature beliefs about what should or should not be done. But such normative components are not the same as the mysterious, if not spurious, "dispositions" we find in traditional attitude research.

The representation and organization problem of an explicit theory of attitude can be solved only when the following assumptions are reviewed first.

Functions of Attitudes

The nature and structure of attitudes derive from their functions in (social) information processing. Whereas frames or scripts provide the necessary knowledge base that enables people to understand events, action, or discourse, attitudes provide the evaluative belief foundation that is needed to assess the (inter)subjective "position" of social members toward such episodes. Such a position, ultimately, is, of course, an important factor in the cognitive monitoring of "survival conditions" for persons as social members: It is crucially relevant to know what objects, persons, or episodes are "good" or "bad," and such information is essential in the planning and execution of (inter)action. For the moment, though, we disregard such fundamental and speculative functions of attitudes and focus on their actual role in processing social information.

Knowledge is both socially and cognitively effective only when it is not specific to ad hoc situations. To a certain extent, it must be context-free and, hence, general and abstract. The same holds for attitudes. This means that attitudes are not ad hoc evaluative beliefs about particular objects, people, or events. Economy and effectiveness in storage, retrieval, and use require that the number of attitudes be limited. The same attitude should be able to handle many different episodes that take place on many occasions during the life of social members. The information stored in attitudes, then, should be general and abstract, and their social relevance requires that they may be socially shared. Attitudes, in our view, are inherently social cognitions. The strategically effective retrieval of such general attitude items for the evaluative tasks to be accomplished in concrete situations involves a process of instantiation in which general information is transformed into particular information. In logical terms, this means that variables are replaced by constants.

Attitudes as Social Schemata

This role of attitudes suggests that they are to be located in semantic (social) memory, along with other forms of general, context-free information, such as concepts, frames, scripts, rules, procedures, norms, values, general goals, and ideologies. Context independence generally also requires independence of exclusively personal contexts, and also implies social relevance. Much like the other forms of abstract, general information in semantic memory, attitudes essentially serve the processing of social information. Concepts, scripts, norms, values, and rules are socially shared, acquired, and applied, and so are attitudes. They essentially serve the adequate participation in communication and interaction.

In contrast, episodic memory represents context-bound, personal experiences (in social contexts or not) and is, therefore, rather a personal or particular memory store (Shoben, 1984). It is this distinction between social and personal memory that also inspires the distinction between attitudes and (particular) opinions. It follows from these assumptions that people do not have purely personal attitudes, much in the same way as people do not have personal scripts, language rules, norms, or values. They only have personal opinions and personal uses or applications of general knowledge and beliefs.

Opinions

The building blocks of attitudes are (general) evaluative beliefs, which we called *opinions*. Attitudes are ordered sets of such general opinions. Like other beliefs, opinions can be represented as a (simple or complex) proposition, that is, as an n-place predicate that organizes *n* arguments. Specific, though, is the presence of an evaluative predicate, which is any predicate that presupposes the application of general norms, goals, or values (Rokeach, 1973). The general belief that "nuclear plants pollute the environment" is an opinion if it presupposes that a clean environment is a socially shared value or goal. Heuristically, opinions may be expressed and signaled by phrases such as "X think (find) that." Opinions may be true (e.g., for those who endorse them) or false (for those who reject them), even when some opinion types, such as norm statements, may have other forms of interpretation or satisfaction (e.g., relevance, effectiveness, and so on).

Opinions may be *general* or *particular*. Particular opinions are about particular objects and are bound to a specific context of evaluation. Therefore, we associate them with information in episodic representations of experienced situations, which we called *situation models*. If I *now* think that the present disposal of toxic waste by *this* nuclear plant pollutes the environment, I entertain a particular opinion, associated with my representation of this nuclear plant and what it does to its environment now. Of course, on another occasion I may (re)activate more or less the same particular opinion, but the specifics of the features of this new context will usually also influence the precise representation of this "same" opinion later.

Attitudes, by definition, only feature general opinions, namely, about generic objects, such as nuclear plants, or about general properties or relations, such as pollution. Attitude "application" takes place through the instantiation of general opinions in situation models. Note, though, that whereas attitudes consist of general opinions, not all general opinions are organized into attitudes. Aside from ad hoc, particular models, we also have generalized models, and these may feature general (personal) opinions that need not be shared with others. "I do not like apples" or "My neighbor is a bore" are examples of such general, personal opinions: They may be inferred from personal experiences and apply to many episodes in which I have to deal with apples or my neighbor, but they are neither inherently related with other general opinions, nor need they be acquired, shared, changed, or used in communication or interaction with other social members (except the targets of the opinions).

The Organization of Attitudes

Attitudes, just like general frames or scripts, are organized so that they can be effectively searched, activated, applied, or changed (Abelson, 1973, 1976; Carbonell, 1979). One major form of organization is hierarchical ordering: There are level differences between more and less general opinions. The opinion "nuclear energy is dangerous," for instance, is more general than "nuclear plants are dangerous" and "nuclear weapons are dangerous." Whereas hierarchical ordering is vertical or top-down/bottom-up, we also may have horizontal ordering principles, for instance, those that represent conditional links between facts about which we have opinions. The opinion that "nuclear plants are unsafe" may be linked with the opinion that "nuclear plants are a threat to the environment," which may again be linked to the opinion that "nuclear plants are dangerous to our health" because these respective opinions are about facts that are conditionally (causally) related. Such conditional "chaining" may be used in argumentation. Note that the conditional link itself may also be evaluative: It may depend on our beliefs about causality, probability, and their relations to norms and values (e.g., of safety and safety precautions and their effects).

Linear and hierarchical ordering are very general organizational principles in memory and are essential for any form of effective search, activation (e.g., spreading activation), or other major operations in information processing. More specific, but often more effective, is categorial organization. That is, each opinion or cluster of opinions may be organized by a category from a limited repertoire. Such categories may again be ordered, both linearly and hierarchically, and define what we call an *attitude schema*. We have discussed the important role of various types of schema above, and this also holds for the schematic organization of opinions in attitudes. The use of categories allows fast and precise operation of search and application strategies, such as partial and context-dependent activation of opinions. The very notion of "cause," for instance, may act as an organizing category in event schemata. Finally, these various organizational properties may also define other well-known structures in attitudes and beliefs, such as those that reflect the "central" or "peripheral" nature of opinions (Rokeach, 1973). Similarly, different applications of organizational principles as well as different strategies of search and activation may also explain why specific opinions may be more relevant for individuals or groups or for specific contexts.

People develop attitude schemata that are crucial for information processing about social life, that is, about interaction, about specific situation and communication types, about other people, about groups, and so on. This social relevance of attitude schemata should also be reflected in their organization and in the prototypical categories that define them. Thus, we develop attitudes about people along dimensions that are recurrently and practically functional in the ways we perceive, categorize, evaluate, and interact with others. Such *person schemata* feature categories that we can effectively apply when "analyzing" people and storing information about them in memory (Hastie et al., 1980). Relevant, for instance, might be categories such as "appearance," "gender," "age," "occupation," "role," or "class," as well as the (inter)actions associated with these categories, which also underlie our prototypical beliefs about other people. And within the category of "character" (or personality), we may again make further subdivisions that may lead to overall evaluative typifications ("shy," "introvert," and so on), which may have a socially shared, commonsense nature of "implicit theories" (Schneider, 1973). Although person schemata as such are part of our general social knowledge, and not specific for the structure of attitudes, categories that organize our knowledge about people may probably also be used to structure our opinions about them.

We have intuitive belief schemata about persons but also about *groups*. Such attitudes are even more effective from a social point of view, because they allow relatively context-free evaluation of possibly large sets of people, even when we do not know their individual members. Stereotypes and ethnic prejudice will be taken below as specific group schemata in social memory.

Finally, we may also develop attitude schema categories for socially relevant object or episode types, such as cars, nuclear plants, or vacations abroad. Such attitude categories may be partly related to our general beliefs (frames, scripts) about such objects or episodes. Whether we find certain cars "beautiful" is a judgment categorizable under an "appearance" node. On the other hand, categories may develop for such attitude objects along the dimensions of goal, value, or interest realization, which they may favor or block. If operating cars and nuclear plants are known to pollute the environment, and if a clean environment is a value we want to maintain or restore, pollution may be seen as "blocking" such a goal (Wegman, 1981). In other words, attitude categories are developed on the basis of our experiences (i.e., models) with the ways persons, groups, objects, or episodes, and their properties "fit" our goals, interests, values, norms, and the perceptions and interactions based on these general criteria. Hence, the structure of attitudes is a cognitive reflection of our social relations to (other) social objects and events. Once acquired, by experiences, cognitive operations (e.g., inferences), or communication, such attitude schemata may become relatively autonomous and, in turn, influence our social perception and interaction. Our major assumption, however, is that the organization of attitudes is a function of the organization of our social life.

Ideological Embedding

Attitudes are seldom isolated. They are related to other socially relevant attitudes and may form organized clusters of attitudes, which we call *ideologies*. Ideologies define coherence relations among attitudes, so that attitude systems are not discretely and arbitrarily organized but feature many relationships that allow fast search and application and effective formation and transformation. Ideologies are generators of specific attitudes: Within an ideological structure, we may develop attitudes about X in analogy with existing attitudes about Y. That is, we may evaluate new social issues by default. The very categorial organization of attitudes allows such coherence relationships. If both cars and nuclear plants are found to be polluting, attitudes about such social objects may be linked through identical evaluations on a specific value, such as that of a clean environment. Attitudes that are thus organized within such a cluster may function as one higher-level unit, for instance, an "ecological" ideology.

Ideologies organize large portions of our social life and are based on fundamental goals, interests, and values. Thus, we also develop ideologies about work, education, the relationships between men and women, or social structure. Hence, ideologies are the cognitive reflections of our social, political, economic, and cultural "position" within the social structure. Typically, ideologies are developed and used in close relation to our fundamental "interests" (Brown, 1973; CCCS, 1978; Kinloch, 1981; Seliger, 1976). This means that ideologies, even less than their component attitudes, are not individual, but group based. Socialization and later social interaction contribute to group-specific ideologies of and about men or women, lower- or middle-class people, Whites or Blacks, labor or capital, and so on. Even sets of ideologies may again be further organized at higher levels and thus may be characterized in general terms, such as "liberal," "conservative," or "radical," depending on the goals and values of social structure shared by attitude clusters. Ideological coherence also allows us to predict, at least to a certain extent, what the overall attitudes of other people might be about X, given their attitudes about Y.

Conclusions

From these informal suggestions about the nature of opinions, attitudes, and their organization, we conclude, first, that such cognitions are inherently social, both in their acquisition and use and in their categorial structures. Second, it appears that the organization of attitudes follows very general principles of cognitive structuring and process, such as hierarchical, linear, and categorial organization. Third, attitudes, knowledge, and beliefs are intimately interrelated: Knowledge categories may also be used to organize doxastic information. Fourth, attitudes are complex structures of general opinions but may themselves also be units in higher-level, or more general, attitude clusters or ideologies. Hence, social cognition, from particular context-bound opinions of individuals to ideological orientations, is highly structured, which allows fast, effective search, retrieval, and application of evaluative beliefs. At the same time, this structure is acquired and applied in social contexts and, therefore, is a structural and strategic function of the major social components of such contexts. In the next sections, we show how these general properties of attitudes and social cognition also hold for ethnic prejudice.

2. Ethnic prejudice as group attitude

2.1. GENERAL PROPERTIES OF PREJUDICE

Now that we have some insight into cognitive processing, in general, and into the nature of attitudes, in particular, we can start to analyze a special type of attitude: *ethnic prejudice*. A first property of prejudice is that it is a "group attitude"—it is shared by members of a social group (the "in-group"). This means that prejudice in our approach is not (a set of) personal opinions. Second, the objects of the attitude are one or more other groups ("out-groups") that are assumed to be different on any social dimension. For ethnic (racial) attitudes, this means that this difference is attributed to ethnic or racial characteristics of the out-group. Third, the overall (macro) evaluation dominating the group attitude is negative. According to the definition of opinion and attitude, this implies that the perceived ethnic differences of the out-group are valued negatively relative to at least some of the norms, values, interests, or goals of the in-group. Fourth, the negative opinions of the ethnic attitude are generalizations based on lacking, insufficient, or biased models. This bias may result from types of social information processing that are normatively sanctioned for judgments about in-group members, such as the use of wrong, irrelevant, or incomplete data, false attribution, or unwarranted inference. And finally, the ethnic attitude is acquired, used, and transformed in social contexts and functions as the cognitive program for intergroup perception and interaction that are structurally favorable for the in-group and its members. This social function of prejudice may involve the maintenance of in-group dominance, power, and exploitation, or the protection of interests or privileges. In this respect, ethnic prejudice is the cognitive foundation of racism.

The Limitations of a "Definition"

This first more or less intuitive characterization combines some of the features of our own approach, which is partly inspired by current research on ethnic stereotypes as social cognition (e.g., Hamilton, 1981), with some of the components in traditional definitions of prejudice (Allport, 1954; Bagley et al., 1979; Bagley & Verma, 1979; Brigham, 1971; Ehrlich, 1973; Estel, 1978; Jones, 1972). Yet, it is often insufficiently understood that "definitions" cannot replace serious theory formation. This means that definitions are always and necessarily incomplete or wrong. A good definition is, at most, a good summary of the main theses of an explicit theory. Starting theory formation about a phenomenon by trying to define that phenomenon is, therefore, an illusory undertaking and only betrays quasi-explicitness. Definitions are only relevant for the component terms of a theory that are not further analyzed within that theory (e.g., the notion of "strategy" in a theory of prejudice, which, however, requires further analysis in a more embracing cognitive theory). Initial definitions of the things we want to theorize about, then, are either a summary of the main points we want to attend to in the theory, or they are a form of (semi-)intuitive marking of the empirical or conceptual "boundaries" of the phenomenon we want to study (the original Latin meaning of *definition*). Thus, our initial description of some main properties of ethnic prejudice is meant only to distinguish it from (a) personal opinions, (b) other (non-prejudiced) group attitudes, (c) stereotypes, and (d) prejudices against other social groups. Each component in such a provisional description needs further theoretical analysis. We first briefly discuss some of these components of prejudiced attitudes, also against the background of traditional approaches, and then attend to the major contribution of this section, namely, the structural organization of prejudice. Then, in the next section, we advance from the structural to the dynamic dimension of prejudice and deal with the strategies of prejudiced social information processing and the actual contents and uses of ethnic attitudes.

Social Categorization

Attitudes and, hence, also prejudice, may develop about practically any socially distinctive group. This presupposes that group members perceive real or imagined differences, along one or more social dimensions, between their own group and the out-group. The "others," thus, may be assumed to differ in nationality, origin, "race," ethnicity, class, language, gender, occupation, status, education, class, role, personality, or appearance (differentiation). Thus, in prejudiced thought, perception, or interaction, out-group individuals are primarily *categorized* as members of the group defined by any of these perceived differences (Deschamps, 1977, 1983; Howard & Rothbart, 1980; Tajfel, 1978, 1981a, 1981b, 1982; Tajfel & Forgas, 1981; Taylor, 1981; Turner & Giles, 1981; Wilder, 1981). Prejudiced categorization implies that properties attributed to such groups are assumed to hold for all or at least for most of its individual members (instantiation). And, conversely, negative evaluations of individual members may be assumed to hold for the group as a whole (generalization). In both cases, prejudiced categorization involves a perceived reduction of differences between out-group members (Tajfel, 1981a, 1981b; Tajfel, Sheikh & Gardner, 1964).

Negative Evaluation

These evaluations, however, are not arbitrary. People judge groups relative to what may be called the "social principles," that is, the basic goals, norms, and values of their own in-group. If a particular out-group is assumed to have properties that are (thought to be) incompatible with these principles, these properties are evaluated negatively. In other words, prejudiced attitudes imply fundamental ("principled") negativization of differentiation and categorization.

Negative generalization is neither limited to individuals nor to single social properties. It is also pervasive in structural terms. A negative evaluation on one dimension or category may "spread" to other categories and to the higher levels of the group schema. This is the reason that prejudice is a group attitude that features high-level (macro) negative opinions, dominating more specific negative opinions. At the same time, such a structural expansion of negativity also allows for the possibility that on less relevant or isolated points, opinions may be neutral or positive (typically, "Blacks are musical").

Negative evaluation is usually associated with affect: Much like other attitudes, prejudice is taken not only as a cognitive schema but also as a particular set of feelings about out-groups (Adorno et al., 1950; Allport, 1954; Berkowitz, 1972; Bettelheim & Janovitz, 1964; Fiske, 1981). Although it is undoubtedly true that people's prejudgments are often accompanied by various forms of affect (feelings, emotions), we argued earlier that this is not always and, hence, not inherently, the case. Dutch in-group members may think that foreigners are favored in housing, but such an opinion need not always be accompanied by a negative feeling or particular emotions, such as frustration, anger, or indignation. Such forms of affect may be personally variable, and are typically context-bound. If people tell a story in our interviews, retrieval of a concrete model or this general opinion may trigger anger, and the same may be true when they have tried in vain to get an apartment, then witness a Turkish family moving into an apartment across the street. In other words, the prejudiced opinion may or may not trigger emotions in particular circumstances. For instance, people from wealthier neighborhoods may share the prejudice that foreigners take houses but, at the same time, they may very well have this opinion without associated affect, which would accompany the threat of losing one's house. The more permanent and general (negative) opinion merely represents evaluation of an assumed fact with respect to general norms and values (e.g., "No group should be favored in social resources," or "Dutch people have priority in taking advantage of 'our' social resources"). Of course, emotionally based personal experiences may be potent factors in the acquisition and maintenance of prejudiced opinions.

Empirical "Bias"

There is a third form of generalization that characterizes the formation and uses of ethnic prejudice. In-group members not only generalize from individual out-group members, or single properties, but also from single situations. In our theoretical terms, this means that they may generalize directly from particular situation models, that is, from single experiences, to generalized models and attitude schemata. However, this generalization only applies for negative instances: The (negative) generalization must fit into a generally negative attitude schema.

But even such a single situation model need not be present. That is, overgeneralization is just one possibility of prejudice formation. People may also directly derive a (new) ethnic schema by analogy with previous ethnic schemata. If they have prejudices against Turks, they may simply specify a new prejudice schema against Moroccans without any direct experiences, encounters, or perceptions, often on the basis of fragmentary models derived from (mass media) communication. Such a fragmentary model would, for instance, feature a few similarities with the existing attitudes about the group already known: Mediterranean origin, darker appearance, immigrant workers, and Islamic religion.

And third, these forms of what may be called the *empirical bias* of ethnic prejudice, also and perhaps most importantly, affects the very processes of model formation through perception, interpretation, and evaluation. That is, even a single particular model constructed under the influence of a monitoring prejudiced attitude may in many ways be biased itself. This intuitive notion of bias needs explication in terms of prejudiced social information processing. Such processes may involve selective, incomplete, one-sided, unbalanced, or, again, negative interpretations, attributions, or other forms of normatively inadequate mental representation of out-groups and their actions. We return to these processes and strategies in the next section.

Self-Norm Violation

Traditional definitions of prejudice were sometimes criticized because they were assumed to contain normative evaluations: Prejudice and its characteristic properties are found to be "wrong" (see, e.g., Apostle et al., 1983). In everyday life, prejudices are usually attributed only to others. In our examples, we found that people will usually deny that they are prejudiced themselves. Hence, in this analysis of prejudice, overgeneralization, empirical bias, and the well-known property of psychological "rigidity" attributed to prejudiced individuals, are all instances of "wrong" social or cognitive behavior. They are "errors."

Our approach to this problem is somewhat different. First, we do not agree with the general assumption that social analysis should not feature evaluative or normative statements. As soon as the respective values or norms on which they are based are made explicit, they can be inferred from prior statements just like any other statements of a theory. In this sense, the critical analysis of prejudice and racism is no less "scientific" than medical pathology.

Second, the notion of "wrongness" is not just a question of "morals." In the case of prejudice, discrimination, and racism, it can easily be operationalized in terms of social pathologies of the in-group (Bowser & Hunt, 1984) and even more important, in terms of the many negative social effects for the out-group. Indeed, without such negative effects summarized under the concepts of dominance or power, prejudice would have no social function, and this social function is also part of the definition of prejudice. It all depends on (group) perspective: Only for White social scientists did the "normative" nature of the concept of prejudice constitute a problem, mainly because it would unacceptably blame the dominant (White) in-group of which they are a part.

Third, even without such considerations there is no problem. Prejudice can also be described (partly) in normative terms with respect to the norms of the in-group. That is, the various biases signaled above violate the principles of social information processing about in-group members. To put it very simply: Prejudices are "wrong" because people find that they should not have similar opinions or judgments about people of their own group or would resent it if other groups would have such prejudices about them. Our interviews repeatedly show that people are very much aware of such norms. In other words, even from a purely descriptive point of view, prejudice is a form of social self-norm violation. This violation also extends into the forms of ethnic group interaction as the kind of differential treatment we call discrimination. Hence, concepts like prejudice and discrimination are no less scholarly defensible than many other notions in the social sciences.

Cognitive Errors?

Finally, another point must be made. Many of the features of ethnic prejudice mentioned above are similar to social information processing in general. People often make overgeneralizations, have biasing perception and representation, or have special attention for negative information. Effective information processing requires differentiation, categorization, and fast heuristics (Nisbett & Ross, 1980). According to such an approach, prejudiced thinking and judgment would simply be one set of cognitive "errors" among many others. We return to these cognitive strategies in the next sections.

However, in our view, this approach would be too limited, to say the least. It is undoubtedly true that in ethnic information processing, including the formation and uses of prejudices, people rely on basic cognitive strategies that enable effective processing of new, complex, difficult, or incomplete information, as is often the case in intergroup perception and interaction. However, this is not the whole story. First, the strategies predominantly lead to negative "outcomes" for out-group members in model or schema (trans)formation, which is not inherent in effective cognitive processing. Second, similar situations, events, actions, or persons of the in-group are not processed in the same (strategic) way. Thus, the application of the prejudiced cognitive program essentially depends on the perceived out-group status of the ethnic minority group or its members. Third, the resulting negative attitudes are socially functional. They may be used to plan, execute, or justify equally negative actions against minority groups.

This suggests that, in addition to the usual cognitive strategies, there is a higher-level monitoring device that controls ethnic information processing in such a way that the actual or general beliefs about ethnic minorities consistently contribute to an overall attitude that is most appropriate as a program for such acts of discrimination. Overall in-group goals, interests, or societal structures of inequality, thus, may be represented so that in-group members generally follow a self-serving strategy, both in action and in attitude formation and use. In other words, "biased" processing of information about ethnic groups is not just an "error." On the contrary, they are often unconscious, unplanned, yet strategic ways of attuning social attitudes to the basic principles of the in-group. In that sense, they may be very effective in providing a

The Cognitive Dimension 201

cognitive program for the multiple (inter)actions of dominance and discrimination in situations and social structure.

Irrationality and Rigidity?

For similar reasons, we do not share the traditional point of view that prejudices are *irrational* or *rigid* beliefs about out-groups. To be sure, personality differences may probably affect the structures and the strategies of prejudiced information processing. Also, in our interviews, we have found that under very similar social circumstances, individual people may nevertheless have different types or degrees of ethnic prejudice. Yet, such individual differences, as they were traditionally attributed to childhood experiences and education (Adorno et al. 1950), cannot explain the general, and socially shared, ethnocentrism and prejudice in whole groups (featuring individuals with very different personalities) (Pettigrew, 1958). From a sociocognitive point of view, then, prejudices are not always irrational either. They may be very rational and functional ways of organizing information about out-groups that must be kept "out or under," even if prejudiced generalizations about groups cannot "rationally" be inferred from observations.

The same is true for rigidity. The strategies that handle ethnic information are by definition flexible and not rigid: People must accommodate often conflicting information, such as negative opinions, with neutral or positive experiences (models). In our interviews, we have seen that they must combine conflicting goals of positive self-presentation and negative other-presentation. In everyday action, they must try to figure out how to combine negative prejudices with the rather strict rules of interaction (politeness, and so forth), at least in a society where overt and blatant racist action is formally prohibited. With lack of interpersonal or social control, and no possibilities of sanctions or retaliation, these forms of control may, of course, be reduced, as ethnic minority group members experience in their everyday life (Essed, 1984). These different forms of social information processing are possible only when people deal with information in a flexible way, even when the outcome may often be stereotypical. And again, this is independent of the rigidity of the personality of the prejudiced group members. Due to their important social functions, however, group attitudes and especially prejudices, indeed, do not change easily. But in that sense of rigidity, they are very similar to other basic social attitudes and ideologies. Thus, the contents of prejudiced attitudes may remain stable or stereotypical even in the face of conflicting evidence, and this conflict may be resolved through flexible strategies of (re)interpretation.

Social Functions

These last issues have reminded us again of a final constitutive component of ethnic prejudice—its very specific social functions and its role in the structural nature of racism in society. These social functions explain why personal prejudices against people who wear glasses are fundamentally different from in-group prejudices against social out-groups such as Blacks, women, the elderly, or squatters. The similarity, indeed, is only one between partially similar forms of social information processing (categorization, differentiation, and associated evaluations). It is essential to distinguish between individual prejudices of the first kind and the group-based, socially functional ones of the second kind (Gardner, Taylor, & Feenstra, 1970). According to our analysis of attitude, the first is not even an attitude and, hence, not a prejudice, but simply a set of personal opinions that are part of generalized personal models. These are not and need not be systematically formulated, expressed, tested, and persuasively conveyed in in-group talk, neither do they lead to consistent and consensual interaction of people without glasses against people who do wear glasses. Indeed, prejudices against people with glasses are not needed to explain or justify the social status or power of people who don't wear glasses. Similar remarks hold for prejudices we may have about other categories of people. For instance, ethnic prejudice is also fundamentally different from opinions about occasionally stigmatizing properties of appearance, such as having red hair or being overweight. Only when group and societal processes are also at stake, such as (perceived) competition or conflict, differential access to social resources, and so on, group attitudes may be qualified as prejudices in our sense, because in that case they are systematically (and not incidentally) related to structural intergroup relationships such as power and domination (Levin & Levin, 1982).

We assume that, without the functional or structural role of ethnic prejudice, we are unable to explain both their organization and their strategic uses in information processing and interaction, as well as their complex relationships with other dimensions of racism in society. For our discussion this means, particularly, that we would be unable to explain why and how ethnic prejudice is formulated in conversational interaction and persuasive reproduction among in-group members.

2.2. THE ORGANIZATION OF ETHNIC PREJUDICE

Ethnic group attitudes are not organized in an arbitrary way. Aside from the usual hierarchical and linear organization of opinions in attitudes that we have discussed before, it is plausible to assume that the acquisition, transformation, and application of ethnic attitudes is structured by strategically effective schematic principles. Part of these principles are general and define how social members form and use group schemata (Hastie, 1981; Wyer & Gordon, 1984). Each time in-group members are confronted with (information about) new, salient out-groups, they need not figure out again what properties of such a group are relevant and about which characteristics opinions should be formed. They have acquired an abstract group evaluation schema, which only needs to be specified with new data for a new group. With a minimum of information, group members are thus able to form relevant and effective belief and opinion systems about the out-group. Obviously, this process is a function of several social structures and processes, such as communication, interaction, goals, and real or imagined social relationships with the out-group. In other words, the organization of ethnic prejudice depends both on general cognitive principles of social information processing and on social (including historical, cultural, and economic) processes of group interaction and societal structure. In this section, we focus on cognitive principles, although we may use arguments derived from the set of social constraints, which we shall deal with in more detail in Chapter 6.

Group schemata may be defined by a number of relevant categories, which are developed as a result of the requirements of social comparison and of goal-dependent and interest-bound intra- and intergroup interactions (Turner, Brown, & Tajfel, 1979). We discuss these categories in an order that partly reflects their social relevance and application.

Appearance

Crucial for the primary identification and differentiation of out-groups is that their members can be recognized in observation and encounters. Appearance, defined as a set of socially salient, visible physical properties, plays an important role in this strategically "fast" process of identification and categorization. Once identified as "Black" and/or "female," further categorization and evaluation of out-group members may follow "automatically." Racial/ethnic categorization is routinely based on this high-level category.

It may be assumed that in-group members often follow a general evaluation strategy that associates greater perceptual "distance" from the (assumed) properties of the in-group with more negative opinions in this category when the categorial dimension is gradual. A Black group, thus, will be evaluated more negatively by Whites—all other things being equal—than a group with lighter skin color, which is "closer" to the White group on this category dimension. At the structural level of analysis, this strategy may emerge in certain societies, of course, through systematic interactions at the micro level as well as through historical and cultural factors, in differential power and status along a color "hierarchy."

Note, though, that this is merely a general strategy holding only for the application of this category. People of very light skin color who for other reasons are categorized as "Black" (or simply as "non-White") are not always evaluated less negatively by Whites if the differentiation process is "all or none," and not gradual. We have seen, above, that group categorization tends to reduce differences among out-group members. Processes of exaggeration and polarization may take place in order to "see" people as Black, even when their skin color or other characteristics can hardly be distinguished from those of at least some of one's own group members. The same is true, of course, for appearance dimensions that are not primarily gradual but categorical in their own right (such as the male-female distinction).

Indeed, this group schema category, like the others to be discussed, is not a purely perceptual or cognitive one but rather a social one. People are assigned the appearance prototypically associated with their ethnic group. It is this sociocultural dimension of appearance features (such as skin color) that underlies the naive group "theories" of "race." Also, for this reason, the appearance category is very important in perception and categorization processes in first or public encounters: It provides directly available information about the probable group membership of other persons.

Appearance is an attitude category that also operates in many other group attitudes and prejudices—about women, the aged, the handicapped, and so on. Apart from race, gender is probably the most prominent subcategory of the appearance category and constitutes the basis of the most widespread and universal sets of group attitudes and prejudices (among males). We assume, then, that almost all group categorizations are at least tentatively paired with external, visible, markers—if not physically, then at least by dress, makeup, or other socioculturally defined features of this membership category, although we surmise that inherent or permanent properties are more powerful as category markers and may be used in more negative group attitudes.

Because appearance is an inherent property of ethnic groups, and discrimination based on such properties prohibited by the law as well as by general norms, much talk about foreigners avoids naming such properties directly. Indeed, our data show that very rarely are ethnic group members negatively qualified just because of, for instance, skin color. On the contrary, sometimes it is strategically emphasized that the speaker has nothing against Black people per se—but only resents their behavior. As we shall see in other cases, below, not all group attitude categories constitute equally "safe" topics of talk: Negative evaluation of people because of their different culture is more acceptable than such an evaluation that is explicitly based on skin color.

Origin

Whereas appearance defines the physiological boundaries of out-groups for in-groups, origin defines spatial or territorial boundaries, such as those of (one's own) world region, country, town, or neighborhood. In the Netherlands, for example, ethnic minority groups, even those with Dutch nationality, such as most people who immigrated from the former colonies (East Indies, Surinam), are called *foreigners* (*buitenlanders*). Generally, then, aliens are categorized as a literal "out-group" and, hence, as "outsiders" as far as territorial rights or privileges are concerned. As tourists they may be considered as guests, but as guests who should stick to the rules of the host country. As immigrants from other countries, foreigners are automatically assigned fewer rights and privileges than the autochthonous population "who has been here all the time." Racist propaganda in the Netherlands, for instance, plays on emotions and opinions of the White in-group that are categorized by this label: It is "our" country, and, therefore, "we" should have priority rights, and hence the power to send them "home."

Everyday talk about ethnic minority groups is replete with references to the origin of the foreigners. We often find assertions such as "they do not belong here," "they should go back where they come from," or implicit reference to sociocultural differences defined by different origins ("we are not used to that *here*"). Note that categorization by origin is not only nationalistic, but may also pertain to town, neighborhood, or street: In-group members feel especially threatened when new groups come to live in their own neighborhood (Elias & Scotson, 1965). As a general strategy for the application of this category, then, we may postulate that the farther they have come, and the closer they are, the more negative the evaluation—again, all other things being equal. The strategies applied here are well known from the application of ethnic opinions in the so-called social distance scale measurement of prejudice (Bogardus, 1925).

Also, this group evaluation category not only applies to ethnic or racial groups but may also be relevant in the development of opinions about other out-groups, such as in the attitutes of urbans about "provincials" (rurals) or in general interregional attitudes within a country. In other words, coming from elsewhere is another primary category in categorization, differentiation, and, hence, group attitude formation.

It should be noted, though, that the combination of origin and appearance in ethnic categorization produces differentation that is not simply defined by geographical distance. In principle, other Europeans are more accepted in the Netherlands than people from Africa or Asia, but obviously this also holds for those "Europeans" who have emigrated to other continents such as the Americas or Australia. And, within Europe, people from Northwestern Europe are more accepted than immigrants from Southern (Mediterranean) Europe. Conversely, being a close neighbor does not always mean that attitudes are positive: Indeed, often nationals of small states develop negative attitudes about nationals of a dominant, large(r) neighbor, sometimes for historical and political reasons, as is the case between the Netherlands and Germany, between Belgium and the Netherlands, or between Poland and the Soviet Union, respectively.

Identification by geographical or national origin is, of course, less immediate than by appearance but is often marked by linguistic and other cultural differences, which, however, we analyze in a separate category below.

In many situations, origin may take prevalence over appearance, especially when territorial rights, such as space, housing, and social services, are concerned. Thus, along one dimension of analysis, for instance, immigrant workers from other European countries, or from Mediterranean countries such as Turkey or Morocco, may be categorized just as negatively in the Netherlands as Black people from Surinam, even when they pass as "Whites" or "nearly White." Here, origin is combined with social and cultural differences that, relative to Dutch culture, are greater for Turks or Moroccans than for Surinamese. The same holds for Blacks and Latinos in the United States.

Socioeconomic Position

The next major category for the organization of group attitudes is socioeconomic position. It is this category that accounts for the widespread group attitudes among "classes," such as the dominant, middle-class attitude about working-class groups. Some of the prejudices we have found in our empirical work seem to be similar to those that used to, and still do, exist among ruling classes about "lower" classes or castes: lack of education, intelligence, manners, speech, hygiene, and so on, on the one hand, and presence of laziness, aggression, violence or crime, on the other.

For ethnic group attitude formation, this category may organize opinions about the socioeconomic status, goals, and interests of the outgroup (Banton, 1983; Turner & Brown, 1978). For relatively small out-groups, such an evaluation is mostly less relevant, so that, generally, attitudes about very small ethnic minority groups are much less developed and pronounced. Thus, in the Netherlands, prejudice is much more developed against Surinamese (about 185,000) than against the (for White Dutch people, indistinguishable) small group from the Caribbean Dutch Antilles (43,000). The same holds for prejudices against Turks or Moroccans (together about 270,000), when compared to those from, for example, Yugoslavia (14,000) or Tunisia (2,700).

Apart from frequency of encounter, topic frequency in talk and media discourse, or other dimensions of visibility or salience, the socioeconomic position of larger groups is especially relevant in prejudice formation. Large immigrant groups are perceived as more competitive for space, housing, work, and social services. Many of the generalized prejudices formulated in our interviews pertain to the perceived "unfair" claims of minority groups to an equal share in society and the economy: "They take our jobs," "they take our houses," or "they profit from the social welfare systems." In general, then, this category organizes all opinions about socioeconomic threats perceived by the dominant majority. For those in-group members for whom socioeconomic interests are most relevant and most unstable, it is this attitude category particularly that has become very salient. This does not simply mean that the "poor" particularly will topicalize this category in talk. Political and intellectual elites often "preformulate" attitudes based on this category, and spread these through the media in ways that appeal to the economically less privileged (see Chapter 6 for details). Thus, ethnic prejudice tends to be located, if not "transferred," by these same elites from the middle classes to the working classes and the poor inner-city areas.

It hardly needs to be emphasized that it is not the real but only the assumed socioeconomic position of minorities that influences the formation of prejudiced opinions in this category. Socioeconomic "competition" is often mentioned as a "realistic" conflict between majorities and minorities (Banton, 1983; Rabbie & Wilkens, 1971). This means that negative opinions can be easily legitimated, as is indeed the case in our data. The quasi-objectivity attributed to (unfair) competition is an important premise that may be used in defensible argumentation. For the elite, such as for academics who study prejudice, thus, scapegoating of minorities by poor majority group members is, therefore, a preferred explanation. Through this strategy, prejudice can be easily transferred to the socioeconomically oppressed. At least for the Netherlands, with only a small percentage of minorities, there is no real competition for scarce resources such as work and housing. Moreover, it has also been established that the minorities often occupy houses or jobs that majority group members wouldn't want to occupy anyway.

Together with the cultural category to be discussed shortly, the opinions in this category appear to be the most safe in public talk about foreigners. A striking example of this could be witnessed in early 1985, when a few thousand Tamil refugees from Sri Lanka fled to the Netherlands (see Chapter 6 for details). The political (Centre-Right) majority as well as a number of newspapers initiated the major topic about these refugees—whether they were "real" (political) refugees or merely "economic" refugees. This discussion, of course, appealed to existing negative attitudes about foreigners in general, so that in talk and letters to the editor, there were soon widespread negative opinions against a potential minority group even when hardly anybody had ever met a Tamil. Similar categorizations have taken place in the United States with immigrants coming from, for instance, Haiti or Central America. Such examples show, (a) the relevance of the socioeconomic category for attitude and prejudice formation, (b) that it is a safe topic for prejudiced talk, (c) that the formation of negative ethnic attitudes may be programed by the elite and those who control the media, and (d) that negative attitudes may be formed, by prejudice schema transfer, about ethnic groups that are practically unknown.

Socioeconomic status as a category of group categorization meshes class concepts with ethnic ones. The negative attitudes about Turkish and Moroccan workers in Western Europe, thus, are not just defined by Origin or Appearance, but also by their prototypically "lower" class position. They are not expected to be doctors, lawyers, or professors, and our data suggest that less negative attitudes exist about (upper-)middle-class members of such salient groups.

Sociocultural Properties

The next major category people use when organizing beliefs and opinions about other groups may be called the *sociocultural* one. Under this category, in-groups typically store beliefs about assumed norms, values, rules, and habits of the out-group, as well as opinions about language, religion, and other cultural or ethnic information assumed to differentiate the out-group from the in-group.

Our interview data suggest that this is a salient category, especially for in-group members who live in everyday contact with ethnic minority group members. The obvious reason is that, apart from physical appearance, sociocultural properties of out-groups seem to be most "visible." They determine behavior of and, hence, interaction with out-group members. Routine complaints about strange dress, religious habits, family structure and relationships, cooking, child rearing, or communication account for large parts of the interviews with prejudiced in-group members. Everyday differences, thus, seem to be most conspicuous in this category and, at the same time, associated with much affect.

The overall conclusion drawn from the opinions about such cultural differences, therefore, is standard: If they want to live here, they must adapt to our culture; they should at least speak our language, behave as we do, and further arrange their lives so that they don't bother us. Differences in basic norms and values, indeed, are perceived as cultural threats, because they are seen as a possible infringement on the very core of the cultural identity of the dominant in-group. Cultural differences associated with Islam particularly are routinely noted for their disturbing if not "dominant" nature. Assumed cultural threats are also a recurrent theme in racist propaganda, even when only a small percentage of the total population is Muslim.

As with the other categories, cultural differences tend to be exaggerated and polarized in ethnic attitude schemata. Selective attention is paid to sometimes marginal differences, such as dress, cooking, or behavior, and these are then magnified and taken as "typical" (and unacceptable) of the other group as a whole. In the Netherlands, for instance, there is much resentment against use of their own language by Turks and Moroccans, the purported "home slaughtering" of sheep or goats, or the treatment of women according to (assumed) Islamic rule. Norms of religious tolerance, which have a long tradition in the Netherlands, are not usually applied to Muslims. And the fact that women in the Netherlands, until recently, had a hardly less subservient role, is conveniently forgotten in such cultural stereotypes. Indeed, it is interesting to note that these stereotypes about the treatment of women in the out-group culture often do not seem to be inconsistent with quite conservative attitudes about women's liberation in the in-group. Tentatively, one might even assume that it is especially those sociocultural properties of the out-group that are barely superseded within the in-group itself that are resented. Many of the focal opinions against immigrant workers, indeed, were until not too long ago applied against the autochthonous working class as well ("asocial behavior," language use, lack of hygiene, inferior position of women, noise, unemployment, and so on). This suggests that sociocultural prejudices may also be formed as a cognitive defense against negative self-judgments. This phenomenon requires more detailed analysis, but it shows how complex the categorization of ethnic opinions may be.

The sociocultural category of group prejudices also holds for other social groups. Prejudice against various youth groups (from the Mods, Rockers, Hippies, and so on of the 1960s, to the Punks, squatters, football hooligans, and so on of the 1980s) is mostly organized around this category, for example, they dress differently, they have different norms and values, behave differently, and have their own language code or styles.

Personal Characteristics

Finally, ethnic group differences are often associated with "personal" or "personality" characteristics, assumed to be "racially" inherent or closely linked to cultural properties. That is, unlike the behavior attributions that are part of the perception and interpretation of in-group members, such personal properties are not taken to vary across individuals. Rather, they are assumed to hold for the members of the out-group as a whole. This dimension of ethnic prejudice is sometimes seen as its most racist core, because it is along these dimensions that in-group members feel superior to out-group members and, hence, entitled to the priorities, privileges, and power that underlie the other prejudice categories. Thus, out-group members generally tend to be seen as less intelligent, diligent, clean, effective, modern, or law-abiding. Typical, for instance, is the routine assumption of aggressiveness and criminal involvement. Outsiders cannot be trusted, they steal or cheat, abuse social services, are dirty and noisy, and generally are not only different from "us" but are also "lower" than us, both socially and personally. The well-known "attribution error" operates through this category: Negative action of out-group members tends to be attributed to such (inherent) personality characteristics and not to properties of the situation (Pettigrew, 1979, 1981; Stephan, 1977).

Dominant group members know implicitly that attributing negative personality characteristics is typical of racist opinions. In our interviews, therefore, this does not occur very often in its most explicit and overt form. Rather, negative behavior is described and the personality attribution in that case may remain implicit. Standard prejudices such as "they do not work" imply that "they are lazy," and the many "they do not know how to . . ." stories often imply that "they are stupid." Most frequent, both in talk and in the media, however, are the many stories about aggression and crime, which also directly suggest negative personality characteristics. We have seen, above, that for general negative opinions, it is interactionally and normatively safer for speakers to use the permitted opinions about unfair competition and intolerable lack of cultural adaptation to the host country. Apart from the clear, implicit meanings of our own interviews, research among minority group members themselves in particular has shown that the negative personality attributions against minorities systematically appear in the many forms of verbal or nonverbal actions against minority group members (Essed, 1984).

Recall that many of these prejudices are similar to the traditional stereotypes about working-class members: Aggressiveness, crime, or drug (alcohol) abuse, were also the standard conceptions of the poor. This means that, at this point, ethnic and class prejudice may be combined, especially when immigrant groups are predominantly working class and living in poor neighborhoods.

Conclusions

In this section, we have taken the schematic notion of group attitude as a starting point for the theoretical analysis of ethnic prejudice. We emphasized that prejudice is not personal, but group based, and organized by high-level negative opinions that are inferred from biased modeling of out-groups, their members, and their actions. Such prejudices are acquired, shared, and communicated within the in-group in various social (historical, cultural) contexts. Apart from their more general functions in effective social information processing about (other) groups, ethnic prejudices function mainly as cognitive programs for the planning, execution, and justification of negative actions against minority groups by a dominant majority and within a racist social structure.

It was also suggested that, at several points, we do not follow the classical approaches to ethnic prejudice. We do not define prejudice in terms of individual biases in social information processing or personal bigotry. We have argued that prejudices do not imply irrationality and rigidity but, on the contrary, require flexible social information processes. They are not merely cognitive errors but strategic ways of establishing a negative attitude about an out-group. General properties of effective social information processing, for example, heuristics such as overgeneralization (Grant & Holmes, 1981), instantiation, or wrong attributions, are insufficient to explain the forms, contents, and uses of ethnic prejudices. And the "wrongness" of ethnic prejudice cannot simply be established by the observing scientist appealing to universal norms of humanity, but may even be assessed descriptively by concluding that in-group members do not follow the judgmental norms and values they apply to members of the out-group.

The group schemata that form the framework for the storage of beliefs and opinions about ethnic minority groups appears to feature a few basic categories: Appearance, Origin, Socioeconomic, Sociocultural, and Personality characteristics. These categories are not merely effective ways of organizing social cognitions, they have been derived from and are functional in perception, interaction, and evaluation of out-groups. They define physiological, territorial, class, culture, and character differences and, hence, boundaries between in-group and out-group members. They enable everyday identification, categorization, differentiation, exaggeration, and, therefore, negative evaluation of ethnic minority group members and their interactions. The respective categories of ethnic group schemata adequately represent the relevant domains of perception and (inter)action in intergroup relations. The schema is general and abstract and, hence, may be used to form similar prejudices about other ethnic groups.

In these various categories, the opinions are not just negative but also tightly organized and salient. Aside from categorical organization, the opinions may involve common concepts, such as perceived difference, deviance, or threat. Thus, different appearance threatens our expectations about homogeneous physiognomy in everyday perception and requires permanent attention and special information processing. Different origin threatens our territory and related rights and privileges, as do the socioeconomic goals of the out-group. Different culture simply threatens our culture and, hence, our routine perception, interpretation, and interaction in daily life. And finally, perceived negative personal characteristics may involve the most direct, namely, bodily, threat, when foreigners are seen as violent and criminal, or threat to our town or neighborhood, when they are seen as dirty, noisy, or drug addicted.

The categories we have introduced define a structural schema and, therefore, also allow focused retrieval and application. Depending on context, people may activate relevant categories of the prejudice schema, such as socioeconomic properties in a context of work or housing. Within each category, opinions are again organized hierarchically, so that summarizing macro opinions figure on top, and more specific general opinions lower in the hierarchy. The macroproposition, "They are (unjustly) favored"—against, "We are discriminated against"—thus, organizes the many opinions about favored treatment in housing, work, or social services. "They are aggressive" may organize prejudiced opinions such as "They are always fighting," "They carry knives," and so on, whereas "They are criminal" will be the macroopinion on top of a host of microopinions such as "They steal," "They deal in drugs," and so on.

We suggested that the respective prejudice categories have been analyzed in an order that might indicate an order of importance and, hence, of acquisition. This means that with each "new" ethnic group, of immigrants, or any social group for that matter, in-group members will first attend to their appearance and origin (if relevant), then to socioeconomic features, and next to cultural and personality characteristics. This order also shows everyday person and group identification and categorization (the country, race, gender, class sequence) of people. Thus, for the Tamil group immigrating to the Netherlands, the first information provided by the media was about their foreign (Third World) country, and their ethnic (racial) identity (and, hence, mostly implicitly, their appearance), followed by stories about their "goals," namely, as "economic refugees," leading to prejudices about their use or abuse of the social services and their claim on "our" resources. Cultural and personality characteristics were not yet given in that initial state, although frequent mention of their "illegal" entry (or even about their "terrorist" background), of course, already prepared the "criminal" nature of their personality category (van Dijk, 1987b, Ch.4).

The categorial and hierarchical organization of ethnic prejudice allows fast and selective schema retrieval and application. It also enables individual group members and subgroups to develop more specific prejudice schemata or models. That is, for some majority subgroups, cultural differences may be more relevant than socioeconomic ones and that would probably result in a more prominent position in the schema or model of such a more relevant category. Also, the more relevant category will organize more and more-differentiated opinions. Depending on the context, individual group members may strategically activate and apply different portions of the ethnic prejudice. These strategies of the actual use of prejudice are studied in the next sections, where we also pay further attention to the actual contents of ethnic prejudices in the Netherlands and the United States.

3. Prejudiced opinions and their organization

With the theoretical model outlined in the previous sections, we should now be able to construct the general attitudes about ethnic minority groups. Unlike much other current work on ethnic or other stereotypes, we find it important to specify the actual contents and structures of ethnic attitudes. Only such a theoretically based reconstruction allows us to make detailed analyses of prejudiced information processing and persuasive communication. Unlike the classical studies of ethnic "traits" in the research tradition initiated by Katz and Braly (1933), however, we represent prejudices as (evaluative) propositions according to our theory of (prejudiced) opinions given in the previous sections.

As our example, we take the ethnic opinions formulated in the (38) interviews recorded in a high-contact neighborhood of Amsterdam. This does not mean that there are no negative ethnic opinions in low-contact, middle-class neighborhoods, but only that they tend to be more diverse, direct, and sometimes based on immediate observation and interaction in the high-contact neighborhoods. We only retain those opinions that are shared and expressed by two individuals or more, which does not imply that "single" opinions are not also shared by other people.

We first list the negative opinions (together with their frequencies, given only to provide a rough indication about the typicality of such opinions in talk) according to the respective attitude categories we have distinguished above. Note that individual persons express such attitudes in variable combinations, types, and intensity. Also, their attitudes may be mingled with more neutral or positive opinions. This list of prejudiced opinions, thus, is merely an aggregate of occurring opinions in a given neighborhood. As a whole, it would rather represent the attitudes of a prototypically prejudiced in-group member. This also means that the opinions are abstracted from their context of occurrence in the interviews, which, however, we have studied in the previous chapters. Here, we are primarily interested in the prejudiced opinions per se, as well as in their cognitive organization. In the next sections, we shall then pay attention to the cognitive strategies that manipulate such opinions.

General
—They do not bother me/I have nothing against them (22)
—The neighborhood has changed (for the worse) because of them (9)
—They should integrate here (8)
—They do not want to adapt themselves (4)
—We feel threatened by the number of foreigners (4)
—I don't like them (3)
—They want us to adapt to them (3)
—We cannot live together (2)

Appearance
—You see them everywhere in the city (2)

Origin
—They should leave our country (9)

Socioeconomic
—They profit from the social services (11)
—They profit from our welfare state (7)
—They have it better than we have (6)
—They get all the houses (5)

Sociocultural
—They have a different mentality (20)
—They (men) don't have respect for women (15)
—They are a close group, keep to themselves (13)
—They have (too) many children (9)
—Children go to bed late (8)
—They do not adapt to Dutch norms and values (4)
—They make different music (3)
—They do not treat children like we do (3)
—They don't eat what they do not like (2)

—They have many people in their houses (2)
—Mothers cannot raise their children properly (2)

Personal
—They cause a lack of safety (e.g., on the streets) (4)
—They are aggressive, hotheaded (11)
—They fight (with words) (4)
—They fight (physically) (4)
—They are dirty (13)
—They collect all kinds of things from the street (3)
—They are noisy (3)
—They make loud music (3)
—They have parties in the middle of the night (3)
—Their children make a lot of noise (3)
—They are criminal
—They steal (6)
—They are lazy (2)
—They drink (2)

This list of (predominantly negative) beliefs shows that most of the general opinions about ethnic groups can be categorized in the attitude categories we have theoretically distinguished earlier. In addition to the specific categories, there is also a more general category that organizes the global opinions about foreigners, such as "I don't like them" or the strategically important "positive" opinion "I have nothing against them," which is often a signal for negative opinions. These general opinions may also be taken as macroopinions that "summarize" lower-level opinions of different categories.

Note that the Appearance category does not occur very often, as such. Except for comments about the "funny" dress of Turkish women, indeed, there are few explicit evaluative remarks about the physical appearance of ethnic minority groups, probably also because such remarks would usually count as explicitly racist. Yet, many references are made to "Blacks" or "those Blacks," which not only serve as an identification but sometimes also as an implicit negative evaluation. Explicit derogatory remarks that imply negative evaluations about, for example, skin color, are rare. This may partly be explained by the semiformal nature and the social constraints of interview talk, because there is independent evidence that such derogatory remarks indeed occur in informal talk (Essed, 1984; Greenberg & Pyszscynski, 1985).

The lack of explicit slurs or abuse pertaining to skin color or other "racial" features may be interpreted as evidence for a less relevant racist component in interethnic perception and group relations (see, e.g., Wilson, 1980). Because socioeconomic and sociocultural categories dominate, in our interviews also, we should in that case speak of "ethnicism" rather than of forms of racism. It is true that skin color apparently plays a role in the Netherlands, that is comparable at some points with, for example, cultural differences and it would thus be correct to subsume negative attitudes against all ethnic minority groups (including the relatively "White" Turks) under the general heading of ethnicism. On the other hand, negative attitudes against Black Surinamese, for whom the cultural differences with respect to the majority population are much less salient, require an explanatory framework in which "racial" appearance plays an important role. In a sense, this also holds for "dark" Turkish and Moroccan immigrants, even when cultural differences in that case seem more topical in talk. Group attitudes about White foreigners, such as from Northwestern Europe, North America, and Australia, are markedly different in structure, content and orientation, even when there are (comparatively slight) cultural differences. In other words, ethnic prejudice as we understand it is intimately associated with socially valued "racial" features. Opinions based on Origin also have a more indirect nature and appear mostly in opinions such as "They should leave our country" and indirectly in general opinions such as "They should adapt."

As may be expected in a high-contact neighborhood, the opinions about various forms of sociocultural "problems" dominate and are most diverse. Part of these are based on occasional personal observations and, therefore, may be analyzed as overgeneralizations. Next, we have the opinions in the category of Personal characteristics, which also derive from assumptions about the reasons for everyday action and interaction. From the diversity of this list and the frequencies associated with each opinion, we may provisionally conclude that sociocultural and personal properties are given relatively high prominence in this neighborhood. In other words, within the overall ethnic attitudes that have developed in the Netherlands, there may be specific variations depending on the social position of the (group of) people who hold them.

Individual Instantiation

The prejudice contents analyzed above hold rather generally and have been obtained from a group of interviews. Yet, it is also interesting to see in which respects individuals participate in such a consensual attitude. Depending on the person and the interview context, involving the topics initiated by the interviewer in addition, there is, of course, considerable variation. Many people have more moderate versions of the prototypical prejudiced structure outlined above. To compare a "real" person with this constructed ethnic attitude, we now give the ethnic opinions of one person, namely, a 74-year-old man living in another high-contact neighborhood, where we conducted interviews that were specifically aimed at obtaining information about the communication sources of people. The interview is chosen especially because of its "natural" character: It was conducted with him and a (less-prejudiced) friend and approaches a "real" conversation, in which he often persuasively argues against his friend. The opinions he formulates (in different stylistic terms, but presented here in the order of their occurrence in the interview) are as follows, where the pronoun *they* replaces both pronouns and full identifying descriptions of different ethnic groups, mostly Surinamese and immigrant workers from Turkey and Morocco:

(1) We have invited them to come here, we cannot just throw them out.
(2) They won't go back, they are doing fine here.
(3) They are here only for the money.
(4) They (Tamils) have no right to complain about the way they have been received here.
(5) They have too many children.
(6) There are generation conflicts between them and their Westernized children.
(7) They oppress their women.
(8) They behave in an authoritarian way against their children.
(9) They need our help to adapt.
(10) It is difficult to get into contact with them.
(11) They can adapt, but they do not want to.
(12) They do as if they do not understand you.
(13) They live as cheaply as possible.
(14) They do not take care of their houses (neighborhood pauperizes).
(15) They are lazy.
(16) They are asocial.
(17) They (Surinamese) have so much money, because they deal in drugs.
(18) They (Surinamese) have expensive clothes and cars because they are pimps.
(19) They (Moroccans) are dirty.
(20) The authorities are too tolerant; they do not understand the problems.
(21) They are themselves the cause of discrimination.
(22) They are favored in housing and welfare allowances.
(23) They may as well all drown them.

Let us now try to organize this list into the categories we have introduced earlier.

General: 9, 10, 11, 20, 21, 23
Origin and Appearance: 1, 18
Socioeconomic: 2, 3, 13, 14, 22
Sociocultural: 5, 6, 7, 8, 12, 14, 16
Personality: 4, 15, 17, 18, 19

We see that, in principle, all opinions can be fit into the prejudice schema categories. All opinions are (very) negative, except the standard opinion of "tolerated presence": We have invited them (the immigrant

workers) here, so we cannot throw them out—categorized here as belonging to Origin. For appearance (associated with socioeconomic status,
and personality) is the negative opinion about the expensive or flashy
clothes of Surinamese "pimps." The socioeconomic opinions are stereotypical: They are here only to make money, live on welfare, and they
are favored in housing. Also, the sociocultural opinions are standard:
They have too many children, oppress their women, their children have
become "Westernized," and they do not take care of their houses as we
do. The personality characteristics are sometimes straightforward: asocial, dirty, lazy, criminal (drugs, stealing, cheating), and ungrateful (as
in example 4). The high-level general category mainly features opinions
of general resentment and its inferences ("they might as well drown
them"), and the standard opinions about adaptation and the government
not doing anything about it. Another general inference is that if they are
discriminated against, it is their own fault. The closeness of fit between
the overall prejudices and those endorsed by this man is such that he is
close to the prejudice prototype. Rather exceptional, though, is his overtly
racist conclusion that they might as well all drown. This kind of talk is
very rare in our interviews: Similar opinions of a violent kind are formulated "only" three times in more than 150 interviews. The man he is
talking to knows that his friend is going "too far" and protests against
this kind of talk. The most negative consensual "conclusion" drawn
from negative prejudices is usually "to send them back where they came
from," and a less negative one "They can stay, if they adapt (or, do not
bother me)."

The opinions expressed by this man imply more dimensions of prejudice than just the categories mentioned above. Note, for instance, that
several of the opinions imply the assumed inferiority of ethnic groups
(laziness, but also having too many children, which implies that they
have no sexual restraint nor use birth control). Next, inferiority allows
treatment as second-class citizens (they should not complain) and at
most a patronizing attitude (they need our help to adapt). In other words,
there are several ways to organize ethnic prejudices further, and the
ordering, relevance, or hierarchy of the opinions may be personally and
contextually variable. We return to these further dimensions of organization below.

In this way, we obtain different prejudice "profiles." Each consists
of the same attitude schema, featuring the same categories and similar
opinions, only in variable degrees of strength, orientation, and elaboration. Thus, at the general level, prejudiced people agree that foreigners
somehow create problems; at the socioeconomic level, they agree that
foreigners cost us money (live out of our pocket) and are favored by the
authorities; and at the sociocultural level, there is agreement that they
should adapt to our culture (language, norms), that they have too many
children, oppress their women, and have strange habits of cooking, eat-

ing, or living. At the personal level, people will at least agree that foreigners tend to be more aggressive, less honest and dependable, and less clean and diligent. Profile differences may show, for instance, in that some people maintain that foreigners should adapt completely, whereas others hold that they should adapt a little bit (e.g., learn the language, respect the law and our fundamental norms). But whatever the differences in degree, the fundamental group attitude structure is fairly similar across different prejudiced individuals. This is one of the reasons we have assumed that prejudice is not personal but group based. The very consensual nature of the opinions formulated by different interviewees can only be explained in terms of shared social cognitions. Personal and contextual variation, then, explains the differences between the prejudice profiles of individual group members.

Further Analysis

To get a somewhat more abstract picture of the structure of ethnic prejudice, we may try to organize further the opinions we have found above at higher levels, as we did, also, in our thematic analysis in Chapter 2. In this case, we do not deal with thematic hierarchies but with attitudinal ones. The more abstract organization of ethnic prejudice may be rendered as follows, where the higher-level categories (on the left) may be taken as general inferences from the lower categories and their contents:

General:
  I do not like them
  They should adapt to us
  The neighborhood (town, country) has deteriorated because of them

  Origin/Appearance:
    They look different
    They do not belong here
    There are too many of them

    Socioeconomic:
      They profit from our social system (work, housing, welfare)
      We have priority in using social resources

      Sociocultural:
        They are different—do not respect our norms and values (living, family life, religion, language, and so on)

        Personal:
          They are different/inferior—aggressive, criminal, dirty, noisy

This simple hierarchical prejudice structure is fairly general and applies to many ethnic minority groups, not only in the Netherlands. Depending on historical and social circumstances, these categories and their contents may be specified in variable ways. This basic structure reveals a number of general sociocognitive features that characterize all dominant group relationships and their cognitive representation in dominant group members:

(1) *Difference and inferiority.* They are from a different country, look different, have different (inferior) norms and values, act differently, and have a different mentality.

(2) *Competition.* They occupy—and are favored to occupy—our country, town, neighborhood, jobs, houses, and welfare system.

(3) *Threat.* They threaten us with their presence, numbers, culture, and behavior, and, thus, threaten our territory, cultural identity, safety, well-being, and material interests.

These organization features can be found in each category and also appear, as such, in talk—of course, in different lexical variations. Competition and Threat may even be further integrated, because Competition may involve a threat to our basic goals and interests, that is, the basic sociocultural and socioeconomic resources of the dominant ingroup. The feature of Difference may be polarized to intolerable Deviance, which also organizes unacceptable differences of culture and personality, such as aggression and crime, which we also find under Threat.

It seems plausible that inclusion of negative ethnic opinions in a given category passes through a conceptual filter of social criteria: If some act or property is seen as different, as competitive, or as a potential threat, then it may be included in the attitude category. The overall criterion, determined by the higher-level negative evaluations, is that the opinion should, in principle, contribute to this overall negative evaluation of the ethnic group. It is this organizational (as well as acquisitional) criterion that guarantees that the attitude remains coherent.

We see that the organization of ethnic attitudes has several conceptual levels and perspectives. This also suggests that such opinions can be accessed in different ways, depending on general or particular context of interaction or communication. The overall normative conclusion inferable from these fundamental categories and features is either "They should leave" or "They should adapt," that is, avoid competition and threat, try to reduce or conceal their difference, and, finally, accept second-class status. Because this is not always possible (or even impossible a priori) the most fundamental opinion may remain: "They are not like us" or "They are members of another, opposed group." Despite the frequent normative claim "that they must adapt," it may be asked whether in-group members really want (full) integration and (hence?)

equality of the out-group. Maybe this claim expresses a form of cognitive dissonance: The speaker is aware of the negative evaluation of, for instance, cultural differences, and, at the same time, knows that such a negative judgment is not quite according to the norm of tolerance. The claim of adaptation in that case may function as a "solution" to that predicament: I would not dislike them as I do if only they would adapt to our culture. At the same time, the prejudiced dislike is transferred to the other group: They are the cause of my negative feelings. The most "tolerant" form of this normative conclusion would be "They can stay if they do not bother us," which, however, also implies that the minorities accept secondary position. Note also that there is another implicit organizational feature that runs through the various categories: *Inferiority*. Difference is not simply neutral difference, difference at the same level, or positively valued difference. The different culture, goals, norms, and behavior are inferior to those of the in-group, and so is their assumed socioeconomic and personal behavior: They profit, steal, are criminal or aggressive, and, hence, less "civilized" than the dominant in-group. As may be expected, the notion of inferiority does not explicitly appear very often in the interviews, because it is normatively prohibited to talk about other people in such terms. Yet, it does emerge, especially in those passages in which foreigners are assumed to be favored, a circumstance that is rejected vehemently with expressions such as "As if we were less than they are." From these passages, as well as from the organization and contents of the prejudiced opinions, however, we may read that there is at least a basic judgment of inequality between in-group and out-group. These various properties of the contents and organization of ethnic prejudice also show why a simple list of attributed ethnic "traits" would be inadequate (even for the account of personality stereotypes). Prejudiced opinions may be rather complex, featuring both in-group (us) and out-group (them) and relevant ethnic relationships. Indeed, another basic dimension of the organization of the ethnic group schema is the polarized nature of in-group and out-group properties (Linville & Jones, 1980; Lord, Ross, & Lepper, 1979; Meindl & Lerner, 1984).

Finally, our analysis also shows how basic ethnic prejudices reflect the norms, goals, and interests of intra- and intergroup interaction and societal structures. The basic organizational setup of negative ethnic attitudes is geared toward the development of prejudiced opinions that can be used as ideological protection against infringements by the out-group on the interests of the in-group. Ethnic stereotypes are not just arbitrary overgeneralizations or innocent opinions about minority group members. They represent the power and dominance dimension of the intergroup conflict, where the White autochthonous population claims to protect its territory, material resources, norms, and values, and other sociocultural and economic interests. Such a cognitive structure not only allows and favors majority group members in perceiving their social environment and possibly threatening groups as such, but also provides the data that may be used in goal setting, planning, and (inter)action execution, that is, in possibly discriminatory acts and their moral justification. We shall return to these interactional and social functions of ethnic prejudice in later chapters, but it should be stressed here that such social functions are preprogrammed cognitively (here we find the classical "conative" dimension of attitudes). In this sense, ethnic prejudice is the mental program of racism. This also means that the contents and structures of ethnic prejudice cannot be fully understood without an analysis of this wider context of their acquisition and application. This also holds for the analysis of prejudiced talk, which is one of the fundamental social expressions and functions of negative ethnic attitudes.

4. Ethnic prejudice in other countries

Our theoretical analysis predicts that similar historical, political, economic, and social circumstances, combined with the same cognitive strategies of social information processing, would result in similar attitudes against ethnic minority groups in other countries. For the countries of Northwestern Europe and those elsewhere where European groups dominate (North America, Australia, and South Africa), called, in brief, the *Northwest,* the (colonial) history, culture, and socioeconomic context is rather similar. Therefore, we may expect that ethnic prejudices in these countries will resemble each other in several respects. Before we continue our discussion of prejudice with an analysis of its cognitive strategies, let us briefly examine how widespread such prejudices are in different countries.

Reliable empirical data, however, are scarce. Available are only the results of the usual questionnaire type of survey research or laboratory research about national or ethnic stereotypes. Little systematic analysis has been made on the basis of informal talk, in-depth free interviewing, or the analysis of other types of discourse. A real survey and analysis of dominant ethnic attitudes in the Northwest, then, would require an entirely different setup and another book or series of books (see also Castles, 1984, for a more general, and especially socioeconomic, account of minority groups in Western Europe). Therefore, we only consider a few studies that actually yield some insight into the ethnic opinions as expressed in questionnaires and interviews.

Before we start that brief discussion about a few selected countries, a more general observation is in order. Social psychological research that we refer to in this chapter suggests that ethnic prejudice results from specific properties of social information processing about out-groups. This might imply that negative group stereotyping is a very general, if not universal, phenomenon (see also Brewer & Campbell,1976; LeVine & Campbell, 1972). To a certain extent, this is indeed the case. Anywhere where ethnically different groups live together, there will be forms of mutual out-group stereotyping. Economic, historical, and sociocultural factors may further support this process, often in such a way that dominant groups develop stereotypes that may be functional in the maintenance of power and privileges (Levin & Levin, 1982). Yet, these same factors have engendered rather specific ethnic prejudice in the Northwest, especially against racial or ethnic minority groups in these countries. Here, ethnic categorization has long been associated with explicit or more implicit beliefs about White superiority, which appeared to be most functional in the contexts of colonialism, imperialism, and capitalism (Robinson, 1983).

Current prejudices about minority groups still embody part of this historical and cultural legacy and are further specified by the actual socioeconomic position of (White) dominant groups and minority groups of color. The ethnic prejudices in such a context, then, are rather different from those in, for instance, many Third World countries where there are conflicts and prejudices among different ethnic groups (e.g., also based on caste, class, religious, or linguistic differences). Such ethnic conflicts are usually local or regional, whereas White racism is a more global problem, related to the equally problematic military, economic, and cultural dominance of a majority of color by a White minority. The point of this admittedly too brief statement is also to emphasize that White prejudice and racism in the Northwest cannot simply be "excused," as is the case in some racist discourse referring to the "universal," if not "natural" character of racism, ethnicism, or ethnocentrism (see, e.g., the critical analysis in Seidel, 1985, of such discourse of the British far right).

The same is true for possible stereotypes in minority groups about the majority. The socioeconomic and historical basis of such stereotypes is fundamentally different. Majority prejudices in the Northwest are associated with political, economic, and social power, and it is their embeddedness in the social structure that engenders the specific form of racism and domination in these countries. Also, for purely social-psychological reasons, minority group beliefs about the dominant group tend to be less prejudiced, simply because minority group members interact with majority group members frequently and in a variety of social contexts. Also, such prejudices are not supported by a general consensus, such as through the (dominant) media. That is, many general beliefs about the dominant group may have the form of correct judgments. For resistance and survival, indeed, minority group attitudes about majorities in this case better be correct.

224   Communicating Racism

The United States

Despite the vast number of studies
about prejudice and racism in the United States, there are few qualitative
studies that enable us to analyze the contents and structures of ethnic or
racial attitudes in that country (see, e.g., Wellman, 1977, for an in-depth
discussion of a few cases selected from a large number of interviews).
Most data about "racial attitudes" have been collected in surveys that
use (preformulated) questionnaires, as used by, for example, Gallup,
The National Opinion Research Center (NORC), and the Institute for
Social Research (ISR). Moreover, in order to study trends and developments, these organizations also tend to use the same questions throughout the approximately four decades of research into racial attitudes, such
as about (de)segregation or federal intervention for schools, jobs or
neighborhoods, intermarriage, busing, and civil rights.

Schuman, Steeh, and Bobo (1985) recently summarized these surveys of White and Black racial attitudes in the United States. They first
conclude that over the last 40 years, attitudes about general principles of
racial equality and integration have steadily improved. Thus, in the
1980s, the vast majority (more than 90%) of Americans think that Black
and White people should be able to go to the same school, compete for
the same jobs, or use the same public facilities, whereas such opinions
were held by less than 50% of the (White) Americans until the 1950s.
Similarly, most (White) Americans, namely, about 70%, disagree with
the opinion that Whites are allowed to keep Blacks out of their neighborhood. Of course, this leaves millions of White Americans who actually
do think that they should be allowed to keep Black people out of their
neighborhoods. While I was writing this section, indeed, this was illustrated most concretely by a mob of hundreds of White youths that threatened a Black and White mixed couple that had come to live in a White
poor neighborhood of Philadelphia.

This incident, which is characteristic of several U.S. cities (most
compellingly described in Lukas' novel [1985] about the recent history
of racial integration in Boston), also points to the second general conclusion drawn by Schuman et al. Whereas adherence to general principles
of racial equality has grown over the years, there has been much less
support for the actual implementation of the policies that have developed
from these principles, such as affirmative action programs, busing, and
neighborhood desegregation, except for government action in public
accommodations. Indeed, most people rejected such forms of government intervention, and the authors surmise that part of this rejection
should be understood as a more general reluctance to accept government
"interference with private matters" (see also Jackman, 1978).

These general tendencies in U.S. race relations, however, require explanations that go beyond superficial observations in terms of opposition against federal policies. Apparently, conflicts between official norms and their "implementation" in actual ethnic attitudes are involved. One explanation is embodied in the notion of *symbolic racism* introduced by Sears and his associates (e.g., Kinder & Sears, 1981; Sears & Allen, 1984; Sears, Hensler, & Speer, 1979). This symbolic racism is no longer expressed in explicit statements favoring segregation or discrimination, mostly because such statements are no longer culturally acceptable, but surfaces in opinions that oppose affirmative action or busing (whether or not people have personal interest in such issues). Shuman et al. especially take issue with the implication that if 90% of (White) people are against busing, the vast majority of the (White) population would be (symbolically) racist.

This is a crucial point. Given their own conclusions regarding the undoubtedly clear trends toward more racial tolerance, they have difficulty in accepting the little-flattering assumption that this might only be sociocultural veneer. As soon as real interests are concerned (whether those of your own family or of your own group—a distinction that, unfortunately, is not given enough stress by Sears and associates), people will show their actual feelings and attitudes (see also Wellman, 1977, for a similar conclusion drawn from qualitative interviews). In several studies about the ethnic situation, both in the United States and in the Netherlands, we have found similar academic, and generally elite, reluctance in accepting that, despite undeniable but superficial changes in the racial status quo, social structure and consensus is still racist or prejudiced when principles or policies are tranformed into the "real thing" of actually having Black neighbors, colleagues, superiors, or in-laws (see, e.g., Bovenkerk et al., 1985). Of course, even when in the United States many people (or corporations) reject federal intervention in many domains, they do so mostly for those areas where they feel threatened in their interests (taxes, EPA regulations, and so on), and not for those actions that might protect them (such as federal crime or terrorism prevention or health programs). We, therefore, find confirmation in the survey research summarized by Schuman et al. for the assumption, supported by much qualitative evidence and analysis, that social norms have changed toward more racial tolerance, but that actual opinions, attitudes, and feelings may still be prejudiced. Indeed, this prejudice has a functional role in a society that still has important racist structures underlying its White group dominance in all fields. It should also be borne in mind that questionnaire statements about the implementation of racial equality and integration may well be more positive than people's actual actions. Shuman et al. do not examine the studies conducted by

ethnic minority scholars that show the actual extent of racism in education, employment, housing, culture, and so on, experienced by minority
groups, both individually and collectively. We have reason to assume,
therefore, that their study implies a subtle academic denial of racism,
which we also found in our interviews and especially among (White)
academics.

California

There are also some survey data more
specifically about California. Several of our interviewees stressed that
racial as well as other social attitudes in California are more tolerant
than in the rest of the United States (taken as a whole). Therefore, we
briefly examine some results of a recent study by Apostle, Glock, Piazza,
and Suelze (1983), who surveyed people in the Bay Area. These authors
are particularly interested in the explanations people give for racial
"facts" and assumptions, assuming that such explanations tap underlying beliefs and opinions about other ethnic groups. Thus, if Black unemployment is high, a question about the causes may reveal prejudices
among White respondents about the perceived lack of intelligence or the
laziness of Black people. The authors distinguish several explanatory
modes, such as radical, supernatural, individualistic, environmental,
genetic, and cultural (or combinations of these), which are labels that
summarize the kind of explanations typically given for the disadvantaged status of Blacks. The radical mode would typically attribute causes
to White dominance, the supernaturals would invoke God, the individu-
alists would blaim the victim by attributing lack of success to lack of individual endeavor, and the other modes would similarly attribute causes to
the genetic makeup of the other group (the classical case of racist ideologies), or to the social environment or the (minority) culture. In our interviews, both in Amsterdam and in San Diego, we have found most of
these explanatory modes in the, sometimes implicit, arguments people
use to explain the ethnic situation in the neighborhood. Indeed, among
blatantly racist people and liberals alike, we consistently find the
explanatory opinion that (many) Blacks and minorities don't try hard
enough. In the Apostle et al. study, to a hypothetical question about a
case in which a Black man became successful, most (60% or more in
each mode) answers are in the environmental mode (less discrimination
in the United States), cultural mode (family and friends different from
other Blacks), or individualistic mode (people with ambition in the
United States can make it).

One result of the Bay Area survey, however, was that Californians in the
early 1970s are generally more in favor of government-induced actions

to promote racial equality. Thus, 38% of the respondents are in favor of a more strict enforcement of existing discrimination laws, whereas 18% are in favor of stricter laws, and 21% of the people think that enough or too much is being done already. A surprisingly high percentage, 33%, appears to accept busing, whereas more than 40% would be willing to pay more taxes and nearly 70% would sign a petition urging passage of strong laws to prevent discrimination in housing. Note, though, that 62% of the respondents would disapprove of or object to their child marrying a Black person.

Another typical finding of the Bay Area study was that traditional stereotypes of Blacks are rejected by the majority of the respondents, but that most people also think that most other Americans still have such prejudices, a phenomenon that we analyzed as a move of transfer in a positive self-presentation strategy. Thus, 24% of the people think that Blacks are more likely to steal or cheat, but 70% think that most Americans have that opinion. On the other hand, although 47% of respondents find Blacks and Whites equally ambitious, 40% think Whites are more ambitious and 2% that Blacks are more ambitious. So, although the "no difference" answer to stereotypical descriptions usually obtains a majority of the responses, the percentages are in the 50% to lower-60% range only, whereas the stereotypes that are negative for Blacks may reach 24% (or even 58% when asked about the value of owning a big car) and those positive for Whites, 40%.

On the whole, thus, it may be concluded from the Bay Area study that, especially as far as implementation of racial policies of equality are concerned, Californians appear more tolerant than most other Americans. On the other hand, among substantial segments of the population (about 25%), such as those espousing genetic, supernatural, or individualistic explanations for the disadvantages of Blacks, negative stereotypes remain prominent. In agreement with our own California interviews, even more people think that Blacks, for whatever reason, do not take sufficient advantage of the (assumed) opportunities, do not value education or ambition highly enough, and, therefore, should partly be blamed themselves. The "radical" explanation, which on the whole explains the status of Blacks in terms of racism of the White minority, is given by only a small group (about 6%) of respondents, much less than the well-known attribution to, for instance, an assumed "Black culture." Thus, blatantly racist stereotypes have become less prevalent, but remnants of such opinions may still be detected in more indirect forms of perception and explanation, such as a lack of ambition, a lack of educational or entrepreneurial values, or other personal and cultural characteristics of Blacks that explain their current socioeconomic position.

Great Britain

In a brief report of the Community Relations Commission, aptly entitled "Some of my Best Friends" (CRC, 1976), we find some survey data about the ethnic opinions expressed by different ethnic groups in Britain about "race relations." As usual in such surveys, there is a tendency for people to give the socially expected, normative answers, which also explains the marked absence of differences between White and Black people interviewed, on a number of points. About half of the White Britons, in fact, found race relations good or very good, especially outside of Greater London, whereas the other half of each group didn't know or had no answer. Even more Black ("colored") people told the (White?) interviewers that race relations were good or very good (up to 70%), and even less than 10% that they were bad or very bad. For this survey research, the comments made in the preliminary, informal interviews were perhaps most interesting. A major topic in White talk about Blacks was "cultural differences" as was also the case in our interviews. Comments were made about appearance (dress) and language. About half of the Whites, especially the older ones, agreed with the statement that wearing Western dress makes Black people more accepted by Whites, and even more thought so about speaking good English. Young White people, who also have much more contact with their Black peers, are more skeptical about this condition of acceptance.

Qualitatively more satisfactory field research was undertaken by Phizacklea and Miles (1979, 1980) in a working-class area in Northwest London. They extensively interviewed both Black and White workers about for instance, issues of class and "race" consciousness, political action, the unions, and racism. Contrary to other sociological work on racism, this study provides frequent quotations from interview statements, which allow us to compare ethnic or racial opinions with those we have found in similar areas in Amsterdam. One of the main theses of the author is that racism in this area cannot be fully grasped only in terms of a historically and culturally transmitted expression of superiority inherent in the colonial past of the British Empire (Rex & Tomlinson, 1979). Rather, ethnic attitudes should (also) be embedded in the present socioeconomic context of White (and Black) British labor and the decline of the area. In this context, racism is also the result of perceived competition for scarce resources, especially housing and work. That is, the authors assume an independent, socioeconomically rooted, racism of the working class, and reject the thesis that this racism is (fully) fed to the working class by the racism of the state or the elite. This does not mean, however, that the authors deny or belittle the racism of the state, but only that the working class through its experiences provides its own contributions to the pervasiveness of racism.

Although partly in agreement with this assumption, we show in Chapter 6 that the role of the elite and the media, *also* in the preformulation of typical scapegoating beliefs, should not be underestimated. Whereas unemployment and the general decline of urban areas is most certainly a fertile soil for the development of socioeconomic ethnic prejudices, "real" circumstances, such as actual percentages of jobs or houses for which there is competition, do not explain the racial resentment in such areas. This is most clearly illustrated by the pervasiveness of prejudice in Southern California, where unemployment is low and housing problems far less serious than elsewhere. That is, consensual models are in part also preformulated elsewhere (in state or city politics, in the media), and then easily adopted by people in the area to blame their socioeconomic predicament on the minorities. Without such preformulations and reproductions through the media, the prejudiced opinions would probably not be as widespread and homogeneous, nor would they be so similar to those expressed in areas where the ethnic and socioeconomic situation are very different.

That ethnic affairs are important in the area studied by Phizacklea and Miles may be inferred first from the fact that, of all social and economic changes the (White) respondents desired for Great Britain, stopping immigration scored highest (36%), much higher than having more houses or more jobs. A typical statement:

> I don't like all these immigrants coming over. There are just too many. I don't mind a few . . . I'm not prejudiced at all. I like them but they are in my country taking something from me. (Phizacklea & Miles, 1980, p. 156)

The general feeling that there are "too many coloreds" (Phizacklea & Miles, 1980, p. 167) is also repeatedly formulated in the working-class inner-city areas in Amsterdam in which part of our interviews were held.

Phizacklea and Miles estimate that about 75% of the respondents formulate at least some sorts of racist beliefs (in a similar area in Amsterdam we found a somewhat lower percentage of 63%). And 38% of the people in Northwest London blamed Blacks for the local problems in their area. More specific are the frequent complaints, endorsed by 42% of the White respondents, that Black people (West Indians, Asians) got preferential treatment in housing by the authorities, a form of prejudice we also encounter in Amsterdam (in London there is a waiting list for council housing like in Amsterdam). Accordingly, 24% of the respondents attributed the local housing problem to Blacks (Phizacklea & Miles, 1979, p. 109). Blaming minorities for unemployment, both locally and nationally, was much less widespread, however (17%, but see the 1979 study, where a percentage of 22% is reported), whereas both Whites and Blacks partly attributed unemployment to laziness or the ease of getting social benefits. Similarly, the authors found few explicit statements expressing the traditional racial stereotypes that could have been attributed to a long sociocultural past, such as inferiority and lack of civilization, whereas "only" 11% of the respondents expressed negative opinions about Blacks' life-styles.

We also found that, in their most direct form, such prejudices are not often formulated, for obvious reasons of face-keeping (note in the example just quoted that in Britain also speakers are well aware of the antiracist norm, and use similar quasi-denials as moves: "I'm not prejudiced, but . . ."). However, our interview technique focused less on "official" politics, class consciousness, or similar topics, but let people speak more about everyday experiences with foreigners, so that we recorded more stories that imply cultural differences, including the assumed cultural inferiority of minorities.

Finally, another topic that also comes up both in Britain and in the Netherlands is that the authorities "don't do anything about it." The concept of "priority" we have met earlier is explicitly formulated by the following speaker:

> They [i.e., the government] ought to think about their own people first and then the coloured people next. (Phizacklea & Miles, 1979, p. 116).

We tentatively conclude from this brief discussion that despite the ethnic differences between the two countries, prejudices in similar social contexts are surprisingly similar. Whether people of Southern Asia, East Africa, or the West Indies are involved in Britain, or Mediterranean immigrant workers and Surinamese in the Netherlands, the dominant prejudices, as well as their strategic formulation in talk, are sometimes literally identical in the different countries.

West Germany

The immigration of workers from Turkey especially makes the ethnic situation in the Federal Republic of Germany similar to that in the Netherlands (where on the other hand, the presence of "West Indian," i.e., Surinamese Blacks, and "East Indian" people from Indonesia, is reminiscent of the English situation). The discussion in Germany about the role of racism should in part be understood against the background of Nazi racism against Jews and other groups. Perhaps even more than in the Netherlands, this explains why the notion of racism is taboo in Germany. Most studies that deal with prejudice and discrimination against immigrant workers (*Gastarbeiter*), especially those from Turkey, are, therefore, using the more specific term *Ausländerfeindlichkeit,* that is, hostility against foreigners (Hoffmann & Even, 1984; Meinhardt, 1982, 1984; Tsiakalos, 1983). The use of the term *foreigners* is similar to that in the Netherlands, in this case. Most of these studies are again sociological, or documentaries, and few deal explicitly with ethnic prejudices in everyday talk. There is, however, one brief report of (ethnographic) field research that is similar to our own study about "foreigner talk" (Keim, 1984), in fact, this is the only study we have been able to find in the literature.

Keim (1984) first signals that a great deal of foreigner talk features stereotypical utterances that we have analyzed as moves of impression management, such as "They're people too," and "I don't really have anything against foreigners, but . . . ." People interviewed focused, just like in Amsterdam, on the differences in the area now that the foreigners have moved in: "In those days, you always walked on the street, you didn't have to be afraid, you knew everybody. But today the foreigners live everywhere" (p. 266). And just like in the Netherlands, the autochthonous people have difficulty distinguishing various ethnic groups, although in Germany this categorization leads to overall inclusion within the Turkish group. Finally, the overall stereotypes used to describe Turks are also similar to those in the Netherlands: they are dirty, loud (in the Netherlands, this is especially attributed to the Surinamese), and come in crowds. They dress differently, their children make a lot of noise, and they may take over our houses if not the whole neighborhood. And finally, just as in England and in the Netherlands, the government is blamed for not taking action against this kind of immigration.

For our discussion, it is most striking that the statements made about these topics are sometimes literally identical with those we have found in our interviews. This suggests that in Western Europe, ethnic attitudes as well as communication about them have become stereotypical in their own right. In line with the thesis of Phizacklea and Miles (1980), we may explain part of this striking similarity in terms of similar socioeconomic contexts. But on the other hand, the different political and historical contexts in these countries, as well as the differences between ethnic groups (Mediterraneans versus West Indians versus Asians), are such that these contexts can hardly explain all facets of these similarities. At the same time, more deep-rooted historical and cultural attitude schemata and evaluation criteria must be involved that explain part of the pervasiveness of ethnic prejudices in Western Europe. These also suggest which topics tend to be attended to in talk, whereas a combination of cognitive and social constraints on conversational interaction about such topics explain the similarity of description and self-presentation strategies.

Vink (1984), in an article intended to counter current prejudices against foreigners in Germany, lists a number of myths people often believe: they take our jobs, they are lazy or do not want to work, they abuse our social welfare system, and, in general, use too much of the national resources, their children lower the level of education in the schools, they cause the high crime rate, do not want to integrate, and, in general, there are "too many of them." This last opinion especially, which also has dominated ethnic prejudice in Switzerland (Ebel & Fiala, 1983), is usually conceptualized as *Überfremdung* (which may be loosely translated as *overalienization*). Again, this list is practically identical to the one we found for the Dutch situation, and this similarity suggests that people in Western Europe react more or less in the same way against the immigration of people from other countries, especially those who are ethnically different. The similarity between prejudices against (White) immigrant workers from other cultures and against Black immigrants from former colonies also suggests that racism, ethnicism, and ethnocentrism are progressively combined into a homogeneous form of negative attitudes against all those who come from elsewhere and who are "different."

A more theoretical approach to *Ausländerfeindlichkeit* has been formulated by Hoffmann and Even (1984). They analyze ethnic attitudes and expressions against the background of phenomenological conceptions of society, for example, in terms of Schutz (1971) and Garfinkel (1967). They reject the assumption that such negative attitudes can be accounted for in terms of ideologies, prejudices, or perceived competition. Rather, they try to identify them in terms of taken-for-granted notions that are reproduced in everyday language. The immigration of foreign workers especially has challenged this commonsense conception of German society as culturally and ethnically homogenous. The negative attitude, thus, results in the refusal to grant foreigners equal rights and equal status as long as they have not adopted German identity. Through examples taken from letters to the editors of several newspapers and magazines, Hoffmann and Even (1984) illustrate how Germans express these commonsense "theories" about their own identity, and how they deny or doubt the necessary passage of status and identity into German society. As a whole, these letters express opinions that seem more extremist than the English and especially the Dutch data we have examined. Many of them have a blatantly racist slant that we did not even find in the "worst" of our interviews. Part of this may, of course, be explained in terms of the interactional moderation typical for face-to-face interviewing, but even in Dutch letters to the editor, we rarely find passages like:

They multiply like rats and they eat everything bare like grasshoppers. (p. 46) When such a Turk stupidly looks at me, my hand tends to hit him. They show archaic behavior, they are illiterates, from a completely alien "cultural" context, and have Islam as their religion. Did Europe in 1683 conquer the Turks so that they now get children's allowance, rent allowance, social welfare, and return premiums . . .? The best policy for these Turks is: kick in the ass and out.

In everyday language as well as in the more formal statements of politicians or other elites, both reported in the press, we find expressions of attitudes such as: There are too many of them, we are losing our German identity, they are *Gastarbeiter* and, therefore, should behave like guests, they do not want to integrate, they have too many children, they will soon take over here, they take our jobs, houses, and space, and the government doesn't do anything about this. We see that these attitude contents organize around the same basic categories and concepts we found earlier.

As in many studies by White sociologists, the analysis Hoffmann and Even provide seems to imply a tendency to minimize the racist dimension of these attitudes. The confrontation with people from a different culture, and the refusal to change one's commonsense conception of society, is more than just cultural conflict and conservatism. Other foreigners, also those with different norms and culture, such as those from other Western European countries, are not conceptualized in this way. The reluctance to draw historical parallels with Nazi fascism, and the justified hesitation to compare actual discrimination against Turks with the holocaust, obscure the fact that similar attitude contents and structures are being formed and enacted against ethnic out-groups. Characteristic of many passages that can be drawn from the current documents of *Ausländerfeindlichkeit* (e.g., Meinhardt, 1982, 1984) is not (only) cultural conflict, perceived competition, or a challenged social identity; rather, "foreigners" (Turks) are perceived and treated as inferior in all domains of society. Yet, despite the more extremist attitudes shared by parts of the German population, it should be emphasized again that, generally, the prejudices are similar to those in, for example, the Netherlands, Great Britain, or Scandinavian countries such as Sweden (Lange & Westin, 1981; Oberg, Bergman, & Swedin, 1981; Westin, 1984). And, these attitudes are largely independent of the specific target groups: If they are of color, come from abroad, are poor, are many, and/or have a different culture, practically each out-group will be attributed similar characteristics, be evaluated similarly, and be treated similarly. Further comparative research will be necessary to study in detail what variations under what conditions exist between the ethnic attitudes and their racist contexts in the respective countries of Western Europe (Castles, 1984).

Finally, it should be stressed that our brief review of some tendencies in ethnic attitude formation in several Western countries does *not* pertain to specific opinions of the extreme political right or of explicitly racist parties, such as the National Front in Britain and in France, the NPD in Germany, or the Centrum Party in the Netherlands. On the contrary, we analyze the common, everyday opinions of the population at large—of people who belong to all political parties, come from all neighborhoods and from all occupations. In other words, we do not identify racism with individual persons nor with small extremist groups. The prejudices we analyze, whether more blatant or those expressed in more subtle and indirect terms, are part and parcel of (dominant, White groups in) societies of which the underlying structures as well as many of the individual and institutional practices are racist. The fundamental similarities between the ethnic attitudes shared among the dominant peoples of most Northwestern countries against those who are categorized as racially or ethnically different suggest that such attitudes are not just isolated incidents, bigoted opinions of small groups, or frustrations of those who feel socially and economically threatened. It would be interesting to investigate how such attitudes are reproduced also across national boundaries.

5. Strategies of prejudiced information processing

Ethnic prejudice should not be accounted for only in terms of negative opinions organized in group attitudes. Perhaps more important still are the strategies people use when processing information about ethnic minority groups and their members. Of course, these strategies are themselves fed by information from ethnic attitudes, but it is interesting to analyze exactly how this information is used in different contexts of action and communication. In section 3, for instance, we assumed that operations such as differentiation, exaggeration, or polarization take place. That is, when ethnic groups are attributed certain properties, in-group members tend to stress differences rather than similarities with respect to their own group, while at the same time minimizing the differences between ethnic groups, and between ethnic group members. Let us examine, in somewhat more detail, the strategies that characterize prejudiced opinion formation and use in social information processing.

5.1. THE STRATEGIC INTERPRETATION OF (TALK ABOUT) ETHNIC ENCOUNTERS

In our brief account of information processing outlined in section 2, we characterized strategies as flexible, hypothetical, goal-directed operations that apply to variable information from different sources (see van Dijk & Kintsch, 1983, for detail). Thus, people make use of strategies to interpret sentences without having to go through the complex and cumbersome task of applying, one by one, rules and categories at variable levels of analysis. Rather, they make fast guesses about the most plausible meaning of words, phrases, and clauses and, thereby, rely on some strategically relevant signals from various levels such as lexical units, word order, plausible meaning, overall topic, context, and various sorts of presupposed knowledge.

The same holds for the interpretation of actions and episodes. Within the last decade, many studies analyzed such strategies of (social) information processing, mostly under the label of *heuristics* (see Kahneman, Slovic, & Tversky, 1982; Nisbett & Ross, 1980; for reviews). Many of these studies have a normative, rather than a descriptive focus. They show how "bad" observers, judges, or statisticians people are. People judge simply on the basis of availability, representativeness, and vividness of single examples, and ignore base rates, and other criteria for making justified inferences. From a somewhat different point of view, we also paid attention to such normative "deviations" of the social information processor. This deviance is not so much defined, however, in terms of what social members should do as naive scientists, but rather what they do (not do) when interpreting out-groups in contrast to the (also imperfect) interpretation of their own group members and in contradiction to their own norms of adequate social judgment. The deviation, thus, is not from academic norms, but from social norms. And it is not merely a set of expedient cognitive heuristics, but a coherent and cooperating system of socially functional strategies geared toward the maintenance of dominance.

When in-group members interpret "ethnic encounters," their goal in doing so is not primarily to establish a truthful and reliable representation of "what is really going on." Rather, just as in the interpretation of other encounters, people construct a model that is subjectively plausible, which is coherent with previous models of ethnic encounters, and is a partial instantiation of general knowledge and attitude schemata. The overall strategic goal, then, is not so much to test such presupposed models and schemata for disconfirming evidence, but to establish models that contain self-confirming information (Gurwitz & Dodge, 1977; Lord, Ross & Lepper, 1979; Rothbart, Evans & Fulero, 1979; Snyder, 1981a, 1981b). Both cognitively and socially, this overall strategy is more effective than having to change general opinions and attitude schemata. The question we must try to answer, then, is what more specific strategies contribute to this overall goal of "biased" information acquisition. Within our framework, we focus here on the biased interpretation of discourse, which is the core of the reproduction of racism, but the strategies are similar for the interpretation of interaction and episodes in general.

Structural and Strategic Constraints of Models

The interpretation, that is, the understanding and evaluation, of (talk about) ethnic events is controlled by a number of structural and strategic constraints. As for interpretation in general, both external (observational) and internal (memory) data are strategically combined as input for processes of understanding and evaluation. Episodic models provide the structures and contents of previous personal experiences, real or communicated, with ethnic events. Scripts and attitude schemata supply the general, socially shared, knowledge and opinions that are necessary for the interpretation of observed events. Let us first examine how such models and schemata exercise specific control over ethnic information processing.

Models embody our past personal experiences, both particularly and generally. They represent subjectively interpreted situations, that is, both our understanding and our personal evaluation of such situations. Model structures are organized by schematic situation categories, such as Setting, Circumstances, Participants, and Actions/Events, each with their Modifiers, which may contain evaluative propositions (opinions) (van Dijk, 1985d, 1987c). As soon as observers (communicators) are confronted with an event, they search episodic memory for "similar" events. The search cues for this activation and (partial) retrieval of such models of previous experiences with similar events may be variable, depending on the special context, goals, or personal relevancies of the observer. When I go to work, I activate and apply the routine and, therefore, generalized, model(s) of my previous "go to work" experiences. When I visit Athens, Greece, I may be "reminded" (Schank, 1982) of my last visit to that city. Apart from the participation of myself, such models may be retrieved through identical Setting, Circumstance, or (other) Participant concepts, and especially by similar Action or Event concepts. Thus, meeting the same people in different situations will usually lead to the activation of different situation models, even if such models may be "cross-referencing" to each other.

For ethnic encounters, these processes may take particular forms. When observing a Black woman in a supermarket, as is the case in the "bread exchange" story we analyzed in Chapter 3, a White observer may not primarily bring to mind (any) other supermarket situation he or she has experienced, but especially supermarket situations with Black women, or, even more generally, any previous encounter with Black women or Black people. That is, the specific, salient presence of a Black woman in a given situation may activate "similar" situation models in which similarity is not primarily defined by Setting and Event, but rather by a specific participant category. This implies that irrelevant experiences and evaluations associated with other situation models may transfer to the present model under construction, for example, models of crimes committed by Blacks (even Black males) as reported in the press or communicated through everyday talk. The result is at least threefold: (a) specific attention is focused on one particular participant category, namely, a minority member, (b) other (irrelevant) ethnic events may be retrieved, and (c) possibly negative evaluations associated with such previous models may transfer to the actual model. The Black woman, indeed, will be seen as "deviant" if not as "criminal" in a situation that otherwise, that is, for a White participant, might have been interpreted as a routine supermarket event. Or, from the perspective of a female shopper, as a specific event in which a woman was forced to take revenge against the arbitrary decision of a (male) supermarket manager.

We see that fragmentary information from a current event, such as the ethnic category membership of one of the observed participants, may lead to specific ("biased") forms of model search, retrieval, and application. This means that the current situation is interpreted on the basis of other possibly irrelevant models featuring ethnic participants, and if such models are globally or locally negative, then this evaluation may be transferred to the actual model. This is probably one of the theoretical explanations for the concept of illusory correlation (Chapman, 1967) as it has been applied to biased ethnic information processing (Hamilton, 1981; Hamilton & Gifford, 1976; Hamilton & Rose, 1980). Also, the very negative evaluation and possibly negative emotions associated with the perception of ethnic group members, or with previous models, may by itself act as a powerful cue for similarly coded previous models (Bower, 1980).

Similarly, the salience of the ethnic group member in both the actual and the previous models will also lead to higher-level representation of that participant as well as of his or her (negative) evaluations by the observer, even when such a participant only plays a subordinate role in the situation, such as a passenger on the bus. This higher-level representation will again facilitate later retrieval, which is one of the reasons why memory for ethnic encounters is better than for comparable other encounters (Howard & Rothbart, 1980). It is approximately in this way that we theoretically reconstruct the well-known concept of *availability* (Taylor, 1982; Tversky & Kahneman, 1973) that has been used to explain differential memory status and access of ethnic inf nation and evaluation (Duncan, 1976; Hamilton & Rose, 1980; Rotnbart, 1981; Rothbart et al., 1979).

The Role of Ethnic Attitude Schemata

Unlike most other researchers on social cognition (see Fiske & Taylor, 1984), we do not attribute all processing monitoring to (often ill-defined) schemata, but clearly distinguish between the role of episodic models, on the one hand, and the role of schematic belief and opinion schemata in social memory (see, however, a brief passage in Rothbart, Dawes, & Park, 1984, p. 130). Search, access, activation, and application of models and schemata, similarly, are also different, and the same holds for processing "ethnic" information. Whereas models have structures that are abstract representations of situations, knowledge schemata, and especially attitude schemata, may have quite different forms of organization. Thus, for prejudiced attitudes, we have assumed a categorial structure that renders the relevant dimensions of intergroup perception and interaction. Especially for well-developed and frequently used schemata (scripts or attitudes), it may be assumed that they are easier to access than episodic models: They are more general, fit the current data better (due to their default values), are better organized, have more general concepts and propositions, and are systematically related to other knowledge and attitudes (e.g., within ideologies). Only recent or salient models that satisfy specific criteria may be retrieved nearly as fast in ongoing situation analysis. On the whole, however, "reminding" is a more difficult process. Therefore, we assume that ethnic attitudes are accessed first, and help search and retrieve actual models. Indeed, to understand and categorize a minority group member in the first place, general belief and opinions about appearance and group category must be retrieved first, that is, from social memory schemata, which may be prejudiced. Possibly negative "associations" in such schemata, therefore, become directly available (because they dominate the attitude schema at the macro level), and may be used again for the retrieval of other "negative" instances, that is, of other models of ethnic encounters. Here we find another strategic move that contributes to dominantly negative interpretation.

Next, the respective categories of the ethnic attitude schema may become operative as interpretation and retrieval information. Thus, in order to understand a supermarket scene, not only the supermarket script has been activated, but also the relevant attitude category related to sociocultural behavior of ethnic groups. If such a category features high-level propositions that summarize out-group actions as "strange" or "deviant," routine supermarket events, such as exchanging purchased items, may also tend to be interpreted in that way. And if an action can be seen as an instantiation of a general stereotype, such as "they steal," this will be the preferred interpretation of possibly ambiguous actions (Duncan, 1976; Sagar & Schofield, 1980). In fact, people do report events that are *only* instantiations of such ethnic opinions, and that have not actually been represented in models. In other words, schema activation, such as in storytelling, may lead to "fake" models. People tell about these "as if" they were real, and in many respects they are cognitively real, even when they are not derived from real experiences. The consequences for further comprehension, talk, and communication, are even more real (Thomas, 1928/1966).

Not only the prejudiced contents but also the structure of prejudice schemata may play a role in ethnic information processing. We have already seen that highest-level negative opinions associated with prejudiced attitudes may be the first that are accessed, retrieved, and applied. The same holds for constituent schema categories, such as about appearance, origin, socioeconomic position, sociocultural and personal properties. Depending on context and on the specific dominant subgroups, any of these categories may be assigned special relevance. After their identification as "Third World" and "Black," the primary focus of attention, both for the authorities and for newspaper readers, in the "understanding" of the Tamil immigration to the Netherlands was on their socioeconomic position: Do they perhaps come and profit from our social system? This is one of the dominant opinions of this category. In this initial phase of processing, at least, the opinion that "it is difficult to find good housing for them" is probably much less relevant. We may even assume that high-level attitude contents may be used also as special search and activation cues for (nonevaluative) schemata, such as scripts. The refugee script in this case, for instance, may be less accessible than the "living on welfare" script.

We have found that prejudiced models and schemata closely collaborate in the ongoing interpretation of ethnic encounters, and the way the structures and strategies of their representation and application lead to specific focus on ethnic minority participants and on the construction of negative evaluations. Several concomitant processes have been postulated that each contribute to the negative "biases" in prejudiced interpretation, such as irrelevant model retrieval (illusory correlation) and differential availability, search, recall, and application of models and schemata. Against the background of this overall framework of ethnic information processing by prejudiced group members, we briefly discuss some strategies that characterize such interpretations, and then turn to the cognitive consequences of this kind of "biased" processing.

Selection and Focus

One of the most effective strategies of biased information processing is selective focusing and attention allocation. Incoming information is generally monitored by personal or contextual relevance criteria. Information that is recognized as being socially or affectively relevant may be assigned special cognitive treatment. The mere use of words such as *foreigners, Surinamese,* or *Turks* may be sufficient signals to trigger the selection strategy: This message (or fragment of the message) needs more attention. These processes of attention distribution and selection are not much different from those of social information processing in general (McArthur, 1981; Taylor & Fiske, 1978; Taylor et al., 1978). People or groups that are novel, do unusual things, or that are relevant to one's goals are assigned higher salience. Selection procedures can be applied if the relevance criteria they are based on are defined in terms of cognitively prominent ethnic attitudes or models. For attitudes that are highly developed and salient, such relevance in principle may hold in any situation, whereas salient models may be more context-dependent and define specific relevance criteria. In the latter case, an unexpected agent or action, unusual properties of an unknown situation-actor relationship, defined relative to previous models (experiences) may require special attention.

In the interpretation of ethnic encounters, similarly, there may be selective attention for minority actors, such as by the very difference of their appearance or because there are "fewer" of them than majority participants. This special attention may also involve more focused processing of their verbal and nonverbal actions, which may enhance identification of actors and better recall of who did/said what (Taylor, 1981; Taylor et al., 1978). According to our processing model, this differential encoding of minority groups, group members, and their actions, both activates and results in different models of the situation. Minority actors in such models are accorded special properties, such as "different" characteristics, a more active role in action (from victim they may be promoted to agent role), and occurrence in higher-level (macro)propositions: What they do is thus assigned more importance. We have seen that negative evaluations in that case become more prominent and (therefore) more memorable. Such models may in turn confirm and be confirmed by stereotypical attitude schemata that focus on differences and negative properties.

These processes at the same time imply that less attention is paid to in-group members and their properties or actions, so that negative actions of less salient in-group members tend to be represented in a less prominent way in the model and, therefore, tend to be less retrievable. We assume that this also happens in the understanding and representation of stories about foreigners. We have seen in the previous chapter that whatever their attitude, dominant group members recall and reproduce especially negative facts and opinions about foreigners from other sources.

Negativization

We see that negativization may be a (general) processing result of the special attention accorded to minorities. However, salience and attention as such only lead to better organization and enhancement of evaluations. That is, negativization requires previously stored negative models and attitudes. It follows that these processes are more pronounced for those observers or recipients who already have negative models and schemata, which contributes to the self-confirmation of negativization in social encounters and communication. This assumption is confirmed by our analysis of the data in Chapter 3.

In the discourse strategies of interpersonal communication, this special processing may also involve meaning (Eiser & Stroebe, 1972; Eiser & van der Pligt, 1984; van der Pligt & Eiser, 1984). Meanings may associate with negative implications, in accordance with the overall negative "bias" in models and attitudes about ethnic groups. Thus, if an in-group member sees or hears that a Black Surinamese drives a big car, the negative association may be made that the car was stolen, according to the general prejudices about the criminal nature of Blacks. The stereotype of poor Black people (typically on welfare) is inconsistent with an expensive car. Hence the inference that the car was probably stolen, or the inference that (unexpectedly much) money must have been made in illegal ways (typically in drugs or prostitution). And, when information is obtained that a Turkish family has moved into a large apartment down the street, the inference may be drawn that they have probably been favored by the housing authority.

In this way, nearly any neutral attribute or action may be associated with negative conditions, consequences, or other implications that are derived from the general attitude. "Neutral" or "normal," let alone "positive," actors and actions are not coherent with predominantly negative models and schemata and, therefore, need further processing by constructing negative "explanations." The same actions of in-group and out-group members are differently interpreted: People we like are "frank" or "outspoken"; people we dislike are "aggressive" (Duncan, 1976; Sagar & Schofield, 1980; Stephan, 1977). Ethnic group members at leisure may be seen as being lazy, whereas in-group members in the same situation may be seen as having a well-deserved rest from hard work. And whereas Black people without a job may be seen as unwilling to work, Whites may be seen as having the "bad luck" of being out of a job. That is, the very interpretation process, and the conceptualizations of persons and their actions, may be directly controlled by underlying models and attitude schemata. A different perspective may lead to different evaluative associations of the meanings of discourse we hear or read in everyday communication. "Neutral" reports in the press, thus, may be routinely associated with their negative inferences, and these will form the model that is used for further thought, communication, and action.

Discounting

Another strategy of biased information processing is discounting (Kelley, 1972): If information about (causes of actions of) ethnic group members is incoherent with prevalent models or attitudes, this information may be discounted in several ways. Discounting strategies, thus, may involve the converse of selection, namely paying less attention to such information or explaining away such information as less relevant, ad hoc, or as an exception "that confirms the rule." Unlike the interpretation of action by in-group members, the causes or reasons for actions by minority group members do not tend to be interpreted in the most plausible way (Pyszcsynski & Greenberg, 1981). A Black male seen running in the street is not just in a hurry, but maybe running away from a crime or from the police. And indeed, the police themselves often take action on precisely this kind of interpretation (as was the case with an acquaintance of ours being arrested when jogging and jaywalking in Milwaukee, Wisconsin).

Discounting might also be construed as the converse of understanding, explanation, and integration processes, that is, as "singularization." Instead of the routine categorization and generalization that characterize ethnic information processing, focus is restricted to a single (exceptional) individual or special actions. Whereas for "typical" actions, negative models and schemata are being applied and confirmed, neutral or positive actions are not generalized to positive general models or schemata.

An ad hoc, particular model is constructed for one single event or person (Gurwitz & Dodge, 1977). Instead of explaining the action by attribution to inherent personal or group characteristics, special circumstances (such as luck) are taken into account (see below for other aspects of this example of the well-known attribution error). And instead of integrating the information with similar representations, the information is dissociated from such representations, so that it can be easily forgotten by becoming irretrievable.

A special case of discounting in communication is *detopicalization*. This happens when in discourse an overall topic or theme, which might be neutral or positive for ethnic minority groups, is detopicalized and given lower-level status, as a detail rather than as a high-level, prominent theme. We have seen above that the converse may take place for negative information: a negative detail about the out-group may be topicalized, by conferring it macro-level status, whereas negative properties of the in-group—such as racism—typically are deemphasized, for instance, in news reports. An example of the "upgrading" of details that illustrate negative properties of immigrants may be found in a story by a California cabdriver about an accident he had with a Mexican. Instead of being upset about, for instance, the damage to his car, the point of his story was that the other driver didn't speak English, a point he repeated several times and highly emotionally during his story.

Attribution

Selection, negativization, and discounting may cooperate in special processing of episodes in situations or discourse. For instance, if a negative topic is being talked about, and ethnic groups are somehow "involved," the recipient may associate these two topics in such a way that the ethnic group is put in the causal, agentive role, even when they are explicitly mentioned in a victim role. A well-known example is the use and possible interpretation of news stories headlined as "TWO DIE IN GHETTO RIOTS," where the deaths may result from police action (Downing, 1980; Fowler et al., 1979). Yet, violence and riots are conceptually associated, and so are ethnic groups and ghettos, which may lead to the interpretation that the ethnic group "caused" the riots and hence the death of two people.

In general, then, the interpretation of action and action discourse about ethnic groups may involve negative attributions, by which negative characteristics of out-group members are taken as the stereotypical "causes" of negative events. In much recent research on ethnic stereotypes, we find discussion of this kind of "fundamental attribution error" (Ross, 1977): Negative acts of out-group members are attributed to their "inherent" (negative) attributes, whereas the same acts by in-group members tend to be attributed (and hence found less negative) to context or circumstances (Pettigrew, 1979; Stephan, 1977). And the converse holds for positive acts, which we discussed above in the strategy of discounting.

In our data, the strategy of negative attribution prevails especially in the interpretation and evaluation of the situation in the neighborhood or country: urban decay, unemployment, lack of housing, of which also ethnic groups are victims, are often attributed to the very presence of such minority groups. Variants of this strategy are known as *scapegoating* as soon as general social problems are involved, and as *blaming the victim* when minorities suffer from such social circumstances. We assume, however, that it is more general, and may extend to any kind of information processing about out-groups.

Attribution and attribution biases in our theoretical framework are part of a more general theory of social interpretation. The processes involved in the attribution of "causes" of action to "dispositions" of actors or to contextual factors (circumstances) (see, e.g., Jaspars, Fincham, & Hewstone, 1983, for recent reviews and developments) cannot be fully understood without a complete analysis of understanding and evaluation. Causes and reasons should be distinguished, the cognitive processes of action should be further analyzed, and we need to specify in precise cognitive detail what naive theories of action and explanation people use as part of such everyday understanding (Antaki, 1981). Simplistic distinctions between "internal" and "external" causes for action may be less relevant in such more detailed cognitive analyses of complex, situated action understanding. This also holds for the application of attribution theories in explaining strategies of ethnic information processing (e.g., Hewstone & Jaspars, 1982; Stephan, 1977).

Finally, it is also crucial in this case to examine whether attributional strategies and biases also hold for out-group members with respect to in-group members. Much of the literature referred to in this section suggests a generality if not a universality of cognitive principles, even when only White experimenters or subjects are used, that might not hold for the ways ethnic minority groups perceive and judge the majority. In this sense, the general notions of "in-group" and "out-group" used here may sometimes be misleading.

Exaggeration and Polarization

Prejudiced recipients not only tend to select information about minorities for special treatment, but also tend to exaggerate the negative nature of the attribute or action (Sagar & Schofield, 1980). Similarly, when in-group members are involved in the same situation, their negative actions will be minimized, and their positive actions exaggerated. This form of "accentuation" has been repeatedly found in processes of intergroup perception (Eiser & van der Pligt, 1984; Judd & Johnson, 1984; Tajfel, 1981a, 1981b). The result is that group actions and attributes are polarized, even when there are no or even small differences (Linville & Jones, 1980; Lord, Ross, & Lepper, 1979). In storytelling, this strategy leads to dramatization and, therefore, to more effective persuasion. The fundamental distinction, also systematically represented in the situation models such stories are expressing, between "us" and "them" is the core of this polarization strategy (van Dijk, 1985d).

5.2. RESULTS FOR MEMORY REPRESENTATION

Some of the results of prejudiced strategic processing have been partially discussed above. According to the specific interpretation steps taken in such strategies, we may first expect subjectively biased situation and text representations in episodic memory. In text representations, for instance, we may expect that macrostructures are constructed that reflect different relevance assignments, for example, details acquire macrostatus, and main topics may be downgraded. Agentless passive sentences may be interpreted as agentives when ethnic group members are assumed to be the agents of negative actions. Otherwise neutral meanings may receive negative associations. Information from (negative) previous models and prejudiced schemata may suggest "coherence" when there is none ("illusory coherence"), or the reverse. And due to discounting operations, it may well be that negative information about the in-group or positive information about the out-group is not or is only fragmentarily represented. Coherence relations may be established that are based on perceived causes between events or actions, for instance, as a result of biased attributions, as in our riots example: People died because of the riots, instead of as a result of police action or accidents. In other words, the semantic representation of discourse about minorities, whether in conversation or the media, is systematically biased by previous prejudiced models and schemata, as well as by the special interpretive strategies that are based on such information. This also explains why otherwise "neutral" (media) information may objectively engender or confirm negative ethnic opinions.

Biased Modeling

Strategically biased understanding of discourse and encounters, however, is merely instrumental in the formation of prejudiced situation models. Even when language users try to represent what a speaker has actually said and meant—which may be relevant when we represent the communicative situation as a conflict and want to argue against the speaker—their representation of the situation the discourse is about must be in agreement with their own cognitive representations. It is what they think actually happened.

Model formation is predominantly controlled by belief and opinion schemata and by (previous) model use. Under the control of a prejudiced attitude, thus, extant (particular and general) ethnic models are searched, partially activated, applied, and updated with the new information. This means that if the ethnic attitude as well as previous models of ethnic encounters are negative, there will be a tendency to maintain this generalized negativity in the formation of new models. The result is that even models of different situations tend to be similar, if only by their overall negative evaluation propositions (which may be the only dimension of a situation later remembered; see Forgas, 1979). This experiential similarity adds to the general tendency of perceiving the out-group as being more homogeneous than the in-group: Not only do its members all look alike, they also always do the same things, namely, those things "we are not used to here" (Park & Rothbart, 1982; Rothbart, Dawes, & Park, 1984).

Negativity may characterize each node and each level of model representation: It may hold for the situation as a whole, as well as for attributes of circumstances, actors, or actions at lower levels. This means that there will be a tendency to evaluate any situation in which ethnic group members are involved as negative. The processing strategy that applies involves both top-down and bottom-up "negativity spreading." If a social situation as a whole is evaluated negatively, the lower levels of the model may also be affected, such as the participant minority actors and their actions themselves. To wit, the negative opinion about living in a decaying urban area may be selectively attributed "downwards" to the ethnic groups of such an area. And conversely, an event in which minority actors participate may be evaluated "upwards" negatively, if the "foreigners" are evaluated negatively. The processes of (self-)confirmation, self-fulfilling prophecies (Snyder, Tanke, & Berscheid, 1977), or circularity that have been shown to characterize ethnic information processing are also reflected in the interpretive modeling of ethnic situations.

Selection and focusing in interpretation, next, will result in "highlighting" ethnic participants in situation models. Even if in reality they are numerically not very prominent, the situation models in which they are represented may well assign them higher-level, major relevance. This means that they are more likely to be actors in high-level macropropositions that dominate a model. Insignificant everyday actions of minority group members may thus be assigned topical status, as is also clear from the stories we analyzed in Chapter 2. Macro-level representation of minority group members in models is one of the theoretical reasons that recall of minority group members and their actions is relatively superior (Bodenhausen & Wyer, 1985; Howard & Rothbart, 1980; Rothbart, 1981; Taylor, 1981).

Accentuation and polarization result in a representation of participants in two highly differentiated, opposed groups, namely, "us" and "them," where "they" are associated with negative attributes, and "we" with positive attributes. Because topicalization and focusing result in the assignment of agentive roles to "them," it follows that "we" are represented in a stereotypical "victim" role. The structure of stories about minorities precisely confirms this organization of ethnic situation models.

The biases in the new or updated model that result from the various strategies described above typically confirm those in previous models (Snyder & Cantor, 1979). In fact, very little updating is necessary at all. The actual situation will be seen as very similar to the previous ones. The processing result of such comparisons is a tendency to strategic generalization. If a few instances of an ethnic encounter are perceived to be similar, it may be assumed that they are all the same. In this way, we capture one aspect of "overgeneralization," which is traditionally taken to be a core strategy of prejudiced information processing (Allport, 1954; Grant & Holmes, 1981).

Obviously, attitude schemata may play a crucial role in such generalization processes. Instead of taking each ethnic encounter as a unique event, or even as a member of a class of similar events that have been experienced before, it may simply be taken as an instantiation of a general ethnic attitude, filled in with some contextual variables. The event is then seen as (proto)typical for its kind (Cantor & Mischel, 1979). In our theoretical perspective, a prototype is, so to speak, the concretization of an attitude in a model. Models represent experiences, but also our imaginary representations of reality. Prototypes are portraits of imaginary group members, and each group member in a particular model will be compared to this generalized model as it instantiates the abstract schema. The ethnic actor, thus, is not primarily represented as an individual but as a "constructed" group member who embodies the most prominent and distinctive features of his or her group members as represented in the respective categories of the ethnic attitude (Origin: foreigner; Appearance: Black; Socioeconomic status: low job or jobless; and so on).

Generalization and prototypical instantiation are apparently the two sides of the same coin of deindividualization and dehumanization.

All the processes described contribute to further extension of negative evaluations, in the interpretation process, in model building, and in attitude (trans)formation, both for the ethnic actors, as well as for their actions and settings. The cognitive machinery appears to be perfectly attuned to the systematic derogation of ethnic out-group members.

From Model to Schema

At this point, we approach the strategic core of prejudiced information processing. If models of ethnic encounters tend to be taken as "copies" of previous models of such encounters, and if they are simply taken as instances of generalized models or of schemata, further abstraction to attitudes is also easy. One or a few models may then serve as sufficient "evidence" for generalization, decontextualization, and abstraction. In other words, in prejudiced information processing, there are few differences between general attitudes and general models. Little or no experiential evidence, thus, is necessary to develop prejudiced attitudes. Each instance, while being interpreted on the basis of the stereotypical pattern, is a confirmation of this stereotype.

Because contextual specifics do not matter very much, ethnic attitudes themselves may develop along a stereotypical pattern. Prejudiced ethnic group attitudes tend to be very similar even for different ethnic groups. It is at this point that strategic information processing has its most powerful (and, therefore, devastating) cognitive and social effects: Many different situations, actions, and people can be interpreted basically in the same way. "They" are all the same, and always do the same things. A set of interpretation, representation, storage, and retrieval strategies guarantee that such a powerful overall strategy does not run into the obvious danger of creating misunderstanding or incoherence from the point of view of the dominant in-group member. In all phases and at each level of ethnic information processing, various strategic moves guarantee permanent self-confirmation of observation and interpretation. Individual differences can be easily accounted for by strategically discrediting them, for example, by taking them as exceptions to the rule, as irrelevant, as specific subtypes, or by other moves that downgrade the relevance of social information (Crocker, Fiske, & Taylor, 1984; Lord, Ross, & Lepper, 1979). This is one of the cognitive reasons that ethnic attitudes do not change easily. In-group members have become experts in dealing with all the information that is incoherent with the socially shared attitude schemata and their individually copied prototypes.

5.3. CONCLUSION: RELEVANCE FOR THE COMMUNICATIVE REPRODUCTION OF PREJUDICE

It need hardly be spelled out how the theoretical account of attitudes and prejudices proposed in this chapter fits into our general framework of the communicative reproduction of racism. The structures and strategies of ethnic prejudice systematically appear in everyday talk, of course, under the control of interaction strategies. The categories of ethnic attitudes and their contents show in the ways people express generalizations about "foreigners," and the frequencies, order, or spontaneity reveal the relevance or the organization of such prejudiced opinions. Stories show how concrete ethnic situation models have been constructed and retrieved from memory. And the many strategies of talk reveal part of the underlying cognitive strategies of ethnic information processing, such as attention allocation, focusing, selection, accentuation, polarization, instantiation, (over)generalization, discounting, attributional transfer, and especially negativization. Talk shows us how in-group members have interpreted ethnic encounters, and how they have represented them in memory.

Similarly, this chapter also suggests how people interpret such talk in others. We have argued that the basic processes in the understanding and evaluation of discourse and events are similar. It follows that people may be just as "biased" in the interpretation of conversation or media messages. In this case, however, the "input" is already prestructured, and the interpretation of the ethnic actors or events told about already suggested. Whereas the events and situations themselves at least potentially allow a more or less "neutral" interpretation, much of the information that might be relevant for such an alternative interpretation may be absent for prejudiced talk. That is, in such discourse, the minority actor and action may appear even more stereotypical and even more negative. Without counterinformation, it will be difficult to construct alternative ethnic models. At this communicative, and hence social, level, the cognitive processes of interpretation appear to be even more self-confirming. This is exactly what the power of the consensus means. In the next chapter, we investigate in more detail these communicative dimensions of prejudiced cognitions and conversations.

5

The Interpersonal Communication of Racism

1. Communication and persuasion

1.1. THE STRUCTURE OF INTERPERSONAL COMMUNICATION

In this chapter, we analyze the dynamics of the reproduction of racism, namely, the interpersonal communication of ethnic prejudice in conversational interaction. The previous chapters have given us the necessary theoretical instruments for such an analysis, as well as insight into the structural and strategic properties of two major components of the communication process, namely, discourse and ethnic attitudes. We should now relate these components in a theoretical framework that explicitly accounts for the cognitive and interactional strategies involved in the production, understanding, and representation of prejudiced talk in memory, and for the links of such representations with the ethnic attitudes of recipients.

Such a theoretical framework can hardly be construed from scratch. We must make use of classical insights and results from theories of interpersonal communication in general, and from those of persuasion research in particular. However, we also argue that until very recently such approaches were hardly adequate, both from a cognitive and from a discourse analytical point of view. Despite various cognitivistic orientations in social psychology, the analysis of attitudes and attitude change has partly remained under the influence of behaviorist conceptualizations, in which messages were treated as "stimuli," behaviors as their caused "responses," and attitudes as the "mediating" intermediary variables of this connection.

The previous chapters have suggested a different approach to interpersonal communication and persuasion. Attitudes in general, and ethnic prejudice in particular, require systematic and explicit cognitive analysis in their own right. The processes of their acquisition and change cannot be fully understood without a detailed account of the cognitive strategies of social information processing. Because interpersonal communication and persuasion are mainly verbal, it is also crucial to pay special attention to the structures, the strategies, and the processing of the "messages" on which they are based. Also, in the currently reformulated cognitive orientations in communication and persuasion research, this discourse dimension remains underdeveloped. And finally, everyday persuasive conversation is also a specific form of social interaction, which requires independent analysis of speech acts, acts of argumentation, and further social acts performed by speech participants in communicative contexts.

Some elements of this new approach are being provided in current research in social cognition and communication. It has become quite fashionable, for instance, to rephrase old cognitivistic notions in terms of a schema-theoretic framework, and to account for communication in terms of the information processing paradigm. We have argued before, however, that the mere use of a notion like "schema" is far from sufficient. In the majority of the recent studies that use this notion for theoretical and experimental analysis, not a single schema is ever explicitly spelled out. Explanations of person or group perception and memory, or of other forms of social information processing, therefore, remain at a rather superficial and semi-intuitive level. The same is true for the analysis of attitudes and ethnic stereotypes and their uses in communication and interaction. This is one of the reasons we find present developments in social cognition not "cognitive" enough.

On the other hand, current research on cognition and communication is not "social" enough either. We claim that when information is processed about other persons and groups, it is not sufficient to examine in which ways these processes are similar to those of information processing (e.g., about objects) in general, as is the case, for example, in the account of ethnic stereotypes in terms of prototypes, or the explanation of prejudiced biases in terms of illusory correlations or availability heuristics. An account of the social dimension of social cognition must be based on the following assumptions: (a) structures and strategies of social information in memory, for instance, about groups, functionally reflect the role of this information in communication and interaction, and (b) these processes of communication and interaction are structurally embedded in social micro and macro contexts. These two dimensions assign both a functional and a contextual dimension to the nature of social cognition. One of the many consequences of this orientation is, for instance, that people are processing social information not as individual persons, but rather as social members of groups. This is crucial for an explicit account of ethnic prejudice as a form of social cognition. Interpersonal communication, in that perspective, is an enactment of intragroup communication and of intergroup perception and interaction.

Against this background, then, our analysis of the interpersonal communication and acquisition of ethnic prejudice requires a new conceptualization of the major components of this process along the following lines:

(a) The interactive production of prejudiced talk in general, and the persuasive structures and strategies of such conversations in particular, are a function of "underlying" cognitive structures and strategies of ethnic beliefs and attitudes. We summarily call this the *production* component.

(b) Similarly, the processes of understanding, evaluating, and representing talk about ethnic groups are a function of the ethnic representations (models and attitudes) of the recipient. This is the *interpretation* component.

(c) The strategic (trans)formation of ethnic beliefs, opinions, and attitudes is a function of these interpretation and representation processes. This will be called the *transformation* component.

(d) These production, interpretation, and transformation processes are a function of the discursive goals and strategies of conversation in particular and of those of interaction, such as self- and other-presentation in general. This is the *interaction* component.

(e) Finally, the cognitive, discursive, and interactional structures and strategies are a function of the social (micro) situation and, therefore, of societal (macro) structures. We may call this the *social context* component.

After a brief critical discussion of the traditional and more recent approaches in the fields of interpersonal communication, attitude change, and persuasion, we focus our attention on the neglected dimensions of the process of social attitude and prejudice (re)production in conversation. The keywords for this new focus are *structures* and *strategies,* namely, those of text and (in) context, those of social cognition and (in) communication, and those of attitudinal and ideological (re)production. That is, we should show how discursive, cognitive, and social strategies of ethnic attitude (trans)formation within the dominant in-group are interrelated and enacted at the micro level of interpersonal communicative encounters. In the next stage, we then establish the link between this communicative, interpersonal level with the higher, macro levels of the analysis of racism and its social reproduction.

Whereas this might be a nice theoretical program, we as yet hardly have an empirical leg to stand on. We merely have our interviews as the major source for data about such processes. Yet, as approximations of real talk, and as examples of persuasive communications about ethnic minority groups, they at least provide rather natural examples of how in-group members go about expressing and conveying their ethnic attitudes in the social and communicative context. To complement these data, we draw on earlier experimental results obtained by others within different theoretical frameworks. Especially for the important interpretation and transformation components, we only have indirect evidence about how the recipients of persuasive talk about ethnic minorities understand and evaluate such talk and how its cognitive representation interacts with the (trans)formation of ethnic attitudes. In this case also, we must rely on previous experimental work, and on data derived from the ways people reproduce personal and media discourse in their own talk (see Chapter 3). Methodologically, this procedure allows less control and a less-focused study of isolated "variables." On the other hand, it provides the most natural form of interpretation and transformation assessment, namely, through the ways speakers spontaneously display their under-standing, representations, (counter)arguments, and/or (dis)agreement in further talk about such earlier communications.

1.2. TOWARD A COGNITIVE THEORY OF COMMUNICATIVE PERSUASION

The interpersonal communication of prejudice is a special case of the communication of attitudes, a process usually—and somewhat narrowly—captured under the concept of "persuasion." Before we propose a new framework of persuasion processes in general, and of those of ethnic prejudice communication in particular, we critically summarize some major tenets of classical persuasion research. We formulate these comments from our actual point of view, namely, that of social cognition, as well as against the background of our own, discourse analytical and interdisciplinary, approach to interpersonal communication and persuasion. We do not aim, however, to give a review of the literature, which has repeatedly and recently been done elsewhere (Petty & Cacioppo, 1981; Petty, Ostrom & Brock, 1981; Reardon, 1981; Roloff & Miller, 1980).

The Behavioristic Background

Despite a long and respectable "cognitive" tradition in social psychology, many studies of interpersonal communication, persuasion, and attitude change showed methodological inspiration from behaviorism, until the 1970s (Bettinghaus, 1973; Greenwald, Brock, & Ostrom, 1968). And even until today, persuasive intentions of a "source," expressed as verbal or nonverbal behavior, are still described as "stimuli," and persuasive effects on behavior as "responses." In the more cognitivistic approaches, these reponses were taken to be caused or "mediated" by attitudes, conceptualized as the "intermediary variables" in the persuasive process (Petty, Ostrom, & Brock, 1981). The formation and change of attitudes as (or influenced by) "internal" responses to persuasive behavior, typically "messages," thus became analyzed as a form of conditional learning. Experimentally, this meant that message or "source" characteristics were treated as independent variables, and mental, verbal, or behavioral responses as dependent variables. Stimuli, as well as cognitive and behavioral responses, were "measured" and statistically "correlated," but not structurally analyzed and subjected to explicit process analysis. And also, the cognitive analysis was formulated in general notions, such as "balance" or "consistency," which were hardly made explicit in terms of precise cognitive representations or rules of inference.

Also, for the sake of experimental clarity and control, the usual setup of research was to manipulate some characteristic of the source (e.g., appearance, status, credibility, and so on), a property of the persuasive message (e.g., style or argument position), or the type of recipients (varying according to gender, age, education, or "persuasibility"), and to examine whether such controlled variables had an effect on the direction, size, or nature of attitude change, measured verbally (typically by scale responses) or behaviorally.

In this analysis of persuasion processes, the precise role of "verbal" reactions, such as opinion statements of various kinds (affirmations on scales, acceptance/rejections of preformulated opinions, or "free" formulations of opinions in, for instance, interviews), was not quite clear. Usually they were seen as the operationalization, or as the external expression, of attitudes. Hence, the permanent interest in the dichotomy between *attitudes,* defined as "verbal (expressions of) attitudes" on the one hand, and "behavior" on the other hand (Cushman & McPhee, 1980; Zanna, Higgins, & Herman, 1982).

Such an analysis ignored the obvious fact that verbal statements are also (communicative) acts, and in need of analysis like other "behavior caused by" attitudes. And only in 1970 did it become understood that action is not "caused" by attitudes, but that more complex cognitive representations and processes, including beliefs, intentions, and goals, interact with attitudes in the planning and execution of "behavior" (Fishbein & Ajzen, 1975; von Cranach & Harré, 1982). We had to wait until the 1980s, however, before such cognitive analyses of the attitude-action relationship were formulated in explicit terms of representations and processes, and integrated into a general framework of social cognition (Higgins, Herman, & Zanna, 1981; Roloff & Berger, 1982; Wyer & Srull, 1984). Together with impression formation and other interactional strategies, persuasion could in that case be analyzed in terms of (discursive) social information processing.

Early Cognitivistic Approaches

Despite the influence of the behavioristic paradigm until the 1970s, a substantial segment of classical persuasion research had a more cognitivistic flavor. After all, the notion of "attitude" itself implies a cognitive perspective on (influencing) behavior. This approach favored more extensive attention for the nature and organization of attitudes themselves, as well as for the mental processes involved in persuasive communication. Although reference to Bartlett's work (1932) on memory and schemata was not frequent, and despite the fact that especially his analysis of the interpersonal communication of beliefs is seldom acknowledged, he should be considered as one major source of this cognitivistic development. Gordon Allport, in his work on attitudes, rumor (Allport & Postman, 1947), and ethnic prejudice (Allport, 1954), was clearly influenced by Bartlett and always paid a lot of attention to the cognitive dimension of social communication.

The major sources of the cognitivistic approach to persuasion are the various "cognitive consistency" theories of the nature of attitudes, attitude change, and persuasion, such as Heider's balance theory (1946), Festinger's cognitive dissonance theory (1957), or Osgood and Tannenbaum's (1955) congruity theory (see Abelson et al., 1968, for surveys). Common to these approaches is the interest in the organization and the dynamics of attitudes and their formation or change (Rosenberg et al., 1960). That is, sets of beliefs are cognitively in equilibrium (balanced, congruous, or not dissonant) only under specific conditions. When these conditions are not satisfied they will tend to change. People were supposed to strive toward "well-formed" cognitive structures. Elementary "logical" notions such as consistency (not both p and –p), transitivity (for instance, if X likes Y, and Y likes Z, then X likes Z), or rules of "deduction" are involved in this kind of "psycho-logic" (Abelson & Rosenberg, 1958).

However, this form of cognitive analysis of attitudes and their change was highly abstract, despite the application to concrete examples (as in Festinger, 1957). There were hardly any attempts to specify in detail the contents and structures of the cognitive representations of such (in)consistent attitudes. The same holds for the dynamic processes of their change. Which cognitive strategies were actually applied, and how these should be explicitly formulated, was not (yet) made explicit. Of the full communication and persuasion process, only an approximate model was provided, such as by McGuire (1969, 1972). He specified the respective steps or stages of the persuasion process, such as attention, understanding, yielding, and acceptance. What each of these steps amounted to exactly, cognitively, was barely understood. As for the other "cognitive" notions of this rich tradition of attitude and persuasion research, the analysis took place at a generalized, abstract, and often intuitive level. As we have seen in the previous chapter for the analysis of attitude and prejudice structures, or for the heuristics of social information processing, there is a tendency to introduce and use plausible and interesting notions (attribution, availability, illusory correlation, balance, yielding, and so forth), but they often remained unanalyzed.

Thus, the use of cognitivistic terms is not yet the same as a full-fledged cognitive theory. The "cognitive analysis" of classical attitude and persuasion theories appears to be superficial at best and certainly highly fragmentary and incomplete. There was no question of systematic and explicit modeling of the cognitive representation of persuasive messages and contexts, no serious attempts at defining the precise nature of beliefs and attitudes in terms of complex structures, no systematic link between attitudes and the "behaviors" they were assumed to "cause," and no formulation of explicit rules, strategies, or other processes through which these various representations are actively linked among each other, on one hand, and with perception and action, on the other hand. If dynamic principles or even strategies were formulated, they at most had a plausible intuitive nature.

Message Analysis

Within the most influential paradigm of classical persuasion research, namely, that initiated by the Yale School (e.g., Hovland & Janis, 1959; Hovland, Janis, & Kelley, 1953; Hovland & Rosenberg, 1960), there was special interest for the "message characteristics" of persuasive communication. For instance, attention was paid to the effects of the ordering of arguments, leading to the well-known "primacy" versus "recency" dispute: Is information (or are arguments) better recalled when they come first or last in a discourse? Despite these early attempts, we witness another major shortcoming of classical persuasion research, that is, its neglect of the systematic structures and contents of persuasive messages. After all, ordering of arguments, choice of words (style), or the strength of appeals (Janis & Feshbach, 1953) are only some (even rather marginal) aspects of persuasive discourse. Little inspiration was taken from insights in linguistics, or the beginning of discourse analysis in anthropology, semiotics, and literary scholarship, to define the precise nature of persuasive messages. From classical rhetoric, only some major notions were borrowed, for instance, repetition (Cacioppo & Petty, 1979; Sawyer, 1981) or rhetorical questions (Petty, Cacioppo, & Heesacker, 1981). However, these were seldom integrated into a more comprehensive theory of the structures and strategies of persuasive discourse. Indeed, because discourse was merely seen as a message-stimulus, produced by a source (of which the production processes were also ignored), only isolated independent variables were chosen, intuitively, as possible determinants of persuasion (Fishbein & Ajzen, 1981). The way people actually go about persuading each other in natural communicative contexts was also an approach that received little attention.

Recent Cognitive Reorientation

Looking back at this earlier work from the vantage point of the mid-1980s, it is, of course, easy to make critical remarks about the theoretical shallowness and incompleteness of much work on persuasion in earlier decades, especially the research that has a more behavioristic flavor. Also, it is now easier to see why so many experimental results were inconclusive, or why firm experimental findings hardly received satisfactory explanations. It was only in the late 1970s and early 1980s that the dominant views in persuasion research slowly became infected by a more explicit account of cognitive processing, as it had been developed in cognitive psychology and AI since the early 1970s (see e.g., Cappella & Folger, 1980). In Petty, Ostrom, and Brock (1981) we find growing interest for the further analysis of "cognitive responses" in persuasion processes; Reardon's (1981) introduction pays attention to the role of cognitive rules in persuasion and its effects on behavior, whereas in Roloff and Berger (1982), we find various approaches that try to integrate the analysis of communication in the framework of social cognition.

The strength of a dominant paradigm, and the traditions of a discipline, appear to be very powerful, however. Even in the recent cognitivistic approaches to persuasion and communication, the old vocabulary and its biasing associations often remain. We read about "stimuli" and "responses," and cognitions are still studied as "intermediary" variables, and seldom as a problem or as structures in their own right. One reason for these persistent behavioristic remnants in cognitive approaches may be the conceptual analysis of persuasion as changing someone's behavior (response) by a persuasive message (stimulus), through a change of attitude (mediator, intermediary, or internal response). That persuasion primarily involves cognitive (trans)formations of intricately structured knowledge, beliefs, and attitudes, and on the basis of complex discourse structures and their cognitive representations, was not an issue that was high on the research agenda. Persuasion focused on behavior change. And for the sake of experimental (typically short-ranged) research, it was insufficiently recognized that many of the "persuasive messages" people are confronted with do not, or only very indirectly, lead to intended "behavior changes." Conversely, many other types of discourse, including those that are not consciously intended to be persuasive such as news reports in the press or TV programs, may also lead to belief and attitude change. In other words, the theory of persuasion should be embedded into a much broader approach of discursive information processing and cognitive transformation in the interactional and social context.

The Major Components of Persuasion

From this brief discussion of some major tenets in persuasion research, we have concluded that some of the essential components of persuasive communication were not systematically analyzed at all, so that their role in theoretical ideas and experimental testing was permanently neglected, undervalued, or loosely formulated in intuitive terms. Let us briefly comment on some of these components, which will be theoretically dealt with more extensively in later sections.

Message structure. Despite the neglect, briefly discussed above, of systematic discourse analysis, "messages" have always played an important role in persuasion research. Attitude change was seen primarily in a "rhetorical" perspective, that is, as the rather direct result of intentionally persuasive messages in personal or public communication. Less attention was paid to other, for example, nonverbal, forms of communication, or to gradual, long-term, self-induced, changes in attitudes as a result of complex thought and belief processing.

Messages themselves were also conceptualized in ways that are reminiscent of classical rhetoric. Because persuasion often involves the uses of argument, it was not surprising that prevailing attention was paid to the organization of arguments in messages and their effects. We referred earlier to the debate about whether pro or con arguments should be formulated together, or whether they should be presented first or last, respectively, leading to primacy or recency effects (Hovland, Lumsdaine, & Sheffield, 1949; Hovland et al., 1957). However, characteristic of persuasion research and of much communication research in the social sciences in general, was the neglect of the very argumentative structure of discourse. Arguments in messages were identified (or produced in experimental materials) in an intuitive way, and no systematic research was undertaken to analyze in detail the structures of conversational or more formal (written) argumentative discourse. The schematic nature of argumentative structures, their organization and rule- or strategy-governed nature, as well as their links with the semantic content or the more "surface" stylistic (lexical, syntactic) properties of messages, or with the performance of speech acts, were seldom recognized (Kahane, 1971; Toulmin, 1958; van Eemeren & Grootendorst, 1983). A rich tradition of argumentation analysis in philosophy was barely known. In fact, even the content of argumentative discourse was seldom explicitly analyzed, for instance, in relation to the intended persuasive goals (Fishbein & Ajzen, 1981).

The same holds for other "message variables," such as fear appeals or lexical style. No analysis was made of the systematic linguistic correlates of emotions, nor of the essentially contextual (and mostly social) nature of lexical and syntactic variation. This means that the same fear appeals formulated in different terms may have different interpretations and cognitive effects, and that persuasive arguments in one communicative context may have a very different role than the same arguments in another context.

In general, then, messages were not analyzed at all, or characterized in intuitively plausible categories involved in the persuasion process. Persuasion was assumed to take place either by "rational" arguments, or by "irrational" emotional appeals or threats. No systematic, genre- and context-dependent discourse analysis was carried out, so that no distinction was made between different levels of text or dialogue, for instance, in terms of phonology, morphology, syntax, semantics, pragmatics, stylistics, rhetoric, narrative analysis, or other subtheories of grammar and discourse analysis, as we have proposed in Chapter 2. It is obvious that if we want to examine the systematic nature of discursive persuasion, we should formulate the precise nature and the cognitive processing consequences of each of these structural features, or their variable combinations in different personal and sociocultural contexts of communication. Although discourse analysis itself only became seriously developed in the early 1970s, there was sufficient work in linguistics and various branches of discourse analysis in the 1950s and 1960s to warrant more systematic attention to the nature of message "variables." But this would have required interdisciplinary endeavors that have been rare in persuasion research. And even in the 1980s, now that we do have sophisticated discourse theories and analytical methodologies in several disciplines, including psychology and communication research, too little attention is being paid to the organization of the "message" in persuasive communication, despite the recent attention for persuasive message strategies (Burgoon & Bettinghaus, 1980).

Comprehension. Similar remarks hold for the first cognitive "step" in persuasive communication: the understanding and representation of the relevant message and its characteristics. Again, much of our insight into these processes has been gained only in the later 1970s, but there was earlier work on comprehension, and even the developments of the 1970s are not yet translated into persuasion research problems. It was mentioned above that McGuire (1972) and others did recognize that persuasion should be analyzed in terms of several steps or phases of cognitive processing, such as attention, comprehension, acceptance, yielding, or integration. Yet, each of these concepts remained unanalyzed and played only an intuitive role. Exactly how messages were comprehended, and exactly how opinions were inferred from them and accepted or integrated was not spelled out. In other words, the cognitive core of persuasion processes, namely, representations and operations, was dealt with in superficial, summarylike statements. One of the reasons for this neglect of interpretation processing was the repeated finding that understanding, measured as "recall," had little effect on attitude change (Cacioppo & Petty, 1979; Love & Greenwald, 1978). Rather, it was found that cognitive responses, such as "thoughts" or (counter)arguments engendered during message perception, appear to influence persuasion and its persistence over time. Exactly why this is the case is usually not explained, nor do we get explicit descriptions of the representations and strategies involved in such cognitive "responses." As long as we do not specify in detail how a persuasive message is actually processed, and which other social and cognitive factors are involved, we cannot obtain full insight into the persuasive process as a whole. In the previous chapter, we have proposed such a theory of discourse comprehension, which, of course, also holds for persuasive messages.

Representation. The possible "effects" of persuasive discourse are not simply "mediated" through "cognitive responses." According to our cognitive analysis, it is the cognitive representation in episodic memory of interpreted discourse that is (one) starting point for further processing, such as attitude formation or change.

The mental representation of discourse is not a replica of "given" discursive structures. Rather, it is the result of a complex strategic interplay between structures, meanings, and functions assigned in short-term memory decoding and interpretation, on one hand, and other cognitive structures, such as knowledge, beliefs, and existing attitudes, on the other hand. This means that the representation of the persuasive message in memory may be subject to many personal, social, and cultural biases, resulting from personal experiences, social scripts, and cultural norms and values.

Compared to the original discourse itself, textual representations may be structured in a very different way. Meanings may have changed and large parts (e.g., surface structure and local meaning details) may no longer be retrievably stored. It comes as no surprise, therefore, that (detailed) arguments may later no longer be recalled. Even immediately after having read or heard a text, recipients usually cannot produce much more than 25% to 50% of a one-page text (see van Dijk & Kintsch, 1983, for detail). After longer delays, people merely have access to fragments of the macrostructure of a text, that is, a few high-level propositions.

Primacy and recency (of arguments or other information) have very different effects on representations and processing. Initial information is used for the activation of scripts, attitudes, and models, and will lead to the important formation of tentative macrostructures and hence to better recall. Final (recent) information is better recalled especially because of special processing interactions between short-term and episodic memory and the current focus of attention. These and other properties of the cognitive representation of argumentation (or other schemata, such as narration), must be taken into account in a full-fledged theory of persuasion.

Much information stored in the representation may not have been expressed in the original discourse at all, but is inferred from other knowledge and belief sources in memory. In other words, representations of (persuasive or any other) discourse are not replicative, but (re)constructive, an insight already advocated by Bartlett (1932) half a century ago. Each theoretical notion mentioned in this paragraph is merely the tip of an underlying theoretical iceberg, which should be made explicit before adequate analysis of the persuasion process is possible.

Situation models. Discourse processing in general, and persuasion in particular, crucially depend on the previous experiences and opinions of a person relative to the persuasion "topic" (persons, groups, objects, events, actions, and so on). Therefore, we need an explicit mental representation of these "previous experiences," and especially of their opinion components, and must show how these interact with the representation of the persuasive discourse.

Again, neither classical nor present work in persuasion has systematically taken such "personal" representations into account by describing their contents and structures, or by specifying their detailed cognitive roles.

It was suggested earlier that such accumulated experiences and their associated opinions are to be represented as "situation models." Such models embody the coherent, hierarchical, and context-bound subjective understanding and evaluations people construct of each situation in which they are involved. Each particular situation, then, is represented as a particular (unique) model. New information about that situation will be used to update the model. This means that besides particular, ad hoc, models, we have generalized situation models. Models not only feature knowledge or beliefs about situations, but also opinions. In the previous chapter, this led us to stress the difference between opinions and attitudes.

Situation models also play a crucial role in the cognitive process of attitude formation and change. Without such models, we are unable to link general attitudes to particular messages, beliefs, or situations. In other words, what is usually called *attitude change* in persuasion research may either refer to transformations of situation models, involving particular opinions of the hearer (and assumptions about them by the speaker), or else to more general opinions as they organize abstract attitudes. Because in most experimental work, short-range attitude change is aimed at, we may assume that, in most cases, this process should be made explicit in terms of opinion formation in situation models. Of course, this process is in turn based on the activation of general knowledge, beliefs, attitudes, and norms.

Context models. If people construct a mental model of each situation in which they are involved, they do so also for the very communicative situation in which they are participating when reading or listening to a persuasive message. That is, they build a relevant picture of the current context, that is, a context model. This model features the actual (interpreted or intended) goals of the communicative interaction, representations (and evaluations) of self as a speaker (or hearer) and as social member, and of the hearer (speaker) in similar roles, of the type of social context being enacted (e.g., public speech, informal conversation with a friend, or reading the newspaper), as well as many other relevant contextual features. Each of these may decisively influence the interpretation and evaluation of the persuasive discourse and the opinions inferred from them. The usual "source characteristics" identified as influencing "factors" in persuasion require explicit representation in such models. It is this representation and not the "real" ("objective") characteristics of sources that explain possible effects on opinion formation and change.

Credibility of the "source" is one of the classical parameters involved here and paid attention to in much persuasion research (Hovland & Weiss, 1951). It is obvious now that such a notion should be further analyzed and integrated into a context model, namely as (only) one dimension of a rather complex "speaker model" constructed by the hearer. In this speaker (or communicator) model, other relevant dimensions may also be represented, such as attractivity (Chaiken, 1979), power (Kelman, 1958), involvement (Petty & Cacioppo, 1981), expertise (e.g., Norman, 1976), gender, age, status, ethnicity, and other personal and social characteristics (Hass, 1981). We have seen for ethnic actors and events how such representations may be biased. One can imagine how complex a theoretical and especially an experimental account may be when only the features of such a part of the context, namely, of the speaker model, are to be combined in the explanation of the effect of persuasive discourse (Cronkhite & Liska, 1980). Indeed, how persuasive is a young, attractive, Black woman of high status when acting as a doctor . . .? Her attractiveness, expertise, role, and status would predict high persuasion impact, but what about the precise cognitive interaction of such factors with those of her being Black? We have seen that for White people she might primarily be categorized as Black, which may activate shared (negative) prejudices, which again may reduce or fully discredit the role of the other factors. Hence, we need to know about the hierarchy, the power, or the relevance of source factor representations in context models. The number of possible interactions soon runs into the thousands. No wonder that heavily controlled experiments tell us so little about what goes on in "real" persuasive contexts, where all these variables are present at the same time.

Knowledge and beliefs. Due to much recent work in cognitive psychology and AI, we now know that comprehension of social events and discourse crucially depends on our knowledge and beliefs as they are represented and organized in frames, scripts, or similar cognitive constructions (see Chapter 4 for detail). We also suggested that persuasion depends on what people already knew and believed before the persuasive discourse, which means that these knowledge structures should be made explicit. Being persuaded by a professor during a class also presupposes that the student has a script about stereotypical teaching events, about normative goals of teaching interaction, and about his or her own role in such an event. The effects of expertise and in general of credibility are crucially mediated through such script-based expectations. And the same holds when we are being persuaded about events, for instance, when we read a newspaper editorial about Central America. Apart from personal previous experiences (models) of, say, El Salvador, the reader brings to bear knowledge and beliefs about civil war (i.e., about armies, guerrillas, fights, weapons, and so on) and about international politics. After the early work, of, for instance, Abelson (1973, 1976) about scripts and belief systems, little persuasion research has explicitly taken into account the specific structures of such beliefs. It was limited to whether or not communicators had or did not have "previous knowledge" about a topic, but spelled out neither this knowledge nor its cognitive organization.

Opinions and attitudes. Crucial in any account of persuasion is the notion of "attitude." This is a classical insight, which is still valid today. However, we have seen in the previous chapter that despite the scores of books and articles devoted to this notion in social psychology, we know very little about the precise nature of attitudes. Again, despite the sophistication of the experimental or formal models, most analyses of the structures and strategies of attitude and their uses remain more or less intuitive and pretheoretical.

Thus, until today, these analyses may specify that attitudes have a "cognitive," "evaluative (or emotive)," and a "conative" dimension, assessed experimentally, not by systematic structural analysis (Breckler, 1984). Or shorter, attitudes are simply identified with any kind of evaluative proposition (or even "statement"), or as a specific (enduring) "disposition" toward specific behavior. Neither in attitude research nor in work on persuasion based on it do we find the actual representation and analysis of an interesting, socially relevant, and full-fledged attitude. When Fishbein and Ajzen (1975) in their extensive study come up with their seducingly simple definition of an attitude as an "evaluative state of mind towards some object," it should be obvious that such a definition can hardly be short for an explicit theory of attitudes. It does explain, however, how "attitude change," despite its vagueness, can easily be measured as any kind of evaluative reaction to persuasive messages.

Obviously, a theory of attitude, and, hence, of attitude change, should be more sophisticated. First steps toward such a theory have again been made by Abelson (1976) and a few others. We have suggested that the complexity of socially relevant opinions and beliefs about issues or complex social events and states of affairs seem to require a theoretical formulation that is reminiscent of frame or script theories (e.g., Carbonell, 1979). Indeed, we assumed that attitudes are categorially, linearly, and hierarchically organized structures of general, that is, context-free, beliefs and opinions represented in (semantic, or rather social) long-term memory about socially relevant clusters of events and states of affairs. Such attitudes are in turn also organized in more embracing attitude clusters and ultimately into ideologies.

Thus, we also distinguished between (component) opinions, which are general evaluative beliefs about persons, objects, or events, and the more complex attitudes of which they may be part. Similarly, it is obviously relevant to distinguish between general opinions (which may be inserted into attitude schemata), and particular opinions, which are evaluative beliefs about particular (actual) objects, persons, or events. According to the theoretical notion of a situation model, it seems likely that particular opinions should be located in ad hoc, particular situation models, general opinions in generalized models, and in schemalike attitudes if they are combined with other general beliefs and opinions that have interactional and social relevance in other contexts.

Attitude change. Against the background of the critique and the proposals formulated above, it should be obvious that the current accounts of attitude change processes also need further theoretical elaboration. Because attitudes are usually rather complex cognitive structures, they simply don't change that easily, and rarely after one persuasive communication. People may change their particular opinions, though, and this change is recorded in episodic models. If a (changed) particular opinion is generalized, it may be integrated into a more general attitude. This may also require changes in other relevant opinions, for instance, if the person perceives incoherence between opinions ("inconsistency" is a logical notion that is not particularly relevant in a cognitive theory: People may well have coherent opinions that are "inconsistent" from a logical point of view). Such changes may spread through the attitude structure, and may also affect the higher levels. In that case, also overall evaluative (macro) beliefs may eventually change. A theoretically adequate account of such changes, however, should spell out in detail the structural input and output of the transformation in the attitude structure. Also, it should specify the precise conditions for such transformations.

It follows that attitude change is not a discrete, momentaneous process. People modify their cognitive structures all the time, also when no persuasive discourses are being processed, for instance, by simply "thinking" about an issue, or by anticipation (Cialdini & Petty, 1981; McGuire & Papageorgis, 1962). They may also do so long after persuasive discourses have been processed. Opinion changes in one model and context may not generalize to others. These are a few of the reasons that much of the experimental persuasion research is limited to momentaneous, particular opinions as represented in situation models derived from one or two persuasion messages. For complex, long-term processes of attitude change, difficult diachronical research would be needed, and for the study of the continuous changes of attitudes, repeated probing or think-aloud protocol analyses might be necessary.

"Behavior" and action. The final component in traditional theories of persuasion and communication is "behavior." We have stressed that persuasion is often conceptualized as mediating between persuasive messages on one hand and desired behavior of the persuadee, on the other hand, where attitudes are some kind of internal "cause" of the observed behavior. Although there have been attempts, also in persuasion research, to analyze the processes of behavior in somewhat more explicit terms, involving, for example, intentions and goals of action (see, e.g., Fishbein & Ajzen, 1975), the current discussion in persuasion research is still neglecting many fundamentals of the cognitive basis of this behavior.

A long tradition in the philosophy of action is usually ignored (see, e.g., von Cranach & Harré, 1982; von Wright, 1963; White, 1968). In the first place, the notion of behavior is misleading. Behavior also covers things people do when not intending to, when out of control, and so on. Hence, we prefer to speak about actions and interactions. These are conceptually represented units of intentional, controlled behavior. Similarly, we should specify exactly what these action "intentions" are. For instance, our intention to travel to Japan may have a quite different structure than our actual intention to eat this apple. The first intention may involve a complex (macro) plan, consisting of a hierarchical set of action propositions, strategies (e.g., to travel as cheaply as possible), and specific goals (visit a friend, attend a congress). Just as sentences can be analyzed as linguistic units consisting of an expression structure and a meaning structure, thus, actions may be analyzed as a manifest unit of behavior (a "doing"), and a cognitive unit, namely, an intention. Similarly, we may have observable goals of action, such as some change in the "world," on one hand, and a cognitive representation of such a goal, namely, a "purpose," on the other hand. Actions are weakly successful if the results of the doing correspond with the underlying intention or plan, and they are strongly successful if the goals are realized, confirming the purpose of the agent (see van Dijk, 1977, 1981a, for details).

Similarly, intentions do not "come up" spontaneously, but are the cognitive end products of a complex chain of beliefs (about abilities, the action context, goals of others, and so on), preferences, wishes, wants, or other "motivational" structures. Each of these need to be made explicit in an account of (inter)action. Given all this information, the potential agent may form a concrete model of a (future) situation, that is, of the kind of action to be performed in a particular context. Finally, this model may be strategically executed, depending on incoming information about the actual context. In other words, intentions, plans, and purposes are constituent elements of episodic models of future situations.

From this theoretical analysis, we may conclude that there is no direct link between attitudes and action. Attitudes, together with frames or scripts for stereotypical episodes, provide the instantiated beliefs and opinions that may form part of an action model. It is not surprising, therefore, that there are few consistent findings about the famous (mostly missing) link between attitudes and behavior that has inspired so many books and articles (Cacioppo, Harkins, & Petty, 1981). Actual action, hence, may be "inconsistent" with attitudes, but the contextual information in a model may prevent the agent from interpreting this "inconsistency" as such. For the link between ethnic attitudes and ethnic interaction, this inconsistency has already been demonstrated by LaPierre (1933) 50 years ago. Similar observations have been made in our analysis of the interviews, in which people may also often say things that are superficially inconsistent with what they actually believe, because of the constraints of the communicative context.

Actions are not merely controlled by attitudes or values but (also) by general social norms, that is, information about what should or should not be done. Situational norms may be part of scripts (what should we do in the classroom or restaurant), or of attitudes (what should be done against the building of nuclear power plants), but we also have higher-level (meta)norms for action and interaction in general, such as norms for cooperation, politeness, and so on. We assume that these general norms are part of what might be called the *principles of social cognition,* that is, of the ideological base that underlies more specific attitudes.

The same holds for general values, which specify items on a good/ bad dimension or its variants (pleasant/unpleasant, and so forth). Psychologically, norms must be based on values, because the obligation or permission to do A presupposes that the agent or somebody else finds A "better" than –A or B (or prefers the goals realized by A). In other words, norms involve valued action and valued results or consequences of action.

We conclude, then, that an account of (inter)action that might "result from" persuasive communications should be autonomous. There is no direct link, and certainly not a causal one (Miller & Colman, 1981). This is also the reason that simple analyses in terms of "causal" attribution are not adequate for an account of action understanding and planning. People decide to act, plan/intend actions on the basis of very complex information structures, and the execution of such actions is again embedded in very complex action context structures (opportunity, and so on) that together define an action model. This analysis is also crucial for persuasive, communicative (inter)action. Only in very simple cases does there appear to be a phenomenologically direct conditional "link" between a persuasive message and the advocated action. But even then we have to make explicit all the cognitive steps (representations and strategies) that go from message comprehension to the actual execution of an intended act before we can actually say that someone "has been persuaded to *do* something."

Summary

Summarizing our critique of the prevailing tendencies in persuasion research, we may mention the following main points:

(1) Persuasive messages themselves have not been systematically analyzed for structures at various levels. Whereas nearly exclusive attention is paid to argumentative discourse, even these argumentative structures are not explicitly described. Thus, both as to "content" as well as to "form," this major component of the persuasive process remained ignored, and no useful theories were borrowed from linguistics or discourse analysis.

(2) The cognitive processes of persuasion have been dealt with in superficial and incomplete terms. An explicit analysis is seldom made of the relevant representations of discourse, events, episodes, or evaluative beliefs. No account is given of comprehension, integration, or retrieval strategies. No distinction is made between episodic (personal, particular) and more general, semantic or social dimensions of opinions. No explicit description is given of either attitude structures or their transformations. Many features of the communicative context have been neglected, or are not explicitly inserted into a cognitive model. On the whole, the cognitive component of persuasion is still primarily taken as a set of "mediating" variables, and as "responses" to some stimulus. Autonomous analysis of cognitive processes and their relation to the communicative context remains rare or remains at a rather general level of intuitively plausible but theoretically confused terms.

(3) The "consequences" of persuasion have been primarily conceptualized in terms of "behavior," which was often assumed to be "causally" linked to attitudes, instead of as actions and interactions that are programmed, intended, and executed autonomously. The complexity of action programming has been underestimated, and it was not stressed enough that (and how) attitudes are only indirectly linked to action, such as via episodic plans of actions as represented in models.

From these major points, we conclude that despite the vast amounts of work on attitude and attitude change in communication, much of persuasion theory, in the methodologically adequate sense of a "theory," is still on the agenda. Of course, this does not make extant work in persuasion worthless. On the contrary, it has provided experimental evidence about many of the features, mostly of the communicative context, that influence specific dimensions of persuasion, such as short-term opinion changes. Only, many results need new interpretations, and many concepts need further analysis. We try to do so, along the lines of our critical remarks made above, by focusing on persuasion processes involved in the reproduction of ethnic prejudice in informal everyday conversations.

2. Communicating prejudice

The persuasive communication of ethnic attitudes through everyday talk is both an interpersonal and a group-based process. Cognitive and social dimensions are equally crucial in modeling this process. Speakers who talk about ethnic minorities do so not only as individuals, but also as dominant group members. Persuasion, thus, involves the intention to share attitudes with other dominant group members, and should, therefore, be analyzed as a form of intragroup communication. Similarly, the ethnic attitudes involved are not personal, but group attitudes. So are the ideologies in which they are rooted and that define coherence relations with other group-based attitudes. This means, among other things, that the speaker already knows a lot about the norms, values, attitudes, opinions, goals, and other beliefs of the hearer in general, and those about ethnic groups in particular. In conversation, these cognitions will either be tacitly presupposed or used in persuasive strategies, such as the appeal to group norms and values.

Despite shared in-group cognitions, however, ethnic attitudes may display significant in-group variation, for instance, because of different social dimensions of subgroups within the autochthonous in-group, as well as individual variation at the level of personal models. In other words, especially with unknown in-group members, a speaker is never sure whether or not the hearer has the same attitude about foreigners. Also, persuasion in that case may not be unidirectional, but bidirectional: The other participant may be expected to engage in persuasion also as soon as such a "controversial" topic is brought up. Mutual persuasion of this kind may involve strategic attacks but also defensive moves.

From this brief introductory summary of the persuasive nature of in-group talk about ethnic out-groups, it already becomes obvious that the processes involved are very complex. Cognitive planning, execution, and monitoring of such persuasive talk, therefore, is equally complex. Therefore, we split up the problem into the following subproblems:

(a) How is conversation about ethnic groups produced by the speaker and how is it related to ethnic prejudice structures and strategies?
(b) What are the structural, strategic, and functional consequences of this production process for the communicative and persuasive nature of talk about ethnic affairs?
(c) How is discourse about ethnic groups understood and represented cognitively by the hearer?
(d) How is represented talk about minorities linked with ethnic situation models of the hearer? How does model updating take place?
(e) What is the role of ethnic attitudes in the comprehension, representation, and retrieval of conversational information? And, conversely, how

is this information and the ethnic models it affects related to general ethnic attitudes? Under what conditions can we say that ethnic attitude may "change" due to conversation(s)?

(f) What social information of the context of communication and interaction influences the processes mentioned above, and how is this information represented and used by the speech participants?

Part of these questions are dealt with in more detail in this and the next sections of this chapter. Our insights obtained in the previous chapters about the contents and structures of conversations and prejudices about ethnic groups, and about the nature of attitude, attitude change, and persuasion, can now be integrated into a more *dynamic* analysis of the persuasive communication of ethnic attitudes in this chapter.

2.1. PRODUCING PREJUDICED TALK

Although there is impressive research about conversation, on one hand, and about text comprehension, on the other hand, we do not know very much about the specifics of the cognitive basis of everyday talk. The reason for this lack of theoretical and empirical insight is simple: Most people working on conversation have (micro)sociological interests, rather than cognitive psychological ones (see, however, Cicourel, 1980), whereas most psychologists have preferred to work with written, textual materials, which are easier to use in experiments (but see Keenan, MacWhinney, & Mayhew, 1977). Conversations must first be carefully recorded and transcribed, and such transcriptions exhibit many detailed features of talk that do not yet enter cognitive theories of discourse comprehension and representation, for instance, pauses, repairs, hesitation phenomena, or nonverbal cues. This lack of specific knowledge about the role of cognition in conversation, however, does not prevent us from theorizing about this role, for instance, in analogy to what we know about discourse comprehension and production in general.

We start our analysis of persuasive "ethnic" talk with a reconstruction of the production processes involved, because production is the first step in the persuasive process. We do so against the background of our earlier work on the cognitive processing of discourse (van Dijk & Kintsch, 1983) and the notions of cognitive theory summarized in the previous chapter.

Instead of describing the production processes involved in purely theoretical terms only, we shall describe them by using a concrete example taken from one of our interviews. Our analysis, then, is what may be called an informal *simulation* of the processes the speaker must go through in order to produce the subsequent contributions to the interview.

Interpersonal Communication 271

Our example is a story told by a 25-year-old man working in the transport section of an aircraft company, but now on sick leave and living in a poor, high-contact area of Amsterdam. The interviewer is a male student of the same age. As may be obvious from the example, the man is highly prejudiced against Surinamese, and does not dissimulate his negative feelings as much as many others do. The passage is taken from the beginning of the interview, after the interviewer's question about experiences with foreigners. As with previous examples, the translation from Dutch colloquial speech is merely an approximation. "Ungrammatical" sentences have also been translated as more or less corresponding ungrammatical English equivalents.

(1) P-D-1
1 M: Yes, you see them once in a while, you know, and then you say
2 hello, and that's it.
3 I: And other experiences with other foreigners or so?
4 M: Well, never have trouble with Turks and Moroccans, but with
5 Surinamese are concerned, yes plenty of trouble, yes.
6 I: Could you tell something about, a story or so, about your
7 experiences?
8 M: Story, yes I once walked on Nieuwendijk [shopping street in
9 central Amsterdam], with my cousin, still a free man, and well,
10 then came uhh let's see four Surinamese boys. Well, they said
11 something, funny remarks and all that. I said something back, and
12 at once we had a fight. That's why I had a knife cut across here
13 and all that. That's how. So those guys I don't like at all, of
14 course. So. Well, nothing against Surinamese, because my mother
15 is married to a Surinamese man, so, but those young ones among
16 them, that is, yes bragging and fighting and all that. So.
17 I: Anything more you can tell?
18 M: Well, as far as I am concerned they can all fuck off, in that
19 respect. Then the good ones must suffer for the bad ones, but I
20 never have such good experiences with them.
21 I: With other, with other foreigners or so, you don't have
22 M: No, never any problems, no because (???). Those Surinamese,
23 that may fuck off. When you see what is happening. Are married,
24 they are married, they divorce, woman takes from welfare, and he
25 has no job, but is moonlighting. We have have experienced that
26 ourselves, in K* (neighborhood in Amsterdam), with my mother's
27 friend . . . .

The story briefly refers to a fight the storyteller has had with young Surinamese boys, and is followed by an evaluation of young Surinamese in general, and an expression of his dislike of Surinamese in general, who he thinks cheat on welfare. Now, what are the processing steps that might lead to this particular contribution to the conversation?

a. Analyzing and Representing the Communicative Context

Obviously, the story and the opinions of the young man (M) are being produced in response to (interview) questions of the interviewer. The processes of understanding discourse in general, and questions in particular, will be dealt with later. At this point, it is relevant, however, that discourse production takes place in a communicative context, in this case within a more or less informal interview with a university student. In order for M to make a relevant contribution to the conversation, he must first have an adequate cognitive representation of this communicative context, namely, in terms of an episodically stored, particular context model. This model represents, for instance, (a) M himself in his actual role of interviewee, (b) the interviewer, (c) the type of communicative situation and context type (interview), (d) the overall goals of the context, and of M and the interviewer in particular, and so on. At the macro level, this context model will monitor the overall production process, as well as the overall structures and strategies of the interview.

At the local level of this, continuously modified, context model, M also represents the previous dialogical turn(s) of the interviewer. These are questions about M's experiences with foreigners, and more specifically a request for a concrete story. By conversational rule, activated from general semantic (social) memory about the structures and strategies of conversation in our culture, M construes an obligation to respond to the question and request to give personal information about foreigners (Labov & Fanshel, 1977). That is, he must produce a coherent next unit ("reponse") of an adjacency pair. In other words, as part of the communicative context model, M sets up an interactional goal dominated by a proposition such as "I must tell about my experiences with foreigners."

Note that this fragment of the context model is partly derived, top-down, from the understanding of the whole communicative context ("I am participating in an interview"), which also allows the inferences of specific propositions as expectations (e.g., "He will ask some questions about my experiences or opinions"), and partly, bottom-up, from the understanding of the previous turns of the interviewer. This understanding is represented in the "text representation" (or text model) in episodic memory. This interpretation, however, relates to what the text refers to or is about, that is, a situation model. In this case, the interviewer performs the speech acts of a question and a request, and hence refers to the very communicative context itself, as represented in the context model. In other words, situation model and context model at this point are overlapping. How speech acts are cognitively processed will not be detailed here (see below for understanding discourse in general). Relevant, however, is that the question or request is in accordance with the (rules of) conversation, that is, adequate at this stage of the interview context as represented by M in his context model (they would be less adequate if the interviewer had already asked the same question before and M had already answered it fully).

In this initial stage of the production process, M has derived an interactive and conversational goal from the context model, which must and can be reached only by providing requested information through the performance of a specific speech act, namely, an assertion. So, one of the first steps in the actual production of the next contribution (turns, moves, sentences, propositions at different levels of analysis and, hence, of production) to the conversation is the planning of an appropriate speech act.

Expressing requested information in an assertion is an appropriate next turn in an adjacency pair introduced by questions or requests for information, and also agrees with the overall structures and strategies of interview discourse. Hence, M decides that an assertion as his next turn is an appropriate speech act, given the context model at this particular moment. Once checked for appropriateness, the plan may actually be formed, that is, a (macro)proposition is constructed that represents, initially only globally, the (speech) act that will be executed.

However, there is a next constraint to be taken care of by M: The assertion is appropriate only when it can be interpreted as an answer to the earlier question or request of the interviewer. This also means that the information to be conveyed by M must more or less satisfy the lack of knowledge expressed by the interviewer. The proposition(s) expressed by the planned assertion of M, therefore, must provide this information, in this case (personal) experiences with "foreigners." Thus, after the analysis and (re)production of the global and local communicative context and the planning of an adequate (speech) act in that context, the semantic content of the speech act becomes relevant.

b. Macro-Semantic Production

Given the interview context and the previous questions (i.e., as represented cognitively by M), M is conversationally entitled to express more than one single proposition. The question and the request for a story permit him to take the floor for the expression of a whole sequence of propositions, by the performance of a sequence of assertions, and, thereby, by telling a story. It follows that M will probably generate not simply a plan for a single speech act, nor retrieve from knowledge a simple proposition. Rather, planning will take place at the macrolevel, both pragmatically and semantically: M represents a (plan for a) macrospeech act, and a macroproposition for its content. Also, both the earlier request to tell a story, and the questions about personal experiences, trigger the notion of a story, and, therefore, M must also retrieve a story schema and rules that will provide the overall narrative functions of the (global) speech acts and propositions to be expressed in the next turn.

The introductory talk (not transcribed here) leading to the interview proper had already introduced the concepts of "neighborhood," "foreigner" and "personal experiences." This means, first, that the actual questions of the interviewer were expected: M already strategically projects ahead the likely course of the interview. Second, the contents also, as represented by the text model, of such introductory talk already provide the propositions that may be used to activate and possibly retrieve relevant information from memory, namely, about "foreigners." The local question being asked, therefore, is not only expected as a speech act, but also the information requested may already have been activated by M. It is assumed that the general proposition, "I had experiences with foreigners," strategically (hypothetically) construed during the introduction, and now being confirmed by the previous question, is used as a retrieval cue to search through memory.

c. The Situation Model

Because personal experiences are concerned, this information will primarily be searched for in episodic memory. Situation models are scanned for those that feature both M and some ethnic minority group member(s). More specifically, the previous turns had focused attention on Surinamese, who were judged to have caused trouble for M. Hence, the search is more specific and scans models with (a) Surinamese, and (b) negative events, according to the "biased" strategies of ethnic information processing discussed in the previous chapter.

Priming negativity. At this point, it is highly relevant for our discussion to witness that the question of the interviewer (line 3) is apparently interpreted as a question about *negative* experiences with foreigners ("never have trouble . . ."). The explanation for this fact may be given in terms of the overall negative evaluation dominating the "foreigner" attitudes of M: "foreigners are (cause) trouble." Also, for people who do not have negative attitudes about ethnic minority groups, such questions may at least trigger negative concepts, which may be explicitly denied by a strategic move: "I have no trouble with...." That is, negative stereotypes may be known, but not endorsed, in which case a denial is in order. This also happens here in the answer of M, but only for Turks and Moroccans. Another (or an additional) explanation may be sought in the priming of remarkable, interesting, and, therefore, often negative, experiences through the notion of a story. And a third explanation may depend on the circumstance that interviews—for instance, in the press—about experiences with foreigners have often featured questions or answers implying negative evaluations. Hence, apart from one's own negative attitudes, about foreigners in general and about Surinamese in particular, there may be other cognitive and contextual factors that prime the search for negative situation models. So, the negativity bias in this case derives both from general attitude schemata in social memory, activated during the introduction, and possibly old context models about this kind of interview, as well as from the interpretation and representation of the previous turns in the text and context models.

d. From Situation Model to Semantic Representation

With the information about interesting (narratable) negative experiences with Surinamese as a search cue, M indeed finds a situation model that satisfies these conditions. Search time and effort may be detected in the typical hesitating (task repetition) of M's turn beginning in line 8: "Story, yes . . . ." The affirmative "yes" may be interpreted as signaling that the search has been successful and that an appropriate situation model has been found. Together with the current context model, it is this situation model that will control the production of the various phases of the (narrative) turn now initiated. The situation model provides the information requested by the interviewer. Given the plan for an overall assertion, functioning as a narrative, as discussed above, this speech act may now receive its semantic content. Basically, semantic representations in discourse production provide the semantic representations (propositions) of the sentences that will be sequentially produced. This is the reverse process of what happens in discourse understanding, in which propositions of a represented text model will be used to update a new situation model. Now, the situation model is the basis for "new" information to be expressed and conveyed to the other speaker. We shall see shortly that discourse may also express information from other memory sources, such as attitude schemata. Information about personal experiences, however, will be retrieved predominantly from situation models in episodic memory.

e. Model Search and Narrative Schema

Situation models may be very detailed and complex, however. Also, not all information in them may be equally relevant for appropriate assertions (for instance, information the speaker assumes to be already known to the hearer), nor is all information equally "interesting" for storytelling. Hence, a model cannot simply be "read off." A strategic selection must be made, also constrained by search limitations: not all information in the model may (still) be retrievable at this moment. Often, only the higher-level (macro)propositions of the event can be retrieved, which provide information of a summary-like story. This is also the case in our example. M gives very few details about what actually happened. He may not remember more, or more may not be relevant at this moment within the context of the interview. And yet, a story is required, so that for each of the conventional narrative categories (Setting, Complication, Resolution, Evaluation, and so on, see Chapter 2), M must retrieve at least one (macro)proposition. This is exactly what he does, for instance, as follows (we represent propositions here, not the actual expressions of the interview; the propositions between parenthesis are not [fully] explicit in the conversation):

SETTING:	I once walked on Nieuwendijk with my cousin. My cousin is still a free man.
ORIENTATION:	Four Surinamese boys came along. They made a funny [provocative?] remark. I said something [provocative?] back.
COMPLICATION:	We had a fight. (I was cut with a knife.)
RESOLUTION:	—
EVALUATION/ CONCLUSION:	I do not like these Surinamese guys.

We see that the major narrative categories are filled with propositions retrieved from the situation model. As we have witnessed earlier (Chapter 2), the Resolution category is missing. There is no (re)solution to the fight event, except maybe implicitly that he and his cousin lost (he was cut with a knife, and there were four of them and he and his cousin only two). There is no explicit Evaluation either, except perhaps in the subtle stylistic undertone of words such as *funny remark* and the sociolectally specific word used for "entering a fight or a brawl" in Dutch (*matten*). There is, however, a post hoc, evaluative Conclusion, which is the semantic, narrative, conversational, and interactive upshot of M's story: I do not like these (young) Surinamese guys.

At that point, M can return to one of his main goals in the interview: to express negative opinions about foreigners or Blacks. Indeed, the story was told as an appropriate answer to the question of the interviewer, but at the same time, it has the important interactional and persuasive function of providing a "good example" and, hence, a "good reason" for the opinion that "Surinamese are bad." We return to these persuasive strategies below, but it should be borne in mind that the selection of information from situation models, as well as their narrative constraints, already strategically prepare these persuasive moves in talk. Indeed, M will not tell any odd story, and certainly not a story that would represent Surinamese in a good perspective, or M in a bad perspective. M explicitly refers to, and deictically points to a scar that results from the fight. This makes him and his story both credible and narratively interesting, and, therefore, also, his negative opinion more convincing.

We see that the search for the situation model, as well as the search within the model, is very much constrained (and assisted) by a number of semantic, narrative, and persuasive goals or functions. Thus, when planning a story, the superstructure category of the Setting requires the search for time, place, participants, and circumstances. This is precisely what M does as we may see from his initial sentence (line 8): he mentions himself, somebody else, the circumstance (action engaged in), and the location. At this point, there is an interesting and apparently irrelevant remark. He mentions the fact that his cousin is "still a free man" (Dutch: *nog een vrije jongen*), that is, not yet married. Cognitively, this simply suggests that the model schema node featuring his cousin triggers the person schema he has about this cousin. Apparently, the fact that this cousin is unmarried is a high-level proposition in the schema (M himself is married), and, therefore, for M a relevant identification of the cousin. Apart from this identification, there does not seem to be much relevance for the story or for the interview(er), unless the marital status of his cousin is mentioned as an implicit explanation of *why* they were walking on that street in the first place: No time of day is mentioned, but the fact that a knife fight was taking place suggests that it occurred during the evening or night (this narrow shopping street is very crowded during the daytime), which again may be more probable when the cousin is not home with his wife. Also, being on sick leave and, hence, being at home in the daytime may make him more aware of his being married. Similar processes take place for the semantic insertions into the other narrative categories. The Orientation is supplied with the direct circumstances and conditions that lead to the Complicating events, and so the Surinamese, and the conflicting acts, are mentioned. The search for the very relevant number of Surinamese is signaled in the story by the usual expression, "let's see", which also signals that the speaker still remembers exactly (he is counting them "in memory," that is, from the situation model), which is a criterion of credibility and, hence, a persuasive move of narrative credibility enhancement.

The "core" of the story is minimal. A fight and a knife cut are sufficient to express the relevant Complication. The relevance of those events is heightened by the fact that M does not simply say "I was cut with a knife," but directly points to the present result of the cut. The story expresses virtually only the highest relevant macropropositions of the situation model. It is a ministory, which, with its summarizing nature and terseness, may be interpreted as a fast but effective preparation for the evaluative conclusion. This evaluation may as such also be stored in the situation model: M will most certainly have represented the Surinamese, who he claims fought with him, in an overall negative modifier under the "They" participant node in the situation model. The use of a Conclusion marker "So" (Dutch: *dus*), repeated in isolated position several times in his talk, marks the narrative conclusion, but may also signal the evaluative inference about Surinamese from the situation model.

We have now briefly and still informally sketched how the (macro) pragmatic, semantic, and narrative structures of M's conversational story fragment are being produced cognitively. Overall, this storytelling appears to be controlled by the current context model, the (fragmentary and provisional) text model of the previous turns of the conversation, and especially the situation model of a (negative) personal experience. These models tell the cognitive process why, what, when, and how information must be provided by M in the interview. We also saw that many of the aspects of the production process already prepare the strategic dimension of the story for persuasive purposes.

f. The Role of Ethnic Prejudice Schemata

M does not merely tell about personal experiences. Before and after the story that expresses a relevant situation model, he also formulates general opinions about foreigners. Indeed, the story provides "proof" supporting his earlier evaluative belief that "Surinamese cause trouble." The expressions in the first few turns (lines 1-5) suggest that M has generalized models about ethnic encounters. At first, these do not appear to be very specific (you see them, you greet them). This lack of detail and the reference to trivialities may be strategic, though, and an example of the well-known move of avoidance. Then, the encounters become specific, namely, in the sense that they may mean "trouble" or not, a negativity search cue we have discussed above. M makes a distinction, however, between immigrant workers, on one hand, and Surinamese, on the other. It appears as if, at this point, not only generalized models (based on actually experienced models) are used, but also abstract attitude schemata about specific ethnic groups among the "foreigners." These schemata have already been activated in the interview introduction. At this point in talk, it becomes relevant to provide information, and the first overall property activated is whether or not the foreign group causes trouble. This partially confirms the assumptions about the structure of prejudiced ethnic attitude schemata formulated in the previous chapter.

This context-bound activation of prejudiced opinions may again be explained in several ways, as we did for the use of negative models above. First, the attitude (proto)schema for foreigners in general is dominated by overall negative evaluation criteria ("Do they cause trouble?"). Second, the interview context may trigger those properties (having trouble) that are particularly relevant to support other general opinions or to tell a story that illustrates these opinions. Third, M may have a personal relevance structure in his generalized models about foreigners (e.g., whether he has had several fights with them; for him, apparently, having fights is a major evaluation criterion of persons or groups).

This activation of the general prejudices about foreigners and Surinamese may also interact with the search for relevant models of personal experiences. Indeed, the fact that under the control of a negativity strategy, M comes up with a story about a violent fight and the use of a knife, both illustrates and confirms the prejudiced propositions that "Blacks are violent" and that "Blacks carry knives." In other words, retrieved models and, hence, stories about ethnic minority groups are easier to find when they feature instantiations of stereotypical prejudices. This is one of the strategic ways that ethnic prejudices control social information processing and communication about minorities. Much experimental work has found similar results about the role of ethnic stereotypes in memory, such as better recall of negative acts of out-group members (see the previous chapter for references).

Evaluation

After his story, M elaborates on the general evaluation that is both illustrated by and inferred from the story. The negative evaluation about "those guys" is denied for Surinamese as a whole. This may be the usual apparent denial move we discussed in Chapter 2, which is aimed at managing negative inferences by the hearer about the speaker. A denial of generalization in these contexts usually implies a denial of being prejudiced. In many cases, this move is further supported by evidence, such as claims about helping Jews in World War II, or having a Black friend. In this case, the support is more specific and more exceptional: His mother has a Surinamese husband (later called a *friend*). The rest of the interview suggests that his purported lack of general prejudice against Surinamese is rather doubtful. Indeed, it is an expedient cognitive strategy for people to think that they are not prejudiced because they have a Black family member or friend, because otherwise some form of incoherence may result in the cognitive processing of social information: If for all X it would be true that I do not like X, this would also hold for the instantiations of X, namely, A, whom I like. Hence, one of the strategies is to deny that I have a general dislike of foreigners or Blacks. M further supports his claim by specifying the subgroup ("those young ones") he doesn't like, and adds his stereotypical evaluation of that subgroup, namely, their bragging and aggressive behavior. That stereotype, as we have seen above, is in perfect agreement with the particular opinion implied by his model of the fight story, which simply confirms the stereotype of the subgroup (see Crocker, Fiske & Taylor, 1984; Taylor, 1981; for this strategy of subtyping in changing attitude schemata). In our case, subgrouping in talk may express cognitive subtyping in prejudice, but also may be a move of avoiding negative self-presentation.

After a further question from the interviewer, M continues his negative opinions by expressing the highly negative attitude proposition that "all" may leave. The choice of the verb ("fuck off") signals the strength of the opinion. Again, however, this strong statement is somewhat mitigated by the standard expression that the good ones must suffer for the bad ones, which at least implies that there are good ones among them. The negative stereotype is further supported by a generalized opinion derived from his experiences. Of course, this might in principle be true in the sense that M did have only negative experiences, but it is more likely that his generalization is based on selective recall of only a few negative experiences, or that it is a generalized opinion derived from the general ethnic attitude. In other words, in social information processing about ethnic groups, people do not simply provide evidence based on models, but construct evidence by instantiating the general attitude: It is the general negative stereotype that tells me that I must have had only negative experiences. We find that opinions about ethnic groups are processed in a circular way: One negative experience is generalized to a general attitude opinion, and the general opinion conversely warrants the inference that there must have been examples of experiences (models) for which the general opinion must be true.

In the last passage (line 22-27), M repeats that he has no problems with other foreigners, and repeats as well his negative attitude against Surinamese. Yet, this time, he does not seem to single out young Surinamese only. Rather, he generally claims that Surinamese are welfare cheats, again based on an example, which seems to be derived from personal experiences (the friend of his mother) although he does not specify this example in detail. The passage also illustrates the complex interplay between concrete model opinions and general prejudices: From the generic or plural, M shifts to singular personal pronouns and deictics ("he", "in [this] neighborhood").

In this example, we also witness how people represent ethnic encounters or experiences in memory. A fight is not merely represented as a fight, but as a fight with members of a specific group. This means that the properties of such a group, for instance, its aggressiveness, may be assigned to their concrete members, as represented in the model. The Surinamese he fought with were "running to type," and illustrate and prove at the same time that the stereotype is a truthful generalization. The same happens with his purported experiences with Surinamese cheating on welfare.

From Semantic Representations to Surface Formulation

We shall not discuss in detail the complex processes of syntactic and lexical formulation for this example. Once semantic representations have been construed from selected propositions of the situation model, these must be linearly ordered and coherently connected. In our case, the description of the fight follows a more or less natural (conditional, causal) order: setting and first events are told first, and subsequent events are told afterwards. The coherence relationships also derive from the conditional and temporal links between the events, as well as from the narrative perspective ("then four Surinamese boys were coming"). Finally, surface cohesion markers may be used to signal coherence, for instance, referential identity ("we", "they"), causality ("that's why," and "that's how"), and functional relationships such as conclusions ("So"). Some surface features directly signal underlying cognitive processing, such as the repeated "a story," and the "search signal" "let's see."

Finally, prejudice strength, possible affect generated during storytelling, and personal properties of the speaker will determine the lexicalization of the concept "fight" as a sociolectal variant, and of the concept "to leave" as the negative colloquial term *to fuck off*. Some of these surface formulations are apparently controlled by underlying cognitive structures and strategies, whereas others do not have this "expressive" function, but rather serve a communicative-persuasive function: They enhance truth claims, credibility, seriousness, or interestingness of the events or experiences told about. We return to these persuasive discourse strategies below.

Summary

This section has informally explained the cognitive processes involved in the production of prejudiced talk. At each stage of the conversation, the speaker strategically makes use of various types of information, which together define the speech act being performed, the contents being expressed, the style and rhetoric of the formulation, as well as the discourse type, such as a story or an argumentation, being used. The various processes and information types involved, then, may be summarized as follows:

(a) Analysis, interpretation, and representation in a model of the communicative context type, namely, the opinion interview. This context model features the following macroinformation: (a) goals of the (verbal) interaction, (b) model of self as interviewee, (c) model of the other as interviewer, and the following local information, (d) previous speech acts and associated intentions and contents, and (e) present interactional obligations.

(b) Analysis, interpretation, and representation in a text model of the global and local discourse structures, featuring, for instance, the present topic of conversation, the overall style, and the previous sentences and propositions.

(c) Activation and retrieval of particular and general model(s) of concrete experiences with ethnic minority group members, featuring negative opinions about the acts and properties of such members on one hand, and the speaker in a victim role on the other hand.

(d) Activation and partial retrieval or instantiation of a general prejudice schema about ethnic groups, used for the stereotypical interpretation of ethnic encounters, the search for relevant (negative) models of personal experiences, and as an "opinion basis" for the derivation of specific opinions about specific (real or imagined) events.

Each of these strategic processes are very complex and require analysis and interpretation by the speaker at several levels at the same time. Indeed, the various components of the process are not "worked through" systematically or serially, as would be the case for grammatical rules or an algorithmic program. Rather, from each level or representation, some elements are used, hypothetically and at the same time, to perform a specific local task, such as producing one sentence. In a later stage, such hypotheses or provisional plans may be changed or confirmed (executed). For instance, the quasi-denial of negative feelings about Surinamese in lines 14-15, may not be preplanned at all in the story that must illustrate a negative experience. However, the speaker may realize that after the negative conclusion, the hearer might form a negative model of the speaker, and then the local decision may be taken to say something "positive" about Surinamese. The same holds for the argumentative support of this denial. In order to do this, the speaker must register his own current propositions and their possible implications for the evaluation of self, register the current nonverbal acts of the hearer, monitor the role of the hearer, and so on. Indeed, when talking to a close friend with similar opinions, the denial might not be necessary in the "same" story. His analysis, interpretations, and decisions, however, are just expedient guesses: At each point, the speaker cannot be sure what exactly the hearer thinks about him, and how his statements are interpreted. Below, we return to the strategic nature of discourse processing by the hearer when analyzing the processing of understanding persuasive prejudiced discourse.

We have observed that model and schema information may be in constant interplay during conversational interaction, in general and in, for instance, storytelling or argumentation, in particular. At the same time, these cognitive strategies of effective social information processing appear to play a role in the cognitive processing of persuasive and other communicative strategies, such as self-presentation. All these cognitive structures and strategies must be well organized and monitored. This takes place through the overall Control System, which features the main information needed to keep the process running smoothly, such as (a) overall context type (interview) as well as the overall communicative goal(s), (b) topic of conversation, (c) model now active, (d) script(s) now active, and (e) attitude(s) now active. The Control System specifies which information must be activated or retrieved, which information is necessary in STM, which STM interpretations should be stored and where, and so on. For prejudiced discourse production, the overall communicative strategy, such as positive self-presentation or negative other-presentation, is also stored in the Control System. In our case, for instance, the Control System specifies which model of personal experiences is an adequate input for storytelling, or from which perspective the story will be told (imagine, for instance, what the story and the models of the Surinamese involved in the fight would look like).

Finally, we may conclude from this section that a single step in the process of ethnic prejudice reproduction, namely, the cognitive processing of the production of persuasive turns in conversation, already requires a very complex theoretical analysis. This section has only provided a rather informal summary of such an analysis. We may expect, then, that a full account of the ethnic reproduction processes in persuasive communication is a vast enterprise. This might give some further support to our conclusion formulated in the previous section, namely, that even the modern developments in persuasion and communication research are still merely scratching the surface of the complex processes involved.

2.2. THE PERSUASIVE COMMUNICATION OF PREJUDICE

In this section, we turn to the next step of the communication of ethnic prejudice: the persuasive dimension of talk about ethnic groups. In Chapter 2, we already examined part of the discourse features that signal such a persuasive function. Now we analyze these persuasive functions themselves. Also, we extend the cognitive analysis of discourse production, given in the previous section, to the sociocognitive aspects of interpersonal communication. That is, speakers not only produce and express propositions about "foreigners," they do so in conversational interaction, for a hearer, and in a social context. This process is also monitored cognitively. Hence, we pay attention to the interrelationships between (a) communicative and persuasive strategies of talk, (b) the interpersonal functions of such talk, and (c) the cognitive monitoring of these strategies and functions. In still other terms: Whereas the previous section was about what the speaker does, the present section is about what "goes on" between speaker and hearer, and the next section analyzes what the hearer does—understanding and transforming beliefs and attitudes.

Strategies

To understand the discursive strategies of communication in general and of persuasive communication in particular, we first need to specify what we understand by interaction strategies in general. We have seen that cognitive strategies are effective ways of handling complex information (van Dijk & Kintsch, 1983). People in that case have a cognitive goal, such as understanding a sentence, a paragraph, or a whole story, and are able to do so only if they can manage many types of information at the same time. They reduce complex information structures by the application of macrostrategies, they work both top-down and bottom-up, they make expedient guesses based on incomplete information and various textual and contextual signals, and supply possible "missing" information from extant knowledge and beliefs in memory. In this way, as we shall see in more detail in the next section, people understand a sentence, a story, or a speech act even with a minimum of textual or contextual information. Indeed, "a good understander only needs half a word," says a Dutch proverb.

The cognitive notion of strategy derives from the strategic analysis of action and interaction, however. In action analysis, then, strategies are also used to manage complex information in an effective way. (Inter)action sequences have a purpose, represented cognitively by the actor(s) in a specific kind of (future) situation model. Such purposes are the cognitive counterpart of goals that are the wanted consequences of intended (planned) actions. Especially for complex interaction sequences, such goals may be reached in different ways. There are alternative action routes to reach the same goal. Yet, not all these routes are equally "effective." Some are easier, others may be more costly, whereas others again are faster. Also, for complex interaction, we may ignore what might happen during the interaction sequence. If we interact with (free) actors, their actions may significantly influence ours. Such unknown events and actions, thus, may advance or block our own actions leading toward the final goal. Now, strategies are applied to keep control over complex action sequences in such a way that the chance to reach a desired goal is optimal. For instance, if we ignore what actions another actor will perform, we may influence these actions by our own actions, for instance, by "forcing" certain wanted actions of the other actor. Or we may choose an action sequence in which events or actions that may impede ours are unlikely. Such an "easy" route, however, may be devious or costly.

Strategies may be analyzed in terms of moves. Each move is a functionally relevant "step" in a strategy-controlled (inter)action sequence. Thus, if my action goal is to be in Paris tonight, I may plan and execute a sequence of actions that may or may not be moves, that is, that have or have not a function in reaching that goal. Thus, various traveling moves, such as going to the station and taking the train, are functionally relevant to reach this goal. They may be necessary conditions for the final state representing the goal. Buying a novel at the station may be part of my actions during the trip, but it is usually not a necessary action to reach a travel goal. It may, however, be a move within the strategy of having a "pleasant" trip to Paris, because book reading may help in avoiding being bored. And if I want to take a "fast" alternative, I may choose to fly, and then the necessary moves would involve going to the airport, checking in, and so on.

From this informal analysis of the notion of interaction strategy, we conclude that it may be understood as a goal-directed, effective way of organizing and managing complex (inter)actions and their concomitant cognitions (e.g., intentions, plans, and evaluations). Just as actions themselves have a cognitive counterpart, their strategic execution also has a cognitive representation. In that sense, a strategy is a specific dimension of an action plan, that is, an overall constraint imposed on the "kind" of actions or action alternatives planned. These strategic constraints may be conceptually represented, for instance, as "fast," "cheap," "pleasant," and so on. If I want and plan to travel to Paris, I may in addition plan to do it "fast," and, thus, will devise my plan in such a way that the final goal is reached as quickly as possible. During plan construction, this means that of various alternative travel means, I will choose the fastest. Hence, cognitively, action strategies control the construction, the structure, and execution of (complex) action plans. They are, so to speak, the overall (macro)evaluation for the "manner" in which the action is to be executed in order to reach the goal.

Social Interaction Strategies

The abstract analysis of strategic action sketched above needs further specification for an understanding of social interaction. In this case, several actors are involved who may each have their own goal during a stretch of interaction. These goals may be mutually conflicting. To reach one's own goal, each actor, thus, must resort to various strategies, such as the strategic control of the strategies of the other actor. One important condition to control the actions of others is to know their goals. If we know where somebody is heading for, it is easier to plan actions to block the way. Hence, it is strategically important to get to know the plans of other actors, and, therefore, we may want to execute questions, or force others to explain their plans. And conversely, because the other actor may apply similar strategies, we may want to conceal our plans in case knowledge about them may prevent the realization of our goal. Thus, knowledge elicitation (e.g., questioning), and (plan) concealment may be effective moves in these knowledge exchange strategies of social interaction.

Similarly, it may also be expedient, especially in cooperative types of interaction, that the other actors know very well what we are doing, that is, know our intentions, plans, or purposes. Ambiguity of actions, which means that coactors (or observers) attribute the "wrong" intentions to our doings, may not be wanted. In such a case, we make sure that our actions are unambiguous by various moves, such as plan announcements, explanations, self-descriptions, and asking for interpretative feedback. In this way, we make sure that at each point of the action sequence, the other actor knows exactly what we are doing, and where we are heading. In other words, we thus control the model the other actor has of us as an actor, as well as about our actions or the action context.

Whereas belief management moves as described above are vital in social interaction strategies, another set of strategies directly pertains to the control of the very actions of the other actor. Indeed, we may "help" others or "prevent" others from reaching their goals. Except for situations in which actors can physically force others to perform certain actions, however, other actors' acts can be controlled only through socially shared norms or rules. In chess, for instance, we can "force" the other player to make a specific move, simply by the rules of the game, and by the basic strategic principle that blocks viable alternatives. Less constrained, but hardly less effective, is, for instance, the smile that is meant to "force" the other to be friendly or to help. Generally, then, interaction strategies of an actor A are geared toward the blocking of any action of an actor B that may have results or consequences that are not wanted by A, or toward the promotion of any action of B that does have results or consequences wanted by A. This generalization characterizes what may be called self-serving types of interaction. Of course, in altruistic interaction types, the generalization should be reversed.

Impression Management

One of the most influential types of social interaction strategies is the one that manages the "impression" others have about us as a person or as a social actor (Tedeschi, 1981). We have seen earlier that during (verbal or other) interaction, we are constantly busy building models of the interaction context and of our interaction partners. To know whether or not these others are likely to promote or block the execution of our own plans, it is also necessary to have an overall evaluation of them. We know other actors will do the same with us, and it is, therefore, important—again, to better reach our goals— to influence that evaluation. The strategies we have recourse to in that case, are the well-known strategies of impression management, of which self-presentation (or face-saving) strategies are the most prominent example (Goffman, 1967, 1969). Moves in such strategies are executed in such a way that positive evaluative inferences are encouraged, and negative ones blocked. Politeness moves may be seen as examples of this strategic self-presentation: Signals of politeness may encourage others to believe that one is a pleasant person, has respect for them, or follows the norms or rules associated with status or role distribution and interaction (Brown & Levinson, 1978).

There are two basic dimensions of impression management. On one hand, we may want to favor a positive evaluation, and on the other, we may want to avoid a negative one (Arkin, 1981). In talk about controversial issues or delicate topics, such as "foreigners" in our interviews, both dimensions may be involved. On one hand, the speaker may want the recipient to believe that he or she is a kind, tolerant, helpful, or understanding person and citizen. On the other hand, general norms require that the speaker at the same time keeps control over negative impression formation: Practically nobody wants to be seen as intolerant, prejudiced, or racist.

Self-presentation, however, involves more than the management of positive or negative evaluation. People provide information for the construction of a full-fledged person schema (Hastie et al., 1980). In this way, they may display signals that may be interpreted as intended social categorizations. Thus, for the speakers in our interviews, it appeared to be particularly relevant that they be perceived as the innocent "victims" of foreigners. Storytelling in that case may primarily lead to empathy from the recipient. In other words, self-presentation involves the strategic expression of the contextually relevant dimensions of a self-schema (Markus, 1977). For prejudiced talk, additionally, this means appropriate signaling of in-group membership, for instance, by persuasive reference to generally respected group goals, interests, and norms. In other words, self-presentation as a victim not only has a personal persuasive function, but also a social function: It is the whole group that is perceived to be the victim of immigration. And such an evaluation is again an important argument in the legitimation of an active "defense" against the foreigners, that is, of discriminatory practices. Racist politicians, such as Powell in England or Le Pen in France, have shrewdly used such prejudiced opinions in their appeals to keep (or throw) out the foreigners, especially those of color.

Communicative Interaction Strategies: Model Manipulation

What has been said about social interaction strategies also holds for communicative interaction (Higgins, 1981). Indeed, much of the work on strategic social interaction has been done with verbal examples, as is the case for impression management strategies (O'Keefe & Delia, 1982; Schneider, 1981). The obvious specificity in this case is that actors are speakers and hearers, and that the actions are verbal. The same overall conditions hold, however: We want the other to understand what we do/say, and we try to reach an interaction goal as effectively as possible by influencing the acts of the other. Yet, in talk, this control over the acts of speech partners is often not a primary goal. Rather, we must first control the (trans)formation of knowledge, beliefs, or opinions of our interlocutors. These include beliefs and opinions about what we are talking about, but also about ourselves, including our own opinions and attitudes (Hass, 1981). The latter try to control the construction of wanted context (speaker) models, the former the construction of wanted situation (event) models by the hearer.

How, then, can speakers control the construction of situation models by the hearer? Before we return to the interpretation and representation strategies of discourse understanding in the next section, let us pay attention to some of the strategies that speakers apply to influence these processes.

Interpretation Facilitation

Models are constructed from textual representations in memory (and previous models and schemata in memory). This means, first, that such textual representations ("meanings") should be as intended by the speaker. A whole set of strategies are used to facilitate or promote intended meanings and their use in the construction of situation models:

(1) Expression of the vitally important overall meaning (macro)propositions, such as in initial or final summaries—this contributes to global coherence and understanding, and to the preferred macropropositions dominating the textual representation and the situation model. Story summaries, and news report headlines and leads, are well-known examples of such strategies. Also, the expression of macrostructures may block alternative global interpretations by the reader. Once a preferred overall meaning is established, local interpretation can also be controlled (top-down) more effectively.

(2) The same holds for the role of superstructure schemata in understanding. It is, therefore, effective that the speaker shows explicitly which type of discourse is being engaged in now, for instance, by signaling this type directly ("I'll tell you a story . . ."), or by using explicit markers that characterize discourse genres, such as argumentative signals in argumentation, or the explicit category headings (Introduction, Theory, Experiments, Subjects, Materials, and so on) in psychological research reports.

(3) Understanding presupposes the application of previous general knowledge, such as frames and scripts. The speaker must be or make sure that the hearer has such frames or scripts. If not, scriptal information must not be presupposed but expressed. Hence, effective talk will strategically check previous knowledge of the hearer, and insert explanation sequences that supply missing frames or scripts.

(4) The same holds for the role of previous situation models in understanding. Information that is completely "new," in the sense that no similar models are supposed to be known to the hearer, is difficult to understand. One strategy in that case is that of reminding and comparison: the actually described events are compared to those of a situation the hearer is supposed to know already.

(5) Whereas the strategies described above control overall understanding and the very contents of the Control System of the hearer, there are other strategies that facilitate understanding at the local level. The explicit expression of local semantic coherence links, for instance, by using connectives, may help establish such coherence. Ambiguous words

may be disambiguated by further explanation or paraphrases. Pronouns may be made explicit by full descriptions, and importance or relevance may be signaled by various devices, such as repetition or such special expressions as "it is crucial that . . . ."

(6) Finally, syntactic structures and lexical expressions may also be strategically controlled to facilitate comprehension, for instance, by reducing syntactic complexity, by reformulations and paraphrases.

Model Schemata

Models are organized by categorial schemata. From vast amounts of information about situations, events, actions, and people, models may be effectively construed by the application of such categorically organized schemata. This process can also be influenced in the same way as text base formation. Yet, except for the uses of pictures, gestures, maps, or other forms of analogical information, such strategic control of model formation must be indirect, that is, through discursive means. In order to convey the model the speaker has in mind, thus, the formulation, as described earlier, must be such that the basic categories of the model are expressed. Thus, in storytelling it is not only narratively, but also semantically, important to mention explicitly Setting elements such as time, place, circumstances, participants and their roles, as well as the actions or events taking place. The overall organization of the model may be signaled by relevant macropropositions, as we have seen above. Finally, models may have an important evaluative dimension, and it is, therefore, important that the speaker strategically control the evaluations assigned by the hearer to model events or participants. In our interviews, this is typically the case for the persuasive formulation of evaluations about foreigners in storytelling.

Credibility

Intended understanding of the speaker, thus, involves the management of preferred textual representations and situation models. Yet, to understand what a speaker is talking about is not yet to believe that what the speaker says is true or probable. Strictly speaking, each situation model is initially embedded in the context and speaker models: It is a representation of what the speaker says or believes is the case. To adopt such a model as a personal representation of the situation, independently of the speaker model, is what we understand by "believing." Persuasive communication is essentially geared toward this process of acceptance. To influence that process, a number of strategies are applied to enhance the "credibility" of what has been said. One major factor in this case is the manipulation of the general credibility of the speaker, as represented in the speaker model, to be discussed below. Direct model credibility can be enhanced by the following strategic moves:

(1) Show that the model is similar to other particular or general models the hearer has already adopted. Typical phrases marking this comparison are, for instance, "It is just like last time . . .," "It has happened again," or "You know that this always happens like this."

(2) Show that the model is an instance of a general frame or script. A typical phrase marking this instantiation is, for instance: "This is a typical example of . . . ."

(3) Show that the model as a whole or parts of it can be inferred from previous models. This is done by argumentative moves and signaled by the usual argumentative markers such as "so," "it follows that," or "that is why. . . ."

(4) Show that alternative models of the situation are less credible (impossible, inconsistent, and so on). Markers of this strategy are, for instance, denials of the possibility of such alternatives, or modal expressions ("must," "necessarily").

(5) Provide factual evidence for the model and its parts by mentioning facts that must be true (see strategy 1), or that are unlikely to have been imagined, such as direct observation, personal experiences, and so forth ("I saw it myself").

(6) Refer to unbiased others who share the model and can vouch for its truth ("X told me that . . .," "You can ask Y").

From these examples, we see that the basic overall strategy of credibility enhancement for model communication is to refer to other information that may sustain the model, such as by comparison, inference, instantiation, verification, consensus, or necessity. When the model is thus presented as maximally coherent with the other knowledge and beliefs (models, scripts, and so on) of the hearer, its chances of acceptance are highest.

Impression Management Strategies and Speaker Models

We have seen above that speakers manage impression formation by the hearer through the strategic manipulation of the construction of speaker models as part of the overall context model of the communicative situation (Eagly, Chaiken, & Wood, 1981; Hass, 1981). Thus, not only what people say should be credible, but also the speaker him- or herself. This type of credibility is attributed to the speaker on the basis of characteristics that can be strategically controlled only in part, such as (beliefs about) appearance, expertise, status, gender, age, social class, or professional and institutional functions (Cronkhite & Liska, 1980). Speaker credibility, unlike content credibility, is usually context independent, but may be a function of discourse and topic type. A mechanic, thus, is more credible when speaking about cars than a professor is, who again will be more credible when talking about his or her own field of expertise.

Because people can only partly control the inherent physical or social features that influence credibility judgments of hearers, they will first of all tend to remind the hearer of such credibility features: They tactically present their "credentials," if unknown, for the context as a whole, for instance, during presentations, or while presenting evidence for a specific fact in the model to be communicated (e.g., "my experience as a doctor tells me that . . .").

Credibility management, however, is just one strategy type among many forms of impression management. To control not only what is believed by the hearer, but also his or her opinions and attitudes, including the opinions about the speaker, the speaker must aim at the construction of other positively valued personal or social characteristics in the speaker model: honesty, modesty, charm, originality, tolerance, and so on. These attractiveness-enhancing strategies may be verbal or nonverbal (smiles, gestures, and so on). The verbal ones may control discourse content, but are most typical for style in the broad sense: all the (variable) ways a situation model is expressed and conveyed. Assuming that more or less the same "message" must be communicated, which in our theoretical framework means more or less the same text and situation models, the speaker may do so in a more or less tactful, honest, straightforward, modest, friendly, polite, or understanding way.

This means that speaker model manipulation is not just a set of strategies for the construction of a desired person schema dominated by such personality "traits." After all, (semi)permanent person schemata about other people, just like frames or scripts, require many particular models. Yet, here too, fast strategies apply, and a "first impression" is known to be very influential. Hence, first encounters are crucial, and this also holds for the impression management strategies in incidental conversations such as interviews. Although it is less serious to make a bad impression on people we meet only once, even in such occasional encounters, a speaker will make sure to enhance his or her attractiveness, if only to promote the actual goals of the interaction. Thus, it has been found that if the recipient aims at forming an impression of the speaker, the contents of talk will also tend to be better recalled (Hamilton, Katz, & Leirer, 1980). Thus, event and speaker models in the recipient may be interrelated and may mutually enhance credibility and acceptability, including social acceptability. In other words, the person impression management strategy may be context-bound, and typical for the interaction and discourse type. For instance, in requests, the speaker's purpose is to persuade the hearer to accomplish an action in the speaker's favor. In that case, politeness may be more effective than power display or more relevant than aggressiveness, which might be the preferred strategy in ransom notes or other types of threatening speech acts.

Opinion Interviews

In opinion interviews, there are also a series of typical self-presentation strategies. Part of these strategies are similar to those also followed in self-disclosure: giving personal opinions about a delicate matter is also providing delicate information about oneself (Gilbert, 1976; Jourard, 1971). In this case, personality management may focus on characteristics that promote the goal of getting one's beliefs, opinions, attitudes, experiences, and so on respected, if not accepted. To control such internal "belief attributions" by the hearer, the speakers in our interviews have recourse to the following moves:

(1) Provide supporting evidence for any opinion expressed (see above for the situation model strategies).

(2) Show that the opinion (evaluative belief) is based on consensually shared values, and does not conflict with other values.

(3) Show that the opinion is not merely a personal one, but endorsed by many other people.

(4) Show that the opinion is coherent (consistent) with other opinions expressed that are easier to justify.

(5) If opinions expressed may have negative implications for the speaker, formulate them in such a way that these negative implications are denied or mitigated.

(6) Show understanding for other opinions or show why other opinions are wrong.

Strategic Talk About Ethnic Groups

The analysis presented above for strategic communicative interaction also holds for persuasive talk about ethnic affairs, and we already gave a few examples of such strategies. It has been repeatedly assumed during this study that prejudiced conversations about ethnic groups and encounters have two global strategic goals:

(a) the expression of (negative) experiences and opinions about such groups, and, at the same time, (b) the social protection of self by positive face-saving strategies, or rather, the avoidance of negative impressions. Because the social norm that prohibits discrimination and racism is rather strong, most speakers are aware of the possibility that negative stories or opinions about foreigners might be interpreted as signaling underlying prejudices. This is why negative statements appeared to be often accompanied by "qualifications" of different types, such as denials of generalized prejudice, concessions of positive properties of ethnic groups or negative ones of the speaker's group, and so on. In this part of this section, therefore, we further examine these strategies—this time from a cognitive, communicative, and persuasive point of view. We want to know how negative other-presentation and positive self-presentation (or the avoidance of negative self-presentation), which are often contradictory, are managed interactively. How does the speaker take into account possible or actual reactions or assumed inferences of the hearer? We do this, first, by analyzing a few examples in detail, and then giving an overview of the specifically persuasive moves that characterize these strategies.

Let us first analyze the case of a woman and her husband, both about 60 years old, living in a high-contact neighborhood. From the interview, in which initially the woman, who is highly prejudiced against foreigners, talks most, we take all the passages that contain persuasive strategies for negative other-presentation and positive self-presentation. The contents embedded in these strategies are summarized in this case (the interview is 25 transcript pages long). Literal passages are marked with quotes. To each passage we try to assign analytical categories that characterize the moves aimed at the persuasion of the interviewer (a male student). We follow the interview linearly (W: Woman, M: Man, I: Interviewer).

(1) W: We lived in another popular neighborhood for years. "But yet, this lot here can't touch that. I mean that. Yes, excuse me, but then there were not so many minorities yet, as they call it, because you are not allowed to say foreigners of course."

The comparison with the previous neighborhood where the woman lived is negative for the present neighborhood, especially because of "this lot" here, which is identified especially as being ethnic minority groups. As a credibility enhancing move, the comparison provides evidence about a positively valued previous situation model: There were no foreigners there, and, therefore, it was better than here. She is not just making things up: She has evidence from comparisons with another situation. "I mean that" is the usual expression for the persuasive affirmation of both honesty and credibility. The ironical introduction of *minorities*, the formal term that is seldom used outside of political or academic contexts, has several persuasive functions. First, W shows that she knows the formal conventions. Second, the use of this formal term in an informal context expresses irony about the people who talk about foreigners in a neutral or positive way, such as politicians or academics. The implication is that she does not agree with such neutral or positive evaluations, but the rhetorical move of ironical quotation allows her to avoid saying so explicitly. Yet, introducing minorities as the cause of the decay of the neighborhood may be heard as racist, and, hence, she uses the formal apology move, which is literally translated as, "Don't hold it against me," obviously a move of avoiding negative inferences (I know one shouldn't say these things, but I have no alternative). In other words, the comparison, the honesty signal, the ironic formality, and the apology contribute to the goal of enhancing credibility (by model comparison), and positive self-presentation (by conformity to the norms), while at the same time expressing a very negative opinion about foreigners. That is, avoiding negative self-presentation is functionally triggered by negative other-presentation.

(2) My son is living with me now, and we have to move and he doesn't get an apartment. "And those foreigners they take people with them when coming back from their vacation, also the children of other people, and they get a house right away, you know, and many Blacks, not because they are Blacks of course, I have never disliked them, NOW I do. Now I dislike them very much. I live here. Just for fun you have to come and live here for a week when we move, but then you shouldn't sleep at night."

The moves in this passage may be summarized in the following format:

Credibility enhancing moves: Her own experiences, observation of what negative things foreigners do (bring back other people), and favorable treatment of foreigners; appeal to interviewer to try it out for himself (verification);

Positive self-presentation: Negative comparison between us and them: we are the victims (engender empathy) of unfair competition; denial of racist reasons for dislike, stressing "good reasons" for dislike;

Negative other presentation: evidence that they take our houses, and bring back (illegally?) other people and children; intense dislike is defensible.

(3) They should build a police station here. Everybody is free to do as they please, if only they do not offend me. I have my rights. I am not the police, but I could tell a lot, and I see a lot. I hate them.

Credibility moves: hinting at personal experiences and observation;

Negative other-presentation: intentional implicitness ("a lot"). Positive self-presentation: quasi-tolerance (acknowledging other's freedom).

(4) "We had trouble with that [Black] woman there, and I tell you exactly what it was all about, about nothing. And listen, she was air to me, I couldn't stand her. So she provoked it. Once it came to an explosion." Granddaughter passed house of that woman, who says something and granddaughter reacts and a fight results. Son jumps through the open window (destroying window sill) to help granddaughter. Black woman shows a big knife and threatens. "I am always very calm in such moments," and defied her. Her husband didn't dare do anything. Police were phoned and came, and I told them "It was the same little joke as last time," you can go back because we already arranged it. Police warns Black woman. Everybody to police station. Talked to old policeman (longing for his retirement) I know. Scorned the young policemen who do not know to handle the woman who is dressed in a blouse "from which her tits are half hanging outside."

This paraphrase of a long story has been given to show how the woman essentially provides evidence in a story about negative characteristics of a Black woman across the street. Most moves are credibility enhancing, such as emphasis on preciseness of the narration (see the honesty move in an earlier example), a move blaming the other for the cause of the aggression ("she was air to me," i.e., I did not pay attention to her), small details in story (jumping through the window, broken window sill, and so on) that enhance the observational dimension and, hence truthfulness, and so on. The very length and details of the story show how the interviewee has represented the situation, and persuasively shows the interviewer that this is a true experience. It was the Black woman who provoked it, and used a knife (negative other presentation, such as the sexual allegations about confusing the young policemen). Positive self-presentation in the expression of such situation models that represent conflict involves the transfer of guilt or cause to the other group, and the contrastive comparison between the threatening knife-brandishing Black woman, and the very "calm" storyteller.

(5) Some of them have never worked. And if you SEE how they live. My son and daughter work hard, and so do I, and they tell me to go on welfare too to take a rest. "You know what I mean? It is, OK I know, like those Blacks here, I tell you in confidence, but if you SEE what kind of stolen goods are being carried into that house during the night. They enter with four of five people, they come in Surinamese dress, that folklore, and they leave, man, wife and children dressed from top to bottom. You know what I mean? Big cars, they are better off than we are. If anybody is being discriminated against, our children are. That's is what I make of it."

Credibility moves: reporting personal observations (emphasis twice on "see"), appeals to and confidence sharing with interviewer; model is (typical) example of general fact (they are better off); also my children think I am right (consensus);

Negative other-presentation: cheat on welfare, steal, have a good life (nice dress, big cars, as "observable" evidence for their cheating, because people who have those things cannot be on welfare);

Positive self-presentation: contrasted positive characteristic (we work hard), victim role (we are being discriminated against), and altruism (I do it for my children).

(6) Turkish boy of upstairs neighbors spit on me in the face. My son beats him up. His father protests, but after talk also gives him a beating. We help each other. But the kids demolish my husbands's car, which he needs because he is an invalid. "May I be quite honest with you": I was so mad that I said they can all use them to make a new polder. My husband has a small welfare allowance. Has worked hard all his life, always proper. And then they, married and divorced but together, in business and both on welfare. "What do you think about that?"

Here is another story that presents minority group members negatively, such as fights and cheating on welfare, contrasted explicitly with positive "we" image: Her own husband always worked hard. Details (such as husband ate a loaf of bread everyday) to enhance credibility about how hard husband worked; honesty (or frankness) move to formulate very negative opinion; and final appeal to the interviewer, requesting an opinion but also a move that rhetorically asks for agreement. The next passages will be given together:

(7) "But on average the people dislike the what you call it the foreigner like the pest. But you know what. Most people don't dare to talk about it, you know."

(8) You hear people say in shops or in the street that next time they will vote for a racist party. "And when it comes to that, who is to blame? According to me, that whole government. What do they want in fact? What do they want?" These people are here to stay, even when they don't work.

(9) Mother-in-law and daughter tell about bad experiences in streetcar with Blacks. "That kind of things. And look, Dutch youth also demolishes much in streetcars, but on average the foreigners do that. Don't think I am cris—ris—discriminate, because I take [tram] line 3 very often."

(10) "They want their own culture. I also have to adapt when I go to Turkey." Clandestine slaughtering. Neighbors took old refrigerator from the street, which didn't work so that all their meat started to rot, and they put that on the street, so that big bugs were crawling on the street. "WE always get that mess." . . . "Look, those things. Dutch

people should try to do that with them. Try to live here for a week, when we have moved.

M: "Then he can see something here. They steal and rob every-thing. NOT only because they, they are, there are of course also good ones among them, but on the whole is not much, you know."

M/W: [Black?] neighbor is a junkie and has stolen many bicycles which he sells to the students here.

---

(11) M: And what is worse, is that they mug old people. The other night I was walking home, and saw two old people being mugged and I attacked the muggers with my bike "I saw these guys on the back but could see they were dark ones"; I broke one's arm, and the other split.

W: "That's what we have to call minorities."

M: Police came, and I told the story. Old people shocked. To the police station, and then they brought me home.

W: "Yes, I thought it was just a fantasy story. But he came home at three in the night." So I went to the police station, and they told me "Everything is really true."

M: And the old people wanted to give me a new bike because my wheel was bent, but I had repaired that, and so they gave me a new watch.

These further passages from the same interview briefly summarize and occasionally quote from long stories. The woman especially volunteers many narrative "proofs" for her very negative opinion about foreigners. Although her opinions are often stated quite bluntly, she nevertheless takes care to show that her "evidence" is valid, and that her opinions are defensible, that is, she at the same time tries to avoid giving a bad impression to the interviewer. A few of the interaction moves in these passages are as follows:

In example 7, we find the usual generalization move that is used to enhance credibility: This is not a personal opinion, but all people think like that. In other words, the personal model I have about foreigners is a socially shared, and, hence, (more) acceptable one. In example 8, too, reference is made to other people, this time to spell out the (negative?) consequences of the presence of all these foreigners: People say they will vote a racist party (the woman does not use this qualification, of course, but mentions the name of the leader of that—forbidden—party). Yet, the move following this evidence based on "bad consequences" is one of transfer or attribution: It is the government that is to blame. Indeed, throughout this interview, and often in others, we find a general distrust of the government and the authorities "who haven't done anything against it." The government is seen as protecting and favoring minorities. In fact, what we find here is a form of counterattribution: If they blame us for becoming racist, I blame them for letting these foreigners come to our country or neighborhood in the first place. Obviously, this is an important move within the strategy of avoiding negative impression formation.

Example 9 at length details the reported experiences of family members in the Amsterdam streetcar (Blacks bothering other people, trying to pick pockets, and so on). The streetcar situation model, however, also activates the common knowledge that streetcars are constantly being destroyed by youth. The woman directly comments on and evaluates that dimension, and attributes that other negative situation also to young foreigners, despite counterarguments of a streetcar driver she knows. Counterarguing against possible counterarguments of the hearer is a well-known move. This requires, of course, some backing up, so she has recourse to the standard quasi-denial that she doesn't want to discriminate. Such denials show that despite her overt hate of ethnic minority groups, she is also aware of the norms that blaming foreigners for negative situations may be heard as a form of discrimination.

Example 10 features the well-known contrastive comparison move, which emphasizes the differences between *us* and *them:* What they do here, we can- and would not do there. We would adapt ourselves. The repeated invitation to the interviewer to take their place is, of course, a powerful move to enhance credibility for the stories (the interviewer can see for himself in that case), as well as for the defensibility of the opinions based on those experiences. In the same example, the man also starts to contribute to the conversation, and concludes that "they steal," which in the next move is, however, qualified by the standard quasi-concession that there are exceptions.

In the summary of another long story (example 11), we find a number of credibility enhancing moves because the story is so "strong" and "heroic" that it might be disbelieved. The woman has a very effective strategy to prove the truth of the story: She says that she didn't believe it herself, at first, but the fact that her husband did come home very late, and especially the confirmation by the objective authorities, namely, the police, are enough evidence to show that the story was true. Finally, the woman again interpolates scorn about the (positively interpreted) term *minorities,* which she thinks is a ridiculous name for people who mug old people. We see that also during "objective" (truthful) storytelling, people routinely insert subjective evaluations, strategically intended to manage the conclusions and the evaluations of the hearer about the story, and at the same time as a form of their own-opinion-presentation.

Conclusion

From these brief qualitative analyses of a number of passages from a long interview with a highly prejudiced couple, we have found instances of several strategic moves aimed at the enhancement of model-credibility, including negative other-presentation, and the avoidance of negative self-presentation. The overall strategy in this interview is to provide personal (including family) experience stories that are so detailed and concrete that they can hardly have been made up. But we also found that even in such stories, moves are built in to "guarantee" their truth, such as personal observation, evidence from other people (the consensus move), or confirmation by authorities (the authority move). The major goal of these narrative strategies is negative other-presentation. Ethnic minority groups are being systematically accused of stealing, mugging, cheating on welfare, lack of hygiene, laziness, and so on. That is, if the event as (re)presented, that is, the model, is found to be truthful, then this will also enhance the acceptability of the overall evaluations associated with the participants to which these true negative acts are attributed. So, strategies that aim at enhancing credibility indirectly contribute to the enhancement of opinion acceptability.

The second major strategy within the combined overall strategy of negative other-presentation and self-defense is the systematic contrastive comparison between *us* as poor victims and *them* as the perpetrators of crime and as the cause of all our troubles. The others are represented as dressing well (despite their "official poverty"), driving big cars, and as generally being better off than "us." We (mother, father, son, and daughter) either did or now work hard and do not get appropriate housing, and the others get everything for nothing. This comparative contrast is one of the powerful rhetorical devices organizing this conversational interaction. Representing oneself as a victim is apparently a good move in the overall strategy of moral self-defense. In this case, even if we would hate foreigners, we would be justified, and could not be accused of discrimination. Hence, the legitimacy of (negative) opinions further contributes to their acceptability.

Finally, the persuasive nature of these examples is enhanced by stressing the generality of the experiences. Other people also complain and my other family members have similar experiences (consensus), the experiences are frequent and not occasional (frequency and reliability), and they are also typical: They conform with what we may expect from foreigners (typicality). These moves appear to follow well-known criteria of causal attribution (Kelley, 1967, 1983). That is, attribution criteria may be used also for the justification of causal judgments. This strategy, then, allows the inference from particular opinions to general opinions, and from there to the general, negative attitude, summarized as "I hate them." By these moves, the speaker shows that her judgments are not idiosyncratic or personal, but those of a competent and concerned in-group member. For the interviewer, belonging to the same in-group, such a strategy is a further contribution to the acceptability of the opinions expressed: The problems I am talking about are problems for all of "us."

3. Understanding and representing prejudiced communication

In this section, we analyze the final and crucial phase in the interpersonal communication of ethnic prejudice through conversation, namely, the processing of persuasive talk by the recipient. Again, our approach is cognitive: We make explicit the structures and strategies that characterize the representation and uses in the memory of the recipient of information and action interactively displayed by a prejudiced speaker. According to our model of text and information processing outlined in Chapter 4, we may distinguish the following steps in this process of interpretation, of which the last steps (attitude change) will be dealt with in the next section (for details, see van Dijk & Kintsch, 1983):

(a) Understanding and representing the communicative situation (including understanding and representing the speaker);
(b) understanding and representing the speaker's utterances;
(c) construction of a model of the situation referred to;
(d) updating of own previous model(s) of similar situation(s);
(e) possible generalization of the constructed/updated model(s); and
(f) partial change of ethnic attitude contents or structures.

Although there is some temporal and conditional ordering in these steps, it should be emphasized that a strategic theory of (prejudiced or other) information processing assumes that, in principle, understanding may take place, often incompletely, at several levels at the same time, and in a different order. For instance, the recipient will usually interpret the context and the speaker at the same time as interpreting the utterances of a conversation. In fact, the utterances of the speaker may be primarily understood and used to form "impressions" of such a speaker. We have seen earlier that speakers also know this and, therefore, have strategic recourse to many impression managing moves in their talk. They will try to influence the interpretation of the situation, the formation of models and attitudes about ethnic groups, and the formation of (positive) models of themselves. In the same way as speakers may be consciously monitoring such strategies, hearers also may well be aware of specific strategic steps, and may form speaker and event models accordingly.

Processing, thus, takes place "on line," that is, incoming information is decoded and interpreted immediately, unit by unit (e.g., words, sentences, propositions) at several levels, together with the application of general knowledge and attitudes or personal situation models. The results of this on-line interpretation are hypothetical representations that may be revised by following interpretation steps. This is also true for the construction of a speaker model: Previous evaluations of the speaker, as well as initial impressions based on the first fragments of the conversation, may be continually revised later in the conversation, even when "first impressions" usually lead to powerful (macro)evaluations that may be used to monitor further processing. Here too, the revision of initial hypotheses may be difficult: People are usually inclined to seek information that confirms rather than disconfirms such early hypotheses.

The processing steps just summarized presuppose vast amounts of personal and social knowledge, beliefs, experiences, opinions, and attitudes (Eagly, 1981). That is, the persuasive "effects" of prejudiced speakers are not inscribed on some attitudinal tabula rasa. In our earlier account of the structures of attitude and attitude change, we also stressed the fact that attitudes are very complex, and seldom changed, as a whole, due to one communicative event. Cognitive "changes" may be limited to isolated models about personal experiences, or may lead to very indirect and often delayed changes of model-based ethnic opinions. It simply does not occur very often in an ethnically complex society that social members receive completely new information about ethnic minority groups. It is one of the aims of this section, therefore, to show how existing beliefs and opinions interact with information conveyed in talk.

3.1. CONTEXT UNDERSTANDING

We have shown earlier that speech participants represent the communicative situation in a specific, episodic memory model. This model features the current participants (including self), the overall goals and categorization of the interaction type, as well as relevant social constraints on the interaction, and various setting features. For discourse production, thus, it appeared relevant that the speaker in our interviews models the recipient as an institutional representative (interviewer), as a stranger, as a young (male or female) student, and so on. The converse happens with the interviewer, who represents the speaker primarily as selected "interviewee," but also categorizes the speaker socially according to gender, social class, occupation, status, or other characteristics.

Similar processes are at work in informal talk about ethnic affairs. The interview situation fairly closely simulates talk among strangers, as may be the case for talk in public places with unknown people in the neighborhood (on the street, in shops), in offices, or in public transportation. Our evidence about various sources people mention (see Chapter 3) suggests that there is frequent conversational interaction about ethnic affairs in such settings and situations. Strategic representation of others in talk may be crucial for the interpretation of their utterances. For instance, if the recipient believes that elite members are not usually racist, he or she will not expect prejudiced talk, and may even tend to ignore those expressions that might be heard as such from other speakers. And conversely, when the recipient already has information about the speaker and his or her beliefs and opinions, as is the case for press or TV interviews with people who admittedly vote for a racist party, understanding their talk will, of course, be monitored by such a provisional person interpretation.

In both cases, however, a fundamental category in the speaker model will be ethnicity. Speakers who are categorized as belonging to the White in-group are in principle represented *as* in-group members, which also allows inferences about probable opinions and attitudes about out-group members. Direct or media represented talk of ethnic group members, thus, may be less credible for recipients when their opinions are interpreted as being in their own interests. Discounting strategies or other strategies of denying the implications of information given by out-group members may then start to operate during understanding, as we can see in the following example:

(12) *I-F-1/2 (Man/woman, 50/50, hi-con, P4/P5)
      (Not they but the Dutch are being discriminated against)
      M: I don't know whether you heard that radio report last Friday on VPRO [broadcast network]?
      I: No.
      M: There was a Surinamese woman from Utrecht . . . well she really took on on the radio she was being discriminated and she lived in a dump and she had to see a city councilman and well VPRO had arranged that she could talk to one of the councilmen. And the only thing that came from her mouth was I am being discriminated and the Dutch all have good housing, well it is a big lie, it is not true.

The man's denial of the stated experiences of the Black woman suggests how he might have represented the woman as well as her opinions. Because it is obviously not true that all Dutch people have good housing (conflict with his general knowledge), he may easily reject that opinion at the same time as the intended opinion that Black people are being discriminated against in housing. It is the latter opinion that conflicts with his own, stated, opinion that Dutch people and not minority groups are being discriminated against. By giving an example of a communicative situation in which a Black woman is represented as telling lies, he need not even make explicit the speaker model assumption that Black people will either lie in general, or show prejudice against Dutch people. In general, then, we assume that in a racist society, ethnic minority group members are represented as being less credible, in particular when speaking about discrimination and racism, because in that case their topics and goals of speech may be represented as self-serving. This presumption of "bias" is also reflected in the representation of such talk in the media: Accusations of discrimination or racism by minority group members are usually accompanied by quotation marks, or other distance markers. Also in our own data, foreigners represented are seldom modeled as truthful speakers. It is interesting to note, however, that when they are represented as denying racism or as critics of their own group, their credibility is very high, and their utterances often taken as good evidence for the opinions of the speaker, as we see in the following example:

> (13) I-C-6 (Woman, 60, lo-con, P6)
> Alright, you also have good ones because my husband works with uhh . . . well Surinamese and all that, who do a very fine job, but they say themselves: Yes uhh it is a pity but most of those who come here aren't worth much already in their own country . . . .

Note that the credibility of the Black speakers is further emphasized by the woman when she interpolates that the Surinamese her husband work with "do a very fine job." This is surprising when we also note that in general the woman speaks very negatively about ethnic minority groups. This suggests that speaker representation may be flexible and context bound. Obviously, such positive (ad hoc) models have a strategic nature in persuasion. The same speaker would probably not be represented as positively in other situations by the same recipient. If speakers show belief similarity then there will be a tendency to represent them more positively (sometimes even across ethnic boundaries), which is in accordance with well-known experimental findings (Rokeach, 1968). Note, though, that perceived belief similarity need not generalize to the group of the speaker as a whole, nor to overall positive attitudes. In our case, thus, Surinamese are found (more) credible only when they discredit their own group. The converse will be true for White speakers who denounce racism and discrimination of ethnic groups. In our earlier examples (section 2.2), we saw, for instance, that a highly prejudiced woman resents the positive treatment of "minorities" by the government. This suggests that authorities and the elite may be represented by members of nonelite groups as being biased in favor of ethnic groups and, hence, less credible. Here is a good example:

(14) I-G-7 (Man, 45, market vendor, P6)
      A few months ago I saw on TV, there was a minister who tells a Turk, a
      Turkish girl it was I believe in Sonja Barend's show [well-known talk-
      show on Dutch TV] and she says yes but the Dutch they put us off, then
      that minister says, I don't remember his name, but he says but the
      DUTCH have to adapt to those foreigners. I ask you, where are we
      heading like this?

In this example, ethnic group and class factors interact in the ways the
man represents the talk of a Turkish girl and a cabinet minister. Note,
though, that in general, White (elite) speakers who defend the rights of
minority group members or protest against racism are represented as
less credible, or even as "traitors." Whereas they might be more credible due to their elite status (position, expertise), their different ethnic
attitude might be seen as especially damaging to the in-group. This
explains why White antiracists tend to be portrayed very negatively in
(other) elite discourse, such as in the media.

From this discussion and the examples we may provisionally conclude
that speaker models in understanding are topic and context bound. When
"foreigners" are the topic of talk, it matters which group member is
speaking, and what the possible interests of the speaker are. For prejudiced recipients (whether elite or nonelite), "pro-foreigner" in-group
members especially tend to be represented very negatively, and their
utterances, therefore, become much less credible. A final, personal example may illustrate this point. In a letter from the editor of a well-known
Dutch elite weekly (*Intermediair*), read by managers and social scientists, to the author, an article about news analysis and the portrayal of
ethnic group members in the press was being rejected on the basis of
the following revealing arguments (note that the statements rejected
were being supported by much empirical evidence and references to
similar findings in many other publications):

(15) Especially what has been stated for news reports about minorities
      remains unproven and an unacceptable caricature of reality. The thesis
      "that the tenet of most reports is that ethnic groups provide problems
      for us" is in my opinion not only not proven, but simply incorrect.

Theoretically, speaker models of recipients are organized in a way
similar to that of persons or actors in general, such as in terms of a person schema featuring a number of relevant categories (see Hastie et al.,
1980, for details). In addition to the group schema categories (Origin/
Appearance, Socioeconomic status, Sociocultural properties, and Personal characteristics) we have postulated in Chapter 4, individual person schemata may feature information about whether or not a person is

a friend or an enemy, or other categories that determine interpersonal communication and interaction. For speakers in opinion interviews or generally in talk about controversial issues, personal evaluative categories such as honesty, truthfulness, or accuracy may be involved as components under a higher-level category of "credibility." The general group membership categories provide stereotypical evidence for evaluating individual speakers, and we have seen that different ethnic group membership (known or derived from origin/appearance/language), conflicting interests, lower status, and cultural differences may add to the negative personal evaluations about the speaker.

The result of such a very complex speaker model within the overall context model the recipient is constructing of the conversational event is an equally complex interaction with the representation of what is being said by the speaker. For instance, high status may in principle make the speaker more credible, but different beliefs or group allegiances may again reduce credibility. The hearer, therefore, must decide from further text and context analysis which of these attributed characteristics is most relevant in the present context. Thus, when the topic is ethnic affairs, and when the hearer is prejudiced, the high-status speaker may get much attention, but what is said may be discredited on other grounds.

This suggests that other important components must also be represented in the context model. First, the goals of the speaker are, of course, relevant. If the speaker is perceived to be aiming at persuading the recipient, the activation of his or her own topic-relevant attitudes is more relevant than when the speaker is apparently criticizing others. Then, the context type may also be an important factor. When speaking in an official function, in public, or in a formal situation, the speaker may receive more attention, and his or her credibility may be enhanced or reduced when expressing opinions that are inconsistent with those of the recipient. This also explains why people tend to use the media more often as support for their opinions than the personal communications of other arbitrary sources.

The point of this section has been to show that before recipients even start interpreting talk from speakers, they already tend to represent their relevant beliefs about the speaker strategically, and to construct inferences that may predict what the speaker is likely to say. Relevant situation models, attitudes, or other cognitive information in that case are being "prepared" for actual understanding. These expectations may even lead to provisional "counterarguing" (and, hence, to self-confirmation) when the speaker is believed to have different opinions about an expected topic of talk (Cialdini & Petty, 1981). The context model, or at least its main information (macropropositions), finally becomes part of the memory Control System, which monitors the actual participation in, and, hence, understanding of the conversation.

3.2. UNDERSTANDING
PREJUDICED DISCOURSE

Although (full) understanding of per-
suasive discourse appears to be neither a sufficient condition nor a good
predictor of attitude change, we may safely assume that it is mostly a
necessary condition (Eagly, 1974). (We ignore cases where people are
already "persuaded" by a discourse before it is actually uttered and
understood because, in that case, persuasion is based only on people's
assumptions about future communicative events, not on those events
themselves; see Cialdini & Petty, 1981.) No serious insight into the
processes of communicative attitude change is possible, in our opinion,
without an explicit account of the processes of discourse understanding
on which they are based. The memory contents and structures of information derived from discourse are a function of the ways this discourse
is understood in the first place. And we need to know about these contents and structures when we want to account for the formation of, or the
interaction with, opinions and attitude structures. This also holds for
cases in which people are being persuaded by discourse they understand
only in part, such as news reports or other media messages and programs.
This relevance of the cognitive processes of discourse understanding, of
course, implies the fundamental interaction between representations of
discourse structures with other information (models, scripts, attitudes,
and so on) stored in memory. This is also the major reason why further
persuasion processes, such as opinion formation or attitude change,
cannot be explained or predicted from discourse contents or structures
alone. Contrary to the classical studies that defined "persuasibility" in
terms of personality characteristics of the recipient (e.g., authorianism,
self-esteem), however, we emphasize the important role of the contents
and structures of current models and attitude schemata of the recipient,
as well as the (individually variable) applications of strategies for their
change (see Eagly, 1981, for discussion).

The processes operating during understanding and memory representation of prejudiced talk are in part similar to those outlined for the
production of such talk. We just suggested that these processes are monitored by three different kinds of information: (a) discourse structures
and their memory representation (the "text model"), (b) the context
model, representing the "facts" talked about, and (c) previous knowledge, beliefs, and opinions activated and applied during understanding.
When understanding prejudiced talk, a special topic is being constructed and special knowledge and attitude structures are being activated,
namely, those featuring "foreigners" or "ethnic groups" and related
information as concepts. This may mean that nonprejudiced discourse
may be interpreted in a "biased," prejudiced, way (or conversely), or

that prejudiced discourse is similarly or differently understood by a prejudiced recipient. We limit our analysis to an account of the understanding and further processing of prejudiced discourse, by both prejudiced and nonprejudiced recipients. In the first case, recipient prejudices may finally be confirmed or changed, and in the second case, they may be formed (or not) due to the prejudiced discourse.

Phases of Discourse Comprehension

Before we turn to the analysis of more specific cases, let us briefly summarize and further explain the major phases of cognitive discourse understanding. Although we mention these phases in a specific order, it should be recalled that understanding is a strategic process in which information may be processed from various sources and levels at the same time and in varying order, depending on the goals and information required by the strategic operations. In other words: Part of a process mentioned first may be attended to only in later stages of understanding, and conversely. To illustrate the various phases of understanding, we take a concrete example of our data, and theoretically "simulate" how a hearer could interpret such a passage.

(16) (MdU2, W, 50, Hi-Contact, P4)

W: What I find unreasonable sometimes, is uhh . . . I am also a woman on my own. I moved from that other apartment to this one, so I needed money. So I went to welfare and asked if they could help me. But no. But the Surinamese who come to this country they get a check for eight-nine thousand guilders, so that they can decorate their apartment. So then I threw in: "Why do THEY get it?" OK? "These are circumstances." I said "Aren't we circumstances?" Look, those are things . . . I was begging for my children's allowance and then a Surinamese puts, he puts a knife beside you and he gets it right away. And that, that are things . . .

I: That really happened like that?

W: Yes, really, yes, yes, yes, yes

I: That a knife was put down . . . on the table?

W: Because I jumped away. I thought, because he was so aggressive that man. They called him twice. Oh that is the man who was behaving like that last time as well. Well, he puts that little knife on the table, and that little check was already waiting for him. Oh yes, and that indeed is . . . . I am not making . . . I don't tell fantasy stories, but that is true.

I: And that was at the welfare agency?

W: And then I said "Is my color not alright, or what?" Isn't it? Well, he got it. And that happens everyday. If you have a small thing going, and think by yourself you want to redecorate your apartment . . . then you are afraid they might get to know that. And those guys they are driving around in big cars, they hang . . . [makes a gesture indicating big jewels on their fingers].

    This is a very typical story, told by a woman who does not seem very prejudiced on all accounts, but who resents the perceived favorable treatment of Surinamese immigrants. Because such stories give concrete "evidence" for such resentment, they are potentially very persuasive. Let us, therefore, examine how such a story is understood in the first place. For the moment we ignore the context model built by the recipient, as well as the—influential—text and situation models already constructed by the hearer on the basis of the previous parts of the conversation. The current topic is "living with foreigners in the neighborhood" (they get apartments easily, have many children, make a lot of noise, "but I have nothing against them").

Decoding and Analysis

                Once perceived, the sounds of talk by the mechanisms of sensory stores, operations of decoding, and analysis are applied in Short Term Memory (STM), and yield morphematic (word) sequences and part of their syntactic structures (categories, functions, ordering). Although these processes are basically bottom-up, they may be strategically facilitated by topic-controlled local semantic analysis: Word meanings that are predictable from currently established semantic representations can be decoded and analyzed more easily. The knowledge applied here is basically general knowledge of the language and of the regional dialect. Yet, pronunciation and syntax, of course, also yield signals that allow personal and social inferences that may form or change the model of the speaker (e.g., origin, class, and gender, in this case: a poor woman from Amsterdam, probably with little education). We have seen that this speaker model in turn may influence attention, understanding, and processes of opinion (trans)formation.

    In Chapter 2, we have found that talk about ethnic affairs also has a number of surface structure features that might be rather specific, such as pauses, false starts, repairs, hesitations, and so on, for instance, when a specific ethnic group or its properties are being described. We may assume that such signals are partially observable and interpretable by hearers, for instance, as indications of uncertainty and hesitation, or as manifestations of social control in speech. These interpretations may be added to the speaker model, and in general, we may assume that they will reduce the overall credibility of the speaker. Foreigners and opinions about them typically are a delicate topic, for which much social control and self-monitoring may be needed, and such control processes may show in the speech phenomena just mentioned, which allows hearers to make provisional inferences from them about the speaker. We may also hypothesize that these inferences may be more negative for hearers who are less prejudiced than the speaker because, in that case, the speech production "errors" can be interpreted as "uncertainty" or "hesitation" about ethnic affairs in general and about the current events told about in particular, rather than as concern for accuracy and adequate formulation. In other words, before actual semantic interpretation, a hearer can already make many personal and social inferences about the possible social status and ethnic opinions of the speaker on the basis of superficial speech characteristics (Scherer & Giles, 1979).

Semantic Interpretation

Central in understanding, however, is the semantic interpretation of the decoded and analyzed forms of speech: Words, phrases, clauses, sentences, and sequences of sentences are assigned semantic representations, that is, concepts and propositional structures. Words and phrases are interpreted strategically by a complex information input, such as syntactic and intonational information, knowledge of the lexicon of the language, meanings of previous words and sentences, the overall topic, as well as social and personal information from the speaker model. Clausal and sentential interpretation in addition requires propositional schemata and an interpretation of coherence relations, such as functional or conditional relationships between them.

At this point the situation model starts to operate: A sentence can be understood only if the hearer can build a semantic representation that corresponds to a possible state of affairs (events, acts, and so forth) in a relevant situation model. That is, ultimately there is no (full) understanding when people cannot "imagine" what a text or talk is about. This does not mean that partial understanding, for instance, of meanings (as represented in the text model), or of reference (a fragmentary model of the situation), is impossible. Complete understanding may even be only an ideal goal of interpretation, at least in the sense of constructing a model exactly as intended by the speaker. Because all understanding is subjective, thus, communication cannot possibly be "complete" in this sense. Also, there is theoretically no boundary to the completeness of the model (much general knowledge and many previous personal experiences may be inserted into the model) and, hence, no limit to the "depth" or "breadth" of processing. However, contextual relevance and time limitations, of course, usually constrain such processing to manageable proportions.

In our example, the hearer already knows that the woman speaks about foreigners as part of the main topic, and also that she is particularly concerned about their favorable treatment. Unlike other stories, however, this story is not preceded by a summary statement expressing its planned topic (although a general topic of unfavorable treatment is expressed earlier in the interview). So, the hearer cannot yet use such a topic to interpret, top-down, the initial clauses of this passage. Yet, instead of the summary statement about the topic, there is a summary statement of a major category of this kind of story, namely, of the Evaluation. Stories about minorities often start with an Evaluation. This suggests that their point is not primarily a macrostructurally represented event or action, but rather a (negative) opinion. In our example, the first sentence denotes an opinion ("I find") with a specific evaluation ("unreasonable"). The hearer may now expect further information about what the woman finds unreasonable, and because similar concepts have been activated before, the hearer may also provisionally infer that the unreasonableness may be connected to what foreigners do, or what Dutch people do for foreigners.

At this point also, stylistic choice, such as lexicalization, becomes important. Note, for instance, that the use of a word such as *unreasonable* and the added temporal quantifier (*sometimes*) mitigate the opinion, which may be interpreted by the hearer (a) literally, as an expression of an opinion about a minor problem, (b) as a weakly negative opinion, (c) as rhetorical understatement of a strong opinion about a big problem, and/or (d) as an indication of strategically monitored self-presentation in the interaction: Opinions about foreigners are mitigated (as the women did before, more explicitly). Due to several factors, thus, this beginning could result in creating a slightly (more) positive impression of the woman. We see that the cognitive processing of impression management is a continuous, strategic process, also in the hearer, who may constantly "adapt" his or her model of the speaker after each discourse unit (e.g., a sentence). This model will then feed back to the interpretation of the rest of the conversational contributions of the speaker. The strategic, that is, hypothetical, result of the semantic interpretation of the first clause, then, is a high-level evaluative proposition dominating the interpretation of the rest of the story. The woman does not simply tell the story to have something interesting to say, or to portray herself as a hero; rather, the story is presented as an example and as further evidence for what she finds unreasonable about the ethnic situation in the neighborhood and the city. The resulting textual representation of this conversational fragment in episodic memory, that is, the text (story) model, thus, has an evaluative proposition as part of its highest-level macroproposition. This theoretically explains findings in social psychology that suggest that people remember situations primarily in evaluative terms (e.g., Forgas, 1979). In our example, indeed, the notion of "unreasonable aspects of the ethnic situation" may have triggered the situation model containing the event-information this story is expressing.

A high-level evaluative (macro)proposition not only controls understanding, but once represented in the text and situation model, also later retrieval by the hearer. Negative attitudes about ethnic groups, thus, will facilitate both this high-level interpretation, as well as later retrieval of this story (e.g., when used for giving illustrations to others about why favoring foreigners is unreasonable). We return to these "uses" of ethnic information in memory in the next main section, and further limit ourselves to the understanding processes per se.

After the first clause, the woman hesitates and breaks off her sentence, starting a new one. This suggests that instead of directly stating her problem (the content of the dominating "I find . . ." clause in a cleft-sentence construction, "what I find . . ., is . . ."), she takes a less direct option, which strategically and narratively, however, may be more effective: She starts a description of her own personal and social situation. The fact that she is a "woman on her own" adds, for the hearer, to the speaker model, for instance, information from which respect, or pity, may be inferred, but that in production may at least be intended as a functional move that explains the reason that the woman needs money from the welfare agency. Less personal, but also a good reason, is the information in line 2 that she had moved. This piece of information is also functional for the rest of the story, because it shows that her "case" is similar to those of Surinamese, who also "moved" (from Surinam to Holland), and who *did* get money to decorate their apartments.

At this point of the understanding process, the hearer has inferred overall macropropositions about the opinion of the speaker and information about the setting of the events to be told, including further information about the speaker. At the same time, the passage obviously is going to be a story, so that the story schema may be activated, and the first sentences interpreted as Setting for that story. We see that local semantic, global semantic, and schematic (superstructural) interpretation takes place at the same time, in parallel with personal and social interpretation of the speaker as a person and as a social member.

Model Formation

These on-line processes of textual understanding result in a hierarchical text model in episodic memory, but also in the activation or the construction of a relevant situation model: The hearer tries to "imagine" what happened at the welfare agency. We assume that the evaluative (macro)proposition is also used to construct the highest nodes of the situation model and thus represents the overall opinion of the woman about the events told in the story. The model further features the information expressed by the text about the woman and her moving to a new apartment, and her need for money. This information may have activated special frames about "women living alone" or "moving" scripts, which explain why exactly the woman needs money (an explanation that is necessary to interpret the conclusion connective "so"). The model, thus, incorporates instantiated information from previous knowledge of the hearer, maybe even fragments of personal situation models (the hearer's own experiences with moving). The same happens with the interpretation of the subsequent sentences of the story: A model is being reconstructed of the woman going to the welfare agency, asking for money, getting none, and of a Surinamese who does get his money after threats with a knife. This model may be the result of a strategic construction from possible other models, such as experiences with the welfare agency or with people threatening with knives. Details of the model conveyed by the woman are, however, unique, and the first question of the interviewer suggests that the model thus constructed is not exactly routine: he (narratively, or rhetorically) "doubts" whether it is true. In other words, conversationally "credibility" is not a priori "given," but continually negotiated by the speech partners. The interviewer at this point shows that for him, insufficient evidence has been given to accept such an "unbelievable" story (of course, he may actually believe the story, but may tactically say he doesn't in order to get more details, which is a well-known interview move).

Note that the local interpretation of the text, for instance, of clauses such as "and asked if they could help me" requires models and scripts. Helping in this case, therefore, is interpreted as "give money," which is a regular component of the "welfare" script. Together with the brief sentence, "But no," this yields the inferred interpretation that the woman did not get money. Here the overall negative evaluation ("unreasonable") begins to make sense, and top-down provides the further interpretation that the woman did not like to get no money. Narratively, we have moved from the Orientation to the Complication of the story (in fact, the first part may be constructed as a ministory, ending with the unsuccessful Resolution that she didn't get money, but obviously this first part is merely an Orientation for the rest of the story).

Before she starts telling about the narratively and evaluatively "interesting" events, however, the woman strategically interpolates a general statement about Surinamese who easily get money from welfare. This prejudiced opinion is used, in the following sentence (line 7) to make her question ("Why do *they* get it?") intelligible. Although, on its own, this general statement only indirectly coheres with the previous sentence, it establishes coherence between the first part of the story and the second part (I did not get money, but they get money, for instance, that Surinamese man). The rhetorical strategy of the woman, both in the welfare office (note the contrastive stress on *they*) and in her retelling of that situation, is to establish a contrast between herself as a group member (*us*) and Surinamese (*them*), which is in line with the overall structure of ethnic prejudice schemata and models. This also implies the persuasively very effective proposition that she is not simply personally frustrated because of the refusal of the agency; rather, she protests against the unfair treatment of (White) Dutch people in general. That is, unwittingly she speaks for the in-group, which is, of course, less self-serving and, hence, more credible than speaking for her own interests. The actual model being expressed by the woman, thus, appears to be an instance of more general models representing favorable treatment of ethnic minority groups. This is why the story is relevant as an argumentative illustration of the general prejudice that foreigners are being favored by the authorities. We may assume, on the basis of evidence derived from retellings of such stories, that the intended prejudiced models may indeed be represented as such by prejudiced recipients, or provide "good reasons" for having negative opinions against foreigners, at least on this point. Indeed, a substantial number of the people we interviewed do not appear to have many grudges against minorities, except for the prejudiced opinion about their "favorable treatment" by the authorities. Such stories, thus, form or confirm highly relevant socioeconomic attitude propositions.

Representing Opinions

The representation of this situation by the hearer, both in a text and in a situation model, is rather straightforward but, for our discussion, a number of specifics need to be attended to. The opinions of the woman may be inserted into the speaker model of the woman, and/or may be added to the model of the situation, for instance, as part of the participant node. For the hearer, however, the situation as told need not be "unreasonable" at all, for instance, because the unique situation of immigrating Surinamese who have no house or furniture at all cannot be compared to that of Dutch people, even when poor, who want to move to another apartment. Or he may know that it is false that Surinamese got such financial help when they immigrated. In that case, the hearer may agree with the welfare officer who is a participant in the story model. The overall evaluation of the situation may thus change from "unreasonable" to "reasonable," or another evaluation on a scale between these two. This is to say that understanding and representing a story, including opinions expressed in them, may have complex consequences on the processing of opinions by the hearer. No doubt the hearer will understand and, hence, represent the negative evaluation of the woman, but the question is whether or not the situation itself is headed by this same evaluation in the hearer's model of the situation. The hearer, in other words, may "remodel" the situation, and apply transformations derived from his or her own models, knowledge, and ethnic attitudes. We return to this complex problem of opinion formation and change below.

Further Interpretation

From our informal analysis of interpretation and representation processes, we may conclude that understanding (prejudiced) discourse involves a set of strategic mental operations applied on structures of text and context, on the one hand, and on those of memory models or schemata of knowledge and beliefs, on the other hand. These operations accept (even incomplete) information from various levels at the same time, and work with effective guesses about the intended meanings, reference, or functions of utterances. Their goal is to construct a model of the situation referred to by these utterances through the construction of a hierarchical representation of the discourse. The degree of understanding, thus, is determined by the criteria we follow for the construction of situation models: If these are fragmentary, then our understanding is also fragmentary. "Deeper" interpretation of a discourse in that case means that our model is more complete, more complex, and features more details.

In the example of the story about what happened in the welfare office, the hearer may activate and apply detailed knowledge and beliefs about the welfare system in the Netherlands, the immigration of Surinamese, and the actions of the authorities, or about the (reasons for the) interactions of young Surinamese males with these authorities. To understand the prejudiced story, then, also may involve understanding why the woman tells this story, why (or whether) Surinamese get money for decorating their houses, or why the man in the story allegedly puts a knife on the table. A large part of this information is not expressed by the story itself, but is presupposed by the speaker or may be "assigned" to it by the hearer. In this sense, intended meanings and interpreted meanings of a discourse will seldom be identical when by *meaning,* we also understand the model derived from the discourse and from personal and social knowledge and beliefs.

Indeed, to "hear" the story as being prejudiced or not largely depends on the role of these social beliefs of the recipient. If a story about the favorable treatment of an ethnic group, the aggressiveness of a Black man, or the "discrimination" of White in-group members is understood as a typical instance of the negative stereotypes dominant group members have about ethnic minority groups, then the hearer's model evaluation may be dominated by a concept like "prejudiced." For other autochthonous recipients, the same story may be heard as a typical example of what they think is a social fact: The authorities do not pay attention to *us*, but only to *them*. In each case, a different model of the situation will be the result, and it is this model that will be used for further processing, for instance, for retelling the story to others, or for the (trans)formation of ethnic opinions and attitudes.

These representations are in principle hierarchical structures of propositions as they are constructed after the passage. During storytelling itself, only fragments of these models are being constructed, on-line, which allows revision in a later stage of understanding. In other words, the linear structures of the textual and interactional input are transformed to a more abstract, hierarchical structure in memory. It is this form of the text and situation models that will later allow effective search and relevant activations. The highest nodes in the models, for instance, may be used to summarize the story. For hearers that assign particular, prejudice-monitored, attention to the reported aggressiveness of the Surinamese man, this proposition may be represented as the highest-level macroproposition and, therefore, be more easily retrievable for later recall and storytelling, for instance, as "evidence" for the assumed aggressiveness of Black men.

Understanding Discourse Strategies

We have repeatedly found that talk about delicate topics such as ethnic groups is highly strategic. Positive self-presentation, negative other-presentation, and other forms of impression formation and persuasion are the interactive dimension of such conversations. Whereas the "contents" of the story typically result in text and situation models, we may finally ask whether and how such strategies are cognitively represented.

In the analysis of the first sentences of the story, we have already concluded that sentences such as "I am a woman on my own" not only denote the social status of the storyteller, which we assumed to be inserted into the speaker model of the hearer. Rather, volunteering this information is strategic in the sense that it contributes to the "point" the woman wants to make, namely, that she is in a similar situation as the Surinamese, and that despite this similarity, she is treated in a different way. The same holds for the contrast between her deferential behavior (begging) and the aggressive behavior of the Surinamese man.

We assume that these strategies have several cognitive functions in understanding. First, such strategies are intended for the construction of a positive speaker model: The woman wants the hearer to believe that she is rather tolerant (while using the mitigating expression "unreasonable sometimes"), deserves help ("woman on my own"), that she is polite and nonaggressive ("begging for my children's allowance"), justified in her claim (they get so much money), and correct in her evaluation of the Surinamese (the man was said to behave the same last time), and truthful ("I don't tell fantasy stories"). Such strategic moves, then, may contribute to a more positive impression and, hence, to enhanced credibility and especially to enhanced empathy with her problem and her opinions. And the converse is true for the strategic construction of the participant minority model in the situation model: Surinamese profit from welfare (more than we do), are aggressive, have money while being on welfare, and, hence, must be cheating (driving around in big cars and have jewels).

These constrastive "images" of the participants in the situation model, and the positive representation of the woman in the speaker model, not only make the story and the storyteller more credible and, hence, more persuasive, they also contribute to the further organization of the story and model structures themselves. Together with stylistic and rhetorical features, these strategic moves contribute to enhanced organization of the model and, hence, to better storage and retrieval. In intuitive terms, indeed, this makes the story more "dramatic" than if the woman had simply said "I went to the welfare agency to ask for money, but I didn't get it, while an aggressive Surinamese got it right away." Her actual story sketches a more complete situation model, but at the same time focuses on those elements of the model that can be fit into well-structured schemata, such as the competitive contrast between *us* and *them,* and the aggressiveness of foreigners as opposed to our "reasonableness" or own needs. Concrete reference to a knife being put on the table can be more easily interpreted in terms of a concrete memory image (we may assume that situation models are not only propositional but also may feature more analogical types of information, such as imagelike structures). The same is true for her replaying relevant fragments of the conversations at the welfare office. At the same time, the thematic schema is not only more memorable for the hearer because of its internal organization, but also because of its "exemplary" nature as an instance of a generally shared prejudiced opinion about the favorable treatment of ethnic groups. In other words, the strategic moves of the woman contribute to a better-structured and more positive speaker model, as well as to a more complete and better-organized model of the situation. Empathy, sympathy, model structure, and typical (attitude confirming) contents of the model together may contribute to more effective persuasion.

And finally, the moves analyzed above, while contributing to enhanced empathy with the predicament of the woman may also tie in with affective reactions of the hearer. We have no theoretical model of exactly how this is done. Yet, we assume that situation models contain opinions of hearers (and represented opinions of speakers), as well as representations of affective reactions: If the hearer also becomes angry about the treatment of the woman, this is likely to be stored as part of the model about the situation told about. Recent work has shown that episodic models linked with affect are easier to retrieve by subjects in the same mood (Bower, 1980). Actual empathy, thus, may lead to enhanced retrievability and, hence, possible effectiveness. Also, affect might be a factor enhancing involvement (which also presupposes more and more elaborate models and attitudes) with the issue of the speaker. Heightened involvement may contribute to enhanced attention, focus, deeper processing, and better organization of what the speaker says, which again may influence better retrievability and hence more effectiveness (Chaiken, 1980; Petty & Cacioppo, 1979). Alternatively, affect may, of course, take a mental shortcut, and directly associate positive feelings with what the woman says. This would define what may be called *emotional acceptance,* that is, acceptance (or "yielding") even without her strategic moves and arguments that contribute to a better cognitive organization (Zajonc, 1980).

We conclude from this tentative discussion that discursive and interactive strategies have an important function in the understanding and representation of prejudiced conversation. They may contribute to a more positive speaker model, enhanced opposition (competition, conflict) between in-group and out-group in situation models and attitude schemata, more and better structure in the story model and the situation model, and finally to links with affective memory structures that allow empathy with the speaker and better reproduction of the story on later occasions. Overall, these assumptions can be subsumed under the goal of enhanced effectiveness, and, hence, as contributions to the process of persuasion: Chances are greater that the hearer represents the storyteller and her situation model more in the way she intends than in any alternative way. And whereas some of the persuasive strategies have a general nature, others appear more specific for the kind of moves that operate in discourse about delicate topics or in prejudiced talk. Thus, it is essential in such conversations that (a) the story is an instantiation of prejudiced opinions and attitudes, (b) the episodic model clearly organizes around a positive *us* (e.g., as victims) and a negative *them,* (c) the speaker establishes a positive model of self, especially as an in-group member, and (d) that the hearer is constrained to make similar evaluations of the events described. We have seen that the persuasive strategies of the speaker are all geared to these dimensions of "acceptable opinion management," and how these contribute to the organization of prejudiced talk in memory of recipients.

4. Prejudiced opinion and attitude (trans)formation

The last phase in the complex process of persuasive communication can be described in terms of the interaction between text and situation models, on one hand, and previous models and attitudes, on the other hand. In our discussion in Chapter 4 on the structures of opinions and attitudes in memory, we found that what is usually termed *attitude change* is really a very complex process. What are mostly experimentally investigated are isolated changes of opinion. How opinions, or social opinion-complexes such as attitudes or prejudices, are exactly changed is seldom represented in theoretically explicit terms. In this last main section of this chapter, we turn to this problem, although without the ambition of fully accounting for all details and intricacies. Aside from a theoretical analysis, we again use natural data from interviews as part of our empirical evidence about the nature of opinion (trans) formation.

4.1. OPINION CHANGE

Opinions have been analyzed as evaluative beliefs, whereas evaluations were assumed to be based on systems of culturally shared norms and values. If it is a value of our society that "all people are equal under the law," then any situation in which people are not treated equally in the same circumstances may be evaluated negatively, if there is a value-based norm that says that "people should be treated equally under the same circumstances." This is precisely what the storyteller in our example in section 3.2. does, finding her unequal treatment by the authorities "unreasonable." Theoretically, propositions that account for such evaluative beliefs may simply be integrated into the models people have about situations. In our example, the probable macroproposition dominating the woman's model of the situation at the welfare agency would be something like "Welfare did not give me money, but it did give money to an aggressive Surinamese." For the woman, this is further interpreted as an instance of unequal and, hence, unfair treatment, so that in addition to this macroproposition, we find the high-level belief proposition "It is unfair ('unreasonable') that p", in which p is the macroproposition representing what actually happened. The prominence of this opinion proposition in the model may (also) be inferred from the initial position of this clause in the story. It is probably this opinion proposition that was used as an important retrieval cue to find the model representing her experiences at the welfare agency (together with negative propositions about ethnic minority groups, which were already topical earlier in the conversation).

At a lower level of the model, the woman in our example may, of course, have further opinions, for instance, about the aggressiveness of the Surinamese man, about the refusal of the authorities to help her, or about the flashy life-style of Surinamese in general. In these cases, the opinions derive from values such as those of politeness, deference, and modesty, sustaining norms such as "help should be asked for in a polite way" (which makes "aggressive" requests negative), and "if people are poor, they should not show off with rich things" (which makes driving big cars and having jewels negative). The woman has represented and strategically tells these experiences and opinions in such a way that they receive extra focus. Her poverty and lack of money is contrasted with the rich life-style of the Surinamese, the refusal of the authorities to help her contrasted with the high amount (thousands) the Surinamese are believed to get, and her deference contrasted with the aggressive behavior of the Black man. In other words, the story is not primarily about an interesting event, but rather about norms and values being respected by the woman and violated by the ethnic group member and the authorities. The overall opinion implication that can be derived from the story, therefore, is that the woman disapproves of the current ethnic situation in the Netherlands, and especially of (Black) minority groups. These are the (implied) opinion propositions persuasively communicated to the hearer.

We have assumed that the hearer may store such opinions in his or her model of the situation described, as well as in the model of the speaker. Yet, the hearer need not "adopt" or "accept" these opinions of the storyteller. The question of this section, then, is what exactly happens, cognitively, in this manipulation of ethnic opinions by recipients?

Opinion Formation and Confirmation

As a first step in the solution of this problem, we may assume that, in principle, the hearer goes about opinion (trans)formation much in the same way the speaker does. States of affairs, events, and actions, as represented in situation models, are subjected to strategic evaluation procedures based on activated norms and values. These norms and values have a rather general, socioculturally based, nature and are, therefore, stored in semantic (social) memory. In principle, they may be assumed by the speaker to be shared by the hearer. This is one of the reasons that speakers in prejudiced talk often explicitly formulate the relevant norms and values, and do so in typical appeal moves to the hearer:

(17) (MA6). (Rice in a Surinamese shop had become rotten because of a flooded basement. The shop owner threw it in the garden, where rats could get to it.) That isn't, those aren't normal things, are they? You can't do that like that. You can put it with the trash can, so that it will be picked up.

(18) (PD5). (We work hard, and they have never worked like that.) They are married, then divorced, but still live together and they are in business and both are on welfare. What do you think of that?

(19) (RA2). (They have a lot of children.) Well, *you* pay for that. *I* pay for that.

(20) (RA2). (Home slaughtering story.) You are not allowed to slaughter sheep at home. You know that, don't you?

Then, the hearer must analyze the situation and determine whether the events or acts are instances of general norm or value statements. An event such as "X got money, but Y did not get money" may be categorized as an instance of differential treatment, which may be found to conflict with the norm of equal treatment. All other things being equal, the hearer should then draw the evaluative conclusion that the event is conflicting with the accepted norms and, therefore, may be evaluated negatively. In our example, this is precisely the cognitive reaction the woman tries to provoke. And in general such stories may, therefore, lead to the intended opinion formation by the hearer. The result in that case is a situation model that is similar to the one expressed by the woman, dominated by the proposition "It is unfair that . . .." In other words, much in the same way as the events themselves are being "checked" against frames and scripts of prototypical episodes (which make the events at the welfare agency intelligible), also the opinions associated with these events are being checked against prevailing norms and values. In the first case, the result of the check may be that the events are judged to be possible, probable, or just true if they do not conflict with information stored in other models of the hearer, or when they are similar to those in other models (the hearer has had the same or similar experiences). For the evaluation procedure of the opinions, a similar process takes place: Are the events or acts instances of (general) events or acts that are normatively prohibited or do they conform to the values shared in society (or in the group)? If so, the result may be that the opinion expressed is found to be "justified," when additionally it does not conflict with one's own opinions stored in previous models, or when they are similar to similar opinions in similar models. In this case, we say that the relevant (particular) opinion is formed or confirmed, respectively.

At another level, the hearer may already have a more general opinion about the unfair treatment of Dutch people in comparison to foreigners, represented, for instance, in general episodic models about situations of favorable treatment of foreigners. In that case, the story and its evaluation by the woman can simply be heard as a further "instance" of this general opinion of the hearer and, hence, as further support for this opinion. The recipient may even use the woman's story as evidence in talk with other people ("My neighbor told me . . ."), as is often the case in our interviews (see below for examples). The same is true for the more abstract opinions activated from prejudice schemata. The opinion of the hearer about this specific case is a confirming instance of the prototypical opinion.

Conversely, if the hearer has a negative attitude toward ethnic minority groups, but does not yet have a general opinion about unfair favorable treatment of such groups, the opinion conveyed by the story may be (over)generalized toward a corresponding more general opinion, which would be coherent with other negative opinions in the schema about ethnic groups. This process is probably facilitated by opinions conveyed by the story that *do* support the hearer's prejudices. If the hearer thinks Surinamese are aggressive, drive big cars, and wear flashy clothes and jewels, then the story would confirm those opinions and, hence, become more credible and the opinions in it more acceptable. Theoretically, we may, therefore, assume that opinion formation or confirmation is seldom based on single opinions, but often takes place within organized clusters, in which already shared opinions are conveyed to form or support new ones.

Rejection

Whereas the processes described above account for the "standard" case of ethnic persuasion, hearers may, of course, also "disagree" with the speaker and "reject" the proposed opinion conclusions. The very story on which they are based may be found hard to believe. In our example, we find some evidence for this interaction process. The interviewer (a male researcher) throughout the interview has not, as with most other interviews, acted in a "passive" way, but has actively "argued" with the interviewees about their experiences and opinions. Although in some cases, such a reaction may lead to socially desirable statements, more often than not they stimulate the interviewee to substantiate his or her experiences or opinions further.

The expression of real or strategic disbelief by the interviewer in our welfare example does just that. The woman emphatically responds with truth claims ("Yes, really, yes, yes, yes, yes"), and explicitly finishes her further details about the situation with the claim that she is not telling fantasy stories.

We previously discussed that strategies that are aimed at enhancing credibility operate on (a) the construction of speaker models (positive impression formation as an honest, truthful, accurate, and tolerant citizen), and (b) the construction of "probable" situation models. In the latter case, telling about things that are exceptional is narratively very functional but poses the problem that the hearer may not believe you. Hence, the speaker in that case must supply supporting evidence for the truthfulness of the events as told (e.g., independent sources, details that are unlikely to be invented, and so on). This also happens in our welfare story: The very concrete information about what the woman did, what was said, and the fact that the agency officers "recognized" the Black man as a troublemaker, are all "evidence" for the truthfulness of the model. If the hearer finds no models that are inconsistent with the model, and when the model is in principle "possible" (an instance of general frames and scripts), then the hearer will tend to accept the model as true.

Yet, what about the opinions conveyed? Assuming that the hearer shares the same general values and norms, how can he or she *not* accept the same doxastic (opinion) inference the woman makes? Let us consider a few possibilities:

(a) Even when people do not endorse ethnic stereotypes, they usually know them (Sprangers, 1983). The hearer in that case may interpret the story as an example of "all those negative stories about foreigners" and reject it without further consideration, especially when the speaker model is also negative ("prejudiced woman"). In that case, the strategic moves and the contents of the story may be processed less thoroughly, or simply stored with a negative label together with similar context models in episodic memory.

(b) The story as such may be accepted as true, but the specific doxastic conclusion may be found unwarranted, for instance, because a number of premises fail: Unequal treatment in general may be valued negatively, but in special circumstances, "positive" differential treatment of socially disadvantaged or oppressed groups may be an instance of a positive value (namely "helping others"). In that case, the evaluation of the woman may not be shared by the hearer, and the model stored without a specific negative opinion dominating it (it may be stored as an instance of people's lack of understanding of the necessity of positive action, though). Theoretically, this suggests that models are accepted as supporting instances of general opinions only if they illustrate the most *specific* opinions possible and not only higher-level, abstract opinions. In this case, "all people should be treated equally" may be found an "irrelevant" norm as a basis for the opinion; instead, more specific and, hence, more contextually adequate norms such as "people who need it must get extra attention and help." Note that the woman in our example implicitly knows this opinion strategy and, therefore, emphasizes the similarity of her case: She is also poor, has also moved, and also needs money to decorate her house (and not to buy a car). It follows that norm application in opinion formation depends on the "definition of the situation," that is, on the high-level structures of the model conveyed. For the woman, her situation and that of the Surinamese are similar, but her treatment by the welfare authorities is dissimilar, and, hence, the evaluation turns out negative because of the relevant norms. If, however, the similarity of a woman wanting to move and the immigration of people from a former colony is not represented as similar, the norm would not apply, and a negative opinion need not follow. We see that model structures determine opinion formation.

(c) The hearer may neither endorse nor reject general opinions based on norms of positive social action and, therefore, may have no opinion on the (assumed) financial help given to immigrating Surinamese. In that case, the higher-level opinion on equal treatment may take precedence and will facilitate opinion formation that is close to that of the woman: It is unfair that she did not get welfare money. Yet, the opinion may remain particular, and attached to this case (model) or similar cases (models) only. Such an interpretation would be facilitated if the hearer has friends who have similar experiences. According to the principles of balance theory (Granberg, 1984; Heider, 1958; Insko, 1981), negative treatment of a friend is usually evaluated negatively, whatever the higher-level norms one might endorse. The recipient may well accept, for instance, that immigrant children get differential treatment in school by getting extra lessons in both their own and in the second language. Our interviews feature many examples of this kind of differences in opinions about positive action. The negative opinion in this case remains attached to the episodic models and need not be generalized and attached to the general ethnic group attitude. Assumed favorable treatment may be resented only for social domains in which resources are assumed to be scarce. We do not find examples in our interviews, for example, in which foreigners are said to "eat all our food," which would be a more likely prejudice in situations in which food is scarce.

Of course, several other possibilities exist. The principles of ethnic prejudice formation, confirmation, transformation, or rejection should, however, be more or less clear by now. The process is a strategic evaluation of events and opinions with respect to existing models (one's own experiences, previous stories), the speaker model (or generalized models of similar speakers), frames, scripts, and general prejudiced attitudes. Acceptance will be the general tendency if no particular or general opinions in other models and schemata conflict with the opinion and will be facilitated if the opinion is an instance of one's own general opinions. Rejection is more likely if there is such a conflict. And no opinion formation or only particular opinions will result from limited application of general norms or previous models.

Acceptance Bias

The acceptance of prejudiced opinions is obviously the easiest strategy if recipients share the prejudiced attitude: Both the "evidence" and the opinion based on it in that case simply confirm what the recipient thought anyway. Rejection of the opinion may be easy only when no attention is paid to the "evidence," or when the speaker is simply disqualified as being prejudiced. If not, a rather complex process of analysis must take place to subsume the events under a different category, and to arrive at a more positive or neutral evaluation of the events (e.g., as illustration of affirmative action). In that case, the story as told may be accepted as true, but the opinions derived from them as unfounded by these other, more specific, norms and values. Each strategic support in the story for the negative opinion may in that case require separate "reanalysis" in terms of a different opinion. That is, counterargumentation plays a role in that case (see Petty, Ostrom & Brock, 1981, for discussion of such "cognitive responses"). However, when ethnic affairs are concerned, such countermoves may lack sufficient general knowledge, lack specific models, and the automatism of alternative rules of inference. Because many more negative stories about ethnic minority members are told, the recipient will have few instances of "positive" models that might support counteropinions. He or she will have to set up a nonprototypical argument, for which there may be little practice and few examples. In other words, reasoned rejection of fact-based prejudices is cognitively and socially rather difficult and, therefore, rather exceptional. Several people in our interviews report that they do not counterargue with prejudiced people (it is hopeless, I don't know what to say, I feel ashamed, and so forth). In our example, this would be easy only when the normative principles of affirmative action would be generally supported by the authorities, the media, and many citizens, which is not the case. The woman would in that case have no socially shared and legitimated "point" by comparing her case with that of immigrants. Generally, and especially in communication about ethnic minorities, there is a bias toward agreement, simply by the power of the consensus (Essed, 1986) and despite the official (high-level) norm of nondiscrimination. At least people seldom explicitly disagree. This means that prejudiced talk is prevailing even *if* most people would disagree. And it is this prevalence that provides the weight of the ethnic consensus.

Attitude (Trans)formation

Analyzing a concrete example, we have arrived at a number of hypotheses about the processes of opinion manipulation resulting from talk about ethnic groups. It was found that opinions may be limited to a specific model ("the woman was treated unfairly"), or may be generalized to similar models ("Dutch people are treated unequally by the welfare agencies"). We also assumed that general prejudices may in such cases be supported by the opinions and "evidence" supplied by the source. This process of self-confirming, or self-fulfilling, ethnic stereotypes is well-known from the literature, and we have only specified some of its further cognitive properties (Rothbart, Evans, & Fulero, 1979; Snyder, 1981a, 1981b; Snyder, Tanke, & Berscheid, 1977; Word, Zanna, & Cooper, 1974).

When persuasion is defined in terms of more general, and more permanent, changes of attitude schemata, more processing is, of course, needed. It does happen that a single "persuasive" case may be associated with an opinion that may be generalized right away and stored in the attitude schema (Crocker, Fiske, & Taylor, 1984; Rothbart, 1981). In our example, this might be the case for the opinion "Foreigners are treated more favorably by the (welfare) authorities," if this opinion would fit into a schema in which rights are more generally denied to foreigners. In this sense, indeed, prejudice formation is "easy," because it allows the formation of complex schemata on the basis of no or very little experience. It is also "easy" because such opinions and schemata are consensual, despite the general norm of nondiscrimination. That this norm in our interviews is still recognized may be inferred from the many examples in which people say that *they* are being discriminated against. So the norm still holds, but its application in the analysis of the social situation is different. If a single or a few foreigners are witnessed benefiting from social resources such as housing, work, or welfare, and when it is also assumed, more generally, that many Dutch people do not have access to these resources, the conclusion that foreigners are being favored is again "easy."

Apart from providing further support or coherence for general prejudices, such opinion conclusions are also functional: The actions based on them will protect the interests of the in-group. Because in-groups generally try to protect their interests, communication about the actions and strategies that lead to such shared goals is necessary. Consensually confirmed prejudices, thus, also provide the conceptual basis that allows such social interpretations and plans, and these also appear in persuasive talk that allows their reproduction in the in-group.

Ethnic attitude formation based on talk, thus, may in many respects be cognitively and socially easier than attitude formation about other groups or other social targets. In our analysis of the structures of ethnic prejudice, we found that probably such ethnic attitudes are generated from out-group protoschemata, which in an abstract way are already formed on the basis of information acquired during socialization. For new ethnic groups, the relevant (negative) properties only have to be filled into the schema. Each story, especially when repeated and legitimated by publication in the media then may be used as "proof" of the general opinion it implies or expresses. Everyday talk and the media provide ample examples that may be used to form, confirm, or generalize negative ethnic opinions. Positive information, counterarguments, and basic principles of adequate interaction in multiethnic societies, are virtually absent in socialization, communication, and other instances of social information processing. This also explains why challenging ethnic prejudices is much more difficult than accepting them.

This means that if recipients are already prejudiced it will not be easy to change such prejudices. Counterexamples can simply be rejected as "exceptions," that is, as special models that have special circumstances and that, therefore, cannot be generalized (Weber & Crocker, 1983). In other words, overgeneralization of ethnic opinions does *not* hold when positive (or neutral) opinions are being expressed in talk. Second, even if one opinion would be changed both in particular and general models, for instance, on the basis of evidence, arguments, or general principles (norms, laws), this change need not affect the attitude structure. Overall negative prejudice schemata do admit "positive," although often marginal or less relevant, components ("Blacks are musical," "Women are sensitive"), as long as the higher-level propositions are not affected. And even such "positive" attributions may have negative implications: A good feeling for rhythm may be considered as a property that is "close to nature," as opposed to the more "civilized" sense of music of Whites (whereas sensitivity of women may be associated with weakness). To change higher-level macropropositions in ethnic prejudice would require a systematic program that would address the (negative) evaluations in many opinions, which in addition are supported by similar opinions in an overall out-group protoschema. In other words, changes of high-level opinions might require reorganization of vast amounts of social information, schemata, basic principles, and so on. Whereas neg-

ativity spreading is a standard strategy in prejudice formation (one negative opinion is applied also to other categories of the attitude), the same
is not true for positive information transfer. In other words, ethnic attitude change may require complete ideological reorientation, in which
different protoschemata are designed, different norms and values being
developed or put in different relevance position, or information systematically gathered to support the new opinions (Rothbart, Dawes, & Park,
1984). And most basically—the discriminatory actions based on ethnic
prejudice should no longer be tolerated. Prejudiced cognitive programming in that case loses much of its relevance, and ideological reorientation then becomes possible. We discuss these social contexts of the
reproduction (and opposition) of racism in the next chapter.

4.2.   SOME QUANTITATIVE DATA
ON ETHNIC INFORMATION USES

After the theoretical and qualitative
analyses of the previous section, this section gives a few descriptive
quantitative data about the ways recipients process information from
sources. Continuing the analysis of the data reported in Chapter 3, we
have analyzed all passages in which people refer to personal or media
sources, with particular attention to their account of the facts and opinions attributed to those sources, as well as their own reactions, opinions,
and agreement with the facts or opinions of these sources.

We realize that such data provide only a glimpse of what really happened, cognitively, in the recipients during the (persuasive) communications. Yet, we assume that the "version" of the communicative event
as told to the interviewer is probably an expression of what the recipient
recalled and found relevant to retell, and that is precisely what we want
to know. From those accounts, we can tentatively infer some properties
of the structural representations of communicated facts and opinions in
the recipient's memory. Also, such accounts suggest how people tell
such "subjective" (but socially shared) versions to in-group members,
which allows us to obtain insight into the basic processes of the reproduction of racism.

There may, of course, be differences in what is recalled and reproduced by the interviewees, for instance, according to whether the source
was a personal communication or media messages, and according to
gender, neighborhood, and age, which we have added as independent
variables.

Which Facts?

The first relevant question is what type of facts, negative or positive (relative to ethnic groups or relations), are typically being mentioned by the interviewees, and whether or not such facts are believed or not. In Table 5.1, we first find that, in general, the vast majority of the facts reported as being borrowed from other sources is negative (103), whereas only a few facts are positive (18), the others being neutral (or no specific facts mentioned).

In absolute terms, more negative facts are attributed to personal communication than to the media (especially because personal communication is mentioned more often as a source), but in relative terms, the media are also somewhat lower as a source for negative facts. There is no difference between men and women mentioning such negative facts (although women make more references to other sources), but women mention positive facts slightly more often. People in low-contact areas mention negative facts slightly less often (when we take into account the proportion of their source references) and positive facts somewhat more often. Senior citizens proportionally mention positive facts more often than young people. With the exception of people in low-contact areas and young people, the average prejudice score for people mentioning positive facts about ethnic groups is higher than that of people mentioning negative facts. This interesting phenomenon suggests that both negative and positive facts are often mentioned critically by people, as we shall see below. The major conclusion that may be drawn from these data is that information about ethnic groups attributed to other sources is mostly negative. This may mean that most communications are indeed about negative facts, or that people recall negative facts better. Both hypotheses are probably true.

Type of Reactions

From the analysis of the facts reported it already emerges that despite the large amount of negative facts recalled and reported by the interviewees, they need not always believe or accept these facts. People show this by implicit or explicit comments. If we look at the figures of Table 5.2, we first observe the obvious prejudice pattern: People reacting to (negative or positive) facts in a way that is negative for ethnic groups are on the whole more prejudiced (4.2) than those who react positively (2.6).

There are twice as many people who give negative reactions than positive ones. A large part of these reactions are based on personal sources, whereas positive reactions are more often based on media information

TABLE 5.1:   Type of Communicated Facts Mentioned
(average prejudice score between parentheses)

	Negative	Positive
All passages (N = 198)	103 (3.4)	14 (3.8)
Media sources (N = 78)	34 (3.0)	8 (3.4)
Personal sources (N = 136)	76 (3.6)	7 (4.0)
Women (N = 122)	64 (3.6)	10 (3.7)
Men (N = 73)	39 (3.2)	4 (4.0)
Low-contact neighborhood (N = 121)	66 (3.1)	7 (2.9)
High-contact neighborhood (N = 77)	37 (4.1)	7 (4.7)
Age ≥ 50 (N = 103)	50 (4.2)	12 (4.1)
Age < 30 (N = 31)	20 (2.6)	1 (2.0)

TABLE 5.2:   Type of Reactions to Communications

	Negative	Positive
All passages (N = 198)	56 (4.2)	28 (2.6)
Media sources (N = 78)	16 (3.6)	18 (2.6)
Personal sources (N = 136)	42 (4.4)	13 (2.4)
Women (N = 122)	37 (4.3)	15 (2.9)
Men (N = 73)	19 (4.0)	13 (2.2)
Low-contact neighborhood (N = 121)	31 (3.5)	21 (2.2)
High-contact neighborhood (N = 77)	25 (5.0)	7 (3.5)
Age ≥ 50 (N = 103)	34 (4.6)	12 (3.5)
Age < 30 (N = 31)	8 (3.2)	6 (2.0)

(indeed, people who refer to the media are less prejudiced and tend to live in low-contact areas). Women react somewhat more negatively, and comparatively less positively to such sources (although, as we saw, they do mention positive facts more often than men). The same pattern holds for the elderly as compared to people under 30. These data suggest that not only are negative facts mentioned most, but people's reactions also tend to adopt the negative facts as reliable and acceptable information by their sources, especially in personal communications in high-contact areas.

Fact-Reaction Links

Of course, facts and reactions should not be considered only on their own. People may display negative reactions that parallel negative facts reported (suggesting belief, acceptance), but may also react with positive remarks about ethnic groups or group relations after such a negative fact attributed to a source, and the same holds for positive or negative reactions to positive facts. In Table 5.3, we have tabulated the scores for these four combinations.

The first striking feature of these data is that there are very few positive facts reported, and even less reacted to negatively. People focus on negative facts, whether they accept or reject them. This suggests that most people who react critically (and who are low in prejudice) do so against the negative things other Dutch people say. Generally, references to personal or media sources seem to trigger negative situation models. Indeed, positive situation models, when told, are usually based on peoples' own experiences and sometimes attributed to TV. Opposed reactions to negative facts reported by the media are mostly based on negative press portrayal of minorities (in crime news, or in reports about racist people). Negative reactions that support negative facts primarily derive their information from personal communications, especially in the high-contact areas. Positive reactions to negative facts are comparatively frequent in low-contact areas, and usually occur in passages with critical comments about what other people say (generally) about ethnic minority groups. The elderly especially tend to accept negative facts, but also more often than young people accept positive facts. A similar pattern divides men and women. If women in our examples seem to be more conforming, this leads to acceptance of the dominant negative information about ethnic groups, at least in these passages about communicative events (the average prejudice scores for men and women are the same, which suggests that more prejudiced women tend to refer to other sources more often for support of their negative attitudes). Young people tend to be more critical of negative information about minority groups.

Reported Source Opinions

Sources not only provide information about (real or fictitious) facts concerning ethnic minority groups, for instance, in stories, but also give opinions. If we inspect Table 5.4, we find similar tendencies as those reported above for facts, such as higher average prejudice for people mentioning positive opinions of sources.

Negative opinions are recalled or mentioned most often, again mostly

TABLE 5.3:   Type of Communicated Opinions Mentioned

	Negative	Positive
All passages (N = 198)	79 (3.5)	21 (3.7)
Media sources (N = 78)	31 (3.3)	15 (4.0)
Personal sources (N = 136)	59 (3.5)	8 (3.1)
Women (N = 122)	46 (3.7)	15 (3.5)
Men (N = 73)	33 (3.3)	6 (4.2)
Low-contact neighborhood (N = 121)	46 (3.0)	13 (3.2)
High-contact neighborhood (N = 77)	33 (4.2)	8 (4.6)
Age ≥ 50 (N = 103)	39 (4.2)	12 (4.3)
Age < 30 (N = 31)	10 (2.2)	3 (2.3)

based on personal communications (which are seldom used for positive opinions). Men refer to negative opinions comparatively more often (and less to positive opinions). The distribution of negative opinions among men and women, and among high- and low-contact areas is more or less identical. Overall, we may conclude the same as for references to (recall of?) facts: Negative source opinions are mentioned much more often than positive source opinions.

Personal Opinion

To know what the personal opinions are of people who mention these predominantly negative facts and opinions, we not only must look at their immediate reactions to particular stories, but also more generally to their opinions about ethnic minority groups. To be able to compare with the similar rough distinction between positive and negative facts (opinions, reactions), we also categorized these opinions as either positive or negative in such cases. Now, we see more clearly why the proportion of negative reactions (which is still high) is lower than the amount of negative facts mentioned: People with positive opinions about ethnic groups will tend to mention negative facts in a critical way. This usually means that they are critical of Dutch people who are negative about foreigners. Yet, again, the (highly) negative opinions dominate in the references to other sources, as we can see in Table 5.5.

The data also suggest that the same number of people with negative as with positive opinions mention the media as a source, but personal com-

TABLE 5.4:   Opinions in Communication Settings

	Negative	Positive
All passages (N = 198)	50 (4.9)	37 (2.1)
Media sources (N = 78)	20 (5.0)	20 (2.0)
Personal sources (N = 136)	31 (4.9)	23 (2.2)
Women (N = 122)	31 (5.1)	22 (2.3)
Men (N = 73)	19 (4.7)	15 (1.9)
Low-contact neighborhood (N = 121)	22 (4.5)	29 (2.0)
High-contact neighborhood (N = 77)	28 (5.3)	8 (2.4)
Age ≥ 50 (N = 103)	34 (5.0)	11 (2.6)
Age < 30 (N = 31)	1 (3.0)	10 (2.0)

munication remains more frequent as a source for people with negative opinions. Men and women do not differ much on this variable, although, relatively, there are somewhat more men with positive personal opinions about ethnic groups. In the low-contact areas, positive opinions dominate among those who refer to other sources, whereas obviously the inverse is true for the high-contact areas. Dramatic is the difference between the old and the young: There are virtually no young people with negative personal opinions who refer to other sources, whereas relatively many have positive opinions. As may be expected, people with positive opinions have an average prejudice score far below the mean of 3.5, namely, 2.1, and those with negative opinions far above the mean, namely, 4.9. This confirms the correspondence of our rough evaluation of these passages about communicative events with the prejudice scores based on entire interviews. We conclude that, despite the fair proportion of people with positive opinions, the negative opinions are still dominating.

Agreement

To test specifically the amount of (dis)agreement between people and their sources, we have measured the correspondence between personal opinions and opinions as reported about sources (see Table 5.6).

We see that the same number of people agree and disagree with their source opinions. Because most people have negative personal opinions, this implies that people with negative opinions agree more often with others with negative opinions, and people with positive opinions more

TABLE 5.5:   (Dis)agreement with Source Opinions

	Agrees	Disagrees
All passages (N = 198)	43 (4.5)	44 (2.9)
Media sources (N = 78)	18 (4.2)	24 (3.2)
Personal sources (N = 136)	28 (4.6)	26 (2.5)
Women (N = 122)	30 (4.4)	23 (3.2)
Men (N = 73)	13 (4.8)	21 (2.5)
Low-contact neighborhood (N = 121)	21 (4.0)	29 (2.4)
High-contact neighborhood (N = 77)	22 (5.0)	15 (3.7)
Age ≥ 50 (N = 103)	28 (4.7)	19 (3.7)
Age < 30 (N = 31)	2 (2.0)	8 (2.1)

TABLE 5.6:   Fact-Reaction Relationships

	+Fact/+React	−Fact/−React	+Fact/−React	−Fact/+React
All passages (N = 198)	10 (3.4)	52 (4.2)	2 (5.5)	18 (2.1)
Media (N = 78)	6 (3.3)	13 (3.8)	1 (5.5)	12 (2.2)
Personal (N = 136)	4 (3.5)	41 (4.3)	1 (6.0)	9 (1.9)
Women (N = 122)	7 (3.3)	35 (4.3)	1 (6.0)	8 (2.5)
Men (N = 73)	3 (3.7)	17 (4.1)	1 (5.0)	10 (1.8)
Low contact (N = 121)	5 (2.4)	29 (3.7)	0 (0.0)	16 (2.1)
High-contact (N = 77)	5 (4.4)	23 (5.0)	2 (5.5)	2 (2.0)
Age ≥ 50 (N = 103)	8 (3.8)	30 (4.8)	2 (5.5)	4 (3.0)
Age < 30 (N = 31)	1 (2.0)	8 (3.2)	0 (0.0)	5 (2.0)

often disagree with their sources, as is also apparent in the prejudice scores of those who agree and those who disagree. People tend to agree more often with personal sources than with the media. Women show more agreement with the opinions of their sources, as is also the case for the elderly. Disagreeing men and young people also score lower on the prejudice scale than disagreeing women and young people (which suggests that their disagreement tends to focus more often on positive opinions about ethnic groups as shown by their sources). Most marked is the tendency that generally those who agree have higher prejudice scores than those who disagree.

    Given the pattern analyzed above, this means that agreement is agreement with a negative consensus, in which negative facts and opinions are recalled or mentioned most often as information drawn from communication. Apparently, disagreement with negative ethnic opinions requires a more critical attitude, which is also coherent with a less prejudiced attitude. Or in other words, there is a connection between negative ethnic attitudes and agreement with dominant social information. Of course, this is exactly what the dimension of conformism to an ethnic consensus suggests.

Conclusions

From these aggregate data about the relations between recipients and their sources, we may first repeat the conclusion that whatever the reactions and the personal opinions of people, they mention negative information about ethnic groups much more often than positive information. We have suggested that there are several explanations for this fact: (a) there are more negative communications about ethnic groups, (b) people tend to remember negative information much better than positive information, (c) people who refer to other sources, for example, both for support of their positive and for support of their negative opinions, do so especially by accepting or criticizing negative information, and (d) interview questions about information about ethnic groups prime, or are associated with, a stereotype about negative information: Stories about foreigners are known to be negative. Similar conclusions hold for the reference to negative opinions of others: These too are mentioned much more often, although less than negative facts.

The reactions and personal opinions of the people mitigate this dominance of negative information: People sometimes do not accept negative information or disagree with negative opinions. Yet, even then, negative reactions and personal opinions about minorities prevail. This also explains why most communications about foreigners tend to be negative. Most people probably tell other people stories that are just as negative as those they have heard and accepted (believed, and agreed on) themselves.

Although the effects for the different social variables are not dramatic, there is a tendency of conformism among women and the elderly, in that they accept and agree more often with the information they attribute to their sources. Because that information is mostly negative, their reactions also tend to be more negative. The high-contact areas are also the location for more people with higher prejudice scores, who tend to mention and agree with negative information from other sources. People who are more critical of the information from their sources (young, males, low-contact, i.e., better-educated people) also tend to have somewhat lower prejudice scores for these examples.

In the light of our discussion in this chapter about the processes of ethnic persuasion, these results provide some more insight into the overall pattern of communicative relationships between sources and their recipients. People generally tend to believe what others tell them about ethnic groups, especially when this is negative. Their reactions, opinions, and agreement are generally in line with the consensus, which apparently is also reflected in communicative events, especially those of informal personal contacts. People tell or hear hardly any positive things about foreigners, and if they do, they ignore, forget, or disagree with that information. Disagreement with or rejection of negative information is much less frequent, and is typical of those who live outside the high-contact areas (are younger, or better educated).

This analysis again confirms our assumptions about the power of socially shared ethnic prejudices, and about the effects of that consensus on information and communication about ethnic groups, as well as on how people process that information. Negative information is mostly accepted, but even when it is rejected, this mostly happens in a superficially critical and cursory way. Our data suggest that no counterarguments, counterstories, or other forms of counterinformation are given as a form of rejection. If people justify their disagreement with prejudiced opinions, they often merely refer to them as "nonsense" or with "that is, of course, not true." This means also that critical and less prejudiced people do not contribute to a different communication pattern. They often report that they remain passive when they hear negative stories. Very few people actively protest against racist talk. Thus, they participate passively in the racist consensus, despite their personal (private) rejection of prejudice.

From these features of the communicative and persuasive aspects of prejudice, we begin to grasp how racism is reproduced, confirmed, and accepted in society. If the consensus is predominantly prejudiced, then the communications are, and if the communications are, the consensus is permanently confirmed. Few people reject negative communications, and still fewer do so explicitly and publicly. So, there is no communicative countermovement, no counterexamples, no counterarguments, and so no antiracist models and schemata. Negative opinions, thus, are rejected only because they conflict with higher-level norms and values.

4.3 ANALYZING PROCESSING REPORTS

The overall picture of the ways people process information about minorities sketched in the previous section shows general tendencies only. On the basis of a few concrete examples, a more qualitative and theoretical analysis has been made in section 4.1. Let us try to find some more empirical evidence of these processes of prejudiced communication. We do this by paying closer attention to the accounts people give of personal communication events. Obviously, such accounts are often no more than very brief, summarizing statements about what people hear, and seldom detailed self-reports about what they have recalled, what they found relevant, what arguments they have used to accept or reject ethnic information, or what opinions, norms, and values were applied in these processes. For that kind of data, we need special protocol sessions or similar techniques usually carried out in the laboratory, often during or immediately after the special tasks, such as problem solving or reading, the subjects must perform. In natural contexts of communication and reproduction, such data are rare. Thus, in a series of 20 additional interviews carried out in the spring of 1985, we tried to ask people specifically about their sources of information about ethnic affairs. However, few people in these interviews are able to recall detailed information, beliefs, and opinions of such communications spontaneously. It turned out that the results do not differ very much from those obtained in less-focused interviewing.

Let us examine, then, some of the informal interview "protocols" (N = 138) of people who mention personal sources of information and opinions about ethnic minority groups. We have found above that in many (76) of these protocols, people mention negative facts about foreigners, whereas only a few (7) positive facts are recalled from such encounters. The same is true for opinions recalled, as well as for the reactions of the people, who are also predominantly negative. People agree and disagree more or less equally often with their sources, which means that their agreement is mostly agreement with negative opinions, and their disagreement mostly with positive opinions. The question then is *how* do they react or (dis)agree, and how do they reproduce such cognitive reactions in their actual talk?

The large majority of the passages merely feature very general, often implicit forms of reaction and (dis)agreement, such as "It is nonsense of course that . . . ," "That is what you hear all the time," or "I don't pay attention to that." Detailed arguments, opinions, or ethnic attitudes are rare, and often are not distinct from the present, conversational, arguments or opinions people use to justify or explain what happened in the communicative events. Yet, we assume that ethnic opinions are not particularly momentaneous, so that even present reactions, evaluations, or retrospective interpretations have some value as indicators of those of the communicative situation to which is being referred.

Let us discuss a few examples, which this time also include several that react negatively to negative talk in order to see what kind of "defenses" they use in communicative situations; recall that (S) means that a summary is given, not the literal text:

(21) I-C-6 (Woman, 60, low-con, P6)
(Daughter doesn't fall for their charm) She says, they look at you [on the bus] as if they want to undress you with their eyes. They are used to that there, that women and girls are not allowed to go out of the house. DO WE HAVE TO STAY INDOORS BECAUSE THEY ARE NOT USED TO THAT?

(22) III-AB-4x (Man, 77, retired construction worker, low-con, P5)
(S) I hear from people, well-known business people, that Gliphoeve [apartment building in De Bijlmer, neighborhood with many foreigners, especially Surinamese] is being ruined by foreigners, and that it must be restored for 50 million, whereas there is no 7 million for a machine to help people with a kidney condition (I don't like that).

(23) II-PD-5 (Woman/man, 60/65, high-contact, P6/P5)
(S) My granddaughter had a streetcar conductor as a friend who says that most of the people who destroy streetcars are young Dutch punks. But I say that they are Moroccan.

The woman in example 21 summarizes a story told by her daughter, but adds a general statement about the cultural differences between Dutch and foreigners, which explains (and supports the truth of) the experiences of her daughter. At the same time, though, the ethnic belief is expressed as support for her own reaction to that story, in which the woman shows that she will not accept constraints on her freedom because of the ways foreigners treat women. We may assume that this kind of argument may be typically used to accept such negative stories about foreigners. The man in example 22 also reacts by mentioning negative consequences of the "favorable" treatment of Surinamese we found earlier, also this time in the form of a comparison with "poor" (sick) Dutch people, for which there is no money. Acceptance and agreement with the story may indeed by based on such *them-us* comparisons of valuable resources, as we saw for the example of the woman in the welfare office in section 4.1, above. Apparently, such arguments are being taken over by recipients to form similar opinions, and to defend them again for others in later talk (as happens here in the interview). In example 23, the woman flatly refuses to believe the experiences of the streetcar conductor, and brings to bear her prejudices against Moroccans to the communicative situation: Vandalism is not something of which "our Dutch boys" could be guilty. Hence, her rejection of a denial of negative opinions about foreigners is based on the perceived incompatibility of negative opinions of in-group members with a (positive) in-group schema. In other interviews, such a rejection takes a more subtle, strategic form. When people say something negative about minorities, they may use the apparent concession that sometimes Dutch people also "do this." This is the complementary move of conceding that among minorities are also "good ones."

(24) I-Z-1/2 (Woman/Woman, 45/45, housemaid/clerk, low-con, P3/P3)
W2: No, I mean we can't really have an opinion about that. I do have an opinion, I could form an opinion, after all that talk you hear in the streetcar.
W1: Just as I say! You hear so much from others.
W2: Two or three times a week, you are sitting in the streetcar, I had it twice last week. This old lady sitting beside me, a decent old lady, begins to tell stories like that about foreigners, that she doesn't accept them . . . I can see that from all her talk. She simply says that in the streetcar, where everybody can hear her. Did she have it from herself, or did she hear it from others?
W1: Well, I didn't react to that, because it was a woman of over 60 years old.

(25) III-SV-3x (Man, 35, book producer, low-con, P4)
M: (S) I don't react very easily against things I disagree with. At most I feel substitute shame.

Example 24 fairly clearly shows a typical instance of public talk about ethnic groups. The woman in the story presupposes that (very) negative talk about foreigners in public is against the norm, and speculates about the sources of such negative opinions (a "decent" old lady, apparently is not supposed to have those opinions). The other woman, like many of our interviewees, did not react, and also gives a reason. This either suggests that one should not argue with elderly people, or that old people tend to have such negative opinions and one should rather not try to change them: Like a child, she is not responsible for what she says. Also, the brief fragment given in example 25, which closes a long statement of the interviewee about his experiences with talk about minorities, shows that many people, even when they disagree, prefer to remain silent. Interesting in this case is the reference to an emotion such as (substitute) shame: The man is ashamed of the behavior of other Dutch people. Indeed, it might be a typical feature of Dutch society to remain friendly in conversations, and not to react too negatively against what other people say. For racist talk this is, of course, another condition that allows further reproduction. There are occasional exceptions to that, though—if people are afraid to be contradicted in their (negative) beliefs about ethnic minorities, they may also keep silent:

(26) III-MR2-2 (Man, 80, retired bank employee, low-con, P4)
(S) I now admit that I think like that—that I wouldn't like it when it

would be like in De Bijlmer here, when Surinamese would come to live here—I wouldn't say that openly in a group of people, because other people would object and I don't like having an argument about it.

On the other hand, some people do take a more active role in the rejection of negative talk and opinions. The first step in such a process of rejection is doubts about the truthfulness of the stereotypical stories:

(27) III-MR-3 (Man, 36, low-con, P3)
(S) You hear those stories, things that are salient, like how Turks treat their women, or about slaughtering, usually not very positive things. I don't know what to believe of those stories. . . . There is a lot of bullshit among it.

Others report that they do more than that. They just contradict the speaker, become angry, and show how prejudiced talk should be understood:

(28) II-MA-2 (Woman, 30, artist, high-con, P2)
(S) I have never heard concrete stories, only abuse and stereotypical things like "They stink," and "when you start talking about it, or when you want to defend them, then it stops."

(29) II-PD-4 (Woman, 25, student, high-con, P2)
(S) Insurance people asked whether there were also foreigners living in this house, and I was angry because it is because they think the house is less safe when foreigners live there.

(30) II-AC-4 (Man, 65, retired policeman, P4)
(Moroccan neighbors) (S) Children are up late, and then "he [Moroccan] tells them [Dutch neighbors], but I never heard that myself, I only know it from hearsay, that they [Moroccans] say uhh, these Dutch must adapt to us for once, because the government has invited us to come [and work] here. Of course, that is not how it is. They came here by themselves."

(31) III-GE-4x (Man, 17, student, low-con, P2)
(S) Heard somebody tell a prejudiced story about Jews, that they control the banks and finances. We can counter such stories by giving explanations or going against them real hard.

The woman in example 28 first claims that even taking the defense of ethnic groups may be sufficient to stop such negative talk. Because few people report doing this, there are few instances where the reproduction of racism in talk is actually blocked by counteraction. The woman in example 29 explains (in attributional terms) the fact that she became angry with the insurance people. She suspects that the insurance people have prejudices against foreigners, and might charge higher premiums. Hence, in communication, sometimes an "innocent" question may be given its "correct" reading due to a critical analysis of the context by the hearer. A characteristic example of counterargumentation is expressed in example 30, in which the man rejects the stereotypical argument about how the foreigners "came" here. Unfortunately, we cannot see from this and some other examples, whether he actually used this counterargument, based on his knowledge of another ethnic situation model, in the conversations he hears. The boy in example 31 is one of the few who refers to stereotypes about Jews in our data (in his neighborhood there are relatively many Jews), and he suggests that such talk can be countered by good and aggressive arguments.

Note, though, that this kind of critical stance and analysis is rather exceptional. We have found that in most situations, people believe the negative stories of others and agree with prejudiced opinions:

(32) II-PD-5 (Woman/man, 60/65, high-con, P6/P5)
      W: But this is what you get in this neighborhood, and you hear about that very often when you are in a shop or whatever if they are having a chat in the street: Next elections, Glimmerveen [head of a forbidden, racist party] is my party. And then I say, look, listen to me, when it really will come as far as that, who was responsible for that? Only the government, according to me. What exactly do they want? What do they want?

Talk about the racist voting intentions of her neighbors is commented on by this woman in terms an explanation and defense of such intentions. Voting racist, also for her, is going very "far," but she blames such behavior on the government, who "lets all those foreigners in." Apparently, during such talk, agreement with acts that are against the law or the norms may be excused by the participants by attributing the reasons for such actions to an outside force, which make the actors less reponsible. Instead of being racist, the actor then is forced by the circumstances and the authorities.

In the next examples, we find a few more "academic" analyses of communicative situations. Interviewees refer to public places such as bars and public transportation, as well as to the media. Interesting is the repeated mention of "eloquence," which suggests that people who tell negative stories are sometimes not only well spoken, but may also be very persuasive. Thus, the man in example 33 shows that he "understands all that," suggesting that the speaker has a point, but still rejects the conclusions or evaluations, because these would be against the norms ("the way to do it").

(33) III-SV-1x (Man, 59, writer, low-con, P4)
      I: So where do you get that information from? Do you hear it also

among your acquaintances, for instance, or are these things you read in the paper as you just said.

M: Well, you know that those things happen, and those people are being interviewed on television . . . You have both let's say "import Dutch," an unelegant word, but I don't mean anything ugly with "import Dutch" as well as let's say autochthonous Dutch who tell their stories uh on television or in the bar, here or, for instance, in the streetcar, when you get an eloquent person sitting in front of you, and uhh that is how I get to know those stories, and then I think yes, God, then I can understand all that, but we can't we shouldn't reason like that, because that is of, course not, the way to do it.

The other interviewees, both university people, do not tell about concrete communicative experiences, but give general impressions and analyses of these situations. Although neither of them is specialized in the field of prejudice and racism, they show that the kind of prejudiced talk we analyze is fairly well known, as well as the principles of how people get to know ethnic prejudices. The sociologist in example 34 suggests that in the high-contact neighborhood where he lived, talk about foreigners also had the function of "testing" other people, thus, to obtain information about their "ethnic stance" as a member of the community. As with political beliefs, the topic may be delicate, and speakers must know with whom they can talk "openly" (i.e., negatively) about ethnic groups in the community.

(34) III-CB-1x (Man, 34, sociologist, low-con, P2)
(S) Sometimes you hear from people who live there about rags hanging before the windows, and toilet bowls being removed. And when I lived in one of those neighborhoods "you could often hear from people that they resented that, and that was discussed, I mean people all the time were busy forming their opinions about that, say, and testing what you thought about that yourself, and what your own experiences were with others" so that you knew whether people were for or against foreigners, and for what reasons. In that sense people knew more about each other than in this neighborhood.

(35) III-ET-1 (Man, 37, university teacher, low-con, P1)
(Story in newspaper) (S) M: Yes, those stories you read all the time like slaughtering sheep and blood streaming from the walls, type of stories you hear on each point where people have unfounded opinions. You are sitting in the train and somebody starts to talk to you about all those people on unemployment allowances, and then they start telling a story "I KNOW SOMEBODY, a family of 5 persons of which 4 have an allowance, they together make twice as much as we make." Such stories are told a hundred times, until they legitimitize the conclusion that the allowances may well go down, because people live nicely on them and couldn't care less about a job . . . Apparently it is allowed and interesting for people to tell and hear those stories, especially when

they are never contradicted. It is important to react to this, for instance, when in the papers or as I saw recently on TV, people do as if those stories are normal, and that the media just register them so that people are getting used to them and a normal way of storytelling.

In this last example, the interviewee gives a political analysis of the consequences of negative stories about foreigners. They may legitimate concrete social actions against minorities. And the fact that they are not contradicted, as we have indeed found, confirms their consensual nature, that is, their "correctness" as symptoms of a "bad" ethnic situation. The passively reproductive role of the media especially is critically commented on here, a point that is raised more often in the interviews in this neighborhood.

Conclusions

From these examples, we may at least infer some elementary features of communicative effects in "foreigner talk." Standard is the belief and support of negative stories as confirmations of negative stereotypes. Possible counterarguments of a moral nature are strategically rejected by pointing out the negative consequences for Dutch people of favorable treatment, and lack of respect for our norms and values by the foreigners. Hence, perceived deviance of in-group norms is justified with higher-level norms and values that protect in-group identity, interests, or goals.

For other recipients of such talk, the situation is more problematic. They feel that such conversations are at least improper (as also speakers themselves are sometimes aware), and may at least have some skepticism about the truth of such stories. In many situations, however, hearers may remain silent, or may be ashamed. Others activate arguments that contradict opinions in talk, or understand that innocent questions or stories are in fact expressions of negative prejudices. Finally, at a meta-level of understanding, some interviewees show that negative story-telling has become part of a dominant consensus, and may have highly detrimental social consequences. They resent the uncritical reception of such stories, also by the media.

The general pattern, thus, is one of uncritical acceptance or at least passivity. Because only a few people think they should react critically, and still fewer actually do so, negative stories can be safely reproduced in talk, and magnified through the mass media. It appears that there is virtually no standard set of (counter)arguments against racist talk. The dominant consensus does not reproduce such arguments or positive information in talk and the media. People thus can only globally disbelieve and reject racist stories and opinions based on them, but have no alternatives.

Both socially and cognitively, there are no antiracist attitudes and models that are as developed as the prejudiced ones. For the rejection of wrong beliefs, people must sometimes have considerable knowledge, which, however, is hardly provided by the media. And for the overt disagreement with racist opinions, they must challenge commonsense norms, values, and arguments against which other arguments may be powerless while "uncommonsense." Those who defend the rights, the points of views, or the interests of the minority groups may risk being treated as social traitors who don't care about their "own people." The development of antiracist models and schemata, as long as it is not supported by the authorities, educational materials, and practice, and especially the media, will have few chances against the massive daily reproduction and execution of a powerful consensus. In this and the previous chapters, we have examined much evidence that shows why such a consensus is so pervasive and persuasive, and how people cognitively respond to prejudiced talk. To examine the real consequences of such talk, we must however also analyze its social contexts, which we do in the next chapter.

6

The Social and Ideological Context of Prejudice Reproduction

1. Introduction

Ethnic prejudice, discrimination, and racism are primarily social phenomena. They characterize intra- and intergroup relations, and we have repeatedly stressed that even their cognitive "programming" has a social basis. The mental representation and the strategic uses of ethnic attitudes and models are organized as a function of their role in social perception and interaction. Prejudice is not a personal, individual attitude toward ethnic minority groups, but socially acquired, shared, and enacted within the dominant in-group. The same is true for prejudice-based discrimination, both at the micro level of everyday interactions among social members, as well as at the macrolevels of societal institutions, groups, and classes.

Social Context, Situation, and Categorization

Although it is not the main aim of this book to unravel the complex social dimension of racism, this chapter focuses on some features of the social context of prejudiced talk. Conversation and the persuasive communication of group attitudes, as they were dealt with in the previous chapters, are themselves inherently social, despite our attention to the discursive, cognitive, and interactional aspects of these forms of social information processing. We define social context as the organized set of properties of the social situation that are relevant for the structures, strategies, and cognitive processing of discourse as interaction. In other words, social situations are analyzed here as the integration of text and context. After the earlier analysis of the cognitive context of talk, we now must attend to the rest of the social situation in which ethnic prejudice is reproduced.

The theory of social situations, both in sociology and in social psychology, has had important informal predecessors during this century (for historical surveys, see Argyle, Furnham, & Graham, 1981; Forgas, 1979; Furnham & Argyle, 1981). However, only in the last decade have attempts been made to make this theory more systematic and explicit, although results in these two disciplines are still little integrated. Together with interaction, social situations may be considered as the building blocks of social organization and process, and the crucial meeting point of cognition and social action. For our own discussion, this means that it is also the location for the analysis of the communicative reproduction of racism by speech participants as social members in general, and as dominant in-group members in particular.

One task of the analysis of social situations, then, is a further social characterization of participants. Traditionally, this involves specification of class and group membership, gender, age, socioeconomic status, institutional functions or other roles, among other things. This chapter provides only a few figures that give some description of the social groups to which our speakers belong. A more adequate approach, common to cognitive or interpretative sociology as well as cognitive social psychology, would be a "dynamic" analysis of such social dimensions in terms of, for example, strategic interaction, negotiation, shared interpretations, and commonsense categories (Schwarz & Jacobs, 1979). In the conversational communication of ethnic prejudice, the traditional descriptions of the social identities of speech participants are abstractions from ongoing processes, such as self-presentation, impression management, categorization, interpretation, and attribution. People monitor this social membership at several levels at the same time, and may talk simultaneously as a woman, as a professor, as a White in-group member, as a neighborhood member, as a Dutch person, and so on in varying hierarchies of relevance, and enact such self- and other-categorizations in strategically effective ways in their interaction (Tajfel, 1982; Tajfel & Forgas, 1981).

Through further analysis of our interview data, we thus hope to be able to study a few of these social categorizations and strategies of prejudiced group members. Part of this task has already been accomplished in our analysis of self-presentation and impression management strategies of prejudiced communication. Yet, the social dimension of this analysis was still lacking, as if people were only participating in such conversations as individual actors. We must probe deeper, for instance, into the permanent self-presentational moves that aim at the avoidance of social categorizations such as *racist*. Similarly, we must pay more attention to the social constraints of shared norms, values, and ideologies that impinge on conversational interaction among White in-group members.

Between Macro and Micro Levels

Limited attention will be paid to an autonomous sociological account of the ethnic situation at the macro level, which is the main object of research in most studies of discrimination and racism. These studies, it must be noted, were carried out from vastly different theoretical or ideological points of view, which neither this book nor this chapter can discuss, however (among many other publications, see, e.g., Banton, 1983; Bowser & Hunt, 1981; Castles, 1984; CCCS, 1982; Cox, 1948; Husband, 1982; Miles & Phizacklea, 1979; Mullard, 1985; Ratcliffe, 1981; van den Berghe, 1967). It goes without saying, however, that such broader historical, socioeconomical, and sociocultural analyses of ethnic relations and racism form the necessary background for the study of ethnic attitudes at the micro level of talk, communication, and interaction. Of the macro approaches, we only retain the more "cognitive" dimension, namely, ideology. Thus, we are interested in the ways participants of prejudiced talk display their knowledge and beliefs of "ethnic situations" in discourse and interaction, and thus reproduce this situation at the micro level (Knorr-Cetina & Cicourel, 1981). Also, we pay special attention to the role of the elite in the communication of racism.

The Role of Elite Discourse and Racism

The macroanalysis of racism in society dovetails with our micro approach in many significant ways. Both from our own empirical results, as well as from much other recent research, we may conclude that the discursive reproduction of racism can be explained only partly in terms of everyday talk among "ordinary" social members. Within the dominant White group, for instance, there are again dominant subgroups that play a special role in the production phase of racist attitudes and practices, as they are communicated primarily through the mass media: politicians, civil servants, journalists, academics, professionals, members of the various state institutions (judiciary, police, social welfare agencies, and so forth), and all others in control of public and dominant discourse types. In a society in which everyday ethnic encounters of the population at large may still be rare or occasional, they are the groups that often preformulate the categories, the relevancies, the topics, the agenda, and the evaluations with respect to ethnic minority groups. At least, they have the means to make such preformulations public and thus actively shape the ethnic consensus.

Informal talk often is an admittedly active and autonomous reproduction of the ethnic attitudes of the elite. Thus, we have repeatedly seen that people refer to the newspaper or TV both for their ethnic topics and for their ethnic opinions. True, such informal talk sometimes represents personal perceptions, interactions, and evaluations of people who have direct experiences with ethnic minority groups. Yet, it is the elite who actively reinterpret, reformulate, and redistribute such "models" among the autochthonous population at large. Indeed, we have also witnessed that the media often uncritically quote racist opinions and experiences of people in ethnically mixed neighborhoods. Institutional decision making, official discourse, and especially the mass media—these groups provide the dominant definitions of the ethnic situation.

Unfortunately, a consequent analysis of this special role of the state, the authorities, the media, or of other institutions and elite groups, is beyond the scope of this book and this chapter. Among other things, it would require a systematic study of elite discourse types, such as laws, regulations, parliamentary debates, meetings, academic research reports, textbooks, news reports, advertising, propaganda, novels, institutional dialogues, and myriad other types of text and talk that define the daily interactions of elites and institutions (see, e.g., Reeves, 1983).

Again, we are limited to what can be traced of this discourse in our data from everyday talk, and to the display of commonsense understanding by speech participants of such specific social constraints in the persuasive communication of ethnic attitudes. The relevance of such a limited view lies in the assumption that this will also show us the functions and effects of elite discourse and racism in society in general, and in everyday talk and situations in particular. Obviously, the theoretical context for such an investigation also involves an examination of the intricate relationships between race and class (Mullard, 1985). In this sense, this chapter is also intended as a design for a bridge between our interpersonal analysis of ethnic attitude reproduction and the study of the (re)production of racism through institutional and elite discourse types.

2. Social correlates of prejudice

Let us start our analysis of the social dimension of ethnic prejudice and its reproduction in talk by examining some of the classical parameters that may play a role in the levels of prejudice inferred from our interviews, namely, area, gender, age, education, occupation, and so on. We first give some simple descriptive data, which, however, may put us on the trace of more interesting qualitative differences. However, we comment on the quantitative figures, as they are usually also provided by survey research, in terms of what we know about the content of the interviews and hence against the background of the (interpreted) social context of the speakers. Some of the quantitative results have already been studied, especially for people mentioning media or personal sources, in Chapter 3. Here we are interested in these data for all interviewees in Amsterdam. The limited number of American interviews does not allow even such approximate generalizations.

Differences Between Groups

In Table 6.1, we have listed the average prejudice scores for interviewees from different social groups. The overall average is 3.4, which is somewhat lower than the midpoint of our 7-point scale.

The first obvious difference is the one between high- and low-contact areas, the first being well above the average, the second below the average prejudice level. This difference is significant: $F(2, 140) = 8.31$, $p = .0004$. Although this result corresponds with most survey results on the area dependence of ethnic attitudes, it should be interpreted with care. The low-contact areas in this case are mostly middle- to upper-middle-class neighborhoods of Amsterdam, where people generally have higher education and better jobs. This will also effect the score of the areas. Most important, though, the lower scores in the low-contact areas also relate to the way people in these areas talk about ethnic affairs. Often these conversations take place at a meta-level. That is, they do not so much topicalize their own experiences (which people obviously lack), but rather the attitudes or assumed experiences of other people, especially those in the "poor" neighborhoods. Also, the people in the low-contact areas are often more explicitly aware of the social norms for attitudes and talk about ethnic minorities, and, therefore, their statements to (student) interviewers may in part also come out as less prejudiced. Below, we shall see in more detail that there is little reason to believe that generally people in (higher-)middle-class areas are less prejudiced if other topics and experiences are discussed (Wellman, 1977).

We find no confirmation for the well-known hypothesis that living with ethnic minority groups reduces prejudice (see, e.g., Amir, 1976; Stephan, 1977, for discussion). Indeed, such reduction depends, for

TABLE 6.1:   Average Prejudice Scores for Different Social Groups

	N	PRE
All people interviewed	143	3.4
Low-contact areas	72	3.0
High-contact areas	65	3.9
Men	65	3.5
Women	78	3.3
Age ≥ 50	65	3.7
Age ≥ 30 and < 50	43	3.4
Age < 30	35	2.8
Occupation > 4	34	2.8
Occupation ≤ 4	54	3.8
Education > 4	24	2.3
Education ≤ 4	37	3.1

example, on close personal contacts in equal situations with common goals (Pettigrew, 1981, 1986).

The differences between men and women are generally slight, and we have little reason to doubt the results of our quantitative analysis of these differences.

The most robust differences in prejudice level have been found for age. Generally, the elderly show higher prejudice levels, and young people, lower levels, with intermediate age scoring around the overall mean. These differences are significant: $F(2, 140) = 5.12$, $p = .0071$.

Note that our figures for education and occupation are very incomplete: We do not have this information for all interviewees, although in most cases in which information about education and occupation is lacking, people have low education and low occupation scores, are jobless, or retired from low-level jobs. For the data we have, though, high occupation (> 4 on a 7-point scale) and especially high education (also > 4 on a 7-point scale) also seem to condition lower prejudice levels. One of the explanations, in addition to the ones formulated earlier, is that these groups usually have access to more and more varied information, also about ethnic groups, which includes beliefs about the kind of opinions that are normatively acceptable and which are not. For them, the presence of ethnic minority groups is generally a "theoretical" problem only, and many admit that they have no experiences and cannot judge. Note also that the averages for low-contact areas and higher occupation are close to 3.0, which is not dramatically lower than the mean of 3.4. Education and (young) age seem to be the most confident predictors of lower prejudice levels as measured on the basis of what people say in talk: $F(1, 141) = 31.28$, $p = .0000$.

If we break down some of these figures for the two different areas (Table 6.2), we see that these tendencies are confirmed: Men and women remain more or less equally prejudiced in the two types of area, the elderly score higher and younger people lower than the average in the respective areas. Note, though, that younger people in the high-contact areas nevertheless reach the overall mean of 3.4.

The American Interviews

Although our American interviews hardly allow quantitative generalizations such as those made above, a few tendencies may be observed. Of 24 interviewees, 11 lived in high-contact neighborhoods in Southeast San Diego, and 13 in predominantly White, relatively wealthy suburbs (La Jolla, University City, Del Mar). Whereas the overall prejudice score is somewhat lower than in Amsterdam (3.3), the difference between the high- and the low-contact neighborhoods is more pronounced: 4.2 in high-contact neighborhoods, and 2.1 in low-contact neighborhoods. The figure for the high-contact neighborhoods is, however, somewhat biased by three highly prejudiced, if not blatantly racist, men, scoring 6 or 7 on the prejudice scale. The people who express less explicit prejudices not only live in the wealthier suburbs but also tend to have better jobs and higher education levels (college or more), read quality newspapers, and watch quality TV programs. Most of them describe themselves politically as Democrats or liberals (although the man who scores highest on the prejudice scale also qualifies himself as a "liberal"). There are no obvious age or gender differences in this small group, although those who express most prejudice appeared to be male and younger than 40. There is no tendency, as in the Amsterdam data, for the elderly to express more prejudice. Most consistent is the tendency that links education with prejudice levels: All people scoring 4 or higher on the scale have no more than high school. Although these are merely tendencies in our data, they are in line with what we found in Amsterdam, and also correspond with results from quantitative survey research about racial attitudes in the United States and California (see Apostle, Glock, Piazza, & Suelze, 1983; Schuman, Steeh, & Bobo, 1985, and the discussion of this work in Chapter 4.4).

Obviously, there are not only differences between different social groups that have (or have less) prejudice, but also differences between ethnic groups. In the San Diego area, and in South California (or even the United States), generally ethnic attitudes toward Asians are often less

TABLE 6.2:   Prejudice Scores for Combined Variables

	N	PRE
Low-contact areas	74	3.0
men	33	3.1
women	41	2.9
age ≥ 50	30	3.3
age < 30	20	2.5
High-contact areas	65	3.9
men	29	4.0
women	36	3.8
age ≥ 50	35	4.1
age < 30	14	3.4

negative than, for instance, against Mexicans or Blacks. The fact that many Asians recently have been shown to perform "even" better at school or on jobs than (White) Americans, and proved to be able to live up to the American dream ideology of personal success better than any other immigrant group, has made them the "model minority" of the late 1980s (Glazer, 1985). (Indeed, on the day this passage was written, December 19, 1985, a long article in the Los Angeles Times reported figures and anecdotes that seem to sustain that evaluation. It shows that prejudices start to develop against Asians for being "too good," as with prejudices against Jews: They "take [our] educational positions," when they occupy more than 30% of freshman classes in colleges, which is much more than their percentage in the population, and score highest or next highest on SAT tests.)

We have not paid much attention in this book to the specific differences between ethnic prejudices against various ethnic groups, neither in the United States nor in the Netherlands. These differences exist, of course, and Blacks and immigrant workers from Turkey or Morocco are associated with different prejudiced opinions. On the other hand, we were more generally interested in the prejudices, and the communications based on them, that seem so remarkably similar for different ethnic groups and even different countries.

Experiences and Contacts with Ethnic Minority Groups

Theoretically, prejudice is an ethnic attitude that is developed on the basis of (negative) protoschemata for ethnic groups together with strategically processed information derived from the media, personal communication, and personal experiences.

On the basis of the number of experiences or contacts actually mentioned in the interviews, each interviewee was assigned an approximate experience or contact value. Of course, this value, for our data, can only reflect reported interaction, not actual interaction. Hence, the data provided here may represent considerable bias. Nevertheless, to obtain a first impression, we calculated prejudice scores for people with different degrees of experiences and contacts (as indicated by their own interviews; see Table 6.3).

Experience here means direct observation of or interaction with members of ethnic groups, whereas *contact* means that the interviewees have (close) personal contacts with minority group members. Level 0 means no experiences or no contacts of these types, and levels 1 through 3 indicate increasing experiences and contacts. We have tabulated these figures for the different areas, so that the overall notion of "high-" or "low-contact area" could also be compared to these experiences and contacts.

The general tendency in the low-contact areas, as may be expected, is that most people indeed have no personal experiences or contacts with minorities, although incidental contacts with a single minority member is not uncommon in the low-contact areas. Interestingly, even in the high-contact area, real personal contacts are not more frequent than in the low-contact areas (which suggests that our initial choice of the term *high-contact* area, is misleading). Because the chances for such contacts are, however, higher in the high-contact areas, we may conclude that people in that case avoid such contacts more often. This is in agreement with our qualitative analysis of thematic structure: It is a frequent topic of talk in such areas that people "have no contact with them."

Another tendency in Table 6.3 is that increasing personal contacts is an indicator of lower prejudice scores in both area types: $F(3, 139) = 5.53$, $p = .0013$. This confirms the well-known finding that real personal contact may reduce prejudice (under specific conditions), and also agrees with our qualitative analyses, which suggest that people with lower prejudice scores more often tell (neutral or positive) stories about good neighborly or friendly contacts with ethnic minority individuals and families (see N. Miller & Brewer, 1984, for discussion). In these situations, indeed, the level of contact, and the nature of the goals (being good neighbors, having good friends) is such that contact is indeed a reliable indicator of less negative attitudes. Instead of saying that contacts reduce prejudice, it is obvious that also the reverse may hold: People with less prejudice will be inclined to establish more and more friendly contacts with ethnic minority group members. Again, this shows the "circular" and self-confirming nature of ethnic prejudice.

Indeed, another general tendency of the figures in Table 6.3 is that

TABLE 6.3:   The Role of Experiences and Contacts with Minorities in Different Areas

| | Low-contact areas | | High-contact area | |
	N	PRE	N	PRE
Experience 0	47	3.0	11	4.4
Experience 1	20	3.3	22	3.9
Experience 2	5	1.6	20	3.6
Experience 3	2	1.5	12	3.8
Contacts 0	35	3.1	27	4.4
Contacts 1	30	3.0	20	4.0
Contacts 2	5	2.4	13	2.9
Contacts 3	4	1.8	5	2.6

lack of experiences and contacts often correlates with higher prejudice scores. For experiences, this is less marked, however. Especially in the high-contact areas, having more experiences usually means that these might also be interpreted negatively, which, of course, does not result in lower levels of prejudice. We have seen earlier that recall of experiences with ethnic minority group members, typically told in stories, often has a negative bias. That (many) experiences are more frequent in the high-contact areas, is as may be expected, and the negative bias in their recall and reproduction also accounts for a large part of the higher prejudice scores in these areas. Only a handful of people in the low-contact areas have such (frequent) concrete experiences. Qualitatively, this confirms our earlier finding that talk by people from such areas has a more general, "theoretical" or "meta" nature. Conversation in such cases is about general norms and values, about the ethnic situation in general, which rather primes socially desirable (positive) norms regarding attitudes and behavior toward minorities. Concrete storytelling about the (more frequent) experiences in highcontact areas has a negative bias, both because of existing prejudice as well as because of narrative constraints (interesting stories are often about remarkable, and hence negative events).

Generally, we should repeat that all our data are based on rather spontaneous self-reports, often prompted by specific questions. We do not know how often people "really" have experiences and contacts with ethnic minority group members, and there obviously are personal differences between how much individuals can remember during the interview, how "extrovert" they are in general when volunteering information about personal experiences, and so on. Despite these personal differences, we still witness, overall, rather clear tendencies that are rooted in social differences between groups, defined in terms of their socioeconomic status or the nature and frequency of their intergroup perceptions and interactions.

Note finally that we did not distinguish here between degrees of "seriousness" of the negative events. Indeed, many of them are the usual petty "problems" of close neighborly relations, such as noise, (usually attributed to—too many—children), dirtiness, or smells, that characterize poor neighborhoods in general, mostly due to bad housing, lack of facilities, and general urban decay.

Men versus Women

Do men and women have different experiences and contacts with ethnic minority groups? Taking into account that we interviewed more women, we find the same contact scores, with women especially reporting more often frequent contacts (see Table 6.4). Indeed, women are more often personal friends or partners of ethnic minority group members.

The same pattern holds for experiences: Women more often tell about experiences (they tell more stories). The prejudice scores are not consistent in this case. As was concluded before, more (close, equal) contacts generally indicate lower prejudice scores, both for men and women. Yet, with experiences we see a pattern that suggests that a single experience (as told) signals a somewhat higher prejudice level for both men and women. On several scores, men seem to have somewhat higher prejudice levels (indeed their average is 3.5, whereas that of women is 3.3), except when frequent experiences are involved, then women score higher (than men, and than their own general mean). This seems to be the cases when women tell (many) stories about their experiences, which tend to be negative. When interviews are held with couples, it is generally the woman who speaks and tells the stories.

Prejudice Levels

Concluding this section, we may briefly look at the prejudice levels themselves, instead of at the averages for each group. Which groups of people tend to score at specific prejudice levels? (See Table 6.5.)

When we look at the scores of all people together we first find that most people score at level P4, and then at P3, which both indicate neutral to slightly negative opinions about ethnic groups, a few stereotypes, no antiracist or positive opinions, understanding for negative opinions of others, emphasis of cultural differences, and the general consensus that foreigners must adapt themselves. The distribution over the various

TABLE 6.4:   The Role of Experiences and Contacts with Minorities for Men and Women

	Men		Women	
	N	PRE	N	PRE
Experience 0	28	3.4	30	3.2
Experience 1	20	3.8	24	3.4
Experience 2	13	3.5	14	3.1
Experience 3	4	3.0	10	3.6
Contacts 0	28	3.9	35	3.6
Contacts 1	25	3.5	27	3.3
Contacts 2	11	2.5	8	3.0
Contacts 3	1	3.0	8	2.1

TABLE 6.5:   Prejudice Levels for Different Groups

	P1	P2	P3	P4	P5	P6	P7
All people interviewed	7	31	36	40	16	10	1
Low-contact areas	6	17	25	17	6	1	0
High-contact areas	1	12	11	22	10	8	1
Men	6	11	12	22	9	4	1
Women	1	20	24	18	7	6	0
Age < 30	3	11	11	6	2	1	0
Age ≥ 50	2	7	15	26	9	5	0
Occupation > 4	3	6	5	6	0	0	0
Occupation ≤ 4	1	5	15	19	8	4	1
Education > 4	3	9	9	2	0	0	0
Education ≤ 4	3	9	9	8	6	1	0
People mentioning media	4	17	17	10	7	6	0
Mentioning personal communication	4	22	27	21	12	7	1
Experiences	4	21	16	24	11	7	1
Contacts with EM	6	24	18	22	8	2	0

levels is slightly biased to the lower levels: There are more people who show no prejudice and who are antiracist (P1 and P2) than people who are systematically negative and racist (P6 and P7).

The differences at the extreme boundaries coincide largely with the areas: Very negative people live predominantly in high-contact neighborhoods, and antiracist people especially in the low-contact areas (in which case contacts with minority are an important criterion). At the higher prejudice levels, men and women are more or less in balance, but men more often score at the P1 level. As may be expected from the means given earlier, younger people tend to score at the lower levels only, whereas the elderly tend to concentrate on the intermediate P4 level. People with better jobs and better education only score at the lower levels (P4 and lower). The mention of information sources is also distributed in the lower levels, although references to personal communication more often is an indicator of a somewhat higher (P4/P5) score than the use of the media. Indeed, many people with low prejudice scores referring to the media do so critically.

Experiences and contacts with minorities are more or less equally distributed, but as noted before, personal experiences more often signal higher prejudice levels. Those dominating at the lowest level, especially, are men from low-contact areas, both those with lower and those with higher education, and both old and young. Women and older people tend to converge to the middle scores, and we have attributed this to a somewhat greater tendency to conformity. Overall, higher (> P5) prejudice levels are accounted for mostly by older people with little education in high-contact neighborhoods, and people mentioning personal experiences or conversations with others as their source of information.

Provisional Conclusions

Conclusions from these elementary descriptive data can only be very tentative and provisional. Most consistent are the roles of area, age, education, and close personal contact. These factors are, of course, not independent. Older people, for example, generally have less contact with other people, and especially ethnic minority groups, than younger people, who frequently report having ethnic companions at school or as friends. Area is less linked with personal contact (indeed people in high-contact areas appear to have less contacts than expected), but does indicate the amount of experiences. Also, area, of course, is a factor that is not independent of those of education and occupation. Use and mention of (public) information, such as the media, typically for the better educated, signal lower prejudice scores, and the same holds for increased personal contacts (which also implies more information). There are only incidental differences between men and women, but women tend to score at the intermediate levels more often than men (as do the elderly).

Part of these differences are easily explained, others require more thorough theoretical analysis. Some explanations are stereotypical themselves, such as the young being more "flexible" in their attitudes, and hence less associated with the "inflexible" nature of prejudices. Similarly, more education seems to imply and induce the use of more information, also about different (ethnic) groups, such as through more and more diverse media use, which tend to mitigate the more blatantly racist attitudes.

The same factor, however, may explain more experience with or knowledge about interviewing and its purposes. We suspect, thus, that the better educated will show more self-awareness and control over what is said. More than others, they may be concerned with positive self-presentation as tolerant citizens. They have fewer personal experiences and only an occasional contact with ethnic minority groups, and negatively perceived personal experiences especially account for much prejudice in the low-contact areas, where people tend to have less education. In many respects, then, the "distance" of the better educated to foreigners in the Netherlands also shows in their talk: These people seldom speak about themselves or their family, but tend to speak about others, about general ethnic affairs, and in fairly general, theoretical terms. Negative statements at that level are more clearly inconsistent with prohibited negative norms and values regarding minorities. In high-contact areas, people are also aware of such general norms, but in that case, personal experiences (models) may be used "acceptably" to defend prejudiced opinions derived from general attitudes (see Jackman, 1978, for further discussion about the role of education).

As we shall see in somewhat more detail below, research by and about the actual experiences of ethnic minority members suggests that the better educated are just as prejudiced in their interactions, but tend to be so in a more indirect and subtle way, especially in the domains in which their own interests are perceived to be threatened (Essed, 1984). By avoiding blatantly negative general evaluations, and by not speaking about their personal contexts of action, their talk often makes a less prejudiced impression. More than others, the better educated, the elite, follow strategies of positive impression formation. Their self-image features a component of (ethnic or other forms of) "tolerance," which must be upheld especially in public, and in contacts with strangers (such as interviewers). Further discourse analysis of the interviews (and of other, less-monitored) talk will be necessary to trace such subtle indicators of social backgrounds. In the next section, then, we examine in more detail the special role of such elites in the communication of racism.

3. Elites, media, and the (re)production of prejudice

After the more superficial quantitative analysis of social context factors, we should address more fundamental questions about the role of specific social groups or institutions in the reproduction of ethnic prejudice in talk. We have discussed in this book how prejudice is organized and strategically expressed in discourse in communicative situations, but we have ignored the relevant problem of the "origins" of current stereotypes and prejudices in society. This problem is forbiddingly complex and intricately intertwined with a study of the causes and conditions of racism and discrimination in general, which we cannot discuss in this single chapter.

Yet, when the notion of "reproduction" is examined, it seems plausible to inquire into the processes of "production." People do not spontaneously "invent" negative opinions about ethnic minority groups, nor do they express and communicate them in everyday talk without sociocultural constraints. Prejudice and its reproduction in (verbal or other) interaction has specific social functions, which may simply be summarized as the maintenance of dominance or power for the in-group and its members (we analyze these functions in more detail in the next section). And although the reproduction of shared prejudices in a racist society is part of the dominant consensus, this consensus also has a "developmental" dimension. Social knowledge, beliefs, ideologies, and hence also prejudice, are also systematically "produced." In this section, we examine one of these production processes, namely, those in which various elite groups and the media are involved. One of the reasons for this focus is that we want to counterbalance the possible misconception that ethnic prejudice is merely or especially (re)produced by "ordinary" or "bigoted" people, or by lower-class groups, such as those in ethnically varied, poor inner-city neighborhoods, as our own figures in the previous section might suggest (see also Phizacklea & Miles, 1980, for discussion).

The Role of the Media

Against this background, then, it may be asked whether all in-group members or subgroups benefit equally from the effects of the functions of prejudice. For "ordinary" people in everyday life, the prejudiced cognitive programming of interethnic perception, representation, and interaction will usually support minor everyday actions and lead to neighborly conflicts and everyday discrimination of individual ethnic minority members, only. Both their prejudices and the discriminatory practices they monitor are in many respects "local phenomena." In order for these to become shared and integrated into the consensual attitudes and practices of a racist society, other important factors must be at play. In our Northwestern societies this means, for instance, that such attitudes and practices are also represented and reproduced by the mass media. Our interview data have shown that this is indeed the case: People not only defend or legitimate ethnic prejudice with references to the media, but also learn about negative opinions of others from the media, whether they accept them or not (see also Hartmann & Husband, 1974).

The media, however, do not routinely report what "ordinary" people think or do in everyday life (unless they are victims of crime or catastrophes). On the contrary, there is much media research that documents the fact that access to the media is predominantly controlled by various "elite" groups, such as the leading members of government and Parliament, leaders of political parties, various state institutions, large business corporations, academia, and (other) professional groups, and, of course, journalists themselves (Fishman, 1980; Gans, 1979; Galtung & Ruge, 1965; Tuchman, 1978). This also holds for reporting about ethnic affairs. Neither ordinary people nor ethnic minority groups themselves have dominant access to ethnic affairs news. And if, as several of our interviews show, ordinary people are allowed to express their "complaints" about ethnic minority groups publicly in their town or neighborhood, this is possible only if those who control the media, or a larger consensus, deem such complaints legitimate. One could even formulate this assumption in sharper terms: People expressing ethnic prejudice will be represented in the media predominantly if they formulate opinions that are at least partly shared by those who control the media.

This does not mean that every journalist shares the views of those he or she interviews, but only that such views are within a range of opinions that apparently merit attention from the media and the public. Opinions that are definitely outside the consensus either tend to be censored or are embedded in a critical framework. Some of our interviewees have noticed that this is not the case for negative opinions about minorities: Racist people are often quoted without further comments. Our own and other research into the portrayal of minorities in the media confirms this impression (Hartmann & Husband, 1974; van Dijk, 1983a; Wilson & Gutiérrez, 1985). In other words, the media play an important, active, role in the public (re)production of ethnic prejudice (see also our brief survey in Chapter 2).

Media and Elite Discourse

It was, however, assumed that this role is not merely reflective, nor limited to the (re)presentation of ethnic prejudices of people from the "poor inner-city neighborhoods." On the contrary, in the social model constructed by the media, actors, and speakers on ethnic affairs are also the national and local authorities, the state institutions (courts, police, education, welfare offices, and so forth), and all those groups that are equipped to provide routine stories to the news media. In addition, news values and other social and professional ideologies of news makers tend to favor negative topics for groups and countries that are ideologically or ethnically distant, different, or deviant (Cohen & Young, 1981; van Dijk, 1987b). Indeed, in the media also, the standard news items about ethnic minority groups imply or suggest that minorities cause social, cultural, and economic "problems" for the dominant (White) in-group. Just as in everyday talk, stories about crime, aggression, threats, deviance, and many forms of cultural conflict, dominate media news. Crucial in this case, however, is that these stories are (re)formulations of various discourse types provided by the elite groups mentioned above: laws, parliamentary debates, institutional decisions or regulations, police reports, court trials, academic research reports, and so on. That is, most ethnic news stories are not reproductions of the conversational stories we have examined earlier. On the contrary, everyday stories often reproduce media stories. It is in this sense (only) that the media (claim to) provide what the public "wants." What we want to know, then, is how such preferences, attention, and interests among "the public" are shaped in the first place.

Against this background, we have reasons, and empirical evidence, to assume that elite groups provide the initial (pre)formulations of ethnic prejudices in society, and that the media are the major channel and the communicative context for such discourse. To substantiate this claim, another book would be needed, so we shall merely list a few arguments, and references to other work (without repeating too many references given earlier), that may make the hypothesis plausible. The reason we summarize this thesis here is that it is a crucial element in a full-fledged theory of the reproduction of racism through discourse. Indeed, the elites' major type of social action and interaction is discourse. Therefore, if their ethnic attitudes are displayed, this will primarily take place in text or talk.

(1) **Prejudice is sociocultural and communicated.** We have seen earlier that ethnic prejudices are neither innate nor arise spontaneously with individual people. They are part of a sociocultural, shared, consensus defining (dominant) in-groups and their relations to ethnic or racial out-groups. Hence, ethnic prejudice must be socially acquired through processes of socialization, education, communication, and interaction. Given that most people in our Northwestern societies have no daily or even occasional interactions with ethnic groups, the process of social information processing is predominantly communicative and discursive: People hear and read about ethnic groups, and infer their opinions from this information.

(2) Ethnic information is mostly derived from the (news) media. Whereas most social information processing about ethnic groups is discursive, only in specific areas may "direct" information about ethnic groups be based on personal communication, such as rumors and stories. Yet, ethnic prejudices are widely shared in society at large, so that even the forms of personal communication based on "experiences" often go back to media stories or to people interviewed by the media. It follows that for society at large, the major direct or indirect source for information about ethnic minority groups are the mass media.

(3) Other media provide background for ethnic prejudice. Although we here refer especially to the news media, such as TV, radio, the newspaper, and magazines, it goes without saying that an important segment of these media is formed by school textbooks or other educational materials, children books, novels, advertising, and movies (see Chapter 2). Research has shown that the portrayal of ethnic minority groups in these discourse genres is equally negative as that in the news media (see Wilson & Gutiérrez, 1985, for survey and references). This explains part of the ethnic prejudices formed during socialization and education, whereas stereotypes in fictional or advertising discourse are coherent with the negative opinions expressed or implied by the news media. These other media shape social knowledge and beliefs about relatively "unknown" others. This also holds for our beliefs about other, especially geographically or ideologically distant, countries and peoples. It has been shown, indeed, that both the news media and these other media, represent ethnic minority groups and, for instance, Third World countries and peoples in similar ways (Downing, 1980).

(4) Elite discourse is reproduced by the media. From these premises it follows, first, that much information on which ethnic prejudices are based is derived or inferred from media discourses of various types. From the premise that various elite groups especially have access to and control over media contents it follows, second, that the information is primarily derived from the contents of the source discourses (decisions, debates, reports, and so on) provided by these elite groups, and from the ways these are transformed by media workers. These transformations may involve changes that are specifically functional in the framework of news production, such as dramatization, personification, group attribution, and negativization (see, e.g., Cohen, 1980; Hall et al., 1978, for such media transformations of official discourse about social minority groups).

(5) The public tends to adopt dominant elite opinions. Generally, media users do not simply repeat beliefs or opinions represented in the media. Yet, when ethnic information is involved, few other sources of information are available. Dominant topics in the media also appear to be dominant topics of talk. This also holds for the overall structure of ethnic attitudes, which is also acquired, during socialization, education, and communication processes, through discourse about (ethnically) different groups. This, of course, leaves open the possibility that people may vary in the acceptance of more concrete opinions. We have seen in the previous chapter, however, that this is rather difficult in the absence or scarcity of alternative forms of discourse and information, antiracist models, and positive information. In other words, the dominant structures, strategies, and even the contents (information, opinions) of the dominant media have the highest chance of being adopted by most people. They define the "ethnic consensus." Feedback, for example, in letters to the editor or interviews, is preferred for those who speak within the boundaries of this consensus and, therefore, generally confirms the consensus (re)produced by and through the media themselves.

(6) **Elite (discourse) on ethnic affairs.** Analyses of ethnic news and other media discourses have shown which elite groups are preferably (self-)selected as the primary definers of "ethnic situations." First, these are White elite groups. Ethnic minority elites have little access to the media, and practically no access if they represent nonconsensual ("radical") views (Wilson & Gutiérrez, 1985). Second, the national and local governments provide and control most political and economic, as well as much social information, as news source discourses such as about immigration, socioeconomic policies, and social problems (unemployment, housing, welfare, crime, and so on). Debates, decisions, laws and regulations, reports, and other discourse types of the government or legislative bodies regarding ethnic minorities, thus get routine coverage and reformulations in the media. Third, the same is true for most state or public institutions and their representatives, such as the police, the courts, education, research, health authorities, and all other institutions with which ethnic minorities are confronted. They also provide the discursive presentation and legitimation for their policies, decisions, and actions taken with respect to ethnic groups, such as reports, documents, studies, public statements, or interviews. Again, many of these become public, in summarized form, through media stories and background articles. Hence, it may safely be concluded that most of our daily media information about ethnic minority groups has been preformulated by these various elite groups or institutions.

(7) **Absence and censorship of the alternative voice.** Alternative voices, if represented at all, are either within

the boundaries of the ethnic consensus (e.g., in critical statements about details of official policies and action), or are heard through the representation of "political action," preferably violent or otherwise negative. Dissensus, thus, is represented a priori through negative frameworks such as "riots," "terrorism," demonstrations, conflicts, threats, or other "street" action. Minority groups or majority subgroups that have solidarity with them, have no power or facilities (press agents, press conferences, contacts, and so on) that provide access to news workers and news-gathering contexts (Moscovici & Faucheux, 1972). So, if they are represented at all, then this representation tends to be negatively framed in terms of problems, deviance, or crime.

(8) Prejudice categories and their elite preformulations. It is not difficult to show that any cluster of negative opinions or biased information that constitute widespread ethnic prejudice is ultimately derived from corresponding information provided by elite groups, whether or not media users transform this information in a more negative or more positive direction. A few examples:

(a) Immigration. Prejudices that imply that immigrants or refugees "flood" our country, that our country is "full," or that most immigrants are "illegal," are largely inferred from media stories about (the predominantly negative) reactions of the authorities to various immigration events. If the government wants to "keep them out," this is a legitimation to keep them out of our city or neighborhood. And if they live in our neighborhood, this means that the government has not done enough to keep them out: Thus the action values of the authorities will be used against them in their hesitation to take more extreme decisions.

(b) Crime and aggression. Prejudices about aggression and crime of ethnic groups largely derive from biased media stories that mention the ethnic backgrounds of suspects, which are again based on police reports or court trials, as well as on media articles about crime statistics or crime "waves" that are also partly derived from information supplied by the authorities. This is one of the most socially destructive ethnic prejudices, and there is much empirical evidence that the law and the media together help construct public attitudes about crime, deviance, or similar negative properties attributed to ethnic minority groups. People who express fear of ethnic crime often refer to the media as their major source of information.

(c) Unfair competition. Similar remarks hold for prejudices about (favorable treatment in) housing, welfare, health, education, and other social and economic areas. Here, the communication process is somewhat more complex, though. The authorities do not directly preformulate prejudices about favorable treatment, which would be inconsistent with their policies and actions. Rather, in these domains there is systematic emphasis on the "problems" ethnic minorities create, either by their very presence, or by their actions (protests, demands, criticism), combined with a focus on the positive "help" the authorities want to provide despite the "difficult" economic circumstances.

The attitudinal inferences, however, are easy to make, if dominant group people perceive themselves as real or potential beneficiaries of such resources, whether scarce or not. Politicians, professionals, or civil servants, thus, may represent the attribution of social resources to minorities as a favor, as a positive action, and not as a right. Other (often much larger) groups are much less focused on in this case (e.g., the vast sums that are expended to support businesses "in trouble"). By representing minorities as special problem cases, as outsiders, and as particular targets for state interventions, the framework of a "competition" is created, in which the out-group can easily be attributed the "unfair" role. For new immigrant groups, indeed, the major arguments formulated by the authorities is the "fear" that they will burden the socioeconomic resources too much. Emphasis is seldom placed on the potential socioeconomic contributions of the immigrants or minority groups. We have not found (Dutch) government reports, nor media stories, about the net gain for the economy of having employed hundreds of thousands of "guest workers" in low-paid jobs and with an initial minimum of social resources (housing, education, health, and so on). In fall 1985, a Rand Report was published that showed that contrary to widespread prejudices, "illegal aliens" (mostly from Mexico), were probably beneficial for Southern California (as may be expected, some of the media covered such results with skepticism). Neither is there much official discourse that contradicts dominant stereotypes with statistics that could prove otherwise. This means, indeed, that there is no systematic body of information that may yield counterarguments and reasons that may be used against the dominant stereotypes in this field.

For people in high-contact areas, and later for all those who read about them in the paper or see them on TV, these media-induced prejudices may be further sustained by biased inferences from observations of foreigners who *do* get a house, a job, welfare, or other forms of "favorable" treatment. That is, through the media, the elite provides the general interpretive framework, and the people can fill in and "confirm" this schema by its own (biased) observations.

        (d) Cultural conflicts. Prejudices about cultural differences and conflicts only partly derive from immediate observations in a few large city neighborhoods. Rather, portrayal of, for example, Islam, the position of women, family structure, food habits, language use, are predominantly based on media stories inspired by the (cultural) elites and institutions, academic research reports, and other (practically always White) "specialists." It has been shown that much of the "ethnic research" carried out by these specialists is itself often prejudiced against the minority groups studied (Essed, 1986). It often represents these groups, benevolently or patronizingly, as inferior, strange, deviant, different, pathological, and perhaps in need of "help." The public at large adopts lay versions of this dominant "analysis" of sociocultural properties of the minority groups.

At this point, we may even ignore the (legally and politically permitted) overt racist publications of academics (social scientists, biologists, and so on) that still aim to "prove" anything that states or implies the superiority in many domains of their own (White) race, cultural threats of other groups, the impossibility of a multiethnic society, and so on. The same holds for the persuasive uses of these academic "arguments" in racist propaganda of right-wing groups and parties (Seidel, 1985). And yet, although such openly and blatantly racist publications come from small elite groups, mitigated reformulations have been shown to appear in discourse by less extreme, but more influential, political and academic elites, through which they become more respectable and reach the mass media and the public (Reeves, 1983). Indeed, the very "democratic" tolerance for racist groups and parties, despite constitutional and legal prohibition of discrimination and racism, shows that for the dominant ethnic consensus, racism is at most an impropriety, and not a crime. Political terrorism, especially left-wing, for instance, is treated much differently from racist terrorism, especially from the right.

(e) **Personal characteristics: Inferiority.**
Finally, information about personal characteristics of ethnic minorities could in principle only be acquired through social interaction, which is practically nonexistant for most people. Hence, prejudices again must be inferred from various media representations. These will be seldom direct and explicit in news stories, although they are implied in many stories on the topics mentioned above. The same holds for advertising, fiction, film, children's books, and so on, in which various minority group members may still be pictured as stupid, lazy, dependant, treacherous, cheating, uneducated, backward, unreliable, childish, and the like. From research on discourse content, it may be concluded that negative stereotypes about the attributed characteristics of minorities mainly derive from explicit or implied descriptions of their "typical" actions in such media discourses (written by special elite groups). The same holds for the personal attributions derived from other discourse types, such as crime news, reports about educational "disadvantage," unemployment, and any other domain that allows inferences about the capacities of people.

Which Elites?

In the previous paragraphs, we have repeatedly used the notion of "elites" without explicit theoretical analysis. Our definition of the term was merely enumerative: We gave examples of the kind of elites involved in the reproduction of ethnic attitudes, and of the types of discourse they produce. This single section can hardly be the appropriate location for a complete sociological discussion of the notion of elites and their political or social power (see, e.g., Bottomore, 1964; Gouldner, 1979; Lukes, 1974; Mills, 1956). A few further observations will do for our purposes.

From our analysis of their role in attitude reproduction, it may first be inferred that elites are social (minority) groups that have various types of power and control, whether political, economic, social, cultural, or personal. Within the framework of the reproduction of racism in general, the sociopolitical elites are in control of the decisions that directly affect the daily lives of ethnic minority groups and their members, such as in the domains of immigration, residence, work, housing, welfare, health, or education. Their elite power is that of legitimate(d) authority. Yet, for our discussion of the discursive reproduction of ethnic attitudes, other elite groups and other forms of power are relevant as well.

The sociopolitical elite, including members of the national and local governments, legislative bodies, and state or city institutions (education, courts, police, welfare agencies, health institutions, and so on), also routinely formulate and justify their policies and decision making, namely, in many discourse forms, such as policy statements, reports, interviews, or propaganda. Here, the execution of power may also be persuasive: Reasons are formulated for the acceptance of policy and action. Such reasons will, among other things, involve "analyses of the problem situation." This is particularly relevant for the persuasive communication of the dominant interpretations of the ethnic situation. In this discourse, then, professional arguments, such as in statistical terms, may be given in favor of severe limitation of immigration (especially of non-Whites), of reducing child allowances to foreign immigrant workers, or of abolishing special school services for immigrant children. The main (overt) premise in such arguments is economic: lack of money and resources within a (semipermanent) economic crisis. Other arguments are, more tacitly, based on assumptions of social fairness, and derive their acceptability from the very prejudices they induce among the public at large: One group should not be favored over others, and immigrant groups especially have not the same rights as autochthonous ones. We have seen that through media reproduction, such arguments or other discursive strategies may reach and be adopted by the public.

Economic elites, such as corporation directors and managers, have only indirect control over the reproduction mechanisms of ethnic attitudes. Apart from their direct control over investments, hiring practices, and work environment, for minority group members also, and, therefore, over discrimination on the job, they monitor the government's policies on public spending, including the budgets for ethnic group relations.

Finally, the various cultural elites, partially coinciding with the sociopolitical ones, such as in education and state cultural affairs, play a key role in the formulation of justifications, analyses, or other discursive structures that support both the political elite and the ethnic consensus. Media workers, teachers, researchers, writers, and many others are engaged directly in the production and reproduction of knowledge, beliefs, interpretive frameworks, fictional representations, and their persuasive effects. Whether or not they support the political elite in power, they have control over much of the mass-mediated agenda, the dominant topics and interpretations, the public discussion of moral values, and the setting of public goals in society. Even without political power, they may exert control by institutional or personal status, prestige, or celebrity. They exert direct control over the contents and style of nearly all mass-mediated messages, and do so with ethnic media news, advertising, or film, in the ways suggested earlier. As the experts in matters of "formulation," they are the ones who produce the dominant discourse environment of a racist society. Their power, thus, is predominantly symbolic (Bourdieu & Passeron, 1977). If their discourse plays such an eminent role in the preformulation of ethnic attitudes, we witness the interesting group contradiction that consists in the fact that the same elite also recruits those who are the most prominent formulators of antiracism (Gouldner, 1979).

Sears and his associates (see, e.g., Kinder & Sears, 1981; Sears, Hensler, & Speer, 1979) also used the term *symbolic* to refer to the "new" racism of the elite or the liberals, for instance, to explain the general opposition to busing we also found in our own California data. This research argues that such opinions and actions are not so much based on self-interest (people who do not have children also oppose busing), and does not have the traditional blatant forms of color-based racism. Yet, as may be clear from this chapter and other data in this book, as well as from the frequently cited results of Essed (1984) about everyday racism, we have both theoretical arguments and empirical evidence to believe that "symbolic" (or "new") racism, is also racism, maybe of a more subtle form, especially in its expression and public communication, but nevertheless a functional part of racism and its reproduction. This chapter intends to show at least some of the ways these kinds of indirect, more subtle, more "tolerant" ethnic opinions are communicated and interpreted.

This brief description and identification of elite groups derives from analysis of their decision power, and their (sometimes indirect) control over the actions and attitudes of (many) others. The instrument of that power is often discursive (which does not deny the important dimension of physical or legal coercion, for instance, by the police). The effects of their power—the degree of control—then, are defined also in terms of the effects of their discourses. It has become plausible that this effect is both epistemic and attitudinal: They control most knowledge and beliefs, and thus indirectly the information the public has at its disposal to form ethnic opinions and attitudes. Their own decisions and signals for preferred readings suggest that the dominant consensus attitude should be negative, at least in the sense that "minorities/immigrants do not belong here and/or they are a problem." The public still has the freedom to reject (some of) their decisions, policies, and justifications, and will do so if its own interests are at stake or information is available to feed such rejection. In the communication of ethnic knowledge and beliefs, this freedom is highly constrained, however. Counterarguments are only sparsely supported by available information, or must rely on everyday, informal talk and rumors, in which again ethnic prejudices prevail.

On the other hand, elite control is not complete, fully coherent, or one way. The elites do not only express and formulate their own beliefs, opinions, and attitudes, nor do they simply legitimate their own interests. In order to keep control, at least in a more or less democratic social structure, there must at least be an illusion of bottom-up monitoring, and this will also be done—partly—through the media, and mostly by the elite who purport to speak "for the people." Because ethnic prejudices are already, historically and culturally, widespread in society, and the negative consensus well known, the sociopolitical elite also knows what discriminatory actions or opinions are not likely to be met with massive opposition of the (White) dominant group. In other words, part of their discourse may simply *presuppose* existing prejudices, and thus will be more persuasive in the defense or justification of opinions and actions based on them. Only the law, some dominant norms (e.g., those of apparent antiracism), and the possible reactions of the minority groups themselves, will keep their decisions and discourse within previously set, but expandable boundaries. Indeed, the political elite will constantly check "how far it can go," also when ethnic affairs are involved. It follows that the role of preformulators of ethnic attitudes played by several elites leaves considerable freedom in the control of the style and contents of (mass-mediated) ethnic discourse, but that there is implicit bottom-up feedback through occasional mass-mediated "voices of the people." In general, this feedback has a negative orientation, however, and may thus be used to legitimate discriminatory policies. Only occasionally, well-organized action or pressure, especially by large ethnic minority groups, may have some positive feedback control on such policies or at least on the discursive strategies of their public presentation. Therefore, the socio-political elite will make sure that its policy discourses will appear non-discriminatory. This may be done by presenting policies as having general application, even when their actual (negative) consequences particularly affect minority groups. At the same time, these policies must be presented to the (White) majority group as being "fair" (for the majority), which allows various forms of implicit discrimination.

It should be added finally that the various elite groups mentioned above are not always unified, nor do they always pursue the same goals or interests. Their ideology and practices are not sustained by intentional policies and close collaboration. Indeed, there is no "conspiracy," and there may also be difference and variation. There are also smaller elites who actively oppose more conservative and racist elites. However, they may, on each side, be located at the fringes of, or outside the consensual spectrum, of which the reception can be defined in terms of a "latitude of acceptance." The shared nature of the policies and discourses of the various elites within this broad consensus, thus, is not planned but derives from a shared system of general norms, values, and the attitudes and ideologies based on them. Such a common basis allows substantial variation in more specific opinions, and at the same time guarantees their overall coherence. For instance, the dominant elite consensus in our societies is that (overt, blatant) racist talk, opinions, and action are unacceptable. Yet, on the other hand, the subtle racist nature of this consensus shows in its focused rejection of clearly antiracist positions, and by its lack of concerted policies and legal action against prejudice and discrimination. Racism in that case is reduced to its radical, extreme, and incidental (personal) forms, whereas structural racism is systematically denied, especially when it is also attributed to the elites themselves.

An Example: The Tamil "Invasion"

To give a concrete example of the role of the elites in the preformulation of ethnic prejudice, we may briefly examine the case of a group of Tamils seeking refuge in the Netherlands in the spring of 1985. This case is particularly enlightening because the Dutch population at large until the end of 1984 had practically no knowledge about the Tamil minority in Sri Lanka. Hence, although there is a generalized negative attitude against (Black) people from Third World countries, especially when they immigrate as a group, there were no specific prejudiced opinions against this group in particular. Also, the group of about 3000 young men was too small to be known through everyday observation and interaction. In other words, what people knew about Tamils was almost entirely derived from media discourse. This is confirmed by interviews we conducted in the spring of that same year, in which Tamils were brought up spontaneously by several interviewees. Media discourse was in turn only based on various forms of official discourse, and later on independent investigative reporting. In other words, what became publicly known about Tamils in early 1985 was exclusively derived from elite discourses (and) through media reproduction.

Our analysis of the coverage in the Dutch national press of the immigration of Tamils shows that both contents and style were conducive to the formation of a cognitive "Tamil"-model that rather closely exemplifies more general prejudices against minorities in the Netherlands. Politicians, the judiciary, the police, the welfare organizations, city councils, diplomats, academics, and, of course, journalists themselves actively participated in coverage and a "public discussion" that negatively influenced a wider consensus from the outset. This enabled the sociopolitical elites to use this same consensus to legitimate their negative policies against the Tamils and their refugee status. Some of the first Tamils were sent back to Sri Lanka, or to West Germany, through which they had reached the Netherlands. Others are waiting anxiously on a simple bed-and-breakfast scheme (instead of the normal welfare allowance) for the political and legal decisions that will grant or refuse them refugee status. In the summer of 1985, the first (negative) decisions about the applications for refugee status were made for some 100 Tamils. Let us summarize some of the major tenets of the mass-mediated discourses that, sometimes intentionally, helped construct this negative consensus and its concrete discriminatory consequences.

Our observations are based on initial analyses of some 250 newspaper articles published in the nine newspapers of the Dutch national press during the first four months of 1985. Further analysis of these data will be reported elsewhere (van Dijk, 1987b, Ch. 4). Here we focus on the specific role of the elite in the discursive production of ethnic beliefs and attitudes.

Numbers

The first news reports about the immigration of Tamils focused on the numbers of the immigrants. For a new ethnic or immigrant group to become publicly and politically salient, it is important that we know "how many" there are. Although at first only a few came across the easy crossings of the German border (after having flown into East Berlin, and crossed to West Berlin), the newspapers began to "count." As is well known from news analysis, such numbers have specific functions. They are seldom correct (or later corrected), as the large variation among newspapers shows, but function as rhetorical signals for professional objectivity and precision. They are the symbols of truth. At the same time, the repeated strategy of giving "per day" or "per week" estimates suggests a strongly cumulative effect, which has negative implications, especially when minority immigration is involved. This allows—and did result in—conclusions about the number of immigrants who would come "if this trend would continue." Although the absolute numbers were small, headlines that soon mentioned "thousands" thus also signaled "massive" immigration of poor, Black, Third World people. This information nicely fits the prejudice schema category, which also organizes opinions such as "Our country is overpopulated," or "We cannot have more people from abroad," which also applies to extant groups of "foreigners." Instead of playing down the seriousness of the absolute numbers, for instance, by comparing them to numbers of other groups who were accepted more easily (Polish and Vietnamese refugees, coming from communist countries), the press emphasized these numbers and by this strategy alone could trigger a well-practiced and simple inference schema: Many immigrants cause many problems.

The "Flood" Metaphors

An even more effective and stereotypical way to emphasize numbers or masses are the frequently used "flood" metaphors. Especially in the headlines and leads, the Tamils are said to come in *streams* or *waves,* they *flood* or even *invade* the country:

(1) During the past few weeks Western Europe is flooded by thousands of Tamil refugees (*Vrije Volk,* 12-5-84).
(2) Stream of Tamils can hardly be absorbed (*Volkskrant,* 1-22-85).
(3) State police investigates Tamil invasion (*Telegraaf,* 3-2-85).
(4) Emergency after Tamil tide (*Vrije Volk,* 3-20-85).

The negative connotations of such metaphors hardly need comment. Obviously, the immigration is categorized as a natural disaster, and the Tamils are thus dehumanized. Also, tidal waves are a threat to the country and its population, which might "drown." The suggested inference, especially in the Netherlands (with its long tradition of fights against the sea, and its continuous attention for dams and dykes being built against it), is that policies should be enacted that should "stop" such a flood.

The even more negative metaphor of *invasion* implies massive attack by a foreign enemy, and further supports the negative properties of the immigrants as perceived and presented by the responsible elites. Maybe the police used another expression, but for the newspaper this was obviously transformed into a more effective dramatic metaphor. That is, elite discourse, for instance, of the immigration authorities, may have subtly negative implications, which are picked up and dramatized by the press. Together with the well-known number game, such metaphors express the usual "moral panic" (Cohen, 1980). The message to the public comes across loud and clear: We are going to have big problems with these Tamils. Letters to the editor and our own interviews show that this is precisely how a majority of the public understands and accepts the official versions.

Illegality

To enhance the negative properties of the refugees, repeated mention was made of their "illegal" entry across the German border. The Tamils, of course, could not safely have applied for a visa in Colombo (which would probably have been refused), nor did they always have the requested travel documents, as is often the case with more or less spontaneous refuge seeking. Yet, in accordance with a widely accepted usage to denote "illegal" foreign workers, mostly from Turkey and Morocco, the Tamils were also routinely branded "illegal," as we may see, for instance, in the following quotation from *NRC-Handelsblad*, a well-known quality newspaper, which uses the notion three times in one paragraph:

(5) The Department of Justice said to have no idea about the number of illegal Tamils residing in the country. Illegally residing Tamils enter the country especially in the border area between Limburg [A Dutch province] and the Federal Republic. A West German TV news show of last Monday reported a number of fifty illegal border crossings per day, but Justice doubts whether this number is correct. (*NRC-Handelsblad*, 12-6-84)

Real Versus "Economic" Refugees

Soon the media discussion proceeded to its next predictable phase in the discussion: Do the Tamil refugees have the right to be here? Repeated claims were made by various officials that Tamils were not "real" refugees, but "economic" ones. Read—they are "welfare cheats." They only come here because they are poor, and want to live out of our pockets, taking advantage of the civil war in Sri Lanka:

(6) Both the Department of Justice and the police in Limburg have the opin-
     ion that most Tamils come to our country for economic reasons. (*Vrije
     Volk*, 1-11-85)

This "opinion" has been formulated in many versions. And even when
some newspapers published counteropinions by other "specialists,"
such as anthropologists, diplomats, or the U.N. High Commissioner for
Refugees, who showed that Sri Lanka was not safe for (young, male)
Tamils to go back to, the emerging opinion was clear: They might not
even be real refugees. Note that this opinion was not just formulated by
individual journalists, but that it was also being formulated explicitly by
the prime minister, the secretary of foreign affairs, and other high state
officials. A government mission was sent to Sri Lanka, which established after a week of interviewing that the south of Sri Lanka was "safe"
to go back to. In other words, the consequences of the discussion were
already being explored even before the refugee status of the Tamils was
decided: If we send them back, where can we send them? In other words,
the political decision was already made, and the doubts about the refugee status already resolved by the presupposed fact of their safety in Sri
Lanka.
     It has usually been considered a naive point of view to assume that the
political and social authorities, as well as the media, conspire in such
concerted actions. And indeed, it is not likely that the respective phases
in the process of opinion formation have actually been planned and executed methodically and by common decision. On the other hand, the
shared attitudes and the decisions based on them were so coherent that
the impression of conscious and coherent planning could be inferred
from the consequences. It is probable that some newspapers, together
with groups of politicians, in an early phase found that there should be
no place for Tamil refugees (or any other kind of poor, Black, Third
World refugees) in this country, and manipulated their discourse and
communication processes accordingly. Some of the media sent teams to
Sri Lanka to do little more than "prove" what they wanted to find there
anyway, namely, that there was no danger for "ordinary" ("nonter-
rorist") Tamils.
     This example of the Tamil-panic in the Dutch press shows how vari-
ous elite groups, notably conservative politicians, the police, the judiciary, and the social welfare institutions, both use the media and are
unwittingly (and sometimes consciously) helped by the media to create
a definition of the situation that, overall, establishes a negative attitude

against a potential minority group. The public at large thus acquires a media-constructed set of beliefs that leaves little alternative than to conclude that the acceptance of refugees would be catastrophic for the country. In its respective phases of coverage, the media address the main categories of ethnic attitudes: origin, numbers, economic goals, and sociocultural and personal characteristics of the prospective minority group—they come from a Third World country, they are terrorists, they are Black and poor, they are illegal, they only come to profit from the welfare system, and they are associated with crime. In this way, existing ethnic prejudices can simply be copied to form new ones about the Tamils, even in the absence of direct contacts with Tamils.

We see that no everyday experiences or prejudice of the "people" are necessarily "reflected" by the authorities or the media: They are the ones who use routine procedures and discourse to preformulate such attitudes, and to prepare a decision strategically that can then be assumed to be supported by the public.

Most cynical of all was the fact that some politicians and media argued that Tamils could not be admitted because "popular opinion was against them," and the authorities did not want (a) "to provoke people in the poor neighborhoods where the Tamils would eventually come to live," and (b) "to subject Tamils to possible forms of prejudice and discrimination." In other words, as we have argued before, the elite tries to transfer its own racism to others who are socially weak, and uses the attributed racism of that group to make "popular" decisions.

In a fourth set of interviews, conducted in a poor, ethnically mixed neighborhood in Amsterdam during the spring of 1985 after months of media reporting about Tamils, we found that this strategy works (see van Dijk, 1987d, for details). People essentially reproduce both the preferred topics and the dominant opinions of the elite as they are expressed in the media. Especially the assumed support by social welfare and the protests of Tamils against their special "bread-and-bed" regime were very much resented by our interviewees. People who are helped, according to the dominant ideology, should apparently be "satisfied" with all they get "for free." This also implies that immigrants have no social rights.

We have reason to believe that the process of prejudice production for the actual minority groups that are most salient (Surinamese, Turks, Moroccans) has been similarly preformulated by the various elites and specifically transformed by the media to fit into the general ethnic attitudes of the public. In other words, everyday talk and persuasion about ethnic minorities is not an autonomous or closed circuit. It is essentially fed by many types of media(ted) stories that are initially formulated by various elite groups.

Conclusion

Reviewing the major prejudice cate-
gories that we distinguished theoretically in Chapter 4, this section summarized the (complex) arguments that led us to assume that most of
these prejudices are based on information derived from various elite discourse types and/or their reproduction through the mass media. If we
want to explore the social "origins" or "formulation places" for consensual attitudes about ethnic groups, we must indeed look at those groups
that have the power or the control over, and the access to, such discourse
and reproduction types. We have identified a few of those groups, and
informally indicated what kind of discourses form or reinforce what
kind of stereotypes and racist attitudes. A brief analysis of the example
of the "Tamil-panic" in the Dutch press has shown that such attitudes
may be preformulated by the elite even when no concrete experiences
with a minority group can explain existing prejudices among the public
at large.

The complex cognitive and social-psychological processes that underlie the formation and persuasive communication of these types of beliefs
and attitudes have been discussed before, and need not be reviewed here.
We should, however, repeat the well-known fact that people do not passively repeat, nor precisely reproduce, what they hear or read. This also
holds for the contents and the structures of mass-mediated elite text and
talk. Depending on many economic, historical, social, and cultural factors, people may bias their interpretations in a negative or more positive
way. Yet, we have reason to believe that much "neutral" information
about ethnic groups will tend to be interpreted negatively in a racist society. We have argued that most media and elite discourses do not provide
models, opinions, or knowledge that allow large groups in the public to
develop counterarguments and strategies that lead to the demolition of
racist attitudes.

On the other hand, it may well be the case that the converse may also
happen: Antiracist opinions and discourse may also be preformulated
primarily by specific elite groups, even when they are seldom a dominant majority. Evidence for this, however, is at most anecdotal (e.g.,
membership in antiracist parties, demonstrations, and publications) or
requires much further research and analysis (e.g., measured or inferred
lower prejudice of people with higher education). Our data have examples that suggest that antiracist people also justify their opinions on the
basis of information derived from the mass media. This is no proof for
the attitudinal impartiality or innocence of the media, however. On the
contrary, these antiracist interpretations are not preferred readings, but
counteropinions of implied consensus opinions. In other words, the rele-

vant elites also provide the various countermovements against exploitation, prejudice, and racism, but they are a small, although active, minority among a dominant majority that either doesn't care or just performs its routine tasks of government, administration, bureaucracy, teaching, law enforcement, or social work.

These countermovements obviously have much less access to the dominant, consensus media and, therefore, their discourse may only be read or heard in small "radical" newspapers, radio, magazines, and especially books (with small publishing companies), which seldom reach the public at large. Only through the usual ploys of getting the attention of the consensus media (conflicts, original, or "violent" action, demonstrations, public trials, or mass meetings) are they able occasionally to get their message across. Their discourse, however, often presupposes an attitudinal framework that is so different from the dominant one that they are not even understood, or their talk heard as so ridiculous or "exaggerated" that their persuasive effects may be minimal.

The informal discussion in this section, which extends the topic of this book, is a necessary complement to the discourse analytical, cognitive, and social-psychological analyses given in the previous chapters. Without this broader framework, we would have represented everyday talk about ethnic minorities in a historical, socioeconomic, and political vacuum. We would have ignored the origins and production processes of ethnic attitudes and ideologies, and the roles and participation of various social groups in the reproduction process. We assume that in a racist society, prejudices are held and expressed at each level and within each subgroup. Yet, there are differences of content, style of expression, and enactment. Also, there are differences in social control and responsibility. Even the rather mitigated and occasional prejudice expressed by a powerful politician or academic, when mass reproduced by the media, may have vastly more negative consequences on public ethnic opinion than the possibly more blatant statements of individuals in scattered personal communications. In other words, if we do not understand how the agenda, the topics, the style, and even part of the opinions expressed in everyday text and talk are preformulated by various forms of elite discourse, we do not understand how racism is reproduced in society.

4. Social functions of prejudiced talk

Another important dimension of the social context of the conversational reproduction of ethnic attitudes is the various functions of such talk. We have occasionally mentioned such social functions, and analyzed some of them in particular, namely, the communicative and interactional functions, such as persuasion, self-presentation or other-presentation. However, people talk about foreigners with several, implicit or explicit aims. In this section, we finally discuss the major social functions of "foreigner talk" and again try to relate these functions to the structures, strategies, and contents of such conversations by examining a few examples.

Sharing Social Cognitions

Closely related to the interpersonal and interactional functions, prejudiced talk also serves the obvious social purpose of expressing, sharing, and reproducing common cognitions of the in-group. We have assumed throughout this book that ethnic attitudes in general, and prejudice in particular, are not (merely) personal cognitions, but essentially cognitive properties of groups and intergroup relations. This means that people talking about foreigners do so primarily as social members of such groups. Beliefs, opinions, and attitudes about ethnic minority groups are based on shared group experiences, norms, and values, and talk about them establishes and diffuses them in the in-group through informal talk and the media. It is, therefore, crucial that what members learn from others or from the media be transmitted to others when it is relevant to other members of the group (Berger & Bradac, 1982; Roloff & Berger, 1982; Rommetveit, 1984). In this perspective, personal experiences and opinions are also presented as experiences and opinions "we," autochthonous Dutch people have regarding foreigners. Speakers thus display their knowledge about what others know, believe, and have experienced, and confirm or "ratify" these models and schemata by expressing their own as characteristic examples of a consensus and as results of—literally—"commonsense" reasoning. At the same time, they will appeal to hearers by asking for similar confirmation of the shared nature of their own opinions and experiences. It is important in that case that they are presented and understood not as purely individual cognitions, but as generally shared and, therefore, as legitimate opinions and experiences. The process of social cognition sharing is not limited to specific attitudes. It also involves testing and confirming more general norms and values of the group. Indeed, ethnic opinions are often formulated in explicit relation to such norms and values. Argumentatively, reference to shared norms and values may serve to justify ethnic opinions in talk, but socially such references have a broader function for in-group members.

There are several discursive strategies that presuppose or aim at this social sharedness of ethnic opinions. Let us take some examples of interviews held in a high-contact neighborhood:

Presupposed knowledge:
(1) (RA2). A couple of Surinamese live here, and well you know how it is with Surinamese. Last week the police and the ambulance was here . . . and you know how it is with Surinamese [takes deep breath] uhh temperamental kind of people, we know that.

(2) (Foreigners on the market). And then you see the women with the pram and two bags and the gentlemen they walk with their hands in their pockets before or after them, you know how, you know the pattern.

Providing "knowledge":
(3) (RA2). (No contact with foreign women.) You don't get into contact with them. Are not allowed to have contact with Dutch people . . . . I have uhh I uhh read that once here or there, yes in the paper, that uhh well, a women should stay indoors, period.

Shared opinions:
(4) (RA2). (No personal experiences with foreigners.) But the antipathy is rising in the neighborhood, you know, against the foreigners. [I know this] from conversations with people . . . It is the general opinion in the street.

(5) (PD5). But on average the people here hate the what shall we call it the foreigners like the pest, you know.

Knowledge appeal:
(6) (RA2). (Story about sheep slaughtering at home.) You are not allowed to slaughter sheep at home, you know that, don't you!

Social Self-Presentation and Membership

It was observed many times in this study that talk about "delicate" social topics such as minorities takes place with strategies of impression management: People present a positive "face" or try to avoid a negative evaluation from the recipient. Aside from this interpersonal function, self-presentation also has a wider social function. People present themselves as competent social members of the in-group. Display of this competence can take many forms. For instance, speakers may want to exhibit their knowledge of and conformity to accepted norms, values, rules, and goals of the group as we have also seen in the examples just given (Asch, 1951; Deutsch & Gerard, 1955; Moscovici, 1976, 1984).

These functions of talk hold in particular when foreigners are discussed. In that case, it is particularly relevant that the speaker displays competence as an in-group member, which also involves respecting the general norm of tolerance and respect for other groups and, at the same time, defense of the goals and interests of his or her own group. Self-categorization and self-evaluation as an in-group member and expressing solidarity with other in-group members are moves in the complex interactional strategies of talk that exhibit this social membership. A corollary of this function is the function of (negative) other-presentation, which shows not only knowledge and beliefs about this other group, but also involves strategies of comparison and other-categorization, such as by the emphasis on differences in the respective categories of group schemata (origin, socioeconomic goals, and cultural and personal properties of the minority group and its members). Some examples:

Social self- and other-presentation and norms:
   (7) (PD5). (This neighborhood here is a mess compared to where I lived before.) But, excuse me, but there [in the other neighborhood] were not so many "minorities," they call it, because we are of course not allowed to say "foreigners."

   (8) (RA2). Look madam, if those people adapt themselves to our uhh, our Dutch customs and habits, then I don't mind . . . In these difficult economic times, Dutch women are being reminded that they uhh should have no more than one, two children, something like the pill and all that, and then you come outside and you see . . . those old men [with young girls, and a lot of children], and look that is what essentially bothers us all.

Different norms and values, comparison:
   (9) (MA6). (Many foreigners in the neighborhood, also the neighbors.) There has not been a sponge on their windows for years. And in the kitchen you see all these boxes with rubbish, all the time. Well, we are not used to that.

   (10) (PD5.) But they want their own culture. But when I go to Turkey, then I have to adapt myself. Otherwise I shouldn't go. You know what I mean?

Social comparison and identity
   (11) (RA2). (The neighborhood is decaying.) People have come to live here who didn't live here before. . . . there has been some, how shall I, how shall I put it [pause] yes, I should not say asocial, but yet people who are not like us...

   (12) (LM2). Not only foreigners [bother us]. Because Whites are just like that . . . It depends [who it is].

   (13) (SM4). I find it terrib-. . . is is predominantly foreigner in this neighborhood. All Dutch people want to leave. Most are busy to try to get away. There are so many here on this square who want to leave.

Explanation, Justification, and Recommendation

In talk about ethnic groups, people not only express shared group cognitions or various forms of social categorization. They also tell about their own or others' experiences with foreigners. This may involve storytelling about actions, as well as explanations and justifications of such actions as part of the accepted goals of the in-group. Although these justifications also have a self-presentational function, they may also be interpreted as forms of in-group defense, as legitimation for the adequacy or effectiveness of specific courses of (discriminatory) action. In that sense, talk may also function as a form of social recommendation for other in-group members on how to "deal" with "those foreigners." Some examples:

Exemplary reaction:
(14) (SM2b). Because my brother he once was for instance threatened, there on K-square. But OK, he is not afraid and he thinks by himself if I, if you, if someone must be hit, you can have the first one. They probably saw that, and so they walked on. They thought, that is not a willing victim. But otherwise, he would've, then they would, his wife also said that, otherwise he would absolutely have been robbed, because that was of course what they had in mind.

(15) (AC3). (We don't know whether they are just having a normal conversation or whether they are fighting; for instance, once young foreigners were starting a fight in the community center, man intervenes.) I mean, we know of course when somebody is calling another names, and then you think, oh that is going wrong, then you have to act, you know. But with them, you knew, know beforehand, you have to see that they are taking a threatening posture and so on, and then I think, now it is going out of hand.

Rejection of the discrimination argument:
(16) (MA3). (Bike "borrowed" by Moroccan neighbor. Owner threatens to call the police.) Since that time he says "We are being discriminated against." I say: No I know what the matter is. We were not allowed to be angry about that [the stolen bike]. What would you say if I would uhh your car. You wouldn't like that either, would you. I say: We are not used to that kind of thing. I say: We are in our own country, and you have to adapt yourself, like we live, and not like you live. That is impossible. And that is how you get these conflicts.

Conclusion

Talk about foreigners has several important social functions. At the interpersonal level, people tell about their experiences and opinions about foreigners and thereby transmit socially relevant information, arguments, and "evidence" for others to form similar opinions. At the same time, the speaker confirms his or her membership in, and solidarity with, the White in-group, as well as distance or rejection of the target out-group. Personal experiences and attitudes can be compared to those of others. People thus test whether individual cognitions and interactions are valid instantiations of more generally social ones. Shared commonsense rules, norms, and principles are formulated in order to show that the speaker knows them (and belongs to the group), and in order to support evaluations about foreigners. Preferred explanations of the present social situation and its conflicts may be given, such as in terms of unemployment or the economic recession, as various lay versions of theories of discrimination. And finally, stories that have Resolution categories, and general normative statements, may be used to show how foreigners should be "treated," or to justify one's own actions. In other words, such talk combines the personal and practical problems of everyday "ethnic" situations with people, with the higher-level, social, and group-based issues, interests, and goals of speakers as social members of the dominant group. All these forms of social information processing are vital for the formation of beliefs and attitudes throughout the in-group. Together with the role of the media, discussed in the previous section, everyday talk about foreigners is the key to shared social cognitions, prejudices, discrimination, and racism. Just as there would be no discriminination or racism without ethnic prejudice, there would probably be no group prejudices without talk about ethnic out-groups.

7

Conclusions

---

1. What did we want to analyze, and why?

In this final chapter, we briefly highlight and discuss the major conclusions that may be drawn from the respective chapters of this book. Then we sketch some problems and areas of research that have remained unexplored in our study but that are important for future developments in analyzing the communication of racism.

The major rationale for this book was that the communicative reproduction of ethnic prejudices is not merely a complex and fascinating academic topic, but also a crucial social problem that needs thorough and critical inquiry. Most of our "Western" societies have become increasingly multiethnic in the past decades, and the persistence and growth of prejudice, discrimination, and racism against ethnic or racial minorities are threatening not only the rights and the well-being of these fellow citizens, but also the humane and democratic values and goals of our society as a whole. The sociopolitical fight against such deeply rooted, structural tendencies presupposes, however, that we have insight into the complex mechanisms that underlie their reproduction among the dominant White groups.

This study focused on a key element of this process of cognitive and social reproduction, namely, discourse and communication. It has been our main thesis that the ethnic attitudes and prejudices that form the cognitive basis of discrimination and racism cannot become socially acquired, shared, and confirmed without the multiple processes of public and interpersonal communication. Apart from—often minimal or even absent—observation and interaction, White people "learn" about minorities mainly through talk and text. They hear and read about extant minority groups or new immigrants in country, city, and community through myriad discourse types that define the communication lines of our society: parent-child and family talk, conversations with peers, friends, or neighbors, through children's books and comics, movies and TV programs, novels or news reports, political propaganda or academic research reports. Whereas (still too few) previous studies focused on the important role of the mass media, primarily the press, TV, and movies, this book focused on more direct, interpersonal communication among majority group members, namely, on everyday conversation.

The main question we thus try to answer can be simply formulated, as follows: "How do majority people talk about the minority groups in their city or country?" Such a question implies several dimensions. First, *what* do people actually say: What are the contents of such talk? That aspect can be accounted for in terms of a semantic or topical analysis. Second, *how* do people talk about "them"? This question requires further discourse analysis of narrative and argumentative structures, local semantic "moves," style, rhetoric, and other conversational features of spontaneous talk. Third, what and how does such talk *express* or *signal* underlying structures and strategies of prejudice in social cognition? Fourth, what are the communicative *sources* of such conversations: To which persons or media do people refer when they account for their information or justify their opinions? Fifth, what are the real or possible *effects* of prejudiced talk, and what strategies do people follow in the *persuasive communication* of their beliefs, opinions, and feelings about minority groups? And, finally, what are the *social contexts* of such talk: What type of interaction is involved, who are the participants, what are the social functions of prejudiced conversations, and which relations of power are at stake, or what role is played by the elite and the media in this kind of informal reproduction of racism? These are the questions that the respective chapters have sought to answer, sometimes in theoretical and empirical detail, sometimes only in terms of first hypotheses and initial evidence.

Unfortunately, we were unable to record and analyze "real," spontaneous conversations about ethnic minorities. Therefore, in five years of intermittent fieldwork, my students and I have collected some 180 interviews, both in Amsterdam and in San Diego. These interviews were as informal and spontaneous as possible, and proved to yield excellent data for an empirical study of prejudiced talk. The analysis of contents, style, and strategies of the communication of ethnic attitudes was based on these interviews. Similarly, we also used them as evidence for the study of underlying ethnic prejudices in cognition, and as data about communication sources, persuasive strategies, the role of the media, and the social self-presentation and self-definition of speakers. Results of studies of other discourse types, especially the news media, provided additional information about the everyday reproduction of racism in society.

---

2. Discourse analysis

Because the conversations in the form of interviews play such a central role in this research project, it is, of course, of primary importance that we analyze them adequately. The first concern of the project, of which results have been published earlier as well (see, e.g., van Dijk, 1984), was, therefore, a systematic discourse analysis of the interviews. Both at the global and at the local levels of description, we tried to account for some specific properties of prejudiced talk. Thus, at the global level we analyzed the topics and overall opinions people express, the stories about minorities they tell, and the arguments they give to defend their opinions or to justify their actions. At the local, micro level, we paid attention primarily to strategic features of talk, such as semantic moves of positive self-presentation and negative other-presentation, as well as stylistic, rhetorical, and conversational properties of this kind of "delicate" discourse.

Topics

Topics, defined as semantic macrostructures, are essential for the conversational as well as the cognitive organization of information. They tell us what myriad lower-level meanings are "all about," they summarize, provide higher-level abstraction, and define what is most important or relevant in a text or in memory. Hence, a topical or thematic analysis of the interviews is a central concern of the study of prejudiced talk. We found that just as conversation in general, the—often spontaneous, and hence not interviewer-induced—selection of topics is highly stereotypical. A simple experiment told us that we indeed all "know" what people say, even if we don't always agree. What people tell us about the "foreigners" in the Netherlands or the "illegal aliens" or "immigrants" in California is essentially the same, with variations depending on context: Too many of them are (coming) here, immigration should become stricter, they make us feel unsafe on the streets, the neighborhood is being run down by them, they are aggressive and involved in crime, some of them work hard but many of them are lazy and on welfare (for which we pay taxes), they take our houses and jobs and are unfairly favored by the government, they do not adapt to our ways, do not speak our language or do have strange religion and other customs, they do not value education as we do, have too many children, do not respect their women, live in dirty places, and in general are different and have a different mentality—they do not belong here.

This informal sequence summarizes the main topics that people bring up in their talk, sometimes in blatantly negative, sometimes in more understanding, ways. Further abstraction of such topics yields the elementary topic classes: They are different (culture, norms, mentality) and do not adapt; they are involved in negative acts (crime, nuisance); they threaten our interests (take space, housing, jobs, and social facilities). The notion of perceived "threat" can be inferred from many of these topics: They threaten our norms and values, our safety and well-being, as well as our interests. At the same time, the general concept of perceived "competition" is related to this kind of assumed threat: The other group has come to compete with us for our territory (country, city, neighborhood), our housing, living conditions and work, and our culture. Depending on the speakers' social context, goals, and values, they will emphasize different dimensions of these various topics. And most people, of each social background or neighborhood, resent "favorable treatment," for instance, in the form of assumed "easy" welfare or housing, affirmative action, or other "unfair" help or "discrimination" against our "own people."

Fundamental, but carefully implicit—indeed never expressed in most interviews—is, of course, the hidden concept-pair of superiority and inferiority. Changing social values and norms have taught people that other groups are, of course, (no longer) inferior to us. And yet, it is not just perceived threat or competition that otherwise inexplicably motivate the dominant White groups of the Northwest of the globe to keep precisely the people of color (or people with other inherent characteristics assumed to be different), out of the country, the city, the neighborhood, the club, the circle of friends, the family, the job, the company, the high position, social security, decent housing, and so on. This distancing, if not (still) segregation, indirectly expressed in so many topics and seemingly innocuous remarks ("They keep to themselves") also signals the dissimulated feeling of group superiority. These and other basic dimensions of prejudiced topics may also be assumed to organize our cognitive representations and strategies of ethnic information processing, as we shall summarize below.

Storytelling

These topics make "excellent" fabric for stories. Indeed, conversational stories are about our personal expe-

riences, especially if these are somehow weird, strange, funny, dangerous, or otherwise "interesting." The vast majority of the stories about
minorities, then, feature negative Complication categories. The different, if not deviant, foreigner, immigrant, or Black is, of course, a prime
subject to play the role of villain in the most classical stories of threat,
crime, vice, or cheating. Psychological work also shows that we remember negative things better, especially about minorities. The negative
portrayal also shows in the Evaluation category of the stories, which may
be the most salient dimension through which storytellers can show their
prejudiced opinions about minorities.

Yet, the story about "them" is seldom heroic. The protagonist hardly
provides the valiant solution to the threat posed by the resented "other."
Indeed, these stories often lack the canonical Resolution category, signaling that there is no obvious way out of the "ethnic problems." They
are tales of complaint and accusation, of self-pity and resentment, not of
self-aggrandizement or pride. They are the narrative of a group who
portrays themselves as the "real" victim of immigration or desegregation. Told especially by those that do have experiences, hence by people
living in ethnically mixed neighborhoods, and, therefore, often in the
poor inner-city areas, that victim role is easy to assume also for other
reasons. Poor Whites, victimized through the socioeconomic oppres-
sion of their class, will tend to look down, instead of up, for the most
likely causes and agents of their misery. And the dominant consensus,
preformulated by the elite, and distributed, further detailed, and dramatized by the media, will, of course, have little tendency to counterargue
such racist dimensions of the ideology.

Argumentation

Stories about minorities usually do
not occur alone. They often are functional elements in argumentative
sequences, for which they provide the sometimes detailed and, of course,
veridical, while actually experienced, "evidence" that supports a usually negative conclusion. Also, argumentations are being used by people who do *not* have everyday experiences with ethnic minorities, for
instance, while not living in the same neighborhood or because they are
working in an all-White job environment. In such cases, argumentation
is typically based on general statements about properties of minorities.
Argumentation is, of course, an important aspect of the pervasive positive self-presentation and negative other-presentation strategies. Especially negative statements about minorities cannot be made without any
support, and when there is no evidence, people will usually at least mus-
ter some arguments that make their conclusions look plausible. One

effective strategic move in argumentation is, for example, the "empathy" argument: it is for their own good—when they would go back, when they would learn the language, and so on.

Semantic Moves

At the local level of analysis, the management of delicate topics and opinions requires strategic moves to combine the sometimes conflicting goals of positive self-presentation and negative other-presentation. Thus, we get the many variants of the widely known move, "I am not prejudiced, but . . .," which we called an *apparent denial*. Similarly, to lessen negative statements about minorities, people often mitigate them in a next clause or sentence, or they will choose—rhetorically—understatements and other ways to tone or play down negative inferences that might be made about themselves. People make apparent concessions, saying that "we" also sometimes do bad things, or that "you also have good ones among them," but the strategic nature of such moves becomes apparent when they regularly appear to be followed by a rather significant *but*. Similarly, the more tolerant speaker tends to emphasize, sometimes genuinely, sometimes merely as a ploy, that he or she "doesn't mind so much, but other people in the neighborhood (job, school) do." Among the many other moves that thus contribute to the overall goals of conversational interaction and impression management, we may expect several forms of contrast or opposition. "We" are, of course, hardworking, law-abiding citizens, whereas "they" don't want to work and are engaged in all sorts of crime. As for several other semantic moves, this kind of contrastive emphasis also has a rhetorical function, typically signaling the crucial cognitive and social opposition, if not conflict, perceived between *us* and *them*.

Style, Rhetoric, and Features of Spontaneous Talk

These properties of strategic management of delicate talk are also exhibited in style, for example, in lexical selection. Only a few people used blatantly racist language, and more generally it seemed obvious that for relative strangers, people use moderate language. Negative expressions are, of course, necessary in so much negative talk, but either these tend to be mitigated by next moves, or people try to formulate their opinions in generally "acceptable" expressions. Another striking element of style appeared to be some kind of "name taboo": Instead of ethnic group names, people overuse pronouns and demonstratives (*they, these people*). We interpreted these deictic expressions in terms of a strategy of linguistic "distancing." Denying a name or an acceptable description, indeed, seems one of the forms whereby prejudiced people deny individuality or social membership to minority groups.

Of the traditional rhetorical figures, a few seem to have specific significance in prejudiced talk. Those of irony, understatement, and litotes ("life is not exactly nice in this neighborhood") typically emphasize the negative in a positive way, and thereby ideally realize the difficult combination of positive self-presentation and negative other-presentation. Such operations partly overlap with the semantic moves of mitigation. We already noticed that contrasting *us* and *them* is common in prejudiced talk, and this signaling of group identity, competition, and conflict can take place both semantically and rhetorically. This also holds for the frequent ploy of comparison, in which majority people typically assert that "they would also respect the law (learn the language, and so on) when they would go to another country." And it is not surprising that the operation of comparison usually comes out positive for *us* and negative for them.

Speakers appear to be doing many things at the same time. Both socially and cognitively, they have to attend to many different types of information. Especially when topics are delicate and careful self-presentation is required, spontaneous talk often runs into production "problems." People hesitate, make false starts, repair earlier words or word groups, make pauses, and use many filler *uuhhmm*. Indeed, we found that when speakers must mention an ethnic group by name (which, as we saw, they avoid by using pronouns), an ethnic name is often preceded by uhhmm's, hesitations, pauses, or repairs. The same phenomena can be witnessed when negative statements are made about some ethnic group.

At these various local levels of discourse analysis, thus, we have also found that people who speak about minorities are engaged in a highly delicate social task, requiring permanent monitoring of the execution of several major strategies, such as those of positive self-presentation and negative other-presentation. Yet, people not only speak as individuals who want to make a good impression even when saying bad things about others; they essentially talk as group members and speak about others as group members, and this opposition between *us* and *them* also underlies many semantic, stylistic, and rhetorical operations. In general, then, we find that systematic discourse analysis is both a subtle and very powerful tool in the assessment of the expression and communication of ethnic prejudice. At the same time, it allows us, as was obvious in the subsequent chapters as well, to make inferences about underlying cognitive and social properties or constraints of ethnic prejudice and their in-group communication.

3. Sources

More than in most work in communication, we have focused on the "message" itself. For our kind of data, in fact, we have hardly more than what people tell us. We have no experimental ways or other methods to access or control properties of the communicative context, such as sources and their properties or effects of communication. Thus, the information about sources people use for their information and opinions about ethnic groups also had to be drawn from our interviews. This limitation also has an important advantage, though: Using people's own accounts of their sources shows us when, where, how, and why such source mentions are made, and especially how people have interpreted, stored, and retrieved information attributed to specific sources.

Obviously, these sources are multiple and may be any type of discourse or communication in a very diverse communicative environment, ranging from parent-child talk, children's books, comics, novels, movies, and TV programs, to news reports, academic studies, and informal everyday conversation. A systematic analysis of some 200 "source passages" in our interviews suggests, however, that in their own talk, people predominantly refer to conversations with other people and to the media, especially TV and the newspaper. In accordance with other work, we found that the media are typically used for information and as an opinion basis regarding the more public topics of immigration, social issues (welfare, unemployment), crime, and discrimination. Personal information is especially relevant for topics that deal with everyday conflicts in the community, such as noises, smells, decay, children, clothing, food, or typically "ethnic" habits. Such information and opinions are often derived from stories and their evaluative conclusions.

In the majority of cases, people use other sources to mention negative "facts" about minorities, even when they do not agree with such facts or opinions themselves. In other words, it is not only implicitly but even explicitly "known" that talk about minorities is negative. For instance, many people know and acknowledge that the press is sometimes biased, for instance, by mentioning the ethnic background of suspects in crime stories. Generally, at least in the Netherlands, TV is perceived as a somewhat more positive source than the newspaper, which, especially in the high-contact (mixed) neighborhoods is often used as "independent evidence" for people's own stories and opinions.

What people say they hear (and remember) from others is in line with the general ethnic opinions we have derived from conversational topics in general: Minorities live on welfare, cause unemployment, take our houses, and are involved in crime, and they especially do not respect our norms and ways of everyday living. At the same time, speakers sometimes assert both that "you hear that all the time" and "people don't dare to talk about this anymore." This shows that stereotypical talk is known and socially shared in the community, but on the other hand, that people realize that there is also a social norm—if not concrete fear for retaliation—against negative talk about minorities. Note, though, that for different topics and opinions, different personal sources may be cited: General negative talk is attributed to "others" or unspecified neighbors. Family members, friends, and colleagues are typical sources for everyday experiences of competition or nuisances (noise, dirt), especially in the high-contact areas. In the low-contact areas, people understandably refer to the media more often as a source (and generally the more-educated and wealthy people seldom talk about themselves or their family members when experiences or opinions about minorities are involved).

From our analysis of the role of sources in prejudiced talk and the communication of racism, we may first conclude that the media play a decisive role, not only in agenda setting, but also in defining the (negative) dominant consensus and preferred interpretations for many public events. For most dominant group members, especially those from low-contact neighborhoods, they are virtually the only source for ethnic information. Even for stories that usually are communicated in interpersonal talk, such as everyday "nuisance" events, the media provide the—often uncritical—public diffusion among the population at large.

4. The cognitive dimensions of prejudice and prejudiced talk

The next major task of this book has been a sketch of the cognitive structures and strategies of ethnic prejudices and their expression in talk. Prejudice was analyzed as a specific form of negative ethnic attitude, which was described as a hierarchically and categorically organized cluster of negative general opinions in semantic (social) memory. Such prejudice schemata organize socially shared ethnic opinions according to categories such as origin, appearance, socioeconomic status, sociocultural properties, or personal characteristics of ethnic groups and their members. It was stressed, therefore, that prejudice is *not* just an individual attitude of (bigoted) people, but a structurally founded form of social cognition. In addition to such general, social schemata, individual group members interpret ethnic events

392   Communicating Racism

in terms of concrete (situation) models, stored in episodic memory. It is at this point that we can explain why and how people have "biased" representations, and hence biased recall, of such events, for instance, in the stories we analyzed. Thus, at all levels of the (also schematically organized) model of an ethnic event, people may use their general prejudices to represent the setting, the circumstances, and especially the ethnic participants and their actions in a negative way. Even when ethnic agents are unknown, as in many crime or urban decay stories, they can be inserted into the model by default.

Similarly, people follow complex strategies to "reinterpret" ongoing events in ways that are negative for ethnic minorities. Of course, urban decay, housing shortage, and unemployment are routinely blamed on the foreigners, and indeed, such is the way dominant group members often "see" otherwise unclear events, or overgeneralize from single models. In other words, we found that ethnic prejudice not only involves schematically organized negative attitude structures, but also concrete, subjective, personally variable models, on one hand, and more general strategies of ethnic information processing on the other hand.

The systematic discourse analysis of the interviews allowed us to find many textual signals for these underlying structures and strategies. Thus, topical analysis shows what kind of general opinions are used and presupposed and how they may be ordered. Once identified as "foreigners" or as "immigrants" under the category of Origin, and as "looking different" or as "Black" in the Appearance category, the major opinions about minorities are organized by the socioeconomic category (they live off welfare—our money—and take our jobs and houses), the sociocultural category (they have a different mentality, do not respect our norms and values, do not speak our language, and so on), and the "Personal" category (they are deviant, aggressive, criminal). Depending on context, and hence allowing personal variation, these socially shared opinions may be further organized by concepts such as "threat" or "competition," as well as by the usually implicit notion of "inferiority."

Despite historical and socioeconomic differences between different countries, we finally found that prejudices, and their structures and strategic uses, are very similar in different countries of Western Europe and North America. People say sometimes identical things about Mexican immigrants in the United States or California, and about Turkish "guest workers" in the Netherlands or Western Germany. We have interpreted such ethnic prejudices as functional in the maintenance of power and privileges of the dominant White majorities in these countries.

5. Interpersonal communication

Based on the results of the analysis of prejudiced discourse and cognitions, we devised a complex theoretical framework for the interpersonal communication of ethnic attitudes. Earlier work on communication and persuasion was critically examined in the light of these theoretical advances: With a better model of discursive and cognitive structures and strategies, we are able to analyze in more detail which processes are involved in the interpersonal communication of racism. For instance, we now know in more explicit detail how people interpret ethnic encounters as well as accounts, such as stories, about such encounters, and how they organize such information in memory. We have also shown exactly how prejudiced talk is being produced on the basis of biased models and prejudiced schemata, on one hand, and within the framework of cognitively represented models of the communicative situation, on the other hand. Such communicative situation models, for instance, represent the contextual constraints speakers use in the strategic management of self-presentation: They have a dynamic model of the possible models hearers may develop about themselves as speakers and as competent social members. That is, the cognitive and discursive moves of impression management are being analyzed in the wider framework of social interaction. Part of the social membership and competence thus displayed, for instance, depends on the enhancement of credibility, for which people have a wide choice of strategic moves, such as plausible argumentation and convincing storytelling.

The cognitive and interactional analysis also permitted us to design a framework for the acquisition and persuasive changes of ethnic opinions and attitudes. Thus, overgeneralization can be easily defined in terms of model abstraction based on single or isolated models of ethnic encounters, whereas even general attitude formation is possible by analogy with schemata for other ethnic groups. People show in their talk which perceived facts or opinions expressed by others (or the media) are found convincing, and how they dealt with persuasive aspects of prejudiced talk or text. In agreement with much other work on persuasion, we found generally that people tend to focus on, and selectively store and retrieve, the model and schema information that is consistent with their own ethnic attitudes.

This is why they tend to mention other sources primarily as strategic confirmation or justification of their own ethnic opinions. It is in this way that a dominant ethnic consensus is being developed and communicated within the in-group. Both the media and most other people do not provide counterinformation that may be used to give up prevailing ethnic opinions. Indeed, one of the most notable properties of a racist society is that it is not antiracist. At most, the general norms or values may be inconsistent with racism, but actual discourse, such as everyday talk and the media, as well as commonsense interpretations and evaluations are not based on systematically developed knowledge and beliefs about the processes of prejudice and discrimination. People have not learned to contradict racist thought and talk, and our data suggest that they hardly ever do so. The prevailing practices, also in communication, are protective of the status quo, and hence of the dominance of the White majority.

6. The social context

Finally, we briefly embedded the analysis of prejudiced discourse, cognition, and communication in a wider social context. Indeed, a major thesis of this book has been that neither prejudiced opinions, nor the everyday talk based on them, are purely personal or individual, but essentially social and group oriented. The structure of ethnic attitudes in cognition is determined by important social dimensions of groups (origin, socioeconomic status, and so on). Talk about minorities appeared to be functional in social interaction processes of self-presentation. Similarly, prejudiced talk was shown to have multiple social functions, such as the signaling of group membership, the display of social competence, the sharing of socially relevant experiences and cognitions, or the illustration and prescription of effective social action against minorities.

We also examined the role of some traditional social categories in the types of ethnic attitudes, such as neighborhood, gender, age, and education. The results, drawn from a quantified qualitative analysis of the interviews in terms of prejudice levels, show agreement with earlier work on the role of such indicators. There are no significant differences between men and women, although women tend to adhere to the more moderate prejudice patterns. The elderly generally appear more prejudiced than younger people, probably also because of less education and less contact: Especially in the Netherlands, the younger generation is for the first time in history growing up with sometimes substantial numbers of ethnic minorities in the classroom. People in the mixed, high-contact neighborhoods usually score higher on the prejudice scale, but again part of this is probably due to differences in education and socioeconomic status. As such, more experiences and "ethnic contact" do not guarantee lower prejudice levels, but people who appear to mention regular personal contacts with minority group members are usually less prejudiced. Most consistent, also in other research, is the generally positive role of education, which also interacts with other factors, such as age, neighborhood, and occupation, of course.

We have interpreted these results with care, however. Thus, clearly, higher levels of education generally make people more aware of the subtleties of prevailing norms and morals. Even more than for other group members, the better educated resent being qualified as prejudiced or racist: After all, they see themselves as the moral guides of society. Also, they have more practice with specific forms of talk, such as interviews, argumentation, and communicative "meta-statements." Indeed, they hardly ever talk about themselves, but mainly about "others." Independent evidence about the actual prejudices of, and the discrimination by, the better educated, namely, obtained through the systematic analysis of the everyday experiences of minority group members, shows that in the appropriate contexts, the better educated hardly show less negative opinions and actions. And then, such elites have more influence and power, so that their prejudice and discrimination have vastly more negative consequences for minorities than the sometimes more blatant prejudices of the powerless.

Illustrated on the example of the media portrayal of a new group of immigrants, still unknown with the population at large, namely, of Tamil refugees in the Netherlands, we finally postulated that ethnic prejudices in society are preformulated by the elite. Politicians, academics, national or local leaders of government or other institutions, as well as the crucial journalists, are the elite groups that provide first descriptions and interpretations of new or salient ethnic groups. By their routine or easy access to the press, they are able to provide preferred interpretations of immigration, social conflicts, and intergroup relations in general. They are the first to signal the "problems" assumed to be caused by immigration, the strains on the job or housing market or on the welfare system, and they are among those who particularly focus on cultural differences and problems (language, education, religion, and so on). The interviews showed that large parts of the public adopt these interpretations and evaluations: A few people mitigate or even denounce such official reactions, but most will accept or even accentuate such dominant group opinions.

This assumption about the elitist preformulation of ethnic opinions also provides further perspective to the analysis of the everyday, conversational communication of racism. It confirms the importance of the media in the active diffusion of the ethnic consensus, but also provides insight into the sources and the credibility evaluations people assign to their own ethnic opinions: If the elite think so, we have even more reason to adopt that opinion.

7. Open problems and future research

This study has examined many aspects of the discursive, cognitive, and communicative dimensions of ethnic prejudice and racism. We have analyzed a wealth of natural data, and developed new theoretical frameworks across several disciplinary boundaries. New insights into the social problems of prejudice and racism have been obtained, but at the same we have more generally learned about social information processing and the communication of beliefs and attitudes. Most of these aspects, however, have been examined here for the first time, and lack of data or theoretical details forced us to provide only an initial account. Let us, therefore, finally mention a few areas in which problems have remained unresolved, evidence unaccounted for, or theory not yet developed.

Although we now have a reasonably accurate first description of prejudiced talk, each level of analysis needs, of course, more detailed inquiry. We have examined topics, but have not yet analyzed in detail how topics are sequenced and changed or how topics are specified semantically at the micro level. We have found some general properties of stories about minorities, especially at the macro level, but the more local organization of such narratives has been studied only in part. At the global level, the structures of argumentation especially need more attention because these play such a vital role in the "defense" of ethnic opinions. Strategic semantic moves have received extensive analysis, but as for the other structures, we need to assess which of them are characteristic of prejudiced talk, and which appear in "delicate" talk more generally. Stylistic analysis has been reduced to a few observations about lexical choice and the use of "distancing" deictic expressions, whereas a rhetorical analysis did not go beyond the description of a few "figures of style." Together with a more extensive account of the proper conversational properties of spontaneous talk, these are the more "local" elements of prejudiced talk that need detailed analysis in the future.

A more general as well as fundamental problem has been the status of informal interviews as data. We assumed that such interviews are sufficiently close to "real" talk. Yet, there are, of course, differences, and a major task for future research is to obtain such "real" conversations about ethnic minorities, and to study the proper interactional structures of such talk in "real" social contexts. We have found that in interviews, even highly prejudiced people tend to express themselves in a rather moderate way, for instance, because of the now well-established role of positive self-presentation. We need to know, however, how majority group members talk about minorities without such social constraints, such as among family members and close friends.

The sources of ethnic prejudices and their formulation have been analyzed in terms of people's own spontaneous accounts of such interpersonal contacts or media influences. It goes without saying that a complete analysis requires independent evidence about the sources people actually have access to, use, and interpret. Detailed fieldwork, as well as experiments, are necessary to understand how people use the media in the acquisition of ethnic information, and with whom they talk themselves in the diffusion of such information.

The cognitive theory of prejudice presented in this book is a further step in the new developments of the study of the structures and strategies of social, intergroup cognition. Yet, the theory of the memory organization of ethnic attitudes has not yet gone beyond the simple structural analysis of hierarchical categorization. We need to know how organizing concepts such as "threat," "competition," or "inferiority" provide further organization to such attitude structures, and we need to know more about the strategies applied in the formation, retrieval, and uses of ethnic prejudices. Despite our attempt to explain the link between cognition and social structures of racism, we still know very little, also more generally, about the nature of the social constraints on memory organization, and hence about the relationships between prejudice and discrimination.

This lack of complete insight into the cognitive structures and strategies involved also implies that we could only provide partial explanations of the processes of interpersonal communication and persuasion. We have some fair amount of knowledge about the understanding and memory storage of prejudiced talk, and about how people build models of ethnic encounters. However, we do not yet fully understand when and how people "adopt" ethnic opinions or integrate these in more complex attitude structures. The roles of general norms, values, goals, and ideologies have been repeatedly emphasized, but we have no explicit theoretical framework of how such social or group cognitions are related to scripts, attitudes, or episodic models. Again, the deficiencies of a more general theory of social cognition made themselves felt also in the more specific theory of ethnic cognition and communication.

Our final attempt to contextualize the communication of ethnic prejudice within a wider social framework was—intentionally—limited to a few observations. If ethnic prejudice and its communication are essentially social and group based, as we have repeatedly stressed, then, of course, a proper intra- and intergroup theory of prejudice and racism should be the basis for a further account of the functions and processes of prejudiced talk in society. And, of course, we need to know much more about the social mechanisms that underlie the apparent variations in prejudice types or the differences in talk about ethnic minorities. What exactly is the role of education, and, therefore, of the elite, in the formulation and distribution of ethnic opinions? How can such a role be integrated into a wider, macro-level account of the role of institutions in the reproduction of racism? Similarly, how do race and class interact in the acquisition and uses of ethnic prejudices and their communicative reproduction? In other words, many of the crucial, macro-level questions about the nature of racism have remained unanswered in our study.

And yet, our micro-level approach to racism, as well as the new insights obtained about the discursive, cognitive, and communicative dimensions of the reproduction of racism in society, at the same time suggest new ways of analyzing these wider, macro-level problems. For instance, instead of formulating very abstract and general hypotheses about the role of the elite, of the media, or of schooling, we now have a more subtle, more detailed and more powerful set of instruments to examine their contribution to the reproduction of racism, namely, through a detailed analysis of their communicative interactions in society. Similarly, we also have some more insight into the ways structural (macro) constraints operate at the level of the concrete (micro) enactment of racism. It is a major task for future research to spell out such relationships.

Appendix:
Some Information About
Data Collection

The Neighborhoods

The interviews that are used as the major data base for this book were conducted in different neighborhoods in Amsterdam and San Diego. These neighborhoods were selected according to the percentage of ethnic minority groups living in those neighborhoods (according to city statistics of Amsterdam, and the 1980 Census for San Diego). In Amsterdam, four groups of interviews were conducted between 1980 and 1985. The first group, which was exploratory, was held in different neighborhoods all over the city, in both ethnically mixed (De Pijp, Dapperbuurt, Bijlmermeer), and predominantly white neighborhoods (Zuid, Buitenveldert, Noord). The second group of interviews was held in a poor, ethnically mixed inner-city neighborhood (Transvaalbuurt). The third group of interviews was conducted in a wealthy neighborhood (Beethovenstraat and surroundings). The last group (of which only a few data were used in this study) was held in another poor, ethnically mixed neighborhood (Staatsliedenbuurt). The reason for interviewing in Amsterdam only, apart from practical reasons, was that in that city, ethnic groups are most salient and diverse, with several neighborhoods with high proportions (up to 25%) of immigrant workers and people from Surinam.

In San Diego, we focused on two different types of neighborhoods as well. We interviewed White people in the Golden Hill area, which according to census data has a substantial number of Blacks and Mexicans or Mexican Americans. In order to be able to compare with similar everyday perceptions and experiences in Amsterdam, we did not interview White people who live in neighborhoods that are nearly completely Black (e.g., in East San Diego) or Mexican (Barrio Logan, San Ysidro). As a predominantly White and socioeconomically more privileged (incomes often more than $50,000) neighborhood, we focused on University City, with some interviews held also in La Jolla and Del Mar. Again, the choice to interview in San Diego was based mostly on practical grounds, such as the presence of the University of California at San Diego, where I was able to spend my sabbatical for research, but it also happens to allow comparisons with Amsterdam, a city of the same size, also a port, and it is just like Amsterdam with an ethnic minority population that is not as high as some other big cities in the United States (though substantially higher than Amsterdam).

The reason these two classes of neighborhoods were chosen were twofold. First, ethnically mixed neighborhoods provide more everyday occasions for perception, interaction, and experiences with regard to ethnic minority group members. Second, the mixed neighborhoods are mostly the poorer inner-city areas where several important social features, such as unemployment, lower-level jobs, urban decay, and "street crime" are more common, and possibly linked to explanations people may have of their ethnic opinions. Conversely, the nonmixed, wealthier neighborhoods would allow us to study how people talk about minorities without actual everyday experiences.

Selection

Interviewees were selected by more or less arbitrarily asking people in a given neighborhood whether they would be willing to participate in an interview (see below, for modes of address). Interviewers went to public places such as cafes, laundromats, shops, and parks, or they went from door to door. Each interviewer, however, had to make sure to balance the choice of interviewees on "observable" characteristics, namely, age and gender, so that both men and women, as well as people from different ages, would be interviewed. Because not all interviews could be held during the evenings or weekends, there is some bias in some of the Amsterdam interview groups toward people who happened to be at home (unemployed, housewives, elderly) during the daytime.

Similar selection took place in San Diego, but there the "door to door" method was much harder for several reasons than in Amsterdam: Simply, especially, of course, in the evening, people are not inclined to let interviewers come in—even females—for well-known "reasons": fear of crime in the United States, especially in the cities, is much more pronounced than in Amsterdam. Second, in the predominantly White and wealthy neighborhoods, people are even less prepared to let in unknown interviewers. One student-interviewer had to try 200 addresses in this way to get 2 interviews! Third, in the mixed neighborhoods, the percentage of minorities is such that just going from door to door would enhance the probability that a member of one of the minority groups would open the door, which would require the application of somewhat difficult strategies (like asking directions, or purportedly looking for family X), to avoid interviewing such persons. After all, the project was dealing with White prejudice and racism, and we are convinced that interviewing minority members regarding their opinions and experiences about such a delicate topic, requires minority researchers (Essed, 1984).

Obviously, this informal method of selection does not yield representative groups of White citizens. Although we took care to interview in socially and economically different neighborhoods (which provides sufficient variation in education, occupation, income, and the like), and to select people from different ages as well as both men and women, we had no way to select people in a more systematic way. In fact, we were glad for every interview people were willing to grant us. Despite this kind of selection, the overall variation of interviewees is substantial and more than satisfactory for the kind of qualitative data we were trying to get.

Interviewers

Most interviewers were students participating in research-oriented classes that focused on different topics of our project. Each research class and hence all fieldwork in a given neighborhood usually lasted three months, with an additional two months for further analysis. Participation was usually in partial fulfillment of a major or minor degree in discourse analysis (in Amsterdam), or as part of the requirements of a communications class (at UCSD). The majority of the students were majoring in one of the humanities or social sciences. Most students were between 20 and 25 years of age (the Californians mostly around 20). Few of the students had previous interview experience, but several instruction, discussion, and practice sessions preceded actual interviewing. For this type of interviewing, we did not find significant or otherwise interesting differences between interviewers who did and who did not have extensive interview experience. Linguistically, this, is of course, hardly surprising, as all students have, of course, more general conversational competence. Experiences we had in the earlier interview groups were very instructive in conducting the later interviews. Interviewers were both male and female, although the research classes mostly attracted more female than male students—a phenomenon which by itself would require interesting explanations (indeed, often female students appeared to be interested because of similarities between ethnic and gender prejudices). Each student conducted about 4 interviews on average, transcribed it, and at the end of a semester wrote a paper based on the interviews—also those by the other students—and against the background of theoretical literature about a specific dimension of the project. Some of the data reported in this book draw on some of these papers.

The Interviews

As we have explained in several chapters of this book, the interviews should be as close as possible to natural conversations people have with strangers. This meant that, although there was a general interview-schema, few questions were previously established, nor was a fixed question-ordering respected. Once the interview was "running," and the topic of "ethnic minorities" had come up, the initiative was mostly left to the interviewees, with occasional follow-up questions by the interviewer. The interviewer, thus, acted like a "visitor" to the neighborhood, and mostly did not have to simulate ignorance when asking about the experiences of people and properties of their neighborhoods. The interviews in Amsterdam, often conducted at the interviewees' homes, lasted about 45 minutes on average. The California interviews, mostly conducted in public places, were usually shorter (30 minutes on average).

Most interviews were requested and started without specific mention of the "ethnic" topic. People were asked to participate in an (anonymous) interview about their opinions and experiences with respect to "this neighborhood" or "this city." After sometimes long introductory sections of the interview, the topic was then shifted to "people" in the neighborhood, which allowed a natural transition to other ethnic groups. In fact, especially in Amsterdam, where ethnic immigration is more recent and more salient, most people would themselves spontaneously introduce "foreigners." Most of the rest of the interview would then remain with that topic. Yet, we also conducted interviews that explicitly announced the topic "ethnic minorities," but we have not found differences in those interviews, nor more or less acceptance of being interviewed. The code numbers of the interviews, only in Amsterdam, of which the main topic was thus overtly announced, are followed by an "x" (for eXplicit). Code numbers for interviews with more than one person are followed by "a," "b," or "c."

The interviewers introduced themselves as what they were—students of the University of Amsterdam, or of the University of California at San Diego, respectively. One strategy of obtaining interviews was to formulate the request in terms of "help" the people could provide by giving an interview the student "had to make for a class." We assumed that such a request for help would have a stronger appeal than a less personal request for an interview (for an institution or company), and would also generate a less formal interview context. Only a few people did probe deeper into the reasons and goals of the interview. In fact, many, especially in the high-contact neighborhoods in Amsterdam, were actually very much willing to talk. In many respects, the interview provided them with an opportunity to air the complaints, resentment, or frustrations they felt about the neighborhood or the minorities, an occasion that seldom arises outside of personal contacts with family members, acquaintances, or neighbors. In several interviews, it was also mentioned that people "don't dare to talk about these things" anymore, for fear of "retaliation." In the low-contact, wealthier neighborhoods, it was generally much more difficult to find people who were willing to grant an interview.

The interview itself was minimally preprogrammed. As soon as the topic "minorities" was brought up, the interviewer usually "followed" the spontaneous talk of the interviewee, only occasionally "coming back" to the main topic after—sometimes lengthy—detours. The topical schema that would guarantee a minimal comparability of the interviews consisted of the—mnemotechnically useful, because the interviewers were instructed not to use notes or read questions—different "contexts" of ethnic experiences and opinions: first next-door neighbors and the neighborhood or the city, then public places such as buses or streetcars or shops, next the job, and finally schools if the interviewee had children. Also sources, such as personal talk and contacts and the media were mostly brought up, often by the interviewees themselves. For each main "contextual" topic, typical questions would pertain to people's reaction to the local (city) or national government's policies regarding minorities.

The second group of interviews (those prefaced by II-), carried out in an ethnically mixed, poor inner-city neighborhood (Transvaalbuurt) in Amsterdam, specifically focused on personal "experiences" people had had, and whether they could tell stories about them. The main aim of that part of the project was to focus on the structures and functions of narratives in talk about ethnic minorities. The third group of interviews, carried out in a White, wealthy neighborhood, placed the focus on reasons and arguments people formulated for their opinions, and in their analysis we paid attention especially to argumentative structures. The fourth group of interviews in Amsterdam focused on information sources, such as family members, acquaintances, friends, neighbors, or the media.

The interviews held in San Diego were, of course, tuned to topics that were specifically salient in the United States and Southern California, such as affirmative action (jobs, education, housing, busing), the immigration of Asians and Mexicans, the position of "illegal aliens" and recent legislation pertaining to "guest labor." The code numbers of these interviews are preceded by "A" (for "America").

Requests to tape the interview were always made and nearly always granted (3 refusals for more than 170 interviews). The interviewees were pledged anonymity and confidentiality of the interview and interview data.

Transcripts

All interviews were transcribed literally, including hesitation phenomena, false starts, repairs, and so on. Yet, lengthy passages that had no direct or indirect bearing to the main "ethnic topic" were not transcribed in order to save time and xerox costs. Transcription conventions were followed, but not the highly precise ones that have become customary in conversational analysis (by which one minute of conversation on average takes one hour of transcription). For hundreds of hours of interviewing, such a method would be both practically impossible and hardly relevant for most of our analytical goals. Moreover, it is impossible to train students to carry out such an expert task in the course of a few weeks. For a more detailed study of typical conversational phenomena, such more detailed transcripts are, however, necessary.

References

Abelson, R.P. (1973). The structure of belief systems. In R. C. Schank & K.M. Colby (Eds.), *Computer models of thought and language* (pp. 287-340). San Francisco: Freeman.

Abelson, R. P. (1976). Script processing in attitude formation and decision making. In J. S. Carroll & J. W. Payne (Eds.), *Cognition and social behavior* (pp. 33-46). Hillsdale, NJ: Erlbaum.

Abelson, R. P., Aronson, E., McGuire, W. J., Newcomb, T. M., Rosenberg, M. J., & Tannenbaum, P.H. (Eds.). (1968). *Theories of cognitive consistency. A sourcebook.* Chicago: Rand McNally.

Abelson, R. P., & Rosenberg, M. J. (1958). Symbolic psycho-logic: A model of attitude cognition. *Behavioral Science, 3,* 1-13.

Adorno, T. W., Frenkel-Brunswik, E., Levinson, D. J., & Sanford, R. N. (1950). *The authoritarian personality.* New York: Harper.

Allport, G. W. (1954). *The nature of prejudice.* New York: Doubleday, Anchor Books.

Allport, G. W., & Postman, L. (1947). *The psychology of rumor.* New York: Holt.

Amir, Y. (1976). The role of intergroup contact in change of prejudice and ethnic relations. In P. Katz (Ed.), *Towards the elimination of racism* (pp. 245-308). New York: Pergamon Press.

Anderson, J. R. (1980). *Cognitive psychology and its implications.* San Francisco: Freeman.

Antaki, C. (Ed.). (1981). *The psychology of ordinary explanations.* London: Academic Press.

Apostle, R. A., Glock, C. Y., Piazza, T., & Suelze, M. (1983). *The anatomy of racial attitudes.* Berkeley: University of California Press.

Argyle, M., Furnham, A., & Graham, J. A. (1981). *Social situations.* Cambridge: Cambridge University Press.

Arkin, R. M. (1981). Self-presentation styles. In J. T. Tedeschi (Ed.), *Impression management. Theory and social psychological research* (pp. 311-333). New York: Academic Press.

Asch, S. E. (1951). Effects of group pressure upon the modification and distortion of judgment. In H. Guetskow (Ed.), *Groups, leadership and men.* Pittsburgh: Carnegie.

Atkinson, J. M., & Heritage, J. (Eds.). (1984). *Structures of social action.* Cambridge: Cambridge University Press.

Atwood, E., Sohn, A. B., & Sohn, H. (1978). Daily newspaper contributions to community discussion. *Journalism Quarterly, 58,* 557-576.

Austin, J. L. (1962). *How to do things with words.* London: Oxford University Press.

Bagley, C. (1973). *The Dutch plural society.* London: Oxford University Press.

Bagley, C., & Verma, G. K. (1979). *Racial prejudice, the individual and society.* Farnborough: Saxon House.

Bagley, C., Verma, G. K., Mallick, K., & Young, L. (1979). *Personality, self-esteem and prejudice.* Farnborough: Saxon House.

Banton, M. (1983). *Racial and ethnic competition.* Cambridge: Cambridge University Press.

Bartlett, F. C. (1932). *Remembering*. London: Cambridge University Press.

Bauman, R., & Sherzer, J. (Eds.). (1974). *Explorations in the ethnography of speaking*. London: Cambridge University Press.

Becker, L. (1982). The mass media and citizen assessment of issue importance: A reflection on agenda-setting research. In D. C. Whitney, E. Wartella, & S. Windahl (Eds.), *Mass communication review yearbook* (pp. 521-536). Beverly Hills, CA: Sage.

Beinstein, J. (1975). Conversations in public places. *Journal of Communication*, (Winter), 85-95.

Berger, C. R., & Bradac, J. R. (1982). *Language and social knowledge*. London: Arnold.

Berkowitz, L. (1972). Frustrations, comparisons, and other sources of emotional arousal as contributors to social unrest. *Journal of Social Issues, 28*, 77-92.

Bernstein, B. (1971). *Class, codes, and control*. London: Routledge & Kegan Paul.

Bettelheim, B., & Janovitz, M. (1964). *Social change and prejudice*. New York: Free Press.

Bettinghaus, E. P. (1973). *Persuasive communication* (2nd ed.). New York: Holt, Rinehart & Winston.

Billig, M. (1976). *Social psychology and intergroup relations*. London: Academic Press.

Black, J. B., Galambos, J. A., & Read, S. J. (1984). Comprehending stories and social situations. In R. S. Wyer, Jr., & T. K. Srull (Eds.), *Handbook of social cognition* (Vol. 1, pp. 119-160). Hillsdale, NJ: Erlbaum.

Black, J. B., & Wilensky, R. (1979). An evaluation of story grammars. *Cognitive Science, 3*, 213-229.

Blumler, J. G., & Katz, E. (Eds.). (1974). *The uses of mass communications*. Beverly Hills, CA: Sage.

Bodenhausen, G. V., & Wyer, R. S., Jr. (1985). Effects of stereotypes on decision making and information-processing strategies. *Journal of Personality and Social Psychology, 48*, 267-282.

Bogardus, E. S. (1925). Measuring social distances. *Journal of Applied Sociology, 9*, 299-308.

Bogle, D. (1973). *Toms, coons, mulattoes, mammies and bucks: An interpretive history of Blacks in American films*. New York: Viking Books.

Bottomore, T. B. (1964). *Elites and society*. London: C.A. Watts.

Bourdieu, P., & Passeron, J-C. (1977). *Reproduction in education, society and culture*. Beverly Hills, CA: Sage.

Bourne, J. (1980). Cheerleaders and ombudsmen: The sociology of race relations in Britain. *Race and Class, 21*, 331-352.

Bovenkerk, F., Brunt, L. et al. (1985). *Vreemde gasten, gemengde gevoelens* [Strange guests, mixed feelings]. Meppel (The Netherlands): Boom.

Bower, G. H. (1980). Mood and memory. *American Psychologist, 36*, 129-148.

Bowser, B., & Hunt, R. G. (Eds.). (1981). *The impact of racism on white Americans*. Beverly Hills, CA: Sage.

Breckler, S. J. (1984). Empirical validation of affect, behavior, and cognition as distinct components of attitude. *Journal of Personality and Social Psychology, 47*, 1191-1205.

Brewer, M. B., & Campbell, D. T. (1976). *Ethnocentrism and intergroup attitudes: East-African evidence*. New York: Halstead Press.

Brewer, W. F., & Nakamura, G. V. (1984). The nature and functions of schemas. In R. S. Wyer, Jr. & T. K. Srull (Eds.), *Handbook of social cognition* (Vol. 1, pp. 119-160). Hillsdale, NJ: Erlbaum.

Brigham, J. C. (1971). Ethnic stereotypes. *Psychological Bulletin, 76,* 15-38.

Brown, G., & Yule, G. (1983). *Discourse analysis.* London: Cambridge University Press.

Brown, L. B. (1973). *Ideology.* Harmondsworth: Penguin Books.

Brown, P., & Fraser, C. (1979). Speech as a marker of situation. In K. R. Scherer & H. Giles (Eds.), *Social markers in speech* (pp. 33-62). Cambridge: Cambridge University Press.

Brown, P., & Levinson, S. C. (1978). Universals in language use: Politeness phenomena. In E. N. Goody (Ed.), *Questions and politeness.* Cambridge: Cambridge University Press.

Brown, R., & Gilman, A. (1960). The pronouns of power and solidarity. In T. A. Sebeok (Ed.), *Style in language* (pp. 253-277). Cambridge: MIT Press.

Burgoon, M., & Bettinghaus, E. P. (1980). Persuasive message strategies. In M. E. Roloff & G. R. Miller (Eds.), *Persuasion: New directions in theory and research* (pp. 141-170). Beverly Hills, CA: Sage.

Button, G., & Casey, N. (1984). Generating topic: The use of topic initial elicitors. In J. M. Atkinson & J. Heritage (Eds.), *Structures of social action* (pp. 167-190). Cambridge: Cambridge University Press.

Cacioppo, J. T., Harkins, S. G., & Petty, R. E. (1981). The nature of attitudes and cognitive responses and their relationship to behavior. In R. E. Petty, T. M. Ostrom, & T. C. Brock (Eds.), *Cognitive responses in persuasion* (pp. 31-54). Hillsdale, NJ: Erlbaum.

Cacioppo, J. T., & Petty, R. E. (1979). Effects of message repetition and position on cognitive responses, recall and persuasion. *Journal of Personality and Social Psychology, 37,* 97-109.

Cantor, N., & Mischel, W. (1977). Traits as prototypes: Effects on recognition memory. *Journal of Personality and Social Psychology, 35,* 38-48.

Cantor, N., & Mischel, W. (1979). Prototypes in person perception. In L. Berkowitz (Ed.), *Advances in experimental social psychology* (Vol 12, pp. 3-52). New York: Academic Press.

Cappella, J. N., & Folger, J. P. (1980). An information-processing explanation of attitude-behavior inconsistency. In D. P. Cushman & R. D. McPhee (Eds.), *Message-attitude-behavior relationship* (pp. 149-194). New York: Academic Press.

Carbonell, J., Jr. (1979). *Subjective understanding: Computer models of belief systems.* Doctoral dissertation, Yale University.

CCCS (Centre for Contemporary Cultural Studies, Birmingham). (1978). *On ideology.* London: Hutchinson.

CCCS (1982). *The empire strikes back. Race and racism in 70s Britain.* London: Hutchinson.

Castles, S. (1984). *Here for good. Western Europe's New Ethnic Minorities.* London: Pluto Press.

Chabrol, C. (1973). *La logique du récit.* Paris: Seuil.

Chafe, W. L. (Ed.). (1980). *The pear stories.* Hillsdale, NJ: Erlbaum.

Chaiken, S. (1979). Communicator physical attractiveness and persuasion. *Journal of Personality and Social Psychology, 37,* 1387-1397.

Chaiken, S. (1980). Heuristic versus systematic information processing and the use of source versus message cues in persuasion. *Journal of Personality and Social Psychology, 39,* 752-766.

Chapman, L. J. (1967). Illusory correlation in observational report. *Journal of Verbal Learning and Verbal Behavior, 6,* 151-155.

Chase, A. (1975). *The legacy of Malthus. The social costs of the new scientific racism.* Urbana: University of Illinois Press.

Chibnall, S. (1977). *Law-and-order news*. London: Tavistock.

Cialdini, R. B., & Petty, R. E. (1981). Anticipatory opinion effects. In R. E. Petty, T. M. Ostrom, & T. C. Brock (Eds.), *Cognitive responses in persuasion* (pp. 217-236). Hillsdale, NJ: Erlbaum.

Cicourel, A. V. (1964). *Method and measurement in sociology*. New York: Free Press.

Cicourel, A. V. (1973). *Cognitive sociology*. Harmondsworth: Penguin.

Cicourel, A. V. (1980). Three models of discourse analysis. The role of social structure. *Discourse Processes, 3,* 101-132.

Coenen, A.W.M., & van Dijk, J.J.M. (1976). *Misdaadverslaggeving in Nederland* [Crime reporting in the Netherlands]. The Hague: Ministry of Justice, WODC (Scientific Research and Documentation Centre).

Cohen, S. (1980). *Folk devils and moral panics* (2nd rev. ed.). Oxford: Robertson.

Cohen, S., & Young, J. (Eds.). (1981). *The manufacture of news. Deviance, social problems and the mass media* (2nd rev. ed.). London: Constable/Sage.

Communications 8 (1966). L'analyse structurale du récit. Paris: Seuil.

Corbett, E.P.J. (1971). *Classical rhetoric for the modern student*. New York: Oxford University Press.

Coulthard, M. (1977). *Introduction to discourse analysis*. London: Longman.

Cox, O. C. (1948). *Caste, class & race*. New York: Doubleday.

CRC (Community Relations Commission). (1976). *Some of my best friends. A report on race relations attitudes*. London: Author.

Critcher, C., Parker, M., & Sondhi, R. (1977). Race in the provincial press: A case study of five West Midlands papers. In *UNESCO, ethnicity in the media* (pp. 25-192). Paris: Unesco.

Crocker, J., Fiske, S. T., & Taylor, S. E. (1984). Schematic bases of belief change. In J. R. Eiser (Ed.), *Attitudinal judgment* (pp. 197-226). New York: Springer Verlag.

Cronkhite, G., & Liska, J. R. (1980). The judgment of communicant acceptability. In M. E. Roloff & G. R. Miller (Eds.), *Persuasion: New directions in theory and research* (pp. 101-140). Beverly Hills, CA: Sage.

Cushman, D. P., & McPhee, R. D. (Eds.). (1980). *Message-attitude-behavior relationship*. New York: Academic Press.

de Beaugrande, R., & Dressler, W. U. (1981). *Introduction to text linguistics*. London: Longman.

den Uyl, M., & van der Wurff, A. (1984). Ethnische attitude in informele gesprekken [Ethnic attitude in informal conversations]. *TTT, 4,* 147-176.

De Mott, J., & Roberts, R. (1979). *White racism, blacks, and mass communication: An instruction source bibliography*. Paper presented at the annual meeting of the Association for Education in Journalism, Houston, TX, August.

Deschamps, J-C. (1977). *L'attribution et la catégorisation sociale*. Bern: Peter Lang.

Deschamps, J-C. (1983). Social attribution. In J. Jaspars, F. D. Fincham, & M. Hewstone (Eds.), *Attribution theory and research* (pp. 223-240). London: Academic Press.

Deutsch, M., & Gerard, H. B. (1955). A study of normative and informational social influence upon individual judgment. *Journal of Abnormal and Social Psychology, 51,* 629-636.

Dik, S. C. (1978). *Functional grammar*. Amsterdam: North Holland.

Dixon, R. (1977). *Catching them young. I. Sex, race and class in children's fiction*. London: Pluto Press.

Doise, W. (1984). Social representations, inter-group experiments and levels of analysis. In R. M. Farr, & S. Moscovici (Eds.), *Social representations* (pp. 255-268). Cambridge: Cambridge University Press.

Downing, J. (1980). *The media machine.* London: Pluto Press.

Duncan, B. L. (1976). Differential social perception and attribution of intergroup violence: Testing the lower limits of stereotyping Blacks. *Journal of Personality and Social Psychology, 34,* 590-598.

Duranti, A. (1985). Socio-cultural dimensions of discourse. In T. A. van Dijk (Ed.), *Handbook of discourse analysis* (Vol 1, pp. 193-230). London: Academic Press.

Eagly, A. H. (1974). Comprehensibility of persuasive arguments as a determinant of opinion change. *Journal of Personality and Social Psychology, 29,* 758-773.

Eagly, A. H. (1981). Recipient characteristics as determinants of responses to persuasion. In R. E. Petty, T. M. Ostrom, & T. C. Brock (Eds.), *Cognitive responses in persuasion* (pp. 173-196). Hillsdale, NJ: Erlbaum.

Eagly, A. H., Chaiken, S., & Wood, W. (1981). An attributional analysis of persuasion. In J. Harvey, W. Ickes, & R. Kidd (Eds.), *New directions in attribution research* (Vol. 3). Hillsdale, NJ: Erlbaum.

Ebel, M., & Fiala, P. (1983). Sous le consensus, la xénophobie (Memoires et documents 16). Lausanne: Institut de Sciences Politiques.

Ehlich, K. (Ed.). (1980). *Erzählen im Alltag.* Frankfurt: Suhrkamp.

Ehrlich, H. J. (1973). *The social psychology of prejudice.* New York: John Wiley.

Eiser, J. R. (Ed.). (1984). *Attitudinal judgment.* New York: Springer.

Eiser, J. R., & Stroebe, W. (1972). *Categorization and social judgement.* London: Academic Press.

Eiser, J. R., & van der Pligt, J. (1984). Accentuation theory, polarization, and the judgment of attitude statements. In J. R. Eiser, (Ed.), *Attitudinal judgment* (pp. 43-63). New York: Springer.

Elias, N., & Scotson, J. L. (1965). *The established and the outsiders.* London: Cass & Company.

Emler, N. (1982). *The interpersonal origins of knowledge.* Paper presented at the conference on "New Perspectives in the Experimental Study of the Social Development of Intelligence," Geneva, June. Unpublished manuscript, University of Dundee, Department of Psychology.

Emler, N. (1983). *Why gossip is important: The role of gossip in managing relations with a network of acquaintances.* Paper presented at the second International Conference on Social Psychology and Language, Bristol, July. University of Dundee, Department of Psychology.

Erickson, F., & Shultz, J. (1982). *The counselor as gatekeeper: Social interaction in interviews.* New York: Academic Press.

Ericsson, K. A., & Simon, H. A. (1984). *Verbal reports as data.* Cambridge: MIT Press.

Essed, P.J.M. (1982). Racisme and feminisme. *Socialisties—Feministiese Teksten* (Sara Publications, Amsterdam), *7,* 9-41.

Essed, P.J.M. (1984). *Alledaags racisme* [Everyday racism]. Amsterdam: Sara. (English translation in preparation.) Claremont, CA: Hunter House.

Essed, P.J.M. (1986). *The Dutch as an everday problem.* Amsterdam: University of Amsterdam, Center for Race and Ethnic Studies.

Estel, B. (1983). *Soziale Vorurteile und soziale Urteile.* Opladen: Westdeutscher Verlag.

Farr, R. M., & Moscovici, S. (Eds.). (1984). *Social representations.* Cambridge: Cambridge University Press.

Ferrara, A. (1985). Pragmatics. In T. A. van Dijk (Ed.), *Handbook of discourse analysis* (Vol. 2, pp. 137-158). London: Academic Press.

Ferro, M. (1981). *Comment on raconte l'histoire aux enfants à travers le monde entier.* Paris: Payot.

Festinger, L. (1957). *A theory of cognitive dissonance*. Stanford, CA: Stanford University Press.
Fine, G. A. (1985). Rumors and gossiping. In T. A. van Dijk (Ed.), *Handbook of discourse analysis* (Vol. 3, pp. 223-237). London: Academic Press.
Fischer, P. L., & Lowenstein, R. L. (Eds.). (1967). *Race and the news media*. New York: Praeger.
Fishbein, M., & Ajzen, I. (1975). *Belief, attitude, intention and behavior*. Reading, MA: Addison-Wesley.
Fishbein, M., & Ajzen, I. (1981). Acceptance, yielding and impact. In R. E. Petty, T. M. Ostrom, & T. C. Brock (Eds.), *Cognitive responses in persuasion* (pp. 339-359). Hillsdale, NJ: Erlbaum.
Fishman, M. (1980). *Manufacturing the news*. Austin: University of Texas Press.
Fiske, S. T. (1981). Social cognition and affect. In J. Harvey (Ed.), *Cognition, social behavior and the environment*. Hillsdale, NJ: Erlbaum.
Fiske, S. T., & Taylor, S. E. (1984). *Social cognition*. Reading, MA: Addison-Wesley.
Forgas, J. P. (1979). *Social episodes*. London: Academic Press.
Forgas, J. P. (1981). Affective and emotional influences on episode representations. In J. P. Forgas (Ed.), *Social cognition* (pp. 165-180). London: Academic Press.
Forgas, J. P. (Ed.). (1981). *Social cognition. Perspectives on everyday understanding*. London: Academic Press.
Fowler, R., Hodge, B., Kress, G., & Trew, T. (1979). *Language and control*. London: Routledge & Kegan Paul.
Furnham, A., & Argyle, M. (Eds.). (1981). *The psychology of social situations*. Oxford: Pergamon Press.
Galtung, J., & Ruge, M. H. (1965). The structure of foreign news. *Journal of Peace Research, 2,* 64-91.
Gans, H. (1979). *Deciding what's news*. New York: Pantheon Books.
Gardner, R. C., Taylor, D. M., & Feenstra, H. J. (1970). Ethnic stereotypes: Attitudes or beliefs? *Canadian Journal of Psychology, 24,* 321-334.
Garfinkel, H. (1967). *Studies in ethnomethodology*. Englewood Cliffs, NJ: Prentice Hall.
Gilbert, S. J. (1976). Empirical and theoretical extensions of self-disclosure. In G. R. Miller (Ed.), *Explorations in interpersonal communication* (pp. 197-215). Beverly Hills, CA: Sage.
Glazer, N. (Ed.). (1985). *Clamor at the gates. The new American immigration*. San Francisco: ICS (Institute of Contemporary Studies) Press.
Glock, C. Y., & Siegelman, E. (Eds.). (1969). *Prejudice U.S.A.* New York: Praeger.
Goffman, E. (1959). *The presentation of self in everyday life*. Garden City, NY: Doubleday.
Goffman, E. (1967). *Interaction ritual*. Garden City, NY: Doubleday.
Goffman, E. (1969). *Strategic interaction*. Philadelphia: University of Pennsylvania Press.
Goody, E. N. (Ed.). (1978). *Questions and politeness*. London: Cambridge University Press.
Gouldner, A. W. (1979). *The future of intellectuals and the rise of the new class*. London: Macmillan.
Granberg, D. (1984). Attributing attitudes to groups. In J. R. Eiser (Ed.), *Attitudinal judgment* (pp. 85-108). New York: Springer.
Grant, P. R., & Holmes, J. G. (1981). The integration of implicit personality theory, schemas and stereotype images. *Social Psychology Quarterly, 44,* 107-115.
Greenberg, B. S., & Atkin, C. (1978). *Learning about minorities from television*. Paper presented at the annual meeting of the Association for Education in Journalism, Seattle.

Greenberg, B. S., & Mazingo, S. L. (1976). Racial issues in mass media institutions. In P. A. Katz (Ed.), *Towards the elimination of racism* (pp. 309-340). New York: Pergamon Press.

Greenberg, J., & Pyszczynski, T. (1985). The effects of an overheard ethnic slur on evaluations of the target: How to spread a social disease. *Journal of Experimental Social Psychology, 21,* 61-72.

Greenwald, A. G. (1968). Cognitive learning, cognitive response to persuasion and attitude change. In A. G. Greenwald, T. C. Brock, & T. M. Ostrom (Eds.), *Psychological foundations of attitudes.* New York: Academic Press.

Greenwald, A. G., Brock, T. C., & Ostrom, T. M. (Eds.). (1968). *Psychological foundations of attitudes.* New York: Academic Press.

Gurwitz, S. B., & Dodge, K. A. (1977). Effects of confirmations and disconfirmations on stereotype-based attributions. *Journal of Personality and Social Psychology, 35,* 495-500.

Gutiérrez, F. (1978). *Through Anglo eyes: Chicanos as portrayed in the news media.* Paper presented at the annual meeting of the Association for the Education in Journalism, Seattle.

Hall, S., Critcher, C., Jefferson, T., Clarke, J., & Roberts, B. (1978). *Policing the crisis: Mugging, the state and law and order.* London: Methuen.

Hamilton, D. L. (1976). Cognitive biases in the perception of social groups. In J. S. Carroll & J. W. Payne (Eds.), *Cognition and social behavior* (pp. 81-94). Hillsdale, NJ: Erlbaum.

Hamilton, D. L. (1979). A cognitive-attributional analysis of stereotyping. In L. Berkowitz (Ed.), *Advances in experimental social psychology* (pp. 53-84). New York: Academic Press.

Hamilton, D. L. (1981). Illusory correlation as a basis for stereotyping. In D. L. Hamilton (Ed.), *Cognitive processes of stereotyping and intergroup behavior* (pp. 115-144). Hillsdale, NJ: Erlbaum.

Hamilton, D. L., & Gifford, R. K. (1976). Illusory correlation in interpersonal perception. *Journal of Experimental Social Psychology, 12,* 392-407.

Hamilton, D. L., Katz, L. B., & Leirer, V. O. (1980). Organizational processes in impression formation. In R. Hastie, T. M. Ostrom, E. B. Ebbesen, R. S. Wyer, D. L. Hamilton, & D. E. Carlston (Eds.), *Person memory: The cognitive basis of social perception* (pp. 121-154). Hillsdale, NJ: Erlbaum.

Hamilton, D. L., & Rose, T. L. (1980). Illusory correlation and the maintenance of stereotypic beliefs. *Journal of Personality and Social Psychology, 39,* 832-845.

Hamilton, D. L. (Ed.). (1981). *Cognitive processes in stereotyping and intergroup behavior.* Hillsdale, NJ: Erlbaum.

Harré, R. (1979). *Social being.* Oxford: Blackwell.

Harré, R., & Secord, P. F. (1972). *The explanation of social behavior.* Oxford: Blackwell.

Hartmann, P., & Husband, C. (1974). *Racism and the mass media.* London: Davis-Poynter.

Hass, R. G. (1981). Effects of source characteristics on cognitive responses and persuasion. In R. E. Petty, T. M. Ostrom, & T. C. Brock (Eds.), *Cognitive responses in persuasion* (pp. 141-172). Hillsdale, NJ: Erlbaum.

Hass, R. G. (1981). Presentational strategies and the social expression of attitudes: Impression management within limits. In J. T. Tedeschi (Ed.), *Impression management. Theory and social psychological research* (pp. 127-146). New York: Academic Press.

Hastie, R. (1981). Schematic principles in human memory. In E. T. Higgins, C. P. Herman, & M. P. Zanna (Eds.), *Social cognition. The Ontario Symposium* (Vol. 1, pp. 39-88). Hillsdale, NJ: Erlbaum.

Hastie, R., Ostrom, T. M., Ebbesen, E. B., Wyer, R. S., Hamilton, D. L., & Carlston, D. E. (Eds.). (1980). *Person memory: The cognitive basis of social perception*. Hillsdale, NJ: Erlbaum.

Hastie, R., Park, B., & Weber, R. (1984). Social memory. In R. S. Wyer, Jr., & T. K. Srull (Eds.), *Handbook of social cognition* (Vol. 2 pp. 151-212). Hillsdale, NJ: Erlbaum.

Heider, F. (1946). Attitudes and cognitive organization. *Journal of Psychology, 21*, 107-112.

Heider, F. (1958). *The psychology of interpersonal relations*. New York: John Wiley.

Heritage, J. (1984). A change-of-state token and aspects of sequential placement. In J. M. Atkinson & J. Heritage (Eds.), *Structures of social action* (pp. 299-345). Cambridge: Cambridge University Press.

Hewstone, M. (1983). The role of language in attribution processes. In J. Jaspars, F. D. Fincham, & M. Hewstone (Eds.), *Attribution theory and research: Conceptual, developmental and social dimensions* (pp. 241-260). London: Academic Press.

Hewstone, M., & Jaspars, J. (1982). Explanations for racial discrimination: The effect of group discussion on intergroup attributions. *European Journal of Social Psychology, 12*, 1-16.

Higgins, E. T. (1981). The "communication game": Implications for social cognition and persuasion. In E. T. Higgins, C. P. Herman, & M. P. Zanna (Eds.), *Social cognition. The Ontario Symposium* (Volume 1, pp. 343-392). Hillsdale, NJ: Erlbaum.

Higgins, E. T., Herman H. P., & Zanna, M. P. (Eds.). (1981). *Social cognition. The Ontario Symposium*. (Vol. 1), Hillsdale, NJ: Erlbaum.

Himmelfarb, S., & Eagly, A. H. (Eds.). (1974). *Readings in attitude change*. New York: John Wiley.

Hoffmann, L., & Even, H. (1984). *Soziologie der Ausländerfeindlichkeit*. Weinheim and Basel: Beltz.

Hovland, C. I., & Janis, I. L. (Eds.). (1959). *Personality and persuasibility*. New Haven: Yale University Press.

Hovland, C. I., Janis, I. L., & Kelley, J. J. (1953). *Communication and persuasion*. New Haven, CT: Yale University Press.

Hovland, C. I., Luchins, A. S., Mandell, W., Campbell, E. H., Brock, T. C., McGuire, W. J., Feierabend, R. L., Anderson, N. H. (Eds.). (1957). *The order of presentation in persuasion*. New Haven, CT: Yale University Press.

Hovland, C. I., Lumsdaine, A. A., & Sheffield, F. D. (1949). *Experiments on mass communication*. Princeton: Princeton University Press.

Hovland, C. I., & Rosenberg, M. J. (Eds.). (1960). *Attitude organization and change*. New Haven, CN: Yale University Press.

Hovland, C. I., & Weiss, W. (1951). The influence of source credibility on communication effectiveness. *Public Opinion Quarterly, 15*, 635-650.

Howard, J. & Rothbart, M. (1980). Social categorization and memory for ingroup and outgroup behavior. *Journal of Personality and Social Psychology, 38*, 301-310.

Husband, C. (Ed.). (1982). *"Race" in Britain*. London: Hutchinson.

Hyman, H. H. (1975). *Interviewing in social research*. Chicago: University of Chicago Press.

Hymes, D. (1962). The ethnography of speaking. In T. Gladwin & W. C. Sturtevant (Eds.), *Anthropology and human behavior* (pp. 13-53). Washington, DC: Anthropological Society of Washington.

Insko, C. A. (1967). *Theories of attitude change*. New York: Appleton-Century-Crofts.

Insko, C. A. (1981). Balance theory and phenomenology. In R. E. Petty, T. M. Ostrom, & T. C. Brock (Eds.), *Cognitive responses in persuasion* (pp. 309-338). Hillsdale, NJ: Erlbaum.

Jackman, M. R. (1978). General and applied tolerance: Does education increase commitment to racial integration? *American Journal of Political Science, 22,* 302-324.

Jaspars, J., Fincham, F. D., & Hewstone, M. (Eds.). (1983). *Attribution theory and research: Conceptual, developmental and social dimensions.* London: Academic Press.

Jaspars, J., & Fraser, C. (1984). Attitudes and social representations. In R. M. Farr & S. Moscovici (Eds.), *Social representations* (pp. 101-124). Cambridge: Cambridge University Press.

Janis, I. L., & Feshbach, S. (1953). Effects of fear-arousing communications. *Journal of Abnormal and Social Psychology, 48,* 78-92.

Johnson-Laird, P. N. (1983). *Mental models.* Cambridge: Cambridge University Press.

Jones, J. M. (1972). *Prejudice and racism.* Reading, MA: Addison-Wesley.

Jones, R. A. (1982). Perceiving other people: Stereotyping as a process of social cognition. In A. G. Miller (Ed.), *In the eye of the beholder. Contemporary issues in stereotyping,* (pp. 41-91). New York: Praeger.

Jourard, S. (1971). *Self disclosure: An experimental analysis of the transparent self.* New York: John Wiley.

Judd, C. M., & Johnson, J. T. (1984). The polarizing effects of affective intensity. In J. R. Eiser (Ed.), *Attitudinal judgment* (pp. 65-82). New York: Springer Verlag.

Kahane, H. (1971). *Logic and contemporary rhetoric.* Belmont, CA: Wadsworth.

Kahneman, D., Slovic, P., Tversky, A. (Eds.). (1982). *Judgment under uncertainty: Heuristics and biases.* Cambridge: Cambridge University Press.

Kahneman, D., & Tversky, A. (1973). On the psychology of prediction. *Psychological Review, 80,* 237-251.

Katz, D., & Braly, K. W. (1933). Racial stereotypes of 100 college students. *Journal of Abnormal and Social Psychology, 28,* 280-290.

Katz, E., & Lazarsfeld, P. F. (1955). *Personal influence.* New York: Free Press.

Katz, E., & Szecskö, T. (Eds.). (1981). *Mass media and social change.* Beverly Hills, CA: Sage.

Katz, P. A. (1976). The acquisition of racial attitudes in children. In P. A. Katz (Ed.), *Towards the elimination of racism* (pp. 125-154). New York: Pergamon.

Katz, P. A. (Ed.). (1976). *Towards the elimination of racism.* New York: Pergamon.

Keenan, J. M., MacWhinney, B., & Mayhew, D. (1977). Pragmatics in memory: A study of natural conversation. *Journal of Verbal Learning and Verbal Behavior, 16,* 549-560.

Keim, I. (1984). Talking about foreigners. Some ethnographic remarks. In P. Auer & A. di Luzio (Eds.), *Interpretive sociolinguistics. Migrants—children—migrant children* (pp. 259-283). Tübingen: Narr.

Kelley, H. H. (1967). Attribution in social psychology. *Nebraska Symposium on Motivation, 15,* 192-238.

Kelley, H. H. (1972). Attribution in social interaction. In E. E. Jones et al. (Eds.), *Attribution: Perceiving the causes of behavior.* Morristown, NJ: General Learning Press.

Kelley, H. H. (1983). Perceived causal structures. In J. Jaspars, F. D. Fincham, & M. Hewstone (Eds.), *Attribution theory and research: Conceptual, developmental and social dimensions* (pp. 343-369). London: Academic Press.

Kelman, H. C. (1958). Compliance, identification and internalization: Three processes of attitude change. *Journal of Conflict Resolution, 2,* 51-60.

Kieras, D. E. (1982). A model of reader strategy for abstracting main ideas from simple technical prose. In T. A. van Dijk (Ed.), *New developments in cognitive models of discourse processing* [Special issue]. *Text 2,* (1/3), 47-82.

Kinder, D. R., & Sears, D. O. (1981). Prejudice and politics: Symbolic racism versus racial threats to the good life. *Journal of Personality and Social Psychology, 40,* 414-431.

Kinloch, G. C. (1981). *Ideology and contemporary sociological theory.* Englewood Cliffs, NJ: Prentice-Hall.

Kintsch, W. (1977). *Memory and cognition.* New York: John Wiley.

Kintsch, W., & Greene, E. (1978). The role of culture-specific schemata in the comprehension and recall of stories. *Discourse Processes, 1,* 1-13.

Kintsch, W., & van Dijk, T. A. (1975). Comment on se rappelle et on résume des histoires. *Langages, 40,* 98-128.

Kintsch, W., & van Dijk, T. A. (1978). Toward a model of text comprehension and production. *Psychological Review, 85,* 363-394.

Kintsch, W., & Yarbrough, J. C. (1982). The role of rhetorical structure in text comprehension. *Journal of Educational Psychology, 74,* 828-834.

Knopf, T. A. (1975). *Rumors, race and riots.* New Brunswick, NJ: Transaction Books.

Knorr-Cetina, K., & Cicourel, A. V. (Eds.). (1981). *Advances in social theory and methodology. Towards an integration of micro- and macrosociologies.* London: Routledge & Kegan Paul.

Kreckel, M. (1981). *Communicative acts and shared knowledge in natural discourse.* London: Academic Press.

Labov, W. (1972). The transformation of experience in narrative syntax. In W. Labov, *Language in the inner city* (pp. 354-396). Philadelphia, PA: University of Pennsylvania Press.

Labov, W., & Fanshel, D. (1977). *Therapeutic discourse.* New York: Academic Press.

Labov, W., & Waletzky, J. (1967). Narrative analysis. Oral versions of personal experience. In J. Helm (Ed.), *Essays on the verbal and visual arts* (pp. 12-44). Seattle: University of Washington Press.

Ladner, J. A. (Ed.). (1973). *The death of white sociology.* New York: Random House, Vintage Books.

Lange, A., & Westin, C. (1981). *Etnisk diskriminering och sosial identitet.* Stockholm: Liber Forlag.

LaPierre, R. T. (1933). Attitudes vs. actions. *Social Forces, 13,* 230-237.

Lausberg, H. (1960). *Handbuch der literarischen rhetorik* (Vols. 1-2). Munich: Hueber Verlag.

Lawrence, E. (1982). Just plain common sense: The roots of "racism." In CCCS (Centre for Contemporary Cultural Studies, Birmingham), *The empire strikes back. Race and racism in 70s Britain* (pp. 47-94). London: Hutchinson.

Leech, G. N. (1983). *Principles of pragmatics.* London: Longman.

Levelt, W.J.M. (1983). Monitoring and self-repair in speech. *Cognition, 14,* 41-104.

Levin, J., & Levin, W. (1982). *The function of discrimination and prejudice* (2nd ed.). New York: Harper & Row.

Levine, P. W., & Campbell, D. T. (1972). *Ethnocentrism: Theories of conflict, ethnic attitudes and group behavior.* New York: John Wiley.

Levinson, S. C. (1983). *Pragmatics.* Cambridge: Cambridge University Press.

Lindsay, P. H., & Norman, D. A. (1972). *Human information processing.* New York: Academic Press.

Lingle, J. H., & Ostrom, T. M. (1981). Principles of memory and cognition in attitude formation. In R. E. Petty, T. M. Ostrom, & T. C. Brock (Eds.), *Cognitive responses in persuasion* (pp. 399-420). Hillsdale, NJ: Erlbaum.

Linville, P. W., & Jones, E. E. (1980). Polarized appraisals of out-group members. *Journal of Personality and Social Psychology, 38*, 689-703.

Lord, C., Ross, L., & Lepper, M. E. (1979). Biased assimilation and attitude polarization: The effects of prior theories on subsequently considered evidence. *Journal of Personality and Social Psychology, 37*, 2098-2109.

Love, R. E., & Greenwald, A. C. (1978). Cognitive responses to persuasion as mediators of opinion change. *Journal of Social Psychology, 104*, 231-241.

Lukas, J. A. (1985). *Common ground*. New York: Knopf.

Lukes, S. (1974). *Power. A radical view*. London: Macmillan.

Mandler, J. M. (1984). *Stories, scripts, and scenes: Aspects of schema theory*. Hillsdale, NJ: Erlbaum.

Mandler, J. M., & Johnson, N. S. (1978). Remembrance of things parsed: Story structure and recall. *Cognitive Psychology, 9*, 11-151.

Markus, H. (1977). Self-schemata and processing information about the self. *Journal of Personality and Social Psychology, 35*, 63-78.

Marslen-Wilson, W., Levy, E., & Tyler, L. K. (1982). Producing interpretable discourse: The establishment and maintenance of reference. In R.J. Jarvella & W. Klein (Eds.), *Speech, place and action* (pp. 339-378). Chichester: Wiley.

Martins, D. (1982). Influence of affect on comprehension of text. In T. A. van Dijk (Ed.), *New developments in cognitive models of discourse processing*. [Special issue]. *Text, 2* (1/3), 141-154.

Maynard, R. A. (1974). *The Black man on film: Racial stereotyping*. Rochelle Park, NJ: Hayden Book Co.

McArthur, L. Z. (1981). What grabs you? The role of attention in impression formation and social attribution. In E. T. Higgins, C. P. Herman, & M. P. Zanna (Eds.), *Social cognition. The Ontario Symposium* (Vol. 1, pp. 201-246). Hillsdale, NJ: Erlbaum.

McCombs, M. E., & Shaw, D. L. (1972). The agenda-setting function of the press. *Public Opinion Quarterly, 36*, 176-187.

McGuire, W. J. (1969). The nature of attitude and attitude change. In G. Lindzey & E. Aronson (Eds.), *Handbook of social psychology: Vol. 3. The individual in a social context* (2nd ed.) Reading, MA: Addison-Wesley.

McGuire, W. J. (1972). Persuasion, resistance and attitude change. In I. de Sola Pool & W. Schramm (Eds.), *Handbook of Communication* (pp. 216-252). Chicago: Rand McNally.

McGuire, W. J., & Papageorgis, D. (1962). Effectiveness of forewarning in developing resistance to persuasion. *Public Opinion Quarterly, 26*, 24-34.

McLaughlin, M. L. (1984). *Conversation. How talk is organized*. Beverly Hills & London: Sage.

Meindl, J. R., & Lerner, M. J. (1984). Exacerbation of extreme responses to an outgroup. *Journal of Personality and Social Psychology, 47*, 71-84.

Meinhardt, R. (1982). *Ausländerfeindlichkeit. Eine Dokumentation*. Berlin: EXpress Edition.

Meinhardt, R. (Ed.). (1984). *Türken raus? Oder verteidigt den sozialen Frieden. Beiträge gegen die Ausländerfeindlichkeit*. Reinbek bei Hamburg: Rowohlt.

Miles, R. (1982). *Racism and migrant labour*. London: Routledge & Kegan Paul.

Miles, R., & Phizacklea, A. (Eds.). (1979). *Racism and political action in Britain*. London: Routledge & Kegan Paul.

Miller, A. G. (Ed.). (1982). *In the eye of the beholder: Contemporary issues in stereotyping*. New York: Praeger.

Miller, G. R. (Ed.). (1976). *Explorations in interpersonal communication*. Beverly Hills, CA: Sage.
Miller, N., & Brewer, M. B. (Eds.). (1984). *Groups in contact. The psychology of desegregation*. New York: Academic Press.
Miller, N., & Colman, D. E. (1981). Methodological issues in analyzing the cognitive mediation of persuasion. In R. E. Petty, T. M. Ostrom, & T. C. Brock (Eds.), *Cognitive responses in persuasion* (pp. 105-126). Hillsdale, NJ: Erlbaum.
Mills, C. W. (1956). *The power elite*. London: Oxford University Press.
Milner, D. (1983). *Children and race. Ten years on*. London: Ward Lock Educational.
Minsky, M. (1975). A framework for representing knowledge. In P. Winston (Ed.), *The psychology of computer vision*. Chicago: McGraw-Hill.
Moscovici, S. (1976). *Social influence and social change*. London: Academic Press.
Moscovici, S. (1984). The phenomenon of social representations. In R. M. Farr & S. Moscovici (Eds.), *Social representations* (pp. 3-70). Cambridge: Cambridge University Press.
Moscovici, S., & Faucheux, C. (1972). Social influence, conformity bias, and the study of active minorities. In L. Berkowitz (Ed.), *Advances in experimental social psychology* (Vol. 6). New York: Academic Press.
Mullard, C. (1985). *Racism, power and resistance*. London: Routledge & Kegal Paul.
Neisser, U. (Ed.). (1982). *Memory observed. Remembering in natural contexts*. San Francisco: Freeman.
Nisbett, R. E., & Ross, L. (1980). *Human inferences. Strategies and shortcomings of social judgment*. Englewood Cliffs, NJ: Prentice-Hall.
Nisbett, R. E., & Wilson, T. D. (1977). Telling more than we can know: Verbal reports on mental processes. *Psychological Review, 84*, 231-259.
Norman, D. A., & Rumelhart, D. E. (Eds.) (1975). *Explorations in cognition*. San Francisco: Freeman.
Norman, R. (1976). When what is said is important: A comparison of expert and attractive sources. *Journal of Experimental Social Psychology, 12*, 294-300.
Norton, R. (1983). *Communicator style*. Beverly Hills, CA: Sage.
Oberg, K., Bergman, E., & Swedin, B. (Eds.). (1981). *Att leva med mångfalden*. Stockholm: Liber Förlag.
O'Keefe, B. J., & Delia, J. G. (1982). Impression formation and message production. In M. E. Roloff & C. R. Berger (Eds.), *Social cognition and communication* (pp. 33-72). Beverly Hills, CA: Sage.
Osgood, C. E., & Tannenbaum, P. H. (1955). The principle of congruity in the prediction of attitude change. *Psychological Review, 62*, 42-55.
Packard, V. (1957). *The hidden persuaders*. New York: Pocket Books.
Park, B., & Rothbart, M. (1982). Perception of out-group homogeneity and levels of social categorization: Memory for the subordinate attributes of in-group and out-group members. *Journal of Personality and Social Psychology, 42*, 1051-1068.
Pearson, F. H. (1976). A content analysis of the treatment of Black people and race relations in United States history textbooks. Doctoral dissertation, University of Minnesota, Minneapolis.
Pettigrew, T. F. (1958). Personality and sociocultural factors in intergroup attitudes: A cross-national comparison. *Journal of Conflict Resolution, 2*, 29-42.
Pettigrew, T. F. (1979). The ultimate attribution error: Extending Allport's cognitive analysis of prejudice. *Personality and Social Psychology Bulletin, 5*, 461-476.
Pettigrew, T. F. (1981). Extending the stereotype concept. In D. L. Hamilton (Ed.), *Cognitive processes in stereotyping and intergroup behavior* (pp. 303-331). Hillsdale, NJ: Erlbaum.

Pettigrew, T. F. (1987). *New patterns of racism. American race relations since 1960.* Cambridge, MA: Harvard University Press.

Petty, R. E., & Cacioppo, J. T. (1979). Issue involvement can increase or decrease persuasion by enhancing message-relevant cognitive responses. *Journal of Personality and Social Psychology, 37,* 1915-1926.

Petty, R. E., & Cacioppo, J. T. (1981). *Attitudes and persuasion: Classic and contemporary approaches.* Dubuque, IA: Wm. C. Brown Co.

Petty, R. E., & Cacioppo, J. T., & Heesacker, M. (1981). The use of rhetorical questions in persuasion: A cognitive response analysis. *Journal of Personality and Social Psychology, 40,* 432-440.

Petty, R. E., Ostrom, T. M., & Brock, T. C. (Eds.). (1981). *Cognitive responses in persuasion.* Hillsdale, NJ: Erlbaum.

Phizacklea, A. & Miles, R. (1979). Working class racist beliefs in the inner city. In R. Miles & A. Phizacklea (Eds.), *Racism and political action in Britain* (pp. 93-123). London: Routledge & Kegan Paul.

Phizacklea, A., & Miles, R. (1980). *Labour and racism.* London: Routledge & Kegan Paul.

Pierce, C.M. et al. (1978). An experiment in racism: TV commercials. In C.M. Pierce (Ed.), *Television and education* (pp. 62-88). Beverly Hills, CA: Sage.

Plett, H. F. (1975). *Textwissenschaft und Textanalyse.* Munich: Fink.

Plett, H. F. (Ed.). (1977). *Rhetorik.* Munich: Fink.

Polanyi, L. (1978). False starts can be true. *Proceedings of the Annual Meeting of the Berkeley Linguistic Society, 4,* 628-639.

Polanyi, L. (1979). So what's the point? *Semiotica, 25,* 207-242.

Polanyi, L. (1985). *Analyzing the American story.* Norwood, NJ: Ablex.

Pomerantz, A. (1984). Agreeing and disagreeing with assessments: Some features of preferred/dispreferred turn shapes. In J. M. Atkinson & J. Heritage (Eds.), *Structures of social action* (pp. 57-101). Cambridge: Cambridge University Press.

Pomerantz, A. (1984). Giving a source or basis: The practice in conversation of telling "How I know." *Journal of Pragmatics, 8,* 607-625.

Propp, V. (1958). Morphology of the folktale. Bloomington, IN: Indiana University Press. (Original Russian work published 1928, Moscow)

Pyszscynski, T. A., & Greenberg, J. (1981). Role of disconfirmed expectations in the instigation of attributional processing. *Journal of Personality and Social Psychology, 40,* 31-38.

Quastoff, U. (1980). *Erzählen in Gesprächen.* Tübingen: Narr.

Rabbie, J. M., & Wilkens, G. (1971). Intergroup competition and its effect on intragroup and intergroup relationships. *European Journal of Social Psychology, 1,* 215-234.

Ratcliffe, P. (1981). *Racism and reaction. A profile of Handsworth.* London: Routledge & Kegan Paul.

Reardon, K. K. (1981) *Persuasion: Theory and context.* Beverly Hills, CA: Sage.

Redmond, R. (1979). *Racisme in kinderboeken* [Racism in children's books]. The Hague: Bibliotheek & Lectuurcentrum.

Rex, J., & Tomlinson, S. (1979). *Colonial immigrants in a British city.* London: Routledge & Kegan Paul.

Reeves, F. (1983). *British racial discourse.* Cambridge: Cambridge University Press.

Robinson, J. P., & Levy, M. R. (1986). *The main source: Learning from television news.* Beverly Hills, CA: Sage.

Robinson, C. J. (1983). *Black Marxism. The making of the Black radical tradition.* London: Zed Books.

Roberts, C. (1975). The presentation of blacks in television network newscasts. *Journalism Quarterly, 52,* 50-55.

Rokeach, M. (1968). *Beliefs, attitudes and values.* San Francisco: Jossey-Bass.
Rokeach, M. (1973). *The nature of human values.* New York: Free Press.
Roloff, M. E., & Berger, C. R. (Eds.). (1982). *Social cognition and communication.* Beverly Hills, CA: Sage.
Roloff, M. E., & Miller, G. R. (Eds.). (1980). *Persuasion. New directions in theory and research.* Beverly Hills, CA: Sage.
Rommetveit, R. (1984). The role of language in the creation and transmission of social representations. In R. M. Farr & S. Moscovici (Eds.), *Social representations* (pp. 331-360). Cambridge: Cambridge University Press.
Rosch, E. (1978). Principles of categorization. In E. Rosch & B. B. Lloyd (Eds.), *Cognition and categorization.* Hillsdale, NJ: Erlbaum.
Rosch, E., & Lloyd, B. B. (Eds.). (1978). *Cognition and categorization.* Hillsdale, NJ: Erlbaum.
Rose, T. L. (1981). Cognitive and dyadic processes in intergroup contact. In D. L. Hamilton (Ed.), *Cognitive processes in stereotyping and intergroup behavior* (pp. 259-302). Hillsdale. NJ: Erlbaum.
Rosenberg, M. J., Hovland, C. I., McGuire, W. J., Abelson, R. P., & Brehm, J. W. (1960). *Attitude organization and change. An analysis of consistency among attitude components.* New Haven, CT: Yale University Press.
Ross, L. (1977). The intuitive psychologist and his shortcomings: Distortions in the attribution process. In L. Berkowitz (Ed.), *Advances in experimental social psychology* (Vol. 10). New York: Academic Press.
Rothbart, M. (1981). Memory processes and social beliefs. In D. L. Hamilton (Ed.), *Cognitive processes in stereotyping and intergroup behavior* (pp. 145-181). Hillsdale, NJ: Erlbaum.
Rothbart, M., Dawes, R., & Park, B. (1984). Stereotyping and sampling biases in intergroup perception. In J. R. Eiser (Ed.), *Attitudinal judgment* (pp. 109-134). New York: Springer Verlag.
Rothbart, M., Evans, M., & Fulero, S. (1979). Recall for confirming events: Memory processes and the maintenance of social stereotypes. *Journal of Experimental Social Psychology, 15,* 343-355.
Rumelhart, D. E. (1975). Notes on a schema for stories. In D. G. Bobrow & A. Collins (Eds.), *Representation and understanding* (pp. 211-236). New York: Academic Press.
Rumelhart, D. E. (1984). Schemata and the cognitive system. In R. S. Wyer, Jr., & T. K. Srull (Eds.), *Handbook of social cognition* (Vol. 3, pp. 161-188). Hillsdale, NJ: Erlbaum.
Sacks, H. (1985). The inference-making machine. Notes on observability. In T. A. van Dijk (Ed.), *Handbook of discourse analysis* (Vol. 3, pp. 13-23). London: Academic Press.
Sacks, H., Schegloff, E. A., & Jefferson, G. A. (1974). A simplest systematics for the organization of turntaking for conversation. *Language, 50,* 696-735.
Sagar, H. A., & Schofield, J. W. (1980). Racial and behavioral cues in black and white children's perceptions of ambiguously aggressive acts. *Journal of Personality and Social Psychology, 39,* 590-598.
Sandell, R. (1977). *Linguistic style and persuasion.* London: Academic Press.
Sawyer, A. (1981). Repetition, cognitive responses, and persuasion. In R. E. Petty, T. M. Ostrom, & T. C. Brock (Eds.), *Cognitive responses in persuasion* (pp. 237-262). Hillsdale, NJ: Erlbaum.
Schank, R. C. (1982). *Dynamic memory.* Cambridge: Cambridge University Press.
Schank, R. C., & Abelson, R. P. (1977). *Scripts, goals, plans and understanding.* Hillsdale, NJ: Erlbaum.

Schank, R. C., & Carbonell, J., Jr. (1978). The Gettysburg Address: Representing social and political acts. In Findler (Ed.), *Associative networks*. New York: Academic Press.

Schary, D. (1969). The mass media and prejudice. In C. Y. Glock & E. Siegelman (Eds.), *Prejudice USA* (pp. 96-111). New York: Praeger.

Schegloff, E. A. (1979). The relevance of repair to syntax-for-conversation. In T. Givón (Ed.), *Syntax and discourse* (pp. 262-288). New York: Academic Press.

Schegloff, E. A., Jefferson, G., & Sacks, H. (1977). The preference for self-correction in the organization of repair in conversation. *Language, 53*, 361-382.

Schenkein, J. (Ed.). (1978). *Studies in conversational interaction*. New York: Academic Press.

Scherer, K. R., & Giles, H. (Eds.). (1979). *Social markers in speech*. Cambridge: Cambridge University Press.

Schiffrin, D. (1985). Everyday argument: The organization of diversity in talk. In T. A. van Dijk (Ed.) *Handbook of Discourse Analysis* (Vol. 3, pp. 35-46). London: Academic Press.

Schneider, D. J. (1973). Implicit personality theory: A Review. *Psychological Bulletin, 79*, 294-319.

Schneider, D. J. (1981). Tactical self-presentations: Toward a broader conception. In J. T. Tedeschi (Ed.), *Impression management. Theory and social psychological research* (pp. 23-40). New York: Academic Press.

Schuman, H., Steeh, C., & Bobo, L. (1985). *Racial attitudes in America*. Cambridge, MA: Harvard University Press.

Schutz, A. (1970). *On phenomenology and social relations*. In H. R. Wagner (Ed.). Chicago: University of Chicago Press.

Schutz, A. (1971). *Gesammelte Aufsätze* (Vol. 1). The Hague: Nijhoff.

Schwartz, H., & Jacobs, J. (1979). *Qualitative sociology*. New York: Free Press.

Searle, J. (1969). *Speech acts*. London: Cambridge University Press.

Sears, D. O., & Allen, H. M., Jr. (1984). The trajectory of local desegregation controversies and Whites' opposition to busing. In M. Brewer & N. Miller (Eds.), *Groups in contact: The psychology of desegregation*. New York: Academic Press.

Sears, D. O., Hensler, C. P., Speer, L. K. (1979). Whites' opposition to busing: Self-interest or symbolic politics? *American Political Science Review, 73:* 369-384.

Sebeok, T. A. (Ed.). (1960). *Style in language*. Cambridge, MA: MIT Press.

Seidel, G. (1985). The concept of culture in the British and French New Right. In R. Levitas (Ed.), *The ideology of the New Right* (pp. 107-135). Oxford: Blackwell.

Seliger, M. (1976). *Ideology and politics*. New York: Free Press.

Shibutani, T. (1966). *Improvised news. A sociological study of rumor*. Indianapolis: Bobbs-Merrill.

Shoben, E. J. (1984). Semantic and episodic memory. In R. S. Wyer, Jr. & T. K. Srull (Eds.), *Handbook of social cognition* (Vol. 2, pp. 213-232). Hillsdale, NJ: Erlbaum.

Sinclair, J. M., & Coulthard, M. (1975). *Towards an analysis of discourse*. London: Oxford University Press.

Snyder, M. (1981a). On the self-perpetuating nature of social stereotypes. In D. L. Hamilton (Ed.), *Cognitive processes in stereotyping and intergroup behavior* (pp. 183-212). Hillsdale, NJ: Erlbaum.

Snyder, M. (1981b). Seek and ye shall find: Testing hypotheses about other people. In E. T. Higgins, C. P. Herman, & M. P. Zanna (Eds.), *Social cognition. The Ontario Symposium* (Vol. 1, pp. 277-304). Hillsdale, NJ: Erlbaum.

Snyder, M., & Cantor, N. (1979). Testing hypotheses about other people: The use of historical knowledge. *Journal of Experimental Social Psychology, 15*, 330-342.

Snyder, M., Tanke, E. D., & Berscheid, E. (1977). Social perception and interpersonal behavior: On the self-fulfilling nature of social stereotypes. *Journal of Personality and Social Psychology, 35,* 656-666.

Sprangers, M.A.G. (1983). *Structuur van negatieve en positieve opinies over etnische minderheden* [Structure of negative and positive opinions about ethnic minorities]. Unpublished manuscript, University of Amsterdam; Laboratory of Psychology.

Stephan, W. G. (1977). Stereotyping: The role of ingroup-outgroup differences in causal attribution for behavior. *Journal of Social Psychology, 101,* 255-266.

Stephan, W. G., & Rosenfield, D. (1982). Racial and ethnic stereotypes. In A. G. Miller (Ed.), *In the eye of the beholder. Contemporary issues in stereotyping* (pp. 92-135). New York: Praeger.

Stinton, J. (Ed.). (1980). *Racism and sexism in children's books.* London: Writers & Readers.

Stubbs, M. (1983). *Discourse analysis. The sociolinguistic analysis of natural language.* Oxford: Blackwell.

Sudnow, D. (Ed.). (1972). *Studies in social interaction.* New York: Free Press.

Tajfel, H. (Ed.). (1978). *Differentiation between social groups. Studies in the social psychology of intergroup relations.* London: Academic Press.

Tajfel, H. (1981a). *Human groups and social categories.* Cambridge: Cambridge University Press.

Tajfel, H. (1981b). Social stereotypes and social groups. In J. C. Turner & H. Giles (Eds.), *Intergroup behaviour* (pp. 144-167). Oxford: Blackwell.

Tajfel, H. (Ed.). (1982). *Social identity and intergroup relations.* Cambridge: Cambridge University Press.

Tajfel, H., & Forgas, J. P. (1981). Social categorization: Cognitions, values and groups. In J. P. Forgas (Ed.), *Social cognition* (pp. 113-140). London: Academic Press.

Tajfel, H., Sheikh, A. A., & Gardner, R. C. (1964). Content of stereotypes and the inference of similarity between members of stereotyped groups. *Acta Psychologica, 22,* 191-201.

Tannen, D. (Ed.). (1981). *Analyzing discourse: Text and talk.* Washington, DC: Georgetown University Press.

Taylor, S. E. (1981). The categorization approach to stereotyping. In D. L. Hamilton (Ed.), *Cognitive processes in stereotyping and intergroup behavior* (pp. 83-114). Hilldale, NJ: Erlbaum.

Taylor, S. E. (1982). The availability bias in social perception and interaction. In D. Kahneman, P. Slovic, & A. Tversky (Eds.), *Judgment under uncertainty. Heuristics and biases* (pp. 190-200). New York: Cambridge University Press.

Taylor, S. E., & Crocker, J. (1981). Schematic basis of social information processing. In E. T. Higgins, C. P. Herman, & M. P. Zanna (Eds.), *Social cognition: The Ontario Symposium* (Vol. 1, pp. 89-134). Hillsdale, NJ: Erlbaum.

Taylor, S. E., & Fiske, S. T. (1978). Point-of-view and perceptions of causality. *Journal of Personality and Social Psychology, 32,* 439-445.

Taylor, S. E., Fiske, S. T., Etcoff, N.L., & Ruderman, A.J. (1978). Categorical and contextual bases of person memory and stereotyping. *Journal of Personality and Social Psychology, 36,* 778-793.

Tedeschi, J. T. (Ed.). (1981). *Impression management. Theory and social psychological research.* New York: Academic Press.

Tedeschi, J. T., & Reiss, M. (1981). Verbal strategies in impression management. In C. Antaki (Ed.), *The Psychology of Ordinary Explanations of Social Behaviour* (pp. 271-309). London: Academic Press.

Thomas, W. I. (1966). Situational analysis: The behavior pattern and the situation. In M. Janovitz (Ed.), *W. I. Thomas on social organization and social personality*. Chicago: Chicago University Press. (Original work published in 1928)
Todorov, T. (1969). *Grammaire du Décaméron*. The Hague: Mouton.
Toulmin, S. E. (1958). *The uses of argument*. London: Cambridge University Press.
Troyna, B. (1981). *Public awareness and the media: A study of reporting on race*. London: Commission for Racial Equality.
Tsiakalos, G. (1983). *Ausländerfeindlichkeit*. Munich: Beck.
Tuchman, Gaye. (1978). *Making news*. New York: Free Press.
Tulving, E. (1972). Episodic and semantic memory. In E. T. Tulving & W. Donaldson (Eds.), *Organization of memory*. New York: Academic Press.
Tulving, E. (1983). *Elements of episodic memory*. Oxford: Oxford University Press.
Turner, J. C. (1981). The experimental social psychology of intergroup behaviour. In J. C. Turner, & H. Giles (Eds.), *Intergroup behaviour* (pp. 66-101). Oxford: Blackwell.
Turner, J. C., & Brown, R. J. (1978). Social status, cognitive alternatives and intergroup relations. In H. Tajfel (Ed.), *Differentiation between social groups: Studies in the social psychology of intergroup relations*. London: Academic Press.
Turner, J. C., Brown, R. J., & Tajfel, H. (1979). Social comparison and group interest in ingroup favouritism. *European Journal of Social Psychology, 9,* 187-204.
Turner, J. C., & Giles, H. (Eds.). (1981). *Intergroup behaviour*. Oxford: Blackwell.
Tversky, A., & Kahneman, D. (1973). Availability: A heuristic for judging frequency and probability. *Cognitive Psychology, 5,* 207-232.
Unesco. (1983). *Racism, science and pseudo-science*. Paris: Author.
van den Berg, H., & Reinsch, P. (1983). *Racisme in schoolboeken* [Racism in textbooks]. Amsterdam: Socialistische Uitgeverij Amsterdam.
van den Berghe, P. L. (1967). *Race and racism*. New York: John Wiley.
van der Pligt, J., & Eiser, J. R. (1984). Dimensional salience, judgment and attitudes. In J. R. Eiser (Ed.), *Attitudinal judgment* (pp. 161-178). New York: Springer.
van der Wurff, A. (1983). Prägnanz in verhalen over etnische minderheden [Prägnanz in stories about ethnic minorities]. Unpublished manuscript, University of Amsterdam, Department of General Literary Studies.
van Dijk, T. A. (1972). *Some aspects of text grammars*. The Hague: Mouton.
van Dijk, T. A. (1976). Philosophy of action and theory of narrative. *Poetics, 5,* 287-332.
van Dijk, T. A. (1977). *Text and context*. London: Longman.
van Dijk, T. A. (1979). Relevance assignment in discourse comprehension. *Discourse Processes, 2,* 113-126.
van Dijk, T. A. (1980a). *Macrostructures*. Hillsdale, NJ: Erlbaum.
van Dijk, T. A. (1980b). Story comprehension: An introduction. In T. A. van Dijk (Ed.), Story comprehension [Special issue]. *Poetics, 8* (1/3), 1-21.
van Dijk, T. A. (Ed.). (1980c). Story comprehension [Special issue]. *Poetics 8* (1/3).
van Dijk, T. A. (1981a). *Studies in the pragmatics of discourse*. Berlin/New York: Mouton.
van Dijk, T. A. (1981b). Pragmatic connectives. In T. A. van Dijk, *Studies in the pragmatics of discourse* (pp. 163-176). The Hague: Mouton.
van Dijk, T. A. (1982a). Episodes as units of discourse analysis. In D. Tannen (Ed.), *Analyzing discourse: Text and talk* (pp. 177-195). Washington, DC: Georgetown University Press.
van Dijk, T. A. (1982b). Toward a model of ethnic prejudice in cognition and discourse. Unpublished manuscript, University of Amsterdam, Department of General Literary Studies, Section of Discourse Studies.

van Dijk, T. A. (1983a). *Minderheden in de media*. [Minorities in the Media]. Amsterdam: Socialistische Uitgeverij Amsterdam.
van Dijk, T. A. (1983b). Cognitive and conversational strategies in the expression of ethnic prejudice. *Text, 3*, 375-404.
van Dijk, T. A. (1983c). *Processes of prejudice and the roots of racism*. Paper presented at SSRC Workshop on Intergroup Theory and British Race Relations, Bristol, 1983-1984. Unpublished manuscript, University of Amsterdam, Department of General Literary Studies, Section of Discourse Studies.
van Dijk, T. A. (1983d). Discourse analysis: Its development and application to the structures of news. *Journal of Communication, 33*, 20-43.
van Dijk, T. A. (1984). *Prejudice and discourse. An analysis of ethnic prejudice in cognition and conversation*. Amsterdam: Benjamins.
van Dijk, T. A. (Ed.). (1985a). *Handbook of discourse analysis*. (Vols. 1-4). London: Academic Press.
van Dijk, T. A. (Ed.). (1985b). *Discourse and literature*. Amsterdam: Benjamins.
van Dijk, T. A. (Ed.). (1985c). *Discourse and communication. New approaches to the analysis of mass media discourse and communication*. Berlin: de Gruyter.
van Dijk, T. A. (1985d). Cognitive situation models in discourse production: The expression of ethnic situations in prejudiced discourse. In J. P. Forgas (Ed.), *Language and social situations*. New York: Springer.
van Dijk, T. A. (1985e). News schemata. In C. Cooper & S. Greenbaum (Eds.), *Linguistic approaches to the study of written discourse* (pp. 210-258). Beverly Hills, CA: Sage.
van Dijk, T. A. (1985f). Structures of news in the press. In T. A. van Dijk (Ed.), *Discourse and communication* (pp. 79-93). Berlin: de Gruyter.
van Dijk, T. A. (1986a). *Schoolvoorbeelden van racisme* [Textbook examples of racism]. Unpublished report. University of Amsterdam, Department of General Library Studies, Section of Discourse Studies.
van Dijk, T. A. (1986b). Ethnic prejudice in cognition and conversation. In M. L. McLaughlin (Ed.), *Communication yearbook, vol. 9*. Beverly Hills, CA: Sage.
van Dijk, T. A. (1987a). *News as discourse*. Hillsdale, NJ: Erlbaum.
van Dijk, T. A. (1987b). *News analysis. Case studies of international and national news: Lebanon, ethnic minorities, refugees and squatters in the press*. Hillsdale, NJ: Erlbaum.
van Dijk, T. A. (1987c). Episodic models in discourse processing. In R. Horowitz & S. J. Samuels (Eds.), *Comprehending oral and written language*. New York: Academic Press.
van Dijk, T. A. (1987d). Elite discourse and racism. In I. Zavala, T. A. van Dijk, M. Diaz-Diocaretz (Eds.), *Discourse, power, literature*. Amsterdam: Benjamins.
van Dijk, T. A. & Kintsch, W. (1978). Cognitive psychology and discourse. Recalling and summarizing stories. In W. U. Dressler (Ed.), *Current trends in textlinguistics*. Berlin: de Gruyter.
van Dijk, T. A., & Kintsch, W. (1983). *Strategies of discourse comprehension*. New York: Academic Press.
van Eemeren, F. H., & Grootendorst, R. (1983). *Speech acts in argumentative discussions*. Dordrecht: Foris.
van Eemeren, F. H., Grootendorst, R., & Kruiger, T. (1984). *The study of argumentation*. New York: Irvington.
Vink, J. (1984). "Die Ausländer nehmen unsere Arbeitsplätze weg" und andere Legenden—Argumente gegen Vorurteile. In R. Meinhardt (Ed.), *Türken raus? Oder verteidigt den sozialen Frieden. Beiträge gegen die Ausländerfeindlichkeit* (pp. 190-200). Reinbek bei Hamburg: Rowohlt.

von Cranach, M., & Harré, R. (Eds.). (1982). *The analysis of action.* Cambridge: Cambridge University Press.
von Wright, G. H. (1963). *Norm and action.* London: Routledge & Kegan Paul.
Weber, R., & Crocker, J. (1983). Cognitive processes in the revision of stereotypic beliefs. *Journal of Personality and Social Psychology, 45,* 961-977.
Wegman, C., (1981). Conceptual representation of belief systems. *Journal for the Theory of Social Behaviour 11,* 279-305.
Wellman, D. T. (1977). *Portraits of white racism.* Cambridge: Cambridge University Press.
Westin, C. (1984). *Majoritet om minoritet. En studie i etnisk tolerans i 80-talets Sverige.* Stockholm: Liber Förlag.
White, A. R. (1968). *The philosophy of action.* Oxford: Oxford University Press.
Wilder, D. A. (1981). Perceiving persons as a group: Categorization and intergroup relations. In D. L. Hamilton (Ed.), *Cognitive processes in stereotyping and intergroup relations* (pp. 213-257). Hillsdale, NJ: Erlbaum.
Wilensky, R. (1983). Story grammars versus story points. *Behavioral and Brain Sciences, 6,* 579-623.
Wilson, C. C., & Gutiérrez, F. (1985). *Minorities and the media.* Beverly Hills, CA, & London: Sage.
Wilson, W. J. (1980). *The declining significance of race* (2nd. ed.). Chicago: University of Chicago Press.
Word, C. O., Zanna, M. P., & Cooper, J. (1974). The nonverbal mediation of self-fulfilling prophecies in interracial interaction. *Journal of Experimental Social Psychology, 10,* 109-120.
World Council of Churches. (1979). *Racism in children's school textbooks.* Geneva: Author.
Wyer, R. S., Jr., & Gordon, S. E. (1984). The cognitive representation of social information. In R. S. Wyer Jr., & T. K. Srull (Eds.), *Handbook of social cognition* (Vol. 2, pp. 73-150). Hillsdale, NJ: Erlbaum.
Wyer, R. S., Jr., & Srull, T. K. (Eds.). (1984). *Handbook of social cognition.* (Vols. 1-3). Hillsdale, NJ: Erlbaum.
Zajonc, R. B. (1980). Feeling and thinking. Preferences need no inferences. *American Psychologist, 35,* 151-175.
Zanna, M. P., Higgins, E. T., & Herman, C. P. (Eds.). (1982). *Consistency in social behavior.* Hillsdale, NJ: Erlbaum.
Zimet, S. (1976). *Print and prejudice.* London: Hodder & Stoughton.

Name Index

424

Subject Index

257

About the Author

Teun A. van Dijk is Professor of Discourse Analysis at the University of Amsterdam. After earlier work in literary theory, text grammar, pragmatics, and the psychology of discourse processing, his current research is especially focused on the social psychological aspects of discourse and communication, with applications mainly in the field of news analysis and the study of ethnic prejudice and racism in various types of discourse. His major books in English include *Some Aspects of Text Grammars* (1972), *Text and Context* (1977), *Macrostructures* (1980), *Studies in the Pragmatics of Discourse* (1981), *Strategies of Discourse Comprehension* (with Walter Kintsch, 1983), *Prejudice in Discourse* (1984), *News Analysis* (1987), and *News as Discourse* (1987). Among his recently edited books are the *Handbook of Discourse Analysis* (4 volumes) (1985), *Discourse and Literature* (1985), *Discourse and Communication* (1985), and *Discourse and Discrimination* (with Geneva Smitherman, in press). He is founder and editor of the international journal, *TEXT*.

NOTES